"A definitive history of Columbine – not just the shootings, which left 13 innocents dead, but everything that led up to the attack and the years of recovery that followed. *Columbine* scrapes away the urban legends and popular analysis, and shows the reader clearly what happened. More importantly, the book does its best to explain why the sons of two stable, middle-class families committed mass murder"
New York Post

"Astonishingly comprehensive . . . It would be a rare and dubious distinction to complete *Columbine* without shedding a tear. One of the significant achievements of Cullen's book is to let the truth contradict many popularly embedded ideas"
Chicago Tribune

"*Columbine* accomplishes an astonishing number of things in compelling, articulate prose . . . a valuable historical reference, but it roils the heart, too, delivering a devastating portrait of the killers"
Miami Herald

"A gripping study . . . To his credit, Mr. Cullen does not simply tear down Columbine's legends. He also convincingly explains what really sparked the murderous rage"
New York Observer

"An engrossing narrative with rich detail . . . interspersing perspectives from victims, investigators and school officials with the killers' writings and videos"
The Denver Post

"For any reader who wants to understand the complicated nature of evil, this book is a masterpiece"
Seattle Times

"Engrossing . . . Cullen's study of Harris and Klebold in the months before the killing is fascinating."
Bloomberg

"A riveting read, on a par with the greatest crime analysis from *In Cold Blood* or *The Stranger Beside Me* – but without the personal asides. It's particularly trenchant in the passages that recreate the events of that day, meticulously heartbreaking in its detail . . ."
Daily Beast

First published in the United States 2009 by Twelve, an imprint of
Hachette Book Group

First published in Great Britain 2009 by
Old Street Publishing Ltd
Yowlestone House, Puddington, Tiverton, Devon EX16 8LN
www.oldstreetpublishing.co.uk

ISBN 978-1-906964-14-6

10 9 8 7 6

A CIP catalogue record for this title is available from the British Library.

Printed and bound in Great Britain

"Masterful . . . *Columbine* is the latest addition to the true-crime page-turner genre exemplified by Norman Mailer's *The Executioner's Song* and Truman Capote's *In Cold Blood*"
Financial Times

"Stunning . . . Through painstaking examination of thousands of pages of evidence – much of it concealed until recently incorporating interviews with psychologists, teachers, survivors and former friends of the killers Eric Harris and Dylan Klebold, and, most importantly, access to their gruesome homemade videos and journals, Cullen has pieced together the real story . . . Blunt, brutal and shocking in equal measure, *Columbine* is a story that peels away the veneer of lazy media stereotyping"
Esquire

"A vivid account of what really happened that day, and the motivation that lay behind it . . . this thoughtful narrative interrogates the preconceptions of a public keen to blame the shootings on Satan, rock music, goths and poor parenting rather than facing the truth – that these two boys hated the world and wanted to kill large numbers of people"
Guardian

"[A] spectacularly gripping account of the Colorado school shooting that shocked America a decade ago . . . Cullen's chilling narrative is too vital to miss, as are his myth-busting revelations: No, the killers were not social outcasts; there was no broader conspiracy; and, yes, the authorities should have known. Read this book for its unflinching honesty, and for the satisfaction, however grim, of setting the record straight"
Oprah Winfrey

"Excellent . . . Cullen leaves us with some unforgettable images – such as the pizza slices floating aimlessly about the school grounds"
Scotsman

"Fascinating . . . Cullen has done an amazing job of assembling a coherent and often gripping narrative out of truckloads of documents and often conflicting testimony"
Irish Times

"As definitive as it is unpleasant . . *Columbine* will remain the single best explanation of the what, how, and why of April 20, 1999"

COLUMBINE

DAVE CULLEN

For Rachel, Danny, Dave, Cassie, Steven, Corey,
Kelly, Matthew, Daniel, Isaiah, John, Lauren, and Kyle.
And for Patrick, for giving me hope.

Contents

Author's Note on Sources ix

I. FEMALE DOWN 1

II. AFTER AND BEFORE 99

III. THE DOWNWARD SPIRAL 171

IV. TAKE BACK THE SCHOOL 237

V. JUDGMENT DAY 303

Timeline: Before 359

Acknowledgments 361

Notes 363

Bibliography 389

Index 405

Author's Note on Sources

A great deal of this story was captured on tape or recorded contemporaneously in notebooks and journals—by the killers before the murders, and by investigators, journalists, and researchers afterward. Much more was reconstructed or fleshed out from the memory of survivors. Anything in quotation marks was either captured on tape, recorded by me or other journalists or police investigators at the time, published in official documents, or, in the case of casual conversations, recalled by one or more of the speakers with a high degree of certainty. When the speaker was less sure about the wording, I used italics. I have abbreviated some exchanges without insertion of ellipses, and have corrected some grammatical errors. *No* dialogue was made up.

The same convention was applied to quotations from the killers, who wrote and taped themselves extensively. Their writings are reproduced here as written, with most of their idiosyncrasies intact.

Passages of this book suggesting their thoughts come primarily from their journals and videos. A multitude of corroborating sources were employed, including school assignments; conversations with friends, family members, and teachers; journals kept by key figures; and a slew of police records compiled before the murders, particularly summaries of their counseling sessions. I often used the killers' thoughts verbatim from their journals, without quotation marks. Other feelings are summarized or paraphrased, but all originated with them. The killers left a few significant gaps in their thinking. I have attempted to fill them with the help of experts in criminal psychology who have spent years on the case. All conjectures about the killers' thinking are labeled as such.

Actual names have been used, with one exception: the pseudonym Harriet was invented to identify a girl Dylan wrote about obsessively. For simplicity, minor characters are not named in the text. They are all identified in the expanded version of the endnotes online.

All times for the massacre are based on the Jefferson County sheriff's report. Some of the victims' family members, however, believe the attack began a few minutes later. The times used here provide a close approximation, and are accurate relative to one another.

I covered this story extensively as a journalist, beginning around noon on the day of the attack. The episodes recounted here are a blend of my contemporaneous reporting with nine years of research. This included hundreds of interviews with most of the principals, examination of more than 25,000 pages of police evidence, countless hours of video and audiotape, and the extensive work of other journalists I consider reliable.

To avoid injecting myself into the story, I generally refer to the press in the third person. But in the great media blunders during the initial coverage of this story, where nearly everyone got the central factors wrong, I was among the guilty parties. I hope this book contributes to setting the story right.

I am a wicked man.... But do you know, gentlemen, what was the main point about my wickedness? The whole thing, precisely was, the greatest nastiness precisely lay in my being shamefully conscious every moment, even in moments of the greatest bile, that I was not only not a wicked man but was not even an embittered man, that I was simply frightening sparrows in vain, and pleasing myself with it.

—Fyodor Dostoyevsky, *Notes from Underground*

The world breaks everyone and afterward many are strong at the broken places.

—Ernest Hemingway, *A Farewell to Arms*

PART I

FEMALE DOWN

i. Mr. D

He told them he loved them. Each and every one of them. He spoke without notes but chose his words carefully. Frank DeAngelis waited out the pom-pom routines, the academic awards, and the student-made videos. After an hour of revelry, the short, middle-aged man strode across the gleaming basketball court to address his student body. He took his time. He smiled as he passed the marching band, the cheerleaders, and the Rebels logo painted beneath flowing banners proclaiming recent sports victories. He faced two thousand hyped-up high school students in the wooden bleachers and they gave him their full attention. Then he told them how much they meant to him. How his heart would break to lose just one of them.

It was a peculiar sentiment for an administrator to express to an assembly of teenagers. But Frank DeAngelis had been a coach longer than a principal, and he earnestly believed in motivation by candor. He had coached football and baseball for sixteen years, but he looked like a wrestler: compact body with the bearing of a Marine, but without the bluster. He tried to play down his coaching past, but he exuded it.

You could hear the fear in his voice. He didn't try to hide it, and he didn't try to fight back the tears that welled up in his eyes. And he got away with it. Those kids could sniff out a phony with one whiff and convey displeasure with snickers and fumbling and an audible current of unrest. But they adored Mr. D. He could say almost anything to his students, precisely because he did. He didn't hold back, he didn't sugarcoat it, and he didn't dumb it down. On Friday morning, April 16, 1999, Principal Frank DeAngelis was an utterly transparent man.

Every student in the gymnasium understood Mr. D's message. There were fewer than thirty-six hours until the junior-senior prom, meaning lots

3

of drinking and lots of driving. Lecturing the kids would just provoke eye rolling, so instead he copped to three tragedies in his own life. His buddy from college had been killed in a motorcycle accident. "I can remember being in the waiting room, looking at his blood," he said. "So don't tell me it can't happen." He described holding his teenage daughter in his arms after her friend died in a flaming wreck. The hardest had been gathering the Columbine baseball team to tell them one of their buddies had lost control of his car. He choked up again. "I do not want to attend another memorial service."

"Look to your left," he told them. "Look to your right." He instructed them to study the smiling faces and then close their eyes and imagine one of them gone. He told them to repeat after him: "I am a valued member of Columbine High School. And I'm not in this alone." That's when he told them he loved them, as he always did.

"Open your eyes," he said. "I want to see each and every one of your bright, smiling faces again Monday morning."

He paused. "When you're thinking about doing something that could get you in trouble, remember, I care about you," he said. "I love you, but remember, I want us all together. We are one large family, we are—"

He left the phrase dangling. That was the students' signal. They leapt to their feet and yelled: "COL-um-*BINE!*"

Ivory Moore, a dynamo of a teacher and a crowd rouser, ran out and yelled, "We are…"

"COL-um-*BINE!*"

It was louder now, and their fists were pumping in the air.

"We are…"

"COL-um-*BINE!*"

"We are…"

"COL-um-*BINE!*"

Louder, faster, harder, faster—he whipped them into a frenzy. Then he let them go.

They spilled into the hallways to wrap up one last day of classes. Just a few hours until the big weekend.

———

All two thousand students would return safely on Monday morning, after the prom. But the following afternoon, Tuesday, April 20, 1999, twenty-four of Mr. D's kids and faculty members would be loaded into ambulances and rushed to hospitals. Thirteen bodies would remain in the building and two more on the grounds. It would be the worst school shooting in American history—a characterization that would have appalled the boys just then finalizing their plans.

2. "Rebels"

Eric Harris wanted a prom date. Eric was a senior, about to leave Columbine High School forever. He was not about to be left out of the prime social event of his life. He *really* wanted a date.

Dates were not generally a problem. Eric was a brain, but an uncommon subcategory: cool brain. He smoked, he drank, he dated. He got invited to parties. He got high. He worked his look hard: military chic hair—short and spiked with plenty of product—plus black T-shirts and baggy cargo pants. He blasted hard-core German industrial rock from his Honda. He enjoyed firing off bottle rockets and road-tripping to Wyoming to replenish the stash. He broke the rules, tagged himself with the nickname Reb, but did his homework and earned himself a slew of A's. He shot cool videos and got them airplay on the closed-circuit system at school. And he got chicks. Lots and lots of chicks.

On the ultimate high school scorecard, Eric outscored much of the football team. He was a little charmer. He walked right up to hotties at the mall. He won them over with quick wit, dazzling dimples, and a disarming smile. His Blackjack Pizza job offered a nice angle: stop in later and he would slip them a free slice. Often they did. Blackjack was a crummy econo-chain, one step down from Domino's. It had a tiny storefront in a strip mall just down the road from Eric's house. It was mostly a take-out and delivery business, but there were a handful of cabaret tables and a row of stools lined up along the counter for the sad cases with nowhere better to go. Eric and Dylan were called insiders, meaning anything but delivery—mostly making the pizzas, working the counter, cleaning up the mess. It was hard, sweaty work in the hot kitchen, and boring as hell.

Eric looked striking head-on: prominent cheekbones, hollowed out underneath—all his features proportionate, clean-cut, and all-American. The profile presented a bit of a problem however; his long, pointy nose exaggerated a sloping forehead and a weak chin. The spiky hair worked against him aesthetically, elongating his angular profile—but it was edgy, and it played well with his swagger. The smile was his trump card, and he knew exactly how to play it: bashful and earnest, yet flirtatious. The chicks ate it up. He had made it to the homecoming dance as a freshman, and had scored with a twenty-three-year-old at seventeen. He was damn proud of that one.

But prom had become a problem. For some reason—bad luck or bad timing—he couldn't make it happen. He had gone nuts scrounging for a date. He'd asked one girl, but she already had a boyfriend. That was embarrassing. He'd tried another, shot down again. He wasn't ashamed to call his friends in. His buddies asked, the girls he hung with asked, he asked—nothing, nothing, nothing.

His best friend, Dylan, had a date. How crazy was that? Dylan Klebold was meek, self-conscious, and authentically shy. He could barely speak in front of a stranger, especially a girl. He'd follow quietly after Eric on the mall conquests, attempting to appear invisible. Eric slathered chicks with compliments; Dylan passed them Chips Ahoy cookies in class to let them know he liked them. Dylan's friends said he had never been on a date; he may never have even asked a girl out—including the one he was taking to prom.

Dylan Klebold was a brain, too, but not quite so cool. Certainly not in his own estimation. He tried so hard to emulate Eric—on some of their videos, he puffed up and acted like a tough guy, then glanced over at Eric for approval. Dylan was taller and even smarter than Eric, but considerably less handsome. Dylan hated the oversized features on his slightly lopsided face. His nose especially—he saw it as a giant blob. Dylan saw the worst version of himself.

A shave would have helped. His beard was beginning to come in, but sporadically, in fuzzy little splotches along his chin. He seemed to take pride in his starter patches, oblivious to the actual effect.

Dylan cut a more convincing figure as a rebel, though. Long, ratty curls dangled toward his shoulders. He towered over his peers. With a ways to go in puberty, he was up to six foot three already, 143 stretched pounds. He could have worn the stature proudly, casting aspersions down at his adversaries, but it scared the crap out of him, all exposed up there. So he slouched off an inch or two. Most of his friends were over six foot—Eric was the exception, at five-nine. His eyes lined up with Dylan's Adam's apple.

Eric wasn't thrilled with his looks either, but he rarely let it show. He had undergone surgery in junior high to correct a congenital birth defect: pectus excavatum, an abnormally sunken sternum. Early on, it had undermined his confidence, but he'd overcome it by acting tough.

Yet it was Dylan who'd scored the prom date. His tux was rented, the corsage purchased, and five other couples organized to share a limo. He was going with a sweet, brainy Christian girl who had helped acquire three of the four guns. She adored Dylan enough to believe Eric's story about using them to hunt. Robyn Anderson was a pretty, diminutive blonde who hid behind her long straight hair, which often covered a good portion of her face. She was active in her church's youth group. Right now she was in D.C. for a weeklong trip with them, due back barely in time for the prom. Robyn had gotten straight A's at Columbine and was a month away from graduating as valedictorian. She saw Dylan every day in calculus, strolled through the hallways and hung out with him any time she could. Dylan liked her and loved the adulation, but wasn't really into her as a girlfriend.

Dylan was heavy into school stuff. Eric, too. They attended the football games, the dances, and the variety shows and worked together on video production for the Rebel News Network. School plays were big for Dylan. He would never want to face an audience, but backstage at the soundboard, that was great. Earlier in the year, he'd rescued Rachel Scott, the senior class sweetheart, when her tape jammed during the talent show. In a few days, Eric would kill her.

Eric and Dylan were short on athletic ability but were big-time fans. They had both been Little Leaguers and soccer kids. Eric still played soccer, but for Dylan it was mostly spectator stuff now. Eric was a Rockies fan and found spring training exciting. Dylan rooted for the BoSox and wore their ball cap everywhere. He watched a whole lot of baseball, studied the box scores, and compiled his own stats. He was in first place in the fantasy league organized by a friend of his. Nobody could outanalyze Dylan Klebold, as he prepped for the March draft weeks in advance. His friends grew bored after the first major rounds, but Dylan was intent on securing a strong bench. In the final week, he notified the league commissioner that he was adding a rookie pitcher to his roster. And he would continue working a trade through the weekend, right up to Monday, his last night. "His life was baseball," one of his friends said.

Eric fancied himself a nonconformist, but he craved approval and fumed over the slightest disrespect. His hand was always shooting up in class, and he always had the right answer. Eric wrote a poem for creative writing class that week about ending hate and loving the world. He enjoyed quoting Nietzsche and Shakespeare, but missed the irony of his own nickname, Reb: so rebellious he'd named himself after the school mascot.

Dylan went by VoDKa, sometimes capitalizing his initials in the name of his favorite liquor. He was a heavy drinker and damn proud of it; supposedly he'd earned the name after downing an entire bottle. Eric preferred Jack Daniel's but scrupulously hid it from his parents. To adult eyes, Eric was the obedient one. Misbehavior had consequences, usually involving his father, usually curtailing his freedom. Eric was a little control freak. He gauged his moves and determined just how much he could get away with. He could suck up like crazy to make things go his way.

The Blackjack Pizza store owner during most of their tenure was acquainted with Eric's wild side. After he closed the shop, Robert Kirgis would climb up to the roof sometimes, taking Eric and Dylan with him, and chugging brewskis while the boys shot bottle rockets over the strip mall. Kirgis was twenty-nine but enjoyed hanging with this pair. They were bright kids; they talked just like adults sometimes. Eric knew when to play, when to get serious. If a cop had ever showed up on that rooftop, everyone would have turned to Eric to do the talking. When customers stacked up at the counter and drivers rushed in for pickups, somebody needed to take control and Eric was your man. He was like a robot under pressure. Nothing could faze him, not when he cared about the outcome. Plus, he needed that job; he had an expensive hobby and he wasn't about to jeopardize it for short-term gratification. Kirgis put Eric in charge when he left.

Nobody put Dylan in charge of anything. He was unreliable. He had been on and off the payroll in the past year. He'd applied for a better job at a computer store and presented a professional résumé. The owner had been impressed, and Dylan had gotten the job. He'd never bothered to show.

But nothing separated the boys' personalities like a run-in with authority. Dylan would be hyperventilating, Eric calmly calculating. Eric's cool head steered them clear of most trouble, but they had their share of schoolyard fights. They liked to pick on younger kids. Dylan had been caught scratching obscenities into a freshman's locker. When Dean Peter Horvath called him down, Dylan went ballistic. He cussed the dean out, bounced off the walls, acted like a nutcase. Eric could have talked his way out with apologies, evasions, or claims of innocence—whatever that subject was susceptible to. He read people quickly and tailored his responses. Eric was unflappable; Dylan erupted. He had no clue what Dean Horvath would respond to, nor did he care. He was pure emotion. When he learned his father was driving in to discuss the locker, Dylan dug himself in deeper. Logic was irrelevant.

The boys were both gifted analytically, math whizzes and technology hounds. Gadgets, computers, video games—any new technology and they were mesmerized. They created Web sites, adapted games with their own characters and adventures, and shot loads of videos—brief little short subjects they wrote, directed, and starred in. Surprisingly, gangly shyboy Dylan made for the more engaging actor. Eric was so calm and even-tempered, he couldn't even fake intensity. In person, he came off charming, confident, and engaging; impersonating an emotional young man, he was dull and unconvincing, incapable of emoting. Dylan was a live wire. In life, he was timid and shy, but not always quiet: trip his anger and he erupted. On film, he unleashed the anger and he *was* that crazy man, disintegrating in front of the camera. His eyes bugged out and his cheeks pulled away from them, all the flesh bunched up at the extremities, deep crevices around the looming nose.

Outwardly, Eric and Dylan looked like normal young boys about to graduate. They were testing authority, testing their sexual prowess—a little frustrated with the dumbasses they had to deal with, a little full of themselves. Nothing unusual for high school.

———

Rebel Hill slopes gradually, rising just forty feet above Columbine, which sits at its base. That's enough to dominate the immediate surroundings, but halfway up the hillside, the Rockies are suddenly spectacular. Each step forward lowers the mesa toward eye level, and the mountains leap up behind, a jagged brown wall rearing straight off the Great Plains. They stand two to three thousand feet above it—endless and apparently impenetrable, fading all the way over the northern horizon and just as far to the south. Locals call them the foothills. This Front Range towering over Columbine is taller than the highest peaks in all of Appalachia. Roads and regular habitation stop suddenly at the base of the foothills; even vegetation struggles to survive. Just three miles away, and it feels like the end of the world.

Nothing much grows on Rebel Hill's mesa. It's covered in cracked reddish clay, broken by the occasional scraggly weed failing to make much of a foothold. Up ahead, in the middle distance, humanity finally returns in the form of subdivisions. On fat winding lanes and cul-de-sacs, comfortably spaced two-story houses pop up among the pines. Strip malls and soccer fields and churches, churches, churches.

Columbine High School sits on a softly rolling meadow at the edge of a sprawling park, in the shadow of the Rocky Mountains. It's a large, modern facility—250,000 square feet of solid no-frills construction. With a beige concrete exterior and few windows, the school looks like a factory from most angles. It's practical, like the people of south Jefferson County. Jeffco, as it's known locally, scrimped on architectural affectations but invested generously in chem labs, computers, video production facilities, and a first-rate teaching force.

Friday morning, after the assembly, the corridors bustled with giddy teenage exuberance. Students poured out of the gym giggling, flirting, chasing, and jostling. Yet just outside the north entranceway, where the tips of the Rockies peeked around the edges of Rebel Hill, the clamor of two thousand boisterous teenagers faded to nothing. The two-story structure and the sports complex wrapped around it on two sides were the only indication of America's twentieth-largest metropolis. Downtown Denver lay just ten miles to the northeast, but a dense thicket of trees obscured the skyline. On warmer days, the sliding doors of the woodshop would gape open. Boys set their cutting tools into the spinning blocks of wood, and the sudden buzz of the lathe machines competed with the exhaust system. But a cold front had swept onto the high plains Wednesday, and the air was hovering around freezing as Mr. D told the students that he loved them.

Cold didn't deter the smokers. Any day of the year, you could find them wandering near, but rarely in, the official smoking pit, a ten-by-eight grass rectangle cordoned off by telephone-pole logs just past the parking lot, just beyond school grounds. It was peaceful there. No teachers, no rules, no commotion, no stress.

Eric and Dylan were fixtures in the smokers' gulley. They both smoked the same brand, Camel filtered. Eric picked it; Dylan followed.

Lately, friends had noticed more cutting and missed assignments. Dylan kept getting in trouble for sleeping in class. Eric was frustrated and pissed, but also curiously unemotional. One day that year, a friend videotaped him hanging out at the lunch table with his buddies. They bantered about cams and valves, and a good price for a used Mazda. Eric appeared entranced with his cell phone, aimlessly spinning it in circles. He didn't seem to be listening, but he was taking it all in.

A guy walked into the crowded cafeteria. "Fuck you!" one of Eric's buddies spat, well out of hearing range. "I hate that putrid cock!" Another friend agreed. Eric turned slowly and gazed over his shoulder with his trademark detachment. He studied the guy and turned back with less interest than he had shown toward the phone. "I hate almost everyone," he replied blankly. "Ah, yes. I wanna rip his head off and eat it."

Eric's voice was flat. No malice, no anger, barely interested. His eyebrows rose at the *Ah, yes*—a mild congratulation for the clever line about to come. He went vacant again delivering it.

No one found that reaction unusual. They were used to Eric.

They moved on to reminiscing about a freshman they'd picked on. Eric impersonated a special ed kid struggling to talk. A busty girl walked by. Eric waved her over and they hit on her.

3. Springtime

Spring had burst upon the Front Range. Trees were leafing, anthills rising, lawns growing vibrant in their brief transition from dormant winter brown to parched summer brown. Millions of mini-propeller maple seedpods twirled down toward the ground. Spring fever infected the classrooms. Teachers zipped through remaining chapters; kids started to stress about finals and daydream about the summer. Seniors looked ahead to fall. Columbine had one of the best academic reputations in the state; 80 percent of graduates headed on to degree programs. College dominated the conversation now: big fat acceptance packets and paper-thin rejection envelopes; last-minute campus visits to narrow down the finalists. It was time to commit to a university, write the deposit check, and start selecting first-semester classes. High school was essentially over.

Up in the Rockies, it was still winter. The slopes were open but the snow was receding. Kids begged their parents for a day off from school for one last boarding run. An Evangelical Christian junior talked her parents into letting her go the day before Mr. D's assembly. Cassie Bernall drove up to Breckenridge with her brother, Chris. Neither one had met Eric or Dylan yet.

Lunchtime was still a big daily event. The Columbine cafeteria was a wide-open bubble of a space protruding from the spacious corridor between the student entrance at the south corner and the giant stone staircase that could fit more than a dozen students across. Kids referred to the area as "the commons." It was wrapped with an open latticework facade of white steel girders and awnings and a decorative crisscross of steel cables. Inside, a hive of activity ignited at lunchtime. At the start of "A" lunch, more than six hundred students rushed in. Some came and went quickly, using it as a central meeting hub or grabbing a pack of Tater Tots for the road. It was packed solid for five minutes, then emptied out quickly. Three to four hundred kids eventually settled in for the duration, in plastic chairs around movable tables seating six to eight.

Two hours after the assembly, Mr. D was on lunch duty—his favorite part of the day. Most administrators delegated the task, but Principal DeAngelis could not get enough. "My friends laugh at me," he said. "Lunch duty! Ugh! But I love it down there. That's when you get to see the kids. That's when you get to talk to them."

Mr. D made his way around the commons, chatting up kids at each table, pausing as eager students ran up to catch his ear. He was down here for the start of "A" lunch nearly every day. His visits were lighthearted and conversational. He listened to his students' stories and helped solve problems, but he avoided discipline at lunch. The one situation where he just couldn't stop himself, though, was when he saw abandoned trays and food scraps. The Columbine Mr. D had inherited was short on frills, but he insisted it stay clean.

He was so irritated by entitlement and sloppiness that he'd had four surveillance cameras installed in the commons. A custodian loaded a fresh tape every morning around 11:05, and the rotating cameras continually swept the commons, recording fifteen-second bursts of action automatically cut from camera to camera. Day after day, they recorded the most banal footage imaginable. No one could have imagined what those cameras would capture just four months after installation.

A terrifying affliction had infested America's small towns and suburbs: the school shooter. We knew it because we had seen it on TV. We had read about it in the newspapers. It had materialized inexplicably two years before. In February 1997, a sixteen-year-old in remote Bethel, Alaska, brought a shotgun to high school and opened fire. He killed the principal and a student and injured two others. In October, another boy shot up his school, this time in Pearl, Mississippi. Two dead students, seven wounded. Two more sprees erupted in December, in remote locales: West Paducah, Kentucky, and Stamps, Arkansas. Seven were dead by the end of the year, sixteen wounded.

The following year was worse: ten dead, thirty-five wounded, in five separate incidents. The violence intensified in the springtime, as the school year came to a close. Shooting season, they began to call it. The perpetrator was always a white boy, always a teenager, in a placid town few had ever heard of. Most of the shooters acted alone. Each attack erupted unexpectedly and ended quickly, so TV never caught the turmoil. The nation watched the aftermaths: endless scenes of schools surrounded by ambulances, overrun by cops, hemorrhaging terrified children.

By graduation day, 1998, it felt like a full-blown epidemic. With each escalation, small towns and suburbia grew a little more tense. City schools had been armed camps for ages, but the suburbs were supposed to be safe.

The public was riveted; the panic was real. But was it warranted? *It could happen anyplace* became the refrain. "But it doesn't happen anyplace," Justice Policy Institute director Vincent Schiraldi argued in the *Washington Post*. "And it rarely happens at all." A *New York Times* editorial made the same point. CDC data pegged a child's chances of dying at school at one in a million. And holding. The "trend" was actually steady to downward, depending on how far back you looked.

But it was new to middle-class white parents. Each fresh horror left millions shaking their heads, wondering when the next outcast would strike.

And then... nothing. During the entire 1998–99 school year, not a single shooter emerged. The threat faded, and a distant struggle took hold of the news. The slow disintegration of Yugoslavia erupted again. In March 1999, as Eric and Dylan finalized their plans, NATO drew the line on Serbian aggression in a place called Kosovo. The United States began its largest air campaign since Vietnam. Swarms of F-15 squadrons pounded Belgrade. Central Europe was in chaos; America was at war. The suburban menace of the school shooter had receded.

4. Rock 'n' Bowl

Eric and Dylan had "A" lunch, but they were rarely around for Mr. D's visits anymore. Columbine was an open campus, so older kids with licenses and cars mostly took off for Subway, Wendy's, or countless drive-thrus scattered about the subdivisions. Most of the Columbine parents were affluent enough to endow their kids with cars. Eric had a black Honda Prelude. Dylan drove a vintage BMW his dad had refurbished. The two cars sat side by side in their assigned spaces in the senior lot every day. At lunch the boys loaded into one with a handful of friends to grab a bite and a smoke.

Mr. D had one major objective on Friday; Eric Harris had at least two. Mr. D wanted to impress on his kids the importance of wise choices. He wanted everyone back alive on Monday. Eric wanted ammo and a date for prom night.

Eric and Dylan planned to be dead shortly after the weekend, but Friday night they had a little work to do: one last shift at Blackjack. The job had funded most of Eric's bomb production, weapons acquisition, and napalm experiments. Blackjack paid a little better than minimum: $6.50 an hour for Dylan, $7.65 to Eric, who had seniority. Eric believed he could do better. "Once I graduate, I think I'm gonna quit, too," Eric told a friend who'd quit the week before. "But not now. When I graduate I'm going to get a job that's better for my future." He was lying. He had no intention of graduating.

Eric had no plans, which seemed odd for a kid with so much potential. He was a gifted student taking a pass on college. No career plans, no discernible goals. It was driving his parents crazy.

Dylan had a bright future. He was heading to college, of course. He was going to be a computer engineer. Several schools had accepted him, and he and his dad had just driven down to Tucson on a four-day trip. He'd picked out a dorm room. He liked the desert. The decision was final; his mom was going to mail his deposit to the University of Arizona on Monday.

Eric had appeased his dad for the last few weeks by responding to a Marine recruiter. He had no interest, but it made a nice cover. Eric's dad, Wayne, had been a decorated air force test pilot; he'd retired as a major after twenty-three years.

For the moment, Blackjack was a pretty good gig—decent money and lots of social opportunities. Chris and Nate and Zack and a mess of their other buddies had worked there. And Eric was alert for hotties. He had been working this one chick for months now. Susan worked as a part-time receptionist at the Great Clips in the same strip mall, so she was always having to pick up the pizza orders for the stylists. Eric saw her at school, too, usually when he was smoking. He addressed her by name there—she wasn't sure how he'd gotten ahold of it—and came by the store now and then to chat her up. She seemed to like him. Eric could not abide embarrassment, so he had been checking with her friends to gauge his prospects. Yeah, she liked him. Business was slow Friday night because of a late spring snowstorm, so they had time to chat when she picked up her order. He asked her for her number. She gave it.

Susan was looking good and Eric's new boss had an announcement, too. Kirgis had sold the store six weeks ago, and things were changing. The new owner fired some of the staff. Eric and Dylan were keepers, but the roof was closed: no more brewskis and bottle rockets. Eric, however, had made a great impression. Kirgis had trusted Eric enough to leave him in charge frequently, but on Friday, the new owner promoted him. Four days before his massacre, Eric made shift manager. He seemed pleased.

Both boys asked for advances that night. Eric wanted $200, Dylan $120, against hours they had already worked. The new owner paid them in cash.

After work, they headed to Belleview Lanes. Friday night was Rock 'n' Bowl, a big weekly social event. Sixteen kids usually showed up—some from the Blackjack circle, some from outside. They jammed into four adjacent lanes and tracked all the scores on the overhead monitors. Eric and Dylan played every Friday night. They weren't great bowlers—Dylan averaged 115, Eric 108—but they sure had fun doing it. They took bowling as a gym class, too. Dylan hated mornings, but Monday through Wednesday he drove to Belleview in the dark. Class started at 6:00 A.M., and they were rarely late, almost never absent. And they still couldn't wait for Friday night: same venue, but no adult supervision. They could get a little crazier. Eric was into all this German shit lately: Nietzsche, Freud, Hitler, German industrial bands like KMFDM and Rammstein, German-language T-shirts. Sometimes he'd punctuate his high fives with "Sieg Heil" or "Heil Hitler." Reports conflict about whether or not Dylan followed his lead. Dylan's friend Robyn Anderson, the girl who had asked him to the prom, usually picked them up at Blackjack and drove them to the alley. But this week, she was still in Washington with her church group.

They went home early that night—Eric had a phone engagement. He called Susan after nine, as promised, but got her mother. The mom thought Eric seemed very nice, until she told him Susan was sleeping at a friend's house. Eric got mad. How odd, the mom thought, that Eric would get so angry so quickly, just because Susan was out. Rejection was Eric's weak spot, especially by females. He wouldn't quite pull a Klebold, but the veil came down, and his anger spilled out. It was just infuriating. He had a long list of betrayals, an actual "Shit List" on his computer of despicable young girls. Susan did not make the list. Her mom offered Eric her pager number, and he pounded out a message.

Susan called back, and Eric was suddenly nice again. They talked about school, computers, and kids who had knifed Eric in the back. Eric went on and on about one kid who had betrayed him. They chatted for half an hour, and Eric finally asked her about Saturday night. Was she busy? No. Great. He would call her early in the afternoon. Finally! Prom night. He had a date!

5. Two Columbines

On Friday nights, Coach Sanders could usually be found in the Columbine Lounge: an ass-kicking strip-mall honky-tonk with the feel of an Allman Brothers club gig in Macon in the 1970s. All ages piled in—mostly rednecks, but blacks and Latinos mixed easily, punkers and skate rats, too. Everybody got along. Biker dudes with gleaming scalps and ponytails chatted up elderly women in floral cardigans. Most nights included an open-mike period, where you could watch an aging drunk strum "Stairway to Heaven," segue into the *Gilligan's Island* theme, and forget the words. The bartenders covered the pool tables with plywood sheets when the band started, converting it all into banquet space. A stack of amplifiers and a mixing board marked off the virtual stage, spotlit by aluminum-clamp lights affixed to the ceiling tile frames. A narrow strip of carpet served as the dance floor. Mostly, it was filled with fortyish women in Dorothy Hamill wedge cuts. They tried to drag their men out there but seldom got many takers. Dave Sanders was the exception. He loved to glide across the carpet. He was partial to the Electric Slide. He was something to see. The grace that propelled him down the basketball court thirty years ago had stuck with him. He played point guard. He was good.

Coach Sanders outclassed most of the clientele, but he didn't think in class terms. He cared about friendliness, honest effort, and sincerity. The Lounge had those in abundance. And Dave liked to kick back and have fun. He had a hearty laugh, and got a lot of use of it at the Lounge.

When Coach Sanders arrived in 1974, he personified the community. He'd grown up in Veedersburg, Indiana, a quiet rural community much like the Jefferson County he found right out of college. Twenty-five years later, it was not such a snug fit. The Lounge sat just a few blocks south of the high school, and in the early days it was brimming with faculty after school or

19

practice. They mixed with former students and parents and siblings of the current ones. Half the town rolled through the Lounge in a given week. The newer teachers didn't approve of that behavior, and they didn't fit in at the Lounge anyway. Neither did the wave of upscale suburbanites who began flooding into Jeffco in the late 1970s, overwhelming Columbine's student body. New Columbine went for fern bars and Bennigan's, or private parties in their split-level "ranch homes" and cathedral-ceilinged McMansions. Cassie Bernall's family was New Columbine, as were the Harrises and the Klebolds. Mr. D arrived as Old, but evolved with the majority to New. Old Columbine remained, outnumbered but unfazed by the new arrivals. Many older families lived in actual ranch houses built half a century earlier on the small horse ranches occupying most of the area when the high school was constructed.

Columbine High School was built in 1973 on a dirt road off a larger dirt road way out in horse country. It was named after the flower that blankets sections of the Rockies. Scraggy meadows surrounded the new building, fragrant with pine trees and horse manure. Hardly anybody lived there, but Jeffco was bracing for an influx. Court-ordered busing had spurred an avalanche of white flight out of Denver, and subdivisions were popping up all along the foothills.

Jeffco officials had debated where the arrivals would cluster. They erected three temporary structures in the wilderness to accommodate the stampede. The high schools were identical hollow shells, ready for conversion to industrial use if the population failed to materialize. Columbine resembled a factory by design. Inside, mobile accordion-wall separators were rolled out to create classrooms. Sound carried from room to room, but students could overcome such minor hardships.

Developers kept throwing up new subdivisions, each one pricier than the one before. Jeffco kept all three temporary schools. In 1995, just before Eric and Dylan arrived, Columbine High School underwent a major overhaul. Permanent interior walls were installed, and the old cafeteria on the east side was converted to classrooms. A huge west wing was added, doubling the size of the structure. It bore the signature new architectural feature: the curving green glass of the commons, with the new library above.

By April 1999, the plain was nearly filled, all the way to the foothills. But the fiercely independent residents refused to incorporate. A new town would only impose new rules and new taxes. The 100,000 new arrivals filled one continuous suburb with no town center: no main street, no town hall, town library, or town name. No one was sure what to call it. Littleton is a quiet suburb south of Denver where the massacre did not actually occur. Although the name would grow synonymous with the tragedy, Columbine lies several miles west, across the South Platte River, in a different county with separate schools and law enforcement. The postal system slapped "Littleton" onto a vast tract of seven hundred square miles, stretching way up into the foothills. The people on the plain gravitated toward the name of the nearest high school—the hub of suburban social life. For thirty thousand people clustered around the new high school, Columbine became the name of their home.

———

Dave Sanders taught typing, keyboarding, business, and economics. He didn't find all the material particularly interesting, but it enabled him to coach. Dave coached seven different sports at Columbine. He started out with boys but found the girls needed him more. "He had this way of making everyone feel secure," a friend said. He made the kids feel good about themselves.

Dave didn't yell or berate the girls, but he was stern and insistent at practice. *Again. Again.* He watched quietly on the sidelines, and when he spoke, they could count on analysis or inspiration. He had taken over as head coach of girls' basketball that semester—a team with twelve straight losing seasons. Before the first game, he bought them T-shirts with ONE IN A DOZEN printed on the back. They made it to the state championship tournament that spring.

When someone crossed Dave Sanders, he responded with "the look": a cold, insistent stare. He used it one time on a couple of chatty girls in business class. They shut up momentarily, but went back to talking when he looked away. So he pulled up a chair right in front of them and conducted the rest of class from that spot, staring back and forth at each girl until the bell rang.

Dave spent almost every night in the gym or the field house, headed back for more on the weekends, and ran summer training camps at the University of Wyoming. Dave was a practical guy. He admired efficiency, tried to do double duty by bringing his daughter to work after school. The basketball girls knew Angela by the time she was a toddler. She hung out in the gym watching Daddy drill the girls: dribbling, tip contests, face-offs... Angela brought her toys with her in a tyke-sized suitcase. By the end of practice, they would be strewn all over the bleachers and the side of the court. The girls let out a big sigh when Dave called out for Angela to start packing up. He worked them hard, and that was the signal that they were nearly done.

Angela treasured those late afternoons. "I grew up at Columbine," she said. Dave was widening out into a big bear of a man, and when he hugged Angela, she felt safe.

Her mom was less impressed. Kathy Sanders divorced Dave when Angela was three. Dave found a home a few blocks away, so they could stay close. Later, Angie moved in with him. It was such a happy divorce that Kathy became friends with his second wife, Linda Lou.

"Kathy's such a sweetheart, and she and Dave got along so well," Linda said. "I asked her one day, 'Why did you two ever get a divorce?' And she said, 'He was never home. I was kind of like married to myself.'"

Linda thrived with the arrangement. Angie was seventeen when she married Dave, and her two girls were nearly raised as well. Linda had been a single working mom for many years and was used to alone time. She grew steadily more dependent on Dave, though. She had been strong when she needed to, but she liked it better with a man to lean on. Independence had been great, but that life was over now.

Linda Lou often met Dave at the Lounge after practice, and they spent the evening together there. She loved the place almost as much as Dave did. They'd met at the Lounge in 1991. They'd held their wedding reception there two years later. It felt like home. Dave felt like home to Linda.

Dave was exactly what Linda had been waiting for: caring, protective, and playfully romantic. He'd proposed on a trip to Vegas. As they'd strolled over a bridge into the Excalibur casino, he'd asked to see her "divorce ring"—which she still wore on her wedding finger. She presented her hand, and he threw the ring into the moat. He asked her to marry him. She gleefully accepted.

Linda and her two daughters moved in, and she and Dave finished raising the girls and Angela. Dave legally adopted Linda's younger daughter, Coni. He considered all three girls his daughters, and they all called him Dad.

Dave's lanky runner's build filled out. His beard grew speckled, then streaked gray. His smile held constant. His blue eyes twinkled. He began to resemble a young Santa Claus. Otherwise, Dave remained remarkably consistent: coaching, laughing, and enjoying his grandkids, but not seeing them enough. He drove an aging Ford Escort, dressed in drab polyester slacks and plain button-down shirts. His hair dwindled, but he parted it neatly on the left. He wore great big oversized glasses with frames from another age. Each night ended with him in his easy chair, chuckling to Johnny Carson, with a tumbler of Diet Coke and Jack Daniel's in hand. When Johnny retired, the Sanderses had a satellite dish and Dave could always find a game to settle down with. Linda waited for him upstairs.

Out of the blue, just a few weeks before the prom, he decided to update his image. He was forty-seven—time for a change. He surprised Linda in a pair of wire-rimmed glasses, the first big fashion statement of his life. He'd picked them out himself. "Woo-woo!" she howled. She had never seen a Dave like *this* before!

He was so proud of those glasses. "I finally made it to 1999," he said.

The big debut came Easter Sunday. He showed up in the glasses at a boisterous family gathering with the grandkids. Nobody noticed.

Alone with Linda that evening, he confessed how badly it hurt.

Dave was planning more changes: No basketball camp this summer. Less coaching, more time with his own girls and his grandkids. There was still time to set it right.

He was trying a new bedtime drink, too: Diet Coke and rum.

The Sunday before the prom, the family threw a birthday party for Angela's four-year-old, Austin. Dave liked making peanut butter and jelly sandwiches for the grandkids. He sliced off the edges, because they liked it fluffy all the way through. Dave would hide a gummi worm in the jelly, which surprised them every time.

Austin called to talk to Grandpa on prom weekend but missed him. Dave called back and left a message on the machine. Angela erased it. She would try again during the week.

———

Prom was scheduled for April 17, but for most kids, it was the culmination of a long, painful dance stretching back to midwinter. Night after night, Patrick Ireland had lain on his bed, phone in one hand, a ball in the other, tossing it up and snatching it out of the air, wishing his best friend, Laura, would take the hint. He kept prodding her about her prospects. *Any ideas? Anybody ask yet?* She tossed the questions back: *Who you going to ask? When? What are you waiting for?*

Indecision was unfamiliar ground for Patrick. He competed in basketball and baseball for Columbine and earned first place medals in waterskiing while earning a 4.0 average. He kept his eye on the ball. When his team was down five points in the final minutes of a basketball game, and he'd just miss an easy layup or dribbled off his foot and felt like a loser, the answer was simple: *Brush it off!* If you wanted to win, you focused on the next play. With Laura, he couldn't focus on anything.

Patrick was modest but self-assured with regard to most things. This mattered too much. He couldn't risk fourth grade again. Laura had been his first love, his first girlfriend, in third grade. It was a torrid romance, but it ended badly and she wouldn't speak to him the next year. It took them until high school to become friends again. For a while, it was friendship, but then his pulse started racing. Had he been right about her the first time? Surely she felt it, too. Unless he was imagining it. No, she was flirting, totally. Flirting enough?

Laura grew impatient. It wasn't just prom night at stake, it was weeks of planning, dress shopping, accessorizing, endless conversations to risk being excluded. The sad looks, the pity—a full season of awkwardness.

She got another offer. She stalled for time, then, finally, accepted. The guy was way into her.

So Patrick asked Cora, just as friends. His whole group was going as friends. No pressure, just a good time.

Prom night arrived. Most groups turned it into a twelve-hour affair: photos, fine dining, the dance, the afterprom. Patrick's gang started at Gabriel's, an old Victorian home in the country that had been converted into an elegant steak and seafood house. They pulled up in a limo and ate like kings. Then it was a long ride into Denver for the big event. The prom committee chose the Denver Design Center, a local landmark known as "that building with the weird yellow thing." The "thing" was a monumental steel sculpture called *The Articulated Wall,* which looked like an eighty-five-foot DNA strand and towered over the shops and restaurants converted from old warehouses.

The trade-off with a famous city location was space. You could barely move on the dance floor. Patrick Ireland's second-most-memorable moment was dancing to "Ice Ice Baby." He had lip-synced to it in a third-grade talent show, so whenever they'd heard it for the next decade, he'd grabbed his buddies and performed the same goofy dance. That was nothing compared to holding Laura. He got one dance. A slow song. Heaven.

———

Cassie Bernall was not asked to prom. She was pretty but, in her estimation, a loser. The church boys from the youth group barely noticed her. At school she got attention, but strictly sexual. Friends were hard to come by. So she and her friend Amanda dressed up anyway, did their hair, and got all glamorous for a work banquet Amanda's mom had going at the Marriott. Then they cruised to afterprom, where dates were optional, and partied till dawn.

6. His Future

Dylan's prom group arranged for a limo, too. Robyn Anderson drove out to pick him up on Saturday afternoon. They shot pictures with his parents before meeting up with the five other couples to head into the city. Robyn wore midnight-blue satin with cap sleeves and matching opera-length gloves. She'd curled her hair in long blond ringlets, swept forward to bounce across her low-cut square neckline—a suburban variation on the classic Pre-Raphaelite style.

Dylan was giddy and beaming getting ready, all cleaned up for once, working to make everything look just right. He tugged his shirt cuffs down, straightened his tuxedo jacket. He'd gone with a traditional black tuxedo, bow tie slightly askew. A small splash of color lightened up his lapel: a pink-tipped rosebud with a tiny ribbon the color of Robyn's dress. His hair was slicked back into a short ponytail that kept giving him grief. He had shaved. His dad followed him around with a camcorder, capturing every move. Dylan looked at him through the lens: Dad, we're going to laugh about this in twenty years.

They rode downtown in a big honking stretch with tinted windows and a mirrored ceiling. Whoa! Dylan held Robyn's hand and compli-mented her on her dress. The first stop was dinner at Bella Ristorante, a trendy spot in Lower Downtown. It was a fun time: jokes and horseplay with table knives and matches, pretending to light themselves on fire. Dylan devoured an oversized salad, a big seafood entrée, and dessert. He gushed about the upcoming reunion for kids from the gifted program in elementary school. It would be fun hooking up again with the childhood smarties. Dylan had volunteered to use his Blackjack connection to get some pizzas.

They finished dinner early. Dylan stepped out for a cigarette. He asked his buddy Nate Dykeman to join him. It was cold out, but nice anyway—a little quiet time, away from all the commotion. Great food, great company, first time in a limo for both of them. "Everything is going perfect, as planned," Nate said later.

Nate was even taller than Dylan, six-four, and considerably more attractive. He had classic features and dark, heavy eyebrows that accentuated his piercing eyes. They talked more about reunions. Everyone was scattering for college. They talked about Dylan heading down to Arizona and Nate across the country to Florida. Nate wanted to work for Microsoft. What would they accomplish before reunion time rolled around? They tossed around the possibilities. "No hints whatsoever that anything could possibly be wrong," Nate recalled later. "We were just having a great time. It's our senior prom. We're enjoying it like we should."

The short ride to the Design Center was a blast: hard rock jamming from the speakers, an adrenaline rush while they riffed on one another. They made fun of pedestrians, flipped them off at random. Nobody could see in; they could see out. What a riot.

Dylan was in a great mood. We've got to stay in touch, he insisted. This group was too fun to let go.

———

Eric pressed his luck. He was crazy for a prom-night date, but he waited till early evening to call Susan. He was confident. Girls liked him. He asked her to come over for a movie. She swung by around seven. His parents had just left, out to dinner to celebrate their anniversary. Eric wanted to show Susan *Event Horizon,* a low-budget gorefest about a spaceship transported back from hell. It was his all-time favorite. They watched it straight through, then sat around his basement bedroom talking.

Eric's parents came home and went down to meet her. It was lots of aimless chitchat, like Eric's dad telling her he got his hair cut at Great Clips. They seemed friendly, Susan thought. They all got along well. After Eric's parents left, he played her some of his favorite tunes. It was mostly banging and screaming to her ear, but then he would mix in some New Age stuff like Enya. He put his arm around her once but didn't go for a kiss. He did lots of thoughtful things, like offering to warm up her car when she had to get home. She stayed until eleven—half an hour after she should have. Eric kissed her on the cheek and said good night.

———

Prom was the standard affair. They crowned a queen, they crowned a king, Mr. D breathed a sigh of relief that they had come through it alive. Dylan and Robyn had fun, but joy wasn't really the objective. Prom was more about acting out some weird facsimile of adulthood: dress up like a tacky wedding party, hold hands and behave like *a couple* even if you've never dated, and observe the etiquette of Gilded Age debutantes thrust into modern celebrity: limos, red carpets, and a constant stream of paparazzi, played by parents, teachers, and hired photo hacks.

For enjoyment, someone invented afterprom. Peel off the cummerbund, step out of the two-inch pumps, forget the stupid posing, and indulge in actual fun. Like gambling. The Columbine gym was outfitted with row after row of blackjack, poker, and craps tables. Parents in Vegas costumes served as dealers. They had ball-toss contests, a jump castle, and a bungee cord plunge. It stayed active till dawn. Afterprom had its own theme: New York, New York. Some parents had built a life-sized maze you had to follow to get into the school, and the entranceway was festooned with cardboard mock-ups of the Empire State Building and the Statue of Liberty. Some of the boys barely saw their dates at afterprom. Some didn't have one. Eric joined Dylan and his limo group. They spent hours in the casino losing fake money. Patrick Ireland hung out nearby. They never met. Dylan kept talking about college, about his future. He kept saying he could hardly wait.

7. Church on Fire

This is a church on fire. This is the heart of Evangelical country. This is Trinity Christian Center, an ecstatic congregation crying out for Jesus in a converted Kmart half a mile from Columbine. As the casino shut down in the school gym, the faithful rose across the Front Range. They spilled out into the aisles of Trinity Christian, heaving and rumbling like an old-time tent revival. The frenzied throng thrust two hundred arms toward the heavens, belting out the spirit their souls just couldn't contain. The choir drove them higher. It ripped through the chorus of Hillsong's burning anthem and the crowd surged.

This is a church on fire . . .
We have a burning desire . . .

No one had the fever like a sunburned high school girl, radiating from the choir like the orchids splashed across her sundress. She threw her head back, squeezed her eyes shut, and kept singing, her lips charging straight through the instrumental jam.

Since pioneer days and the Second Great Awakening, Colorado had been a hotbed on the itinerant ministry circuit. By the 1990s, Colorado Springs was christened the Evangelical Vatican. The city of Denver seemed immune to the fervor, but its western suburbs were roiling. Nowhere did the spirit move more strongly than at Trinity Christian Center. They had a savior to reach out to and The Enemy to repel.

Satan was at work in Jefferson County, any Bible-church pastor would tell you so. Long before Eric and Dylan struck, tens of thousands of Columbine Evangelicals prepared for the dark prince. The Enemy, they called him. He was always on the prowl.

Columbine sits three miles east of the foothills. Closer to the peaks, property values rise steadily, in tandem with decorum. In comparison to Trinity Christian, upscale congregations like Foothills Bible Church mount Broadway productions. Foothills Pastor Bill Oudemolen took stage like the quintessential televangelist: blow-dried, swept-back helmet hair, crisp tie, and tailored Armani suit in muted earth tones. But the stereotype dissolved when he opened his mouth. He was sincere, sharp-witted, and intellectual. He rebuked ministry-for-money preachers and their get-saved-quick schemes.

West Bowles Community Church lay between other megachurches geographically, socioeconomically, and intellectually. Like Oudemolen, Pastor George Kirsten was a biblical literalist. He was contemptuous of peers obsessed with a loving Savior. His Christ had a vengeful side. Love was an easy sell—that missed half the story. "That's offensive to me," Kirsten said. He preached a strict, black-and-white moral code. "People want to paint the world in a lot of gray," he said. "I don't see that in the Scripture."

Religion did not mean an hour a week on Sundays to this crowd. There was Bible study, youth group, fellowship, and retreats. The "thought for the day" started the morning; Scripture came before bed. West Bowles kids roamed the halls of Columbine sporting WWJD? bracelets—What Would Jesus Do?—and exchanging Christian rock CDs. Occasionally, they witnessed to the unbelievers or argued Scripture with the mainline Protestants. The Columbine Bible Study group met at the school once a week; its major challenges were resisting temptation, adhering to a higher standard, and acting as worthy servants of Christ. Its members kept a vigilant eye out for The Enemy.

Pastors Kirsten and Oudemolen spoke of Satan frequently. Reverend Oudemolen called him by name; Kirsten preferred The Enemy. Either way, Satan was more than a symbol of evil—he was an actual, physical entity, hungry for compliant souls.

He snatched the most unlikely targets. Who would have expected Cassie Bernall to fall? She was the angelic blond junior who'd dressed up for a function at the Marriott on Saturday instead of prom. She was scheduled to speak at her church's youth group meeting on Tuesday. Cassie's house sat right beside Columbine property, but it was only her second year at the school. She'd transferred in from Christian Fellowship School. She had begged her parents to make the move. The Lord had spoken to Cassie. He wanted her to witness to the unbelievers at Columbine.

———

Monday morning was uneventful. Lots of bleary eyes from Saturday's all-nighter, lots of chatter about who did what. All Mr. D's kids had made it back. A handful peeked through his doorway with big grins. "Just wanted you to see our bright, shining faces," they said.

Supervisory Special Agent Dwayne Fuselier was a little on edge Monday. He headed the FBI's domestic terrorism unit in Denver, and April 19 was a dangerous day in the region. The worst disaster in FBI history had erupted six years earlier and retaliation followed exactly two years after. On April 19, 1993, the Bureau ended a fifty-one-day standoff with the Branch Davidian cult near Waco, Texas, by storming the compound. A massive fire had erupted and most of the eighty inhabitants burned to death—adults and children. Agent Fuselier was one of the nation's foremost hostage negotiators. He spent six weeks trying to talk the Davidians out. Fuselier had opposed the attack on the compound, but lost. Just before storming in, the FBI gave Fuselier one final chance. He was the last person known to speak to Davidian leader David Koresh. He watched the compound burn.

Speculation raged about the FBI's role in the blaze. The controversy nearly ended Attorney General Janet Reno's career. Waco radicalized the anti-government militia movement, made April 19 into a symbol of perverse authority. Timothy McVeigh sought vengeance by bombing the Murrah Federal Building in Oklahoma City on April 19, 1995. His explosion killed 168 people, the largest terrorist attack in American history to that point.

8. Maximum Human Density

I t's a safe bet that Eric and Dylan watched the carnage of Waco and Oklahoma City on television, with the rest of the country. Those atrocities were particularly prominent in this region. McVeigh was tried in federal court in downtown Denver and sentenced to death while the boys attended Columbine in the suburbs. The scenes of devastation were played over and over. In his journal, Eric would brag about topping McVeigh. Oklahoma City was a one-note performance: McVeigh set his timer and walked away; he didn't even see his spectacle unfold. Eric dreamed much bigger than that.

Judgment Day, they called it. Columbine would erupt with an explosion, too. Eric designed at least seven big bombs, working off *The Anarchist Cookbook* he found on the Web. He chose the barbecue design: standard propane tanks, the fat, round white ones, eighteen inches tall, a foot in diameter, packing some twenty pounds of highly explosive gas. Bomb #1 employed aerosol cans for detonators, each wired up to an old-fashioned alarm clock with round metal bells on top. Step one was planting them in a park near Eric's house, three miles from the school. That bomb could kill hundreds of people but was intended for only stones and trees. The attack was to begin with a decoy: rock the neighborhood and divert police. Every free minute raised the potential body count. The boys were going to double or triple McVeigh's record. They estimated the damage variously as "hundreds," "several hundred," and "at least four hundred"—oddly conservative for the arsenal they were preparing.

Eric may have had another reason for the decoy plan. He was uncannily perceptive about people, and Dylan had been wavering. If Dylan was reticent, the decoy would help ease him in. It was a harmless explosive, no one would be hurt by it, but once they drove off, Dylan would be committed.

The main event was scripted in three acts, just like a movie. It would kick off with a massive explosion in the commons. More than six hundred students swarmed in at the start of "A" lunch, and two minutes after the bell rang, most of them would be dead. Act I featured two bombs, using propane tanks like the decoy. Each was strung with nails and BBs for shrapnel, lashed to a full gasoline can and a smaller propane tank, and wired to similar bell clocks. Each bomb fit snugly into a duffel bag, which Eric and Dylan would lug in at the height of passing-period chaos. Again, Dylan was eased into killing. Clicking over the alarm hinge was bloodless and impersonal. It didn't feel like killing—no blood, no screams. Most of Dylan's murders would be over before he faced them.

The fireball would wipe out most of the lunch crowd and set the school ablaze. Eric drew detailed diagrams. He spaced the bombs out but located them centrally, for maximum killing radius. They would sit beside two thick columns supporting the second floor. Computer modeling and field tests would later demonstrate a high probability that the bombs would have collapsed some of the second floor. Eric apparently hoped to watch the library and its inhabitants crash down upon the flaming lunchers.

As the time bombs ticked down, the killers would exit briskly and flare out across the parking lot at a ninety-degree angle. Each boy was to head for his own car, strategically parked about a hundred yards apart. The cars provided mobile base camps, where they would gear up to unleash Act II. Pre-positioning ensured optimal fire lanes. They had drilled the gear-ups repeatedly and could execute them rapidly. The bombs would detonate at 11:17, and the densely packed wing would crumble. As the flames leapt up, Eric and Dylan would train their semiautomatics on the exits and await survivors.

Act II: firing time. This was going to be fun. Dylan would sport an Intratec TEC-DC9 (a 9mm semiautomatic handgun) and a shotgun. Eric had a Hi-Point 9mm carbine rifle and a shotgun. They'd sawed the barrels off the shotguns for concealment. Between them, they'd carry eighty portable explosives—pipe bombs and carbon dioxide bombs that Eric called "crickets"—plus a supply of Molotov cocktails and an assortment of freakish knives, in case it came down to hand-to-hand combat. They'd suit up in infantry-style web harnesses, allowing them to strap much of the ammo and explosives to their bodies. Each had a backpack and a duffel bag to hump more hardware into the attack zone. They would tape flint match-striker strips to their forearms for rapid-fire pipe-bomb attacks. Their long black dusters would go on last—for concealment and for looking badass. (Later, the dusters were widely referred to as trench coats.)

They planned to advance on the building as soon as the bombs blew. They'd be set back far enough to see each other around the corner—and just barely avoid the blast. They had devised their own hand signals to communicate. Every detail was planned; battle positions were imperative. The 250,000-square-foot school had twenty-five exits, so some survivors would escape. The boys could remain in visual contact and still cover two sides of the building, including two of the three main exits. Their firing lines intersected on the most important point: the student entrance, adjacent to the commons and just a dozen yards from the big bombs.

Positioning yourself at a right angle to the objective is standard U.S. infantry practice, taught to every American foot soldier at the Infantry School in Fort Benning, Georgia. Interlocking fire lanes, the military calls it. The target is constantly under fire from two sides, yet the assault team's weapons are never pointed at confederates. Even if a shooter turns sharply to peg an escaping enemy, his squad mates are safe. From their initial positions, Eric and Dylan could sweep their gun barrels across a ninety-degree firing radius without endangering each other. Even if one shooter advanced more quickly, he would never violate his partner's fire lane. It is both the safest and the most effective assault pattern of modern small-arms warfare.

This was the phase Eric and Dylan were savoring. It was also when they expected to die. They had little hope of witnessing Act III. Forty-five minutes after the initial blast, when the cops declared it was over, paramedics started loading amputees into ambulances, and reporters broadcast the horror to a riveted nation, Eric's Honda and Dylan's BMW would rip right through the camera crews and the first responders. Each car was to be loaded with two more propane devices and twenty gallons of gasoline in an assortment of orange plastic jugs. Their positions had been chosen to maximize both the firepower in Act II and the carnage in Act III. The cars would be close to the building, near the main exits—ideal locations for police command, emergency medical staging, and news vans. They would be just far enough from the building and each other to wipe out most of the junior and senior parking lots. Maximum body count: nearly 2,000 students, plus 150 faculty and staff, plus who knows how many police, paramedics, and journalists.

Eric and Dylan had been considering a killing spree for at least a year and a half. They had settled on the approximate time and location a year out: April, in the commons. They finalized details as Judgment Day approached: Monday, April 19. The date appeared firm. The boys referred to it twice matter-of-factly in the recordings they made in the last ten days. They did not explain the choice, though Eric discussed topping Oklahoma City, so they may have been planning to echo that anniversary, as Tim McVeigh had done with Waco.

The moment of attack was critical. Students liked to eat early, so "A" lunch was the most popular. The maximum human density anywhere, anytime in the high school occurred in the commons at 11:17. Eric knew the exact minute because he had inventoried his targets. He'd counted just 60 to 80 kids scattered about the commons from 10:30 to 10:50. Between 10:56 and 10:58, "lunch ladies bring out shit," he wrote. Then lunch door 2 opened, and a "steady trickle of people" appeared. He recorded the exact moment each door opened, and body counts in minute-by-minute increments. At 11:10, the bell rang, fourth period ended, students piled into the hallways. Moments later, they rushed the lunch lines, fifty more every minute: 300, 350, 400, 450, 500-plus by 11:15. Eric and Dylan's various handwritten timelines show the bombs scheduled to explode between 11:16 and 11:18. The final times are followed by little quips: "Have fun!" and "HA HA HA."

Eric and Dylan expected their attack to puzzle the public, so they left an extraordinary cache of material to explain themselves. They kept schedules, budgets, maps, drawings, and all sorts of logistical artifacts, along with commentary in notebooks, journals, and Web sites. A series of videos were specifically designed to explain their attack. They would come to be known as the Basement Tapes, because the bulk were shot in Eric's basement. Even more illuminating was Eric's twenty-page journal devoted to his thinking. Both chronicles are revealing, but also maddeningly contradictory. They were so disturbing that the sheriff's department would choose to hide them from the public, concealing even the existence of the Basement Tapes for months. Eric and Dylan's true intentions would remain a mystery for years.

———

The date was the first element of Eric's plan to fail—apparently because of ammo. On Monday, he had nearly seven hundred rounds for the four guns. He wanted more. He had just turned eighteen, so he could buy his own, but that fact somehow escaped him. He was used to relying on others, and he thought Mark Manes could help. Manes was a drug dealer who ran some guns and ammo on the side. He had come through with the TEC-9 in January, but he was dragging ass on the ammo. Thursday night, Eric began hounding him to come up with the stuff. Four days later, Eric remained empty-handed.

They could have gone ahead without the extra ammo, but their fire-power would have been impaired. Shotguns are not built for rapid-fire assault. The TEC-9 took twenty- and thirty-round magazines. Dylan could release one with the flick of a button and pop in a new mag with a single sweep of the hand. Real gun aficionados hate the thing. It's too big and bulky for a professional and way too unreliable—a poor man's Uzi. Dealers complain of slapdash design, frequent misfeeds, and a lousy sighting mechanism that is often misaligned and can't be adjusted. "Cheap construction and marginal reliability," says a major Russian gun dealer's Web site. But it was available.

———

Eric and Dylan had a mostly uneventful Monday. They got up before sunrise to make bowling class by 6:00 A.M. They cut fourth hour for an extended lunch at Blackjack, and attended their other classes as usual. That evening, Manes suddenly came through with the ammo. He'd gotten it at Kmart: two boxes, with fifty rounds apiece. Together, they cost twenty-five bucks.

Eric drove to Manes's house to pick up the ammo. He seemed eager to get it. Manes asked if Eric was going shooting that night.

Maybe tomorrow, Eric said.

9. Dads

Dave Sanders had never talked about regret before. Not to Frank DeAngelis. They talked every day, they had been close for twenty years, but they had never gone there.

It came up unexpectedly, on Monday afternoon. Frank strolled out to the baseball diamond to watch his boys take on archrival Chatfield. He had coached the team before he went into administration, alongside his old friend Dave Sanders. And there at the top of the bleachers was Dave watching right now. He had a couple hours to kill until his girls arrived for basketball practice. The season was over, but they were working fundamentals for next year. Dave could have spent the time grading papers, but it was hard to fight the lure of the field.

Mr. D said hi to the kids excited to see him there, then sat down next to Dave. They talked for two hours. They talked about everything. Their entire lives. Coaching, of course. The first time they met, when Frank arrived at Columbine in 1979. He was one of the shortest teachers on the faculty and the principal recruited him to coach basketball. "They needed a freshman coach, and I was on a one-year contract," Frank said. "The principal said, 'Frank, if you do me this one favor, I owe you one.' And what am I gonna say? 'I'll do whatever you want, sir.' So I coached basketball."

The conversation was lighthearted for a long time, Dave cutting up as usual. Then he turned serious. "Do you miss coaching?" he asked.

"Not really." Frank's answer sort of surprised Dave. Coaching was his life, Frank explained, but he had never really left it. He'd just expanded his audience.

"You think so?" Dave wondered.

Oh, yeah, Frank said. You can't really teach a kid anything: you can only show him the way and motivate him to learn it himself. Same thing applies to shortstops turning the double play and students grasping the separation of powers in the U.S. government. It's all the same job. Now he had to coach teachers, too, to inspire their own kids to learn.

"What about you?" Frank asked. "Any regrets?"

"Yeah. Too much coaching."

They shared a good laugh.

Seriously, though, Dave said. His family had come second to coaching. God. His family came second.

Frank suppressed another laugh. His own son, Brian, was nineteen. Frank was confident he had been a good dad, but never enough of one. It had rankled his wife since day one, and recently she had laid into him about it: "When are you going to stop raising everybody else's kids and start raising your own?"

That stung. It was a little hard to share, but this seemed like the moment, and Dave seemed like the guy. Dave understood. It was bittersweet for both of them. They had reached middle age blissfully. They wouldn't change a moment for their own sake—but had they shortchanged their kids? Frank's son was grown now, and Dave's daughters were, too. Too late. But they were still young women, and Dave had five grandkids and was hoping for more. Dave had not told the other coaches he was cutting back yet. He had not announced his decision to take off the first summer in memory. He confided it all to Frank now.

What an amazing guy, Frank thought. He thought about hugging Dave. He did not.

The game was still going, but Dave got up. "My girls are waiting for me," he said. "I have open gym."

Frank watched him walk slowly away.

————

Coach Sanders had something else on his mind. He had held his first team meeting last Friday, and his new team captain, Liz Carlston, had failed to show. He expected to see her tonight. It was going to be a tense conversation, and it wasn't going to be just her.

Sanders sat all the girls down on the court. They talked a lot about dedication. How was it going to look to the freshmen if the team leaders mouthed the words, then failed to show up? He expected a one hundred percent commitment. Every practice, every meeting, or you're out.

He told them to scrimmage. He let them keep at it the entire evening. He sat on a folding chair watching, analyzing, preparing.

At the end of the night, Liz tried to summon the courage to talk to him. She had just blanked on the meeting; she hadn't meant anything by it. She felt guilt and fear and anger. He wouldn't actually cut her, would he? Why hadn't he given her a chance to explain?

She stopped at the baseline to change her shoes. Coach Sanders was right there. She should talk to him.

She walked out quietly. She didn't even say good-bye.

———

Linda Lou was asleep when Dave got home that night. He kissed her softly. She woke up and smiled.

Dave was holding a wad of cash—a thick stash, seventy singles. He flung them toward her and they fluttered down onto the comforter. She got excited. She loved his little surprises, but she wasn't sure what this was about. He went with it for a minute, got her hopes up, and then said she was silly: it was for her mom. Linda's mom was turning seventy on April 20. She liked to gamble. She would like that.

Dave was all laughs that might with Linda. She was shocked when she learned later how tense his evening had been.

"That's how the man could change," she said. "Walk through our door and he was done with basketball. Now he was thinking of my mom."

He went down to fix himself a Diet Coke and rum. He found a game. Linda fell back asleep with a smile.

———

Morning was less pleasant. The alarm buzzed at 6:30. Linda and Dave were both in a rush. Linda had to pick up balloons for her mom's birthday party, and Dave had to drop Linda's poodle off for a haircut.

Dave had no time for breakfast. He snagged an energy bar and a banana for the car. It was trash day—his job, but he was going to be late. He asked Linda if she would do it.

She was too stressed. "I really don't have time today."

"I'm really going to be late," he muttered.

They rushed out to separate cars and realized they had forgotten to kiss good-bye. They always kissed good-bye.

Dave blew her a kiss from the driveway.

10. Judgment

O n Tuesday morning, the boys rose early, as usual. It was dark but warm already, set to soar into the eighties, with blue skies, perfect for their fires. It was going to be a beautiful day.

Dylan was out of the house by 5:30. His parents were still in bed. He called out "Bye," and shut the door behind himself.

They skipped bowling class and went straight to work. Dylan scrawled the schedule into Eric's day planner under the heading "make TODAY count." Eric illustrated it with a blazing gun barrel.

First stop was the grocery store, where they met up to acquire the last of the propane tanks: two for the cafeteria, two for each car, and two for the decoy. The big bombs were the heart of the attack. Eric had designed them months before but had left acquisition to the final morning. The boys had stashed most of the arsenal in Eric's bedroom closet, and he had faced a couple of close calls with his parents already. Hiding a cluster of twenty-pound tanks in there was out of the question.

They returned to Eric's house at 7:00 and then split up: Eric filled the propane tanks, Dylan got the gasoline. They allotted half an hour to assemble the big bombs and set up the cars, and an hour for one last round of gear-up, practice, and "chill." They got something to eat. Dylan apparently had potato skins.

Several friends noticed peculiarities. Robyn Anderson was surprised to see Dylan a no-show for calculus. He had sounded fine on the phone the previous night. Then a friend told her Eric had been missing from third hour. The boys cut an occasional class together, but never an entire morning. Robyn hoped Dylan wasn't sick; she made a mental note to call once she got home.

Their friend Brooks Brown had a stronger reaction. Eric had missed a test in psychology class. *What kind of stunt was that?*

————

Chill time was over. It had gone on too long, perilously over schedule. Shortly before 11:00 A.M., Eric and Dylan set off with the arsenal. Dylan wore cargo pants, a black T-shirt printed with WRATH, and his Red Sox cap turned backward, as usual. His cargo pockets were deep enough to conceal most of the sawed-off shotgun before he pulled on the duster. Eric's T-shirt said NATURAL SELECTION. They both wore black combat boots and shared a single pair of black gloves—the right on Eric, the left on Dylan. They left two pipe bombs behind at Eric's house, six at Dylan's. Eric laid a microcassette on the kitchen counter with some final thoughts. They also left the Basement Tapes, with a final good-bye recorded that morning.

They drove separate cars to a park near Eric's house, dumped the decoy bomb in a field, and set the timers for 11:14. Combat operations were under way.

They hopped back in their cars and headed for the school. They had to hustle now. The last few minutes were critical. They couldn't plant the big bombs until "A" lunch began. Fourth period ended at 11:10. Once the bell rang, they had seven minutes to carry the bombs in, navigate the turbulent lunch crowd, stash the bombs by the designated pillars, get back to their cars, gear up, take cover, and prepare to attack.

Eric pulled into the parking lot at 11:10, several minutes behind schedule. A couple of girls spotted his car as they headed out for lunch. They honked and waved. They liked him. Eric waved back and smiled. Dylan followed him in. No waves.

Dylan drove to his normal spot in the senior lot and parked his BMW directly in front of the cafeteria. When the attack began, this would afford him a clear sweep of the southwest side of the building: the long, wide arc of green-tinted windows that wrapped the commons on the first floor and the library above.

Eric continued on to the small junior lot, about a hundred yards to Dylan's right. Eric had the choice spot, directly facing the student entrance, where the bulk of the survivors would presumably flee. He could also cover the full southeast side of the building and interlock his fire with Dylan's to his left.

Brooks Brown walked out for a cigarette and spotted Eric parking in the wrong lot. Brooks charged up to confront him about the test; by the time he got there, Eric had stepped out and was pulling out a big hulking duffel bag.

"What's the matter with you?" Brooks yelled. "We had a test in psychology!"

Eric was calm but insistent. "It doesn't matter anymore," he said. "Brooks, I like you now. Get out of here. Go home."

Brooks thought that was strange. But he shook his head and walked on, away from the school.

Eric's friend Nate Dykeman also caught sight of him arriving, and also found the circumstances strange.

Eric headed in with his duffel. By 11:12, they were scheduled to be back at their cars, arming up. A surveillance tape time-stamped 11:14 indicates they had still not entered the commons. They had less than three minutes—the timers were set for 11:17. There was only a modest chance that they could make it to safety in time. And they could hardly have hoped to be locked and loaded when the bombs blew.

They could have reset the timers and sacrificed a few casualties. That would have required coordination, as they had parked across the lot from each other and it would be risky to expose the bombs inside the cafeteria. They could have abandoned the plan, but the decoy bombs might already be exploding.

Shortly after 11:14, they entered the commons. They moved inconspicuously enough to go unnoticed. Not one of the five hundred witnesses noticed them or the big, bulky bags. One of the bags would be found inches from two tables strewn with food.

They made it out, and armed quickly. It was just like the drill, except this time each was alone—close enough for hand signals, too far to hear. They strapped on their arsenals, covered them with the dusters. Time was tight and they broke with their drill, leaving the shotguns in the duffel bags. Each boy had a semiautomatic against his body, a shotgun in his bag, and a backpack full of pipe bombs and crickets. This is probably the moment they set the timers on their car bombs. It would just be a matter of seconds now. Hundreds of kids dead. As far as they knew, they had instigated mass murder already. The timers were winding down. Nothing to do but wait.

Surveillance cameras should have caught the killers placing the bombs. They would have, if either the bombers or the custodian had been on time. Every morning, the custodian followed the same routine: a few minutes before "A" lunch, he pulled out the prelunch tape and set it aside for later viewing. He popped an old, used tape into the machine, rewound it, and hit Record. Rewinding took up to five minutes, meaning a brief pause in taping. Kids could leave all the garbage they wanted during that window, but hardly anyone was around to do so.

The custodian was running late on Tuesday. He hit the stop button at 11:14, and no bombs were visible; neither was Eric or Dylan. While waiting out the rewind, the custodian got a phone call. He talked, and the tape sat a little longer. He got the new tape in and hit Record at 11:22, leaving an eight-minute gap. The first frame shows the bombs visible and students near the windows beginning to react. Something peculiar outside has caught their attention.

———

Columbine ran on a bell schedule, and most of its inhabitants followed a strict routine. Several of them had broken it Tuesday morning. Patrick Ireland, the junior afraid to ask Laura to the prom, liked variety. Some days he spent "A" lunch in the library, others in the cafeteria. He had stayed up late talking to Laura on the phone again, and still had to finish his stats homework. So he headed to the library with four of his buddies as Eric and Dylan positioned the duffel bags. Patrick sat down at a table just above one of the bombs.

Cassie Bernall, the Evangelical junior who had transferred to Columbine to enlighten nonbelievers, pulled up a chair near the window. It was unusual to find her in the library at this hour. She was also behind on her homework, trying to complete an English assignment on *Macbeth*. But she was happy she had finished the presentation she would be making to her youth group that night.

Mr. D was oddly absent from the cafeteria. His secretary had booked an interview, delaying his rounds. He sat in his office at the opposite end of the main corridor, waiting for a young teacher to arrive. Mr. D. was about to offer him a permanent position.

Deputy Neil Gardner, the community resource officer, worked for the sheriff's department but was assigned full-time to Columbine. He normally ate with the kids, and "A" lunch was his optimal chance for bonding, a key element of his job. He wore the same security uniform with the bright yellow shirt every day, so he was easy to spot. Tuesday, Gardner took a break from his normal routine. He didn't care for the teriyaki on the menu, so he went for takeout from Subway with his campus boss—an unarmed civilian security guard. It was a beautiful day, lots of kids were outside, so they decided to check out the smokers. They ate their sandwiches in Gardner's squad car, in the faculty lot beside the smokers' pit on the opposite side of the school.

Robyn Anderson sat in her car nearby. She had driven out of the senior lot just about the time Eric and Dylan were hauling the bombs in, but had missed them. She'd swung around the building to pick up two friends. She got antsy—lunchtime was slipping away. Five minutes passed, maybe ten. Finally, the girls appeared. Robyn snarled at them, and they drove off. On the opposite end of the school, shots had already been fired.

A freshman named Danny Rohrbough went to the commons to meet up with two buddies. After a few minutes, they decided to head out for a smoke. If the bombs had worked, that choice might have saved him. He might have gotten out just in time. They headed out a side exit at the worst moment, directly alongside the senior parking lot.

The bombers spent a minute or two by their cars. They knew the diversionary bomb should have already blown three miles to the south. In fact, it had fizzled. A surveyor working in the area had moved it, and then the pipe bombs and one of the spray cans had detonated, producing a loud bang and a grass fire. But the propane tanks—the main explosive force—lay undisturbed in the burning field. The decoy was Eric's only big bomb to ignite at all, but one of his dumber ideas. Officials learned of it just as the shooting started, four minutes before the first call from the school. The chief effect was to alert authorities that something was amiss in the area. Nothing of consequence was diverted.

Eric and Dylan had to proceed on faith.

As far as Eric and Dylan knew, cops were already speeding south. They would see the commons disintegrate, though. Each car was positioned for a perfect view. The cafeteria would explode in front of them; they would watch their classmates be torn apart and incinerated, and their high school burning to the ground.

II. Female Down

At 11:18, the school stood intact. Some kids had already made it through the lunch lines and were strolling outside, settling onto the lawn for a little picnic. No sign of disturbance. The timing devices were not precise. No digital readouts with seconds counting down in red numerals; they were old-fashioned clocks with a third little alarm hand positioned two-fifths of the way between the 3 and the 4. But they should have blown by now.

Hundreds of targets streamed out the student entrance. They hopped into their cars and zipped away. Time for Plan B. There was no Plan B. Eric had staggering confidence in himself. He left no indication that he planned for contingencies. Dylan left no indication that he planned much of anything.

They could just proceed to Act II: mow the departers down in a cross fire and advance on the exits as scripted. They still could have topped McVeigh. But they didn't. The bomb failure appears to have rattled one of the boys.

No one observed what happened next. Either boy might have panicked, but Eric was unflappable, the reverse of his partner. The physical evidence also points to Dylan. Eric apparently acted swiftly to retrieve his emotional young partner.

We don't know whether they employed their hand signals, or how they came together. We know that Eric was in the prime location yet abandoned it to come to Dylan's. And Eric moved quickly. Within two minutes, Eric had figured out that the bombs had failed, grabbed his packs, crossed the lot to Dylan's car, rushed with him to the building, and climbed the external stairs to the west exit. That's the first place they were observed, at 11:19.

Their new position set them on the highest point on campus, where they could survey both lots and all the exits on that side of the building. But it took them away from their primary target: the student entrance, still disgorging students. They could no longer triangulate or advance aggressively without separating.

At 11:19 they opened the duffel bags at the top of the stairs, pulled out the shotguns, and strapped them to their bodies. They locked and loaded the semiautomatics. One of them yelled, "Go! Go!" Somebody, almost certainly Eric, opened fire.

Eric wheeled around and shot at anyone he could see. Dylan cheered him on. He rarely fired. They hit pedestrians among the trees, picnickers to the south, kids coming up the stairs to the east. They tossed pipe bombs down the stairs, into the grass, and onto the roof. And they shared a whole lot of hoots and howls and hearty laughs. What a freaking wild time.

Rachel Scott and her friend Richard Castaldo were the first down. They had been eating their lunch in the grass. Eric shot Richard in the arms and torso. He hit Rachel in the chest and head. Rachel died instantly. Richard played dead. Eric fell for it.

Danny and his smoking buddies Lance Kirklin and Sean Graves were headed up the dirt path toward the stairs. They saw the gunmen firing, but assumed it was a paintball game or a senior prank. It looked like fun. They rushed straight toward the shooters, to get closer to the action. Danny got out ahead, making it halfway up the stairs. Eric pivoted and fired his carbine rifle. A shot tore through Danny's left knee: in the front and out the back. He stumbled and began to fall. Eric fired again and again. As Danny collapsed, he took a second bullet to the chest, and a third to the abdomen. The upper round went straight through him as well, causing severe trauma to his heart. It stopped pumping immediately. The third shot lacerated his liver and stomach, causing major organ damage and lodging inside.

Lance tried to catch Danny, but realized he had been hit, too, multiple times, in the chest, leg, knee, and foot.

Danny's face hit the concrete sidewalk. Death was almost instantaneous.

Lance went down on the grass. He blacked out, but continued to breathe.

Sean burst out laughing. He was sure it was paintball. They were part of the game now.

Sean felt a shot zip by his neck. It left a cool breeze in its wake. He felt a couple of pricks, like an IV needle being pulled out. He did not realize he had been shot. He looked around. Both his friends were down. Pain signals reached Sean's brain. It felt like someone had kicked him in the back. He ran back for the door they had come out. He nearly made it. But the pain overcame him, his legs gave out, and he collapsed. He couldn't feel his legs anymore. He could not understand what had happened. He seemed to have been shot by a tranquilizer gun.

Eric turned again and spotted five kids under a clump of pines in the grass. He fired, and the kids took off running. One fell. He played dead, too. Another took a hit but kept on running. The last three got away clean.

The shooters kept moving. Lance regained consciousness. He felt someone hovering above him. He reached up toward the guy, tugged on his pant leg, and cried for help.

"Sure, I'll help," the gunman said.

The wait seemed like forever to Lance. He described the next event as a sonic blast that twisted his face apart. He watched chunks of it fly away. Breaths came rapidly: air in, blood out. He faded out again.

Dylan made his way down the hill, toward Sean. Several people in the cafeteria saw him coming. Someone ran out, grabbed Sean, and started dragging him in. An adult stopped him. She said it was dangerous to move a seriously injured person. Sean ended up propped in the entrance, with the door pressed against him. Someone tried to step over him on the way out, planted a foot into Sean's back, and said, "Oh, sorry, dude."

A janitor came by and reassured Sean. He held Sean's hand, said he would stay with him, but he had to help kids escape first. He advised Sean to play dead. Sean did.

Dylan fell for it again, or pretended to. He stepped right over Sean's crumpled body and walked inside.

A stampede was under way in there. The lunch crowd had panicked. Most took cover under tables; some ran for the stairs. Coach Sanders heard the commotion in the faculty lounge and ran toward the danger.

"I don't think he even thought about it," his daughter Angela said later. "His instinct was to save his kids."

Dave burst into the commons and tried to take charge. Two custodians followed him to assist. Sanders directed students to get down. He rethought that pretty quickly and yelled, "Run!"

Sanders looked around. There were exits in three directions, but most of them looked bad. There was one plausible option: across the commons and up the wide concrete stairway to the second floor. No telling what was up there, but anything was better than this. Sanders led the way. He ran across the open room unprotected, waving his arms to get the kids' attention and yelling for them to follow. The tables offered little true protection, but they *felt* a lot safer. It was scary out in the open. The kids trusted Coach Sanders, though.

A wave of students swelled behind Sanders. Most of the 488 people in the commons followed him toward the stairs. He bolted to the top and spun around to direct traffic. *To the left! To the left!* He sent them all down the corridor toward the east exit, away from the senior parking lot.

"The whole time he was just saving people," a student said. "He took me and just pushed me into a room."

Some students stopped to warn others; some just ran. Someone ran into the choir room and yelled, "There's a gun!"

Half the kids took cover; the other half fled. A few doors down, in Science Room 3, students were immersed in a chemistry test. They heard something like rocks being thrown against the windows, but the teacher assumed it was a prank. Stay seated and concentrate on your test, he said.

Dave Sanders stayed behind until every kid had passed. The tail end of the mob was just pushing its way to the stairs as Dylan stepped inside the cafeteria.

There were twenty-four steps. About a hundred kids were caught on the staircase, racing for cover on the second floor. They were wedged between each other and the steel railings. Nowhere to take cover. They were arrayed at different heights for easy access. Crouching was not an option—anyone attempting to stop would get trampled. The cafeteria was roughly one hundred feet wide. Dylan was in easy firing range. One or two pipe bombs or one burst from his TEC-9 would have halted the entire advance. Dylan took a few steps in, lifted his weapon up to firing position.

This was the second time since setting the timers that Dylan separated from Eric. For the second time, Dylan appeared to lose his nerve. He swept his rifle in an arc across the room. He watched the students disappear up the stairs. He did not fire. He had only engaged his weapon a few times.

Dylan looked around, then turned and stepped back over Sean in the doorway. The heavy door whacked Sean hard again in its grip. Dylan rejoined Eric at the top of the stairs.

It's not clear why Dylan made his cafeteria excursion. Many have speculated that he came down to see what went wrong with the bombs. But he never went near them. He made no attempt at detonation. It's more likely that Eric sent him in to check for opportunities and rev up the body count.

Dylan did nothing on his own, but Eric amused himself heartily at the top of the stairs, shooting, laughing, and hurling pipe bombs. He spotted a junior named Anne Marie Hochhalter getting up from the curb to make a run for it. Eric hit her with a 9mm round. She kept running, and he hit her again. This time she went down. A friend picked her up, dragged her to the building, and got her out of Eric's sight. Then he let go of her and ran. He ducked behind a car in the senior lot, and a pipe bomb exploded where Anne Marie had first collapsed.

"This is awesome!" one of the killers yelled.

By the time Dylan rejoined Eric, they had used up all the easy targets. Everybody caught outside had run like crazy or hidden. One last pack was still in the open. These students had fled across the senior lot, climbed over the chain-link fence, and were racing across the soccer field near the base of Rebel Hill. Eric had a go at them. They were too far. Not out of range, just too hard to hit. Dylan fired at the distant targets, too, bringing his total shot count up to five. It was 11:23. The killers had enjoyed four heady minutes.

———

Deputy Gardner was the first officer alerted. The custodian radioed Gardner as soon as he started the new surveillance tape and caught sight of kids near the windows. The custodian sounded scared. The first 911 call came through to Jeffco at the same time. A girl was injured in the senior parking lot. "I think she's paralyzed," the caller said. The dispatch hit the police band at 11:23, just as Gardner drove around the building to the commons and Dylan rejoined Eric at the top of the stairs. "Female down," the dispatcher said.

Gardner saw smoke rising and kids running. He heard gunshots and explosions and a flurry of dispatches on his radio. He couldn't quite tell where the commotion was coming from.

———

Four minutes into the mayhem, much of the student body was oblivious. Hundreds were running for their lives, but more sat quietly in class. Many heard the commotion; few sensed any danger. Most found it annoying. The chaos and the solitude went on side by side, often only yards apart. As Dave Sanders ushered kids to the commons staircase, part-time art teacher Patti Nielson paced above him on hall-monitor duty. Sanders herded the lunch crowd up the stairwell toward her, but then down a parallel hallway. Nearly five hundred kids charged the length of the building. Nielson never saw or heard them. She heard the racket outside, though. Some kids ran up saying they heard gunfire. Nielson was annoyed. It was a prank, obviously, or a video shoot. It had gone on far too long. She looked down the corridor to the west exit. Through the large glass panes in the doors she could see a boy with his back to her. He had a gun. He was firing it into the senior lot. She assumed it was a prop, a loud one, and totally inappropriate. Nielson stormed down the hallway to tell him to knock it off. A junior named Brian tagged along to watch.

They approached the exit just as the shooters ran out of targets. There were two sets of doors there, separated by an air lock. Nielson and Brian passed the first set and reached for the second handles. Eric spotted them. He turned, raised the rifle to his shoulder, aimed at Nielson, and smiled. Then he fired. The glass shattered, but the bullet missed. Nielson still thought it was a BB gun. Then she saw the size of the hole.

"Dear God!" she screamed. "Dear God! Dear God!"

She turned to run. He fired again. Another miss, but glass and metal shards and possibly a grazing bullet tore through the back of her shoulder. It burned. Brian had turned, too. Nielson heard him grunt, saw him lurch forward. His back arched, his arms flared, and he hit the floor hard. That looked bad, but he got right up onto his hands and knees to scurry back through the first doors. It was shrapnel, just like hers.

She got down, too, and they crawled the short distance back to the first doors. They got one partially open and squeezed through. Once they had that door behind them, they rose to their feet and ran.

Nielson was desperate for a phone. The library seemed like an obvious destination. It was just around the corner, spanning most of the south hallway, behind a glass wall. Nielson saw dozens of kids milling about inside, plainly visible to the shooters she pictured on her heels. She never looked back to see.

Nielson ran into the library to warn them. "There's a kid with a gun!" she yelled.

There were no adults. That surprised Nielson. Teacher Rich Long had rushed in moments before, yelled at everyone to get out, and then fled to warn others. Patti Nielson had the opposite instinct. She ordered them down.

Then Nielson grabbed the phone behind the counter and punched in 9-911. She concentrated on details, like the extra 9 for an outside line. *Don't waste a second!*

Nielson expected the shooter to arrive any moment now. But Eric was not following. He had been distracted. Deputy Gardner had pulled into the lot with lights flashing and siren blaring. Gardner had stepped out of his car, still confused about what he was walking into.

Eric opened fire. He got off ten rounds, all misses. Dylan did nothing.

Gardner took cover behind his police car. Eric didn't even hit that. Then his rifle jammed. Eric fought to clear the chamber. Dylan fled into the school.

Gardner saw his opening. He laid his pistol across the roof and squeezed off four shots. Eric spun around like he'd been hit. Neutralized, Gardner thought. What a relief.

Seconds later, Eric was firing again. It was a short burst; then he retreated inside.

It was 11:24. The outside ordeal lasted five minutes. Eric did most of the shooting. He fired his 9mm rifle forty-seven times in that period and did not use his shotgun. Dylan got just three shots off with the TEC-9 hand-gun and two with his shotgun.

They headed down the hallway toward the library.

———

Dave Sanders heard the shots when Eric fired on Patti Nielson. Coach Sanders ran toward the gunfire. He passed the library entrance just moments after Nielson ran in. He spotted the killers at the other end of the hallway. He wheeled around and ran for the corner.

A boy peeked out of the choir room just in time to see him flee. Sanders wasn't just running for it, he was trying to clear students out of the line of fire. "Get down!" he yelled.

12. The Perimeter

The story took twenty-eight minutes to hit local television. The networks quickly followed. Something awful was happening at a high school near Denver. Coverage began with confused reports about a shooting in the outlying suburbs: no confirmation on injuries, but multiple shots—as many as nine—and possible explosions. Automatic weapons might be involved, possibly even grenades. A fire had been reported. SWAT teams were mobilizing.

CNN was locked in on Kosovo. NATO had gone to war over the genocide there. Night had just fallen in Belgrade, and American warplanes were massing on the horizon, about to pulverize fresh targets across the Serb capital. At 11:54 A.M. Denver time, CNN cut to Jeffco and stayed there nonstop, all afternoon. The broadcast networks began interrupting the soaps. Columbine quickly overshadowed the war. No one seemed to know what had actually happened. Was it still happening? Apparently. As the networks went live with the story, gunfire and explosions were erupting somewhere inside that school. Outside, it was mayhem: choppers circled, and police, firefighters, parents, and journalists had descended on the campus. Nobody was going inside. Fresh waves of support troops were arriving by the minute, but they just crowded around the building. Occasionally, students would scurry out.

Local stations kept surveying the area hospitals. "There are no patients yet," a journalist reported from one. "But they are expecting one victim with an ankle wound."

Jeffco 911 operators were overwhelmed. Hundreds of students were still inside the building. Many had cell phones and were calling with conflicting reports. Thousands of parents from all around the area were dialing the same center, demanding information. Many students gave up on 911 and called the TV stations. Local anchors began interviewing them live on the air, and the cable networks picked up their feeds.

Witnesses confirmed injuries. A girl said she watched "like three people" get shot.

"Did it look like they were shooting at specific people?" a reporter asked.

"They were just shooting. They were—they didn't care who they shot at; they were just shooting and then they threw a grenade or they threw something that blew up."

There seemed to be no end of "witnesses," though most had seen chaos but no one causing it. A senior described the first moments of awareness: "OK, I was sitting in math class, and all of a sudden we look out and there's people that are sprinting down the math hall and we open the door, we hear a shot, a loud bang, and then we hear some guy go 'holy crap, there's a guy with a gun!' So everybody starts freaking out, one of my friends goes up to the door and says there's a guy standing there. We evacuate to the corner of our classroom and my teacher just doesn't know what to do because she's so freaked."

There appeared to be several shooters—all boys, all white, all Columbine students. Some were shooting in the parking lot, some in the cafeteria, some upstairs while roaming the halls. Somebody was positioned on the roof. Some of the assault team wore T-shirts; others advanced in long black trench coats. One pair included one of each. Some had hats, and one or two were hiding behind ski masks.

Some of this mix-up was standard crime-scene confusion. Contrary to popular conception, eyewitness testimony is notoriously unreliable, especially when witnesses were under duress. Memories get jumbled and witnesses imagine missing details without realizing they're doing it. But much of this misunderstanding was due to specific factors. Eric discarded his trench coat at the top of the stairs almost as soon as he began shooting. Dylan kept his on until he got to the library. Each costume change created another shooter. The school's location on a hill, with nearby entrances on both floors, allowed Eric and Dylan to be seen upstairs and downstairs almost simultaneously. The long-range weapons scattered gunfire over a shooting radius hundreds of yards wide. Distant witnesses had no idea where the shooters were; they only knew they were under attack. Some witnesses listened carefully and correctly located the source of the turbulence—but the bomb blasts often led them astray, particularly when bombs landed on the roof. Several kids were sure something was coming from up there. They spotted a frightened air-conditioner repairman and instantly identified him as the rooftop gunman.

———

Word whipped through the Columbine community. Kids called home on their cell phones the minute they got to safety—or someplace they hoped would remain safe. About five hundred students were off campus, either for lunch or sick or cutting class. Their first sign of a problem came when they hit police barricades as they tried to return. Cops were everywhere. More cops than they had ever seen.

Nate Dykeman was one of the kids heading back in. He was stunned by the stories he heard. Nate had gone home for lunch, same as he did every day. But on the way out, he had seen something peculiar: Eric walking into the building from the wrong parking lot at the wrong time. He should have been walking out. Eric and Dylan had both been missing that morning. They were up to something, obviously. Odd that they hadn't included him, or called, at least. Maybe not Eric, he wasn't the most thoughtful friend, but Dylan was. Dylan would have called.

There had been some weird shit going on between those two lately. Pipe bombs and guns. When Nate heard about the shooting, he got nervous. When someone mentioned the trench coats, that sealed it.

This isn't happening, Nate thought. This can't be happening.

He ran into his girlfriend, who was stopped at an intersection. She was also a good friend of Eric's. She followed Nate home. Then Nate did the same thing nearly everyone was doing: he started dialing friends, checking in to make sure they were all safe. He wanted to call Dylan's house, but that was just way too scary. Soon. He would call soon. He checked on some other friends first.

———

While Deputy Gardner was firing at Eric, he knew help was on the way. "Female down" at a high school unleashed a frenzy of police radio traffic. Jeffco issued a metro-wide mutual-aid request, prompting police officers, firefighters, and paramedics from around the city to begin racing toward the foothills. The police band got so congested so quickly that Gardner couldn't alert dispatch that he'd arrived. After engaging Eric, Gardner got back in his car and radioed for backup. This time he got through. Gardner followed protocol and did not pursue Eric inside.

Deputy Paul Smoker was a motorcycle cop, writing a speeding ticket on the edge of Clement Park when the first dispatch came in. He radioed that he was responding and gunned his motorcycle into the grass. He tore through soccer fields and baseball diamonds and arrived at the north side of the building just moments after Gardner's gunplay. He parked behind an equipment shed, where a bleeding boy had taken shelter. Another patrol car pulled up right behind him, then another. They all wound around the corner from Gardner, just out of sight. The boy told them he had been shot by "Ned Harris." Nobody had any paper, so a deputy wrote the name on the hood of his patrol car.

They ran forward to help another bleeding student lying in the grass. As they approached, they passed into Deputy Gardner's sight line, around the corner. It had been two minutes since Gardner's gun battle with Eric, and he was out of his car with his pistol drawn. Smoker and Gardner spotted each other as Eric reappeared inside the west exit doorway.

"There he is!" Gardner yelled. He opened fire again.

Eric ducked back behind the door frame. He poked his rifle through the shattered pane and returned fire. A couple of students were on the move again, and Eric tried to nail them, too. Smoker could see where Gardner was firing, but the doorway was blocked from view. He maneuvered down to where he could see Eric and got off three shots. Eric retreated. Smoker heard gunfire inside. More students ran out of the building. He did not pursue.

Deputies continued arriving. They attended to the scared and wounded and struggled to determine what they were up against. Witnesses came to them. Kids saw their police cars at the top of the hill and came running. Some were bleeding. All were desperate. They lined up behind the cars and crouched near the officers for protection.

They provided lots of accurate information. Reports on the police radio conflicted wildly, but any one group in one location tended to offer remarkably consistent accounts. These kids described two gunmen in black trench coats shooting Uzis or shotguns and throwing hand grenades. At least one appeared to be high school age, and some victims knew them. Kids kept arriving. The cars were feeble protection, and the crowd was likely to draw attention. The deputies decided it was paramount to evacuate them. They directed some of the boys to tear their shirts into strips and treat one another's wounds while they devised an escape plan. They decided to line several patrol cars up as a defensive wall and shuttle the students to safer ground behind them.

Every cop had been trained for events like this. Protocol called for containment. The deputies broke into watch teams. They could cover a handful of the twenty-five exits and protect those students who were already out. "Setting up a perimeter," they called it. They would repeat the "perimeter" phrase endlessly that afternoon. Paramedics were establishing triage areas away from the school, and the deputies worked on getting the kids there. Cops would lay down suppressive fire to protect evacuations and scare off opportunistic attacks. They had no idea whether the gunmen were still present, or interested. The officers did not observe or engage the gunmen for some time.

Newly arriving officers covered additional exits. Gunfire was audible to the first officers and continued through the arrival of hundreds more. Deafening explosions kept erupting inside the school. The exterior walls along the cafeteria and the library rumbled from some of the blasts. Deputy Smoker could see the green windows buckling. Half a dozen students ran out the cafeteria doors after one shock wave. They made it to another deputy, who was guarding the south exits.

"Are we going to die?" one of the girls asked him. No. She asked again. No. She kept asking.

The deputy thought the shooters might flee the building, cross the field, and hop a chain-link fence separating the school grounds from the first subdivision.

"We didn't know who the bad guy was, but we soon realized the sophistication of their weapons," Deputy Smoker said later. "These were big bombs. Big guns. We didn't have a clue who 'they' were. But they were hurting kids."

When the networks went live around noon, hundreds of uniformed responders were present. Thirty-five law enforcement agencies were soon represented. They had gathered an assortment of vehicles, including a Loomis Fargo armored truck whose driver had been working in the area. One student counted thirty-five police cars speeding past him on his one-mile ride home from school: "Ambulances and police cars barging over medians and motorcycle cops weaving through opposite traffic almost killing themselves," he said.

Half a dozen cops arrived every minute. Nobody seemed to be in charge. Some cops wanted to assault the building, but that was not the plan. Whose plan was this? Where had it come from?

They reinforced the perimeter.

Eric had exchanged fire with two deputies, at 11:24 and 11:26 A.M.—five and seven minutes into the attack. Law enforcement would not fire on the killers again or advance on the building until shortly after noon.

13. "1 Bleeding to Death"

Ribbons of yellow police tape marked the perimeter. No one was getting out of there; the issue became getting in. Onlookers, journalists, and parents were appearing as fast as policemen. They presented little threat to the deputies but significant danger to themselves. Misty Bernall was one of the early arrivals. She did not know that her daughter was in the library, or what that might portend. She only knew Cassie was missing, along with her freshman son, Chris.

Misty's yard backed right up to the soccer field where Eric had fired on students, but she had arrived by a much more circuitous route. Misty was a working mom, so she was not present to hear Eric fire toward her house. But her husband, Brad, was. He had come home sick, heard a couple of pops, but thought nothing of them. Firecrackers, maybe some pranksters. He lived beside a high school. He was used to commotion. He didn't even put his shoes on to have a look.

Half an hour later, Misty sat down to lunch with a coworker and got a disturbing call. It was probably nothing, but she called Brad to check. He put on his shoes. Brad went out back and peered over the fence. Bedlam. The schoolyard was swarming with cops.

Misty Bernall was a tall, attractive woman in her mid-forties with a loud voice and a commanding presence. She had full features and the same curly blond hair as Cassie, worn in a similar style, though shorter, just past her shoulders. She could be mistaken for a much older sister. Brad was taller, with dark hair, and handsome—a big guy with a soft voice and a humble demeanor. They shared an intense faith in the Lord, and they began begging Him to save their kids.

They could cover more ground apart. Misty headed for the high school. Brad hung by the phone.

At the perimeter, officers struggled to hold back the parental onslaught. TV anchors broadcast their entreaties: "As difficult as it may be, please stay away." But fresh waves of moms and dads kept swarming over the hill.

Misty gave up. Two rendezvous points had been set up. Misty chose the public library on the other side of Clement Park. She found very few students. Where were they?

When they poured out of the high school, students had seen two main options: a subdivision across Pierce Street, or the wide-open fields of Clement Park. Hardly anyone chose the park. They crouched behind houses, worked themselves under shrubbery, rolled under cars. Any semblance of protection. Some pounded frantically on front doors, but most of the houses were locked. Stay-at-home moms started waving strangers in off the street. "Kids were piling into houses," one student said. "There must have been a hundred fifty or two hundred kids piled into this house."

The second rendezvous point, Leawood Elementary, sat in the heart of that neighborhood, so most of the survivors gravitated there. Parents were sent to the auditorium, where kids were paraded across the stage. Moms shrieked, hugs abounded, unclaimed kids sobbed quietly backstage. Because the kids were hard to keep in one place, sign-in sheets were posted on the walls, so parents could see evidence in their child's own hand.

There was no parade of survivors at the public library. Misty was conflicted. Leaving for Leawood was risky: the roads had been closed, so everything was by foot now. She could easily miss her kids in transit. A local minister got up on a chair and shouted: "Please stay here!" The fax would arrive any minute, he assured them. They would be much better off waiting. The fax was a copy of the sign-in sheets from Leawood. Misty waited impatiently for its arrival.

The mood stayed tense but restrained. Commotion erupted in little bursts. "Paul's OK!" a woman screamed. She held up her cell phone. "He's at Leawood!" Her husband rushed over. They hugged, they wept. Tears were rare. It was too scary to cry in fear; only reunion allowed release. A clump of students would appear now and then over the hill. If they weren't claimed immediately, a pack of moms would descend to interrogate them. Always the same question: "How did you get out?!"

They needed reassurance there was a way out.

"I didn't know what to do," a young girl said. "We heard guns and I was standing there and the teacher was crying and pointing to the auditorium and everybody was running and screaming and we heard an explosion—I guess that was a bomb or something. I didn't see this but we were trying to find out and I guess they shot again and everyone started running and I was like, *What is going on!* They started shooting again and there was complete panic. People were shoving, they were going into the elevators and people would like push people off and we were all just running…"

Most of the stories sputtered out like that: disjointed flurries of re-created mayhem. The words ran together until the witness ran out of breath. A winsome freshman was different. She was still in her Columbine gym uniform, and recounted her escape dispassionately. She had faced the gunmen in the hall. She was pretty sure one had run right past her, shooting. But there was so much smoke and confusion, she wasn't sure what was happening or where or anything. Bullets ricocheted down the corridor. Glass shattered, metal clattered, chunks of plaster crashed down on the floor.

Moms gasped. Someone asked if she'd feared for her life. "Not really," she said. "Because the principal was with us." She said it matter-of-factly, with earnest conviction. It was just the tone a younger girl might have used to explain that she felt safe with her daddy.

The stories were harrowing, but they reassured the moms. Every escape was different, but they ended the same: the kids escaped. The accumulation was soothing.

Misty questioned every kid. "Cassie!" she shouted. "Chris!" She worked her way across the crowd and back again. Nothing.

————

Command had fallen to the newly elected Jeffco sheriff, John Stone. He had not yet faced a murder case in office. The metro cops were horrified to discover that the county was in charge. Many were open with their disgust. City and even suburban officers thought of sheriff's deputies as security guards. These were the guys who shuttled defendants to court from the jail. They stood guard while the real cops testified about the crimes they had responded to and investigated.

The grousing increased when they learned who was heading the command. John Stone looked the part of an Old West sheriff: a big, burly guy with a large potbelly and a thick gray mustache, weathered skin, and craggy eyes. He wore the uniform, the badge, and the pistol, but he was a politician. He had been a county supervisor for twelve years. He'd run for sheriff last

November and had taken the oath in January. He'd appointed John Dunaway as his undersheriff. Another bureaucrat.

The sheriff and his team defended the perimeter. Gun blasts came and went. The SWAT teams seethed. *When* was somebody going to allow them to advance?

Dunaway named Lieutenant David Walcher incident commander. Operations would now be directed by a man who did police work for a living, with oversight from Dunaway and Sheriff Stone. The three set up a command post in a trailer stationed in Clement Park, half a mile north of the school.

Just after noon, a SWAT team made its first approach on the school. The officers commandeered a fire truck for cover. One man drove the truck slowly toward the building, while a dozen more moved alongside. Near the entrance, they split in half: six and six. Lieutenant Terry Manwaring's team held back to lay down suppressive fire and later work its way to another entrance. At approximately 12:06, the other six charged inside. Additional SWAT team members arrived moments later and followed them.

The team thought they were in striking distance of the cafeteria. They were on the opposite end of the building. Lieutenant Manwaring had been inside Columbine many times, but he was unaware it had been remodeled and the cafeteria moved. He was perplexed.

The fire alarm had not been silenced. The men used hand signals. Every cupboard or broom closet had to be treated as a hot zone. Many doors were locked, so they blasted them open with rifle fire. Kids trapped in classrooms heard gunfire steadily approaching. Death appeared imminent. Parents, reporters, and even cops outside heard the shots and came to similar conclusions. One room at a time, the team worked methodically toward the killers. It would take three hours to reach their bodies.

On the west side, where the killers were active, a fire department team staged a riskier operation. Half a dozen bodies remained on or near the lawn outside the cafeteria. Several showed signs of life. Anne Marie, Lance, and Sean had been bleeding for forty minutes. Deputies along the perimeter moved in closer to provide cover while three paramedics and an EMT rushed in.

Eric appeared in the second-floor library window and fired on them. Two deputies shot back. Others laid down suppressive fire. The paramedics got three students out. Danny was pronounced dead and left behind.

Eric disappeared.

Lieutenant Manwaring's half of the SWAT team had inched around outside the building using the fire truck for cover. They arrived at the opposite side half an hour later. They rescued Richard Castaldo from the lawn around 12:35, an hour and a quarter after he was shot. They made another approach to retrieve Rachel Scott. They brought her back as far as the fire truck. Then they determined she was dead, and aborted. They laid her there on the ground. Finally, they went for Danny Rohrbough, unaware of the prior finding. They left him on the sidewalk.

At 1:15, a second SWAT team charged the building from the senior lot, smashed a window in the teachers' lounge, and vaulted in. The officers quickly entered the adjacent cafeteria but found it nearly deserted. Food was left half-eaten on the tables. Books, backpacks, and assorted garbage floated about the room, which had been flooded by the sprinkler system. Water was three to four inches high and rising. A fire had blackened ceiling tiles and melted down some chairs. They did not notice the duffel bags, held down by the weight of the bombs. One bag had burned away. The propane tank sat exposed, mostly above water, but it blended into the debris. Signs of panic were everywhere, but no injuries, no bodies, no blood.

There were lots of healthy people. The team was shocked to discover dozens of terrified students and staff. They were crouched in storage closets, up above the ceiling tiles, or plainly visible under cafeteria tables. One teacher had climbed into the ceiling and tried to crawl clear through the ductwork out to safety to warn police, but had fallen through and required medical care. Two men were shivering in the freezer, so cold they could barely lift their arms.

The SWAT team searched them and shuttled them out the window they came in. At first that was easy, but the farther they moved, the more officers they had to leave behind to secure the route. They brought in more manpower to assist.

Overhead, circling steadily, chopper blades beat out a steady *thuch-thuch-thuch thuch-thuch-thuch.*

Robyn Anderson watched it all from the parking lot. She had headed to Dairy Queen with her friends, zipped through the drive-thru, and circled back to school. There were a whole lot of cops when they got back. Officers were assembling the perimeter, but the entrance to the senior lot was still open. Robyn pulled into her space. A cop strode up with his gun drawn. Stay where you are, he warned. It was already too late to back out. Robyn and her friends would wait in her car for two and a half hours. Robyn ducked when she saw Eric appear in the library window. She couldn't tell it was him; she was too far back. All she could make out was a guy in a white T-shirt firing a rifle in her general direction.

Who would do something like this? Robyn asked her girlfriends. *Who would be this retarded?*

Robyn looked over to her friends' spaces. Eric, Dylan, and Zack had assigned spots, three in a row. Zack's car was there. Eric's and Dylan's were missing.

———

Nate Dykeman was terrified of who might be responsible. He had called most of his close friends but had held off on Eric and Dylan. He had been hoping to hear from them. Hoping, but not really expecting. Dylan would break his heart. They had been tight for years. Nate spent a lot of time at his house, and Tom and Sue Klebold had looked after him. Nate had a lot of trouble at home, and the Klebolds had been like a second mom and dad.

Dylan did not call. Around noon, Nate dialed his house. Tom Klebold would be home—he worked from there. Hopefully Dylan was with him.

Tom picked up. No, Dylan was not there. He's in school, Tom said.

Actually, no, he isn't, Nate said. Dylan had not been in class. And Nate didn't want to worry Tom, but there had been a shooting. There had been descriptions. The gunmen were in trench coats. Nate knew several kids with trench coats—he was trying to account for all of them. He hated breaking the news, but he had to say it. He thought Dylan was involved.

Tom went up to Dylan's room, checked his closet for the coat. "Oh my God," he said. "It's not here."

Tom was shocked, Nate said later. "I thought he was going to, like, drop the phone. He just could not believe that this could possibly be happening, and his son was involved."

"Please keep me informed," Tom told him. "Whatever you hear."

Tom got off the phone. He turned on the TV. It was everywhere.

He called Sue. She came home. Tom called their older son. He and Sue had kicked Byron out for using drugs—they would not tolerate that behavior—but this was too important.

Tom apparently withheld his fears about Dylan. Byron told coworkers he was terrified his brother was trapped. He was also worried about younger friends still in school. "I've got to see if everybody's OK," he said.

Lots of Byron's workmates were connected to the school. They all headed home.

Tom Klebold called 911 to warn them his son might be involved. He also called a lawyer.

———

The televised version of the disaster was running thirty minutes to an hour behind the cops' view. Anchors dutifully repeated the perimeter concept. The cops had "sealed off the perimeter." But what were all those troops doing, exactly? There were hundreds out there; everyone seemed to be milling about. Anchors started wondering aloud. Luckily, no one seemed to be seriously injured.

Around 12:30, the story took its first grisly turn. Local TV reporters gained access to the triage areas. It was awful. So much blood, it was hard to identify the injuries. Lots of kids had been loaded into ambulances; area hospitals were all on alert.

Half a dozen news choppers circled, but they withheld most of their footage. For a few minutes, stations had broadcast live from the air, but the sheriff's team had demanded they stop. Every room in Columbine was equipped with a television. The gunmen might well be watching. Cameras would home in on the very images most useful to the killers: SWAT maneuvers and wounded kids awaiting rescue. TV stations also held back news of fatalities. Their chopper crews had seen paramedics examine Danny and leave him behind. The public remained unaware.

The stations also caught glimpses of a disturbing scene playing out in a second-story classroom in another wing of the building, far from the library, in Science Room 3. It was hard to make out exactly what was going on in there, but there was a lot of activity, and one disturbing clue. Someone had dragged a large white marker board to the window, with a message in huge block letters. The first character looked a lot like a capital I but turned out to be a numeral: "1 BLEEDING TO DEATH."

14. Hostage Standoff

Around one P.M., word filtered out to reporters that kids were trapped in the building. The situation had escalated into a hostage standoff. Publicly, the nature of the attack changed. No telling what the assailants might try. Where were they? The captives seemed to be held in the commons, but reports conflicted.

Word of the ambulance scenes and the hostage standoff traveled quickly to Leawood and the public library. Parents grew tenser, but they worked together, exchanging information and passing around cell phones. It was tough to get a signal. Cell phones were not ubiquitous in 1999, yet everyone in this affluent community seemed to have one. They pounded at them furiously, grilling neighbors, updating relatives, leaving messages for their children on every conceivable answering machine. Some would hit Redial absentmindedly as they swapped information face-to-face, buzzing their own homes, praying that the machine wouldn't pick up this time. Misty kept calling Brad. Still no word on Chris or Cassie.

Then a fresh story zipped through the pack: twenty students—or thirty or forty—were still inside the school. They were not hostages; they were hiding, barricaded in the choir room with equipment piled high against the door. The parents gasped. Was that good news or bad? Dozens more students were in danger, but dozens more confirmed alive—if it was true. A lot of wild rumors had already come and gone.

At least two to three hundred students were hiding in the school, in classrooms and utility closets, under tables and desks. Some had rigged up protection; others were right out in the open. Everyone was afraid to move. A great number whispered cautiously into cell phones. Many clustered around classroom TVs. They heard banging and crashing and the deafening screech of the fire alarm. CNN carried a live call between a local anchor and a student alone under a desk. What was he hearing? The same thing as you, the student said. "I've got a little TV [and I'm] watching you guys right now." For four hours rumors, confirmations, and embellishments bounced in and out.

The cops were livid. Reporters had no idea hundreds of kids were trapped inside and no concept of the echo chamber in full bloom. The cops knew. The detective force was assembling teams to interview every survivor, and they knew hundreds of their best witnesses were still inside, getting compromised by the minute. But the cops had no means to stop it. This was the first major hostage standoff of the cell phone age, and they had never seen anything like it. At the moment, they were more concerned with information passing to the shooters. Sometimes the kids' revelations scared reporters. On live TV, a boy described sounds he took to be the gunmen: "I hear stuff being thrown around," he said. "I am staying underneath this desk. I don't know if they know I'm up here. I am just staying upstairs for right now, and I just hope they don't know—"

The anchorwoman interrupted: "Don't tell us where you are!"

The boy described more commotion. "There's a little bunch of people crying outside. I can hear them downstairs." Something crashed. "Whoa!"

The anchor gasped. "What was that?!"

"I don't know."

The anchors had enough. Her partner told him to hang up, keep quiet, and try to reach 911. "Keep trying to call them, OK?"

The cops pleaded with the TV stations to stop. Please ask the hostages to quit calling the media, they said. Tell them to turn off the televisions.

The stations aired the requests and continued broadcasting the calls. "If you're watching, kids, turn the TV off," one anchor implored. "Or down, at least."

———

Much of the country was watching the standoff unfold. None of the earlier school shootings had been televised; few American tragedies had. The Columbine situation played out slowly, with the cameras rolling. Or at least it appeared that way: the cameras offered the illusion we were witnessing the event. But the cameras had arrived too late. Eric and Dylan had retreated inside after five minutes. The cameras missed the outside murders and could not follow Eric and Dylan inside. The fundamental experience for most of America was *almost* witnessing mass murder. It was the panic and frustration of not knowing, the mounting terror of horror withheld, just out of view. We would learn the truth about Columbine, but we would not learn it today.

We saw fragments. What the cameras showed us was misleading. An army of police held at bay suggested an equivalent force inside. Hysterical witnesses corroborated that image, describing wildly different assaults. Killers seemed to be everywhere. Cell phone callers confirmed the killers remained active. They provided unimpeachable evidence of gunfire from inside the attack zone. The data was correct; the conclusions were wrong. SWAT teams were on the move.

The narrative unfolding on television looked nothing like the killers' plan. It looked only moderately like what was actually occurring. It would take months for investigators to piece together what had gone on inside. Motive would take longer to unravel. It would be years before the detective team would explain why.

The public couldn't wait that long. The media was not about to. They speculated.

15. First Assumption

An investigative team had assembled before noon. Kate Battan (rhymes with Latin) was named lead investigator. Battan already knew who her primary suspects were. Most of the students were perplexed about who was attacking them, but quite a few had recognized the gunmen. Two names had been repeated over and over. Battan quickly compiled dossiers on Eric and Dylan in the command post trailer in Clement Park. She dispatched teams to secure their homes. Detectives arrived at the Harris place at 1:15, just as the third SWAT team burst into the Columbine teachers' lounge. Eric's parents had gotten word and were already home. The cops found them uncooperative. They tried to refuse entrance. The cops insisted. Kathy Harris got scared when they headed for the basement. "I don't want you going down there!" she said. They said they were securing the residence and removing everyone. Wayne said he doubted Eric was involved, but would help if there was an active situation. Kathy's twin sister was with her. Wayne and Kathy were concerned about the repercussions, she explained; parents of the victims might retaliate.

The cops smelled gas; they had the utility company shut off power, then resumed the search. In Eric's room they found a sawed-off shotgun barrel on a bookshelf, unspent ammunition on the bed, fingertips cut off gloves on the floor, and fireworks and bomb materials on the desk, the dresser, the windowsill, and the wall, among other places. Elsewhere they discovered a page from *The Anarchist Cookbook,* packaging for a new gas can, and scattered glass shards on a slab in the backyard. An evidence specialist arrived that night and spent four hours, shooting seven rolls of film. He left at 1:00 A.M.

The Klebolds were much more forthcoming. A police report described Tom as "very communicative." He gave a full account of Dylan's past and laid out all his friendships. Dylan had been in good spirits, Tom said. Sue described him as extremely happy. Tom was anti-gun and Dylan agreed with him on that—they wouldn't find any guns or explosives in the house, that was for sure, Tom said. The cops did find pipe bombs. Tom was shocked. Dylan was fine, he insisted. He and Dylan were close. He would have known it if anything was up.

The first FBI agent on the scene at Columbine was Supervisory Special Agent Dwayne Fuselier. He had shaken the Cajun accent, on everything but his name. FUSE-uh-lay, he said. Everyone got it wrong. He was a veteran agent, a clinical psychologist, a terrorism expert, and one of the leading hostage negotiators in the country. None of that led Dr. Fuselier to Columbine High. His wife had called. Their son was in the school.

Fuselier got the call in the cafeteria of Denver's Rogers Federal Building, a downtown high-rise thirty minutes away. He was sipping a bowl of bland soup—low-salt, for his hypertension. The bowl stayed on the table. When he got to his Dodge Intrepid, Fuselier swiped his arm under the seat, groping for the portable police light. He hadn't pulled it out in years.

Fuselier headed toward the foothills. He would offer his services as a hostage negotiator, or anything else they might need. He wasn't sure how his offer would be received.

Cops in crisis tend to be thrilled to have a trained negotiator but wary of the Feds. Hardly anyone likes the FBI. Fuselier didn't blame them. Federal agents generally have a high opinion of themselves. Few try to conceal it. Fuselier didn't look like a Fed, or sound the part. He was a shrink turned hostage negotiator turned detective, with an abridged version of the complete works of Shakespeare in the back seat of his car. He didn't talk past the local cops, roll his eyes, or humor them. There was no swagger in his shoulders or his speech. He could be a little stoic. Hugging his sons felt awkward but he would reach out to embrace survivors when they needed it. Smiling came easy. His jokes were frequently at his own expense. He genuinely liked local cops and appreciated what they had to offer. They liked him.

A stint on the domestic terrorism task force for the region proved fortuitous. It was a joint operation between local agencies and the FBI. Fuselier led the unit, and a senior Jeffco detective worked on his team. The detective was one of Fuselier's first calls. He was relieved to hear that Dwayne was on his way and offered to introduce him to the commanders on arrival.

The detective brought Fuselier up to speed before he arrived at the school. There were reports of six or eight gunmen in black masks and military gear shooting everyone. He assumed it was a terrorist attack.

It took a certain voice to talk down a gunman. Agent Fuselier was always gentle and reassuring. No matter how erratic the subject's behavior, Fuselier always responded calmly. He exuded tranquillity, offered a way out. He trained negotiators to read a subject quickly, to size up his primary motivations. Was the gunman driven by anger, fear, or resentment? Was he on a power trip? Was the assault meant to feed his ego, or was he caught up in events beyond his control? Getting the gun down was primarily a matter of listening. The first thing Fuselier taught negotiators was to classify the situation as hostage or nonhostage. To laymen, humans at gunpoint equaled hostages. Not so.

An FBI field manual citing Fuselier's research spelled out the crucial distinction: hostages are a means to fulfill demands. "The primary goal is not to harm the hostages," the manual said. "In fact, hostage takers realize that only through keeping the hostages alive can they hope to achieve their goals." They act rationally. Nonhostage gunmen do not. The humans mean nothing to them. "[These] individuals act in an emotional, senseless, and often-self-destructive way." They typically issue no demands. "What they want is what they already have, the victim. The potential for homicide followed by suicide in many of these cases is very high."

Jeffco officials had labeled Columbine a hostage standoff. Every media outlet was reporting it that way. Dr. Fuselier considered the chances of that remote. What he was driving toward was much worse.

To the FBI, the nonhostage distinction is critical. The Bureau recommends radically different strategies in those cases—essentially, the opposite approach. With hostages, negotiators remain highly visible, make the gunmen work for everything, and firmly establish that the police are in control. In nonhostage situations, they keep a low profile, "give a little without getting in return" (for example, offering cigarettes to build rapport), and avoid even a slight implication that anyone but the gunman is in control. The goal with hostages is to gradually lower expectations; in nonhostage crises, it's to lower emotions.

One of the first things Fuselier did when he arrived was organize a negotiation team. He found local officers he had trained, and fellow FBI negotiators responded as well. A neighboring county loaned them a section of its mobile command post, already on scene. The 911 operators were instructed to put through to the team all calls from kids inside the building. Anything they could learn about the gunmen might be useful. They passed on logistical information they gathered to the tactical teams. The team was confident they could talk the gunmen down. All they needed was someone to speak to.

Fuselier shuttled between the negotiation center and the Jeffco command post, coordinating the federal response. When things calmed down momentarily, Fuselier pitched in questioning students who had just escaped the school. He walked over to the triage unit and flipped through the logs. They had evaluated hundreds of kids. He scanned for kids he knew from the neighborhood or the boys' soccer teams. Everyone he recognized said "evaluated and released." He called their parents as soon as he got a break.

His son's name never came up. Agent Fuselier was grateful to have his hands full. "I had work to do," he said later. "I compartmentalized. Focusing on that kept me from wondering about Brian." Mimi checked in regularly, so Dwayne didn't have to. She had gotten to Leawood, and she had seen a lot of kids. No one had spotted Brian; no one had heard a word.

———

An attack of this magnitude suggested a large conspiracy. Everyone, including detectives, assumed a substantial number were involved. The first break in the presumed conspiracy seemed to come early. The killers' good friend Chris Morris reported himself to 911. He had seen the news on TV while he was home playing Nintendo with another friend. At first he was worried about his girlfriend. And his Nintendo buddy's dad was a science teacher in the building.

The two boys hopped in the car and raced around, trying to find Chris's girlfriend. They kept running into police barricades and collecting scraps of information along the way. When he heard about the trench coats, Chris got scared. He knew Eric and Dylan had guns. He knew they had been messing with pipe bombs. For this?

Chris called 911. He got disconnected. It took a few tries, but he told his story and the dispatcher sent a patrol car by the house. The cops questioned him briefly, then decided to drive him out to the main team in Clement Park. There was a lot of confusion. Who was this kid? "Chris Harris?" a detective asked. Pretty soon he was surrounded by detectives. Cameramen noticed. TV crews came running.

Chris looked the part: squishy features, nerdy, and overwhelmed. He had rosy cheeks, wire-rimmed glasses, and mussy light brown hair just past his ears. The cops cuffed him fast and got him into the back of a patrol car.

By now, many of the killers' buddies suspected them. It was a scary time to be Eric's or Dylan's friend.

———

From the outset, before they even had names or identities for the gunmen, TV reporters depicted the boys as a single entity. "Were they loners?" reporters kept asking witnesses. "Were they outcasts?" Always *they*. And always the attributes fitting the school shooter profile—itself a myth. The witnesses nearly always concurred. Few knew the killers, but they did not volunteer that information, and they were not asked. *Yeah, outcasts, I heard they were.*

Fuselier arrived at Columbine with one assumption: multiple gunmen demanded multiple tactics. Fuselier couldn't afford to think of his adversaries as a unit. Strategies likely to disarm one shooter could infuriate the other. Mass murderers tended to work alone, but when they did pair up, they rarely chose their mirror image. Fuselier knew he was much more likely to find a pair of opposites holed up in that building. It was entirely possible that there was no single *why*—and much more likely that he would unravel one motive for Eric, another for Dylan.

Reporters quickly keyed on the darker force behind the attack: this spooky Trench Coat Mafia. It grew more bizarre by the minute. In the first two hours, witnesses on CNN described the TCM as Goths, gays, outcasts, and a street gang. "A lot of the time they'll, like, wear makeup and paint their nails and stuff," a Columbine senior said. "They're kind of—I don't know, like Goth, sort of, like, and they're, like, associated with death and violence a lot."

None of that would prove to be true. That student did not, in fact, know the people he was describing. But the story grew.

16. The Boy in the Window

Danny Rohrbough had been second to die. As Eric was taking aim at him on the sidewalk, Danny's stepsister was in the building, headed toward him. Nicole Petrone had changed into her gym uniform while the bombs were being laid. It was a beautiful day, and her class was going outside to play softball. Just as Eric finished shooting at Deputy Gardner, the lead girls in Nicole's class turned the corner toward them.

Mr. D arrived in the hallway at the same moment—at the opposite end from the killers. He had just been alerted to the shooting, and had come running to investigate. The girls had not been warned. Mr. D spotted Dylan and Eric coming in the west doors, and the girls blundering into their path.

"They were laughing and giggling and getting ready to walk right into it," he said.

The killers fired. Bullets soared past the girls. The trophy case just behind Mr. D shattered.

"I assumed I was a dead man," he said.

He ran straight into the gunfire, screaming at the girls to turn back. He herded them down a side hallway that dead-ended at the gym. It was locked.

Mr. D had the key, on a chain in his pocket, latched to dozens just like it. He had no idea what it looked like. "I'm thinking, *He's coming around the corner and we're trapped*," DeAngelis said. "If I don't get these doors open, we are trapped." A movie image zipped through his mind: a Nazi concentration camp, with a guard shooting escapees in the back. *We're just going to get mowed down as he comes around the corner*, he thought. He reached in and grabbed a random key. It fit.

He ushered the girls into the gym and scouted around for a hiding place.

They could hear bombs and gunfire and he could only imagine the hell going on outside. He spotted an inconspicuous door on the far wall. There was a storage room behind it, with cages piled with gym equipment. He unlocked the door and led them in.

"You're going to be fine," he told them. "I'm not going to let anything happen to you. But I need to get us out of here. I'm going to shut the door behind me. You don't open that door for anyone!" Then he had an idea. Why didn't they come up with a code word? *Orange,* someone suggested; no, *Rebels,* another girl said; no... A few started quarreling about it. Mr. D. couldn't believe it. He burst out laughing. Girls started giggling. That broke the tension, for a moment.

He locked them in the storeroom, crossed the gym, creaked open the outside door, and poked his head out. "I saw other kids coming out and teachers," he said. "Then a Jeffco sheriff—his car came over that embankment, flying, and I told some of the teachers, 'I have to go back in there! There are kids in there.' So I told the police officer after he got out and I explained. He said, 'You go in.'"

Mr. D brought Nicole's class back out to the same spot with the same cop, but by now he'd realized there were hundreds more still inside.

"I'm going—" he began, but a deputy cut him off.

"No one's going back in."

So Mr. D led the class across a field, over a series of minor obstacles. He stopped at a chain-link fence to boost them over. Other girls assisted from the far side. "Let's go, girls," he said. "Over the fence."

When the last girl was over, they ran across the field until they felt safe. Mr. D found the command post and drew diagrams of the hallways for the SWAT teams. He also described what he had seen. He remembered a guy with a baseball cap turned backward. "They kept saying these guys were in trench coats," Mr. D recalled later, "and I kept saying, 'These guys were not in trench coats! He had a baseball cap turned backwards.'"

Eventually, Mr. D headed to Leawood to be with the kids. He met his wife there, his brother, and a close friend. Tears streamed down everyone's cheeks, except Frank's. That was odd. Frank had always been the emotional one. But the first symptom of post-traumatic stress disorder (PTSD) was already taking hold. He felt nothing.

"I was like a zombie," he said later.

———

John and Kathy Ireland knew Patrick had "A" lunch. But he always ate out. John went looking for Patrick's car. He knew Patrick's spot. If the car was gone, his boy was safe. A deputy stopped him at the perimeter. "Please!" John begged. He promised not to walk as far as the school. "If I can just get to the parking lot…" Pleading was useless. John knew the neighborhood, so he tried another approach. That one was blocked, too. He headed back to Leawood.

Kids kept pouring in there. Mostly the auditorium was filled with parents seeking kids, but there were also kids without parents. John saw several in tears. He chatted with them, and they perked up.

John and Kathy were happy to see kids find their parents. But every reunion raised the odds their boy was in trouble. *Some*body's kids were in those ambulances. John and Kathy refused to indulge in negative thoughts. "I couldn't go to the place that Pat would have been hurt," Kathy said later. "I absolutely felt confident that he was going to be OK. At least I wasn't going to speculate or waste energy on that. I just needed to find him."

John found lots of Patrick's friends, but nobody had seen him. Who was he with? Why hadn't they called?

Patrick had gone to the library to finish his stats homework. Four friends had joined him. None of them had called the Irelands because every one of them had been shot.

———

Agent Dwayne Fuselier was also having no luck locating his son. Mimi had given up on the public library and had run over to Leawood. There were many more kids there, but none had seen Brian.

Dwayne had access to a growing army of law enforcement, but it didn't do him a lick of good. Cops kept an ear out for word of Brian, but none came. Fuselier also had the advantage of knowing a great number of kids were alive and well in the building. He had spoken to many personally, and continued picking their brains about the killers. He was one of the few parents aware of the full danger. Two bodies had been lying outside the cafeteria for hours. He didn't know they were Danny Rohrbough and Rachel Scott, but he knew they had not been moving, and then he heard the

dispatch announcements indicating they were dead. Others described the
1 BLEEDING TO DEATH sign in Science Room 3.

Mimi monitored the stage at Leawood, where talk of death and murder were verboten. She scoured the sign-in sheets and worked the crowd.
Dwayne checked in every fifteen minutes by cell, but did not mention the
murders. She did not inquire.

———

For ninety minutes of chaos, the gunmen seemed to be all over the school
simultaneously. Then it quieted down. The killers still appeared to be roaming, firing at will, but the gunfire was sporadic now, and no one was staggering out wounded. The injured had reached the hospitals. It had taken an
hour to get most of them out of the building, through the triage center, and
into ambulances. Between 1:00 and 2:30 P.M., the injury count fluctuated
between eight and eighteen, depending upon which station you were watching. The numbers varied but kept rising. A sheriff's spokesman announced
that SWAT teams had spotted more students trapped in the building, lying
on the floor, apparently injured.

Suddenly, at 1:44 P.M., the cops finally nabbed someone. "We've got
three [students], with their hands up with two police cars around them,"
a reporter told CNN. "Their hands are up." The cops detained them at
gunpoint.

Word spread quickly to the library. "They surrendered!" a woman
screamed. "It's over!"

They celebrated there briefly. The truth trickled back slowly.

———

Just before 2:30, an officer riding along in a news chopper spotted somebody moving inside the library. He was just inside the blown-out windows,
covered in blood and behaving curiously: sagging against the frame, clearing away shards of glass. He was going to jump!

The officer radioed a SWAT team. They revved the Loomis armored
truck and raced toward the building.

"Hang on, kid!" one of them called. "We're coming to get you."

Patrick Ireland was confused. He heard someone yell, but couldn't see
anyone or figure out where the voices were coming from. He felt dizzy.
His vision was blurry and one big section was blank. He was unaware that

blood was streaming down into his eyes. The shouting inside his head was more important: *Get out! Get out!*

But the muddled outside yelling had caught his attention. Why were they talking so slowly? Everything was deep and mumbly, like his head was underwater. Where was he? Not sure. Something had happened, something horrible. Shot? *Get out! Get out!*

Hours earlier, Patrick Ireland had taken refuge under the table with his friends. Makai and Dan were down there, and a girl he didn't know. Corey and Austin had gone to investigate and ended up somewhere unknown. Patrick put his head down and closed his eyes. The shooting was barely under way in the library when he heard Makai moan. Patrick opened his eyes. Makai's knee was bleeding. Patrick leaned over to administer pressure. The top of his head poked over the edge of the tabletop. Dylan saw him, and fired the shotgun again. Patrick went blank.

Patrick's skull had stopped several buckshot fragments. Other debris lodged in his scalp as well—probably wood splinters torn from the tabletop in the blast. One pellet got through. It burrowed six inches through spongy brain matter, entering through the scalp just above his hairline on the left, and lodging near the middle rear. Bits of his optical center were missing; most of his language capacity was wiped out. He regained consciousness, but words were hard to form and difficult to interpret as well. Pathways for all sorts of functions had been severed. Perception was impeded, so he couldn't tell when he was speaking gibberish or jumbling incoming sounds. The left brain controls the right side of the body, and the pellet cut through that connection. Patrick was paralyzed on the right side. He had been shot in the right foot; it was broken and bleeding—he didn't even know. He felt nothing on that side.

Patrick drifted in and out. He was semiconscious when the killers left the room. All the kids were running for the back exit. Makai and Dan tried to get his attention. He returned a blank stare.

"Come on, man," one of them said. "Let's go!"

It didn't register. They tried to drag him, but both had been shot in the legs and Patrick was limp. They got nowhere. The killers could return any moment. Eventually, they gave up and fled.

Sometime later, Patrick woke up on the floor again. *Get out!* He tried to get out. Half his body refused. He couldn't stand; he couldn't even crawl right. He reached with his left hand, gripped something, and dragged himself forward. His useless side trailed behind. He made a little progress, and his brain gave out.

He came to repeatedly and began again. No one knows how many times. A bloody trail revealed his convoluted path. He started less than two table lengths from the windows, but he headed off in the wrong direction. Then he hit obstacles: bodies, table legs, and chairs. Some he pushed away, others had to be maneuvered around. He kept heading for the light. If he could just make it to the windows maybe someone would see him. If he had to, maybe he would jump.

It took three hours to get there. He found an easy chair beside the opening. It was sturdy enough not to tip, and might provide cover if the killers returned. He wedged his back against the short wall and worked himself upward, then grabbed hold of the chair for a final push. He propped himself against the girder between two large panes and rested awhile to recover his strength. Then he flipped around. He had one more task before he took the plunge.

The problem was that Patrick couldn't jump. There was a waist-high window ledge to get over. The best he could do was lean forward and tumble over it headfirst onto the sidewalk. His gut would bear down on the sill as he rolled over it. It was a jagged mess. The gun blasts had blown out most of the glass, but left shards clinging around the frame. Patrick stood on one leg, braced his shoulder against the girder, and picked away the chunks with the same hand. He was meticulous. He didn't want to get hurt.

That's when he heard the murky voices.

"Stay there! We're gonna get you!"

The armored truck pulled up beneath the window. A squadron of SWAT officers leapt out. Nearby teams provided cover from either side. One group took aim from behind a fire truck; snipers sprawled on rooftops trained their scopes from farther back. If this rescue mission was fired upon, they'd be ready.

Patrick wasn't waiting. He thought he was. He remembers them calling "OK, it's safe! Go ahead and jump. We'll catch you." The rescue team recalls it differently, and the video shows them still scrambling into place.

Patrick collapsed forward. The ledge caught him at the waist, and he folded in half, head dangling toward the ground. The SWAT team wasn't ready, but Patrick was frantic and didn't understand. He wiggled forward, but couldn't get much traction from the inside, because his feet were already up off the floor.

A SWAT officer clambered up the side of the truck and threw his weapon to the ground. Another followed close behind him. As the first man hit the truck roof, Patrick kicked his good leg up toward the ceiling, and reached down for the sidewalk with his arms. That nearly did it. One more thrust and he would be free.

The officers lunged toward him and each man caught one of his hands. Patrick kicked again, completely vertical, and his hips pulled away from the frame. The officers clenched and his hands barely moved. The rest of his body spun around like a gymnast gripping the high bar, until he whacked into the side of the truck. The officers kept hold and eased him down onto the hood. He tried to break away, still desperate to flee. They lowered him down to other officers, but he kicked hard and his legs slammed against the ground.

They pulled him upright, and he tried to climb into the front seat. The SWAT team was confused. What was he trying to do? They assumed he understood he was the patient. He did not. He had to get out of there. Here was a truck; he was ready to go.

They got him to a triage site, and then straight into an ambulance. On the drive to St. Anthony Central Hospital, paramedics cut off Patrick's bloody clothes—everything but his undershorts. They removed his gold necklace with the water-ski pendant. He had six dollars in his wallet. He was not wearing shoes. They confirmed gunshot wounds to his left forehead and his right foot, as well as a number of superficial wounds about his head. His elbow was lacerated. As they worked, they tested Patrick's mental acuity and tried to keep him conscious. *Do you know where you are? Your name? Your birthday?* Patrick could answer those questions—slowly, laboriously. The answers were easy, but he struggled to form them into words. Most of his brain tissue was intact. Sections could function in isolation, but the connecting circuitry was confused. Patrick's brain was less successful forming new memories. He knew he had been shot, by a man in black with a long gun. That was true. The masks he described on the killers' faces were not. He insisted he had been shot at a hospital, in the emergency room.

Speech was a problem. Only one side of his mouth moved, and his brain was inconsistent in retrieving information. Sometimes it got stuck. He gave them all ten digits of his phone number, but his first name was nearly impossible. Paaaaaaaaaaaaaaah...Paaaaaaaaaah...He could not form that second syllable. It sounded like a droning stream of nonsense and then the second syllable spat out suddenly, clear and distinctive: *rick*. Great. Rick Ireland. That caused considerable confusion later.

Just before Patrick's rescue, President Clinton addressed the nation. He asked all Americans to pray for students and teachers in that school. As CNN cut back from the White House, an anchor spotted Patrick: "Look, there's a bloody student right there in the window!" she gasped.

It played out live on television. Patrick's eighth-grade sister Maggie watched. He was so bloody, she didn't recognize him.

Viewers were stunned, but it didn't make much of an impression at the rendezvous points. News of a kid falling out the window never reached most parents, including John and Kathy. They might have gone on searching for hours if Kathy hadn't asked a neighbor to run by the house to check the answering machine. The neighbor found endless messages from Kathy checking for Patrick, plus a recent one from St. Anthony's: *We have your son. Please call.*

Kathy was conflicted: *My son's alive! My son is hurt!* "It was scary," Kathy said later. "But I was relieved to have something to deal with."

She felt much better once she got a nurse on the phone. It was a head wound, but Patrick was awake and alert; he had provided his name and phone number. *Oh, good, it was just a graze,* Kathy thought. "I just went straight to the assumption that it was just the scalp," she said later. "If he was able to talk, then it was just the scalp."

John felt grave danger, no relief. "I just figured anybody shot in the head, it can't be good," he said.

John drove the couple to the hospital. He was a computer programmer, who prided himself on his navigational skill. He was too upset to find the hospital. He knew exactly how to get to St. Anthony's, he said. "And I'm driving down Wadsworth and I can't remember where the hell it is!"

They sat side by side, presuming they shared the same basic assumptions. It was seven years before they discovered that they arrived at St. Anthony's in completely different mind-sets.

John was racked with guilt. "There should have been something I was able to do to protect him," he said. John knew it was irrational, but years later, it still haunted him.

Kathy focused on the present: How could she help Patrick now? But no one even knew exactly what was wrong. Staff kept coming in to check on them, filling them in on the surgery, what to expect in Patrick and themselves. Dead brain cells do not regenerate, but the brain can sometimes work around them, they were told. No one really understands how the brain reroutes its neural pathways, so there's no procedure to assist it.

A projectile to the brain tends to cause two sets of damage. First, it rips away tissue that can never be restored. One path might cause blindness, another logical impairment. But the secondary impact can be just as bad or worse. The brain is saturated with blood, so gunshots tend to unleash a flood. As fluid builds, oxygen is depleted and the pool cuts off fresh supplies. Brain tissue is choked off by the very cells designed to nourish it. Patrick's doctors feared that as he'd lain on the library floor, his brain had been drowning in its own blood.

Patrick Ireland had brain damage; that was a fact. His symptoms indicated severe impairment. The only question was whether those functions could return.

The surgery was scheduled to take about an hour, but lasted more than three. It was after 7:00 P.M. when the surgeon came out to advise John and Kathy of the results. He had cleared out buckshot fragments and debris from the surface. One pellet had penetrated Patrick's skull. It was far too perilous to dig out. That lead would be in him for life. It was hard to tell how much damage the pellet had wreaked. Swelling was the main indicator. It looked bad.

———

As one SWAT team rescued Patrick Ireland, another squad reached the choir room. The rumor was true: sixty students were barricaded inside. A few minutes later, sixty more were discovered in the science area. SWAT teams led them through the hallways, down the stairs, and across the commons.

At 2:47, three and a half hours into the siege, the first of those kids burst out the cafeteria doors. News choppers homed in on them instantly. The anchors and the TV audience were perplexed. Where were these kids coming from?

More followed, single file in quick succession, running down the hillside as fast as they could with their hands on the backs of their heads, elbows splayed. They kept coming and coming, dozens of them, tracing the same winding path, first away from the school, then back toward a windowless corner surrounded by squad cars and ambulances. They huddled there for several minutes, sobbing, waiting, clinging to one another. Police officers patted them down and then hugged them. Eventually, cops packed groups of three to five kids into squad cars and shuttled them to the triage area a few blocks south. The kids had to run right past two bodies on the way out, so at some point, an officer moved Rachel farther away.

The SWAT team reached the 1 BLEEDING TO DEATH sign on the same sweep through the science area that freed all those kids. The sign was still against the window. The carpet in Science Room 3 was soaked in blood. The teacher was alive, barely.

17. The Sheriff

The Columbine crisis was never a hostage standoff. Eric and Dylan had no intentions of making demands. SWAT teams searched the building for over three hours, but the killers were lying dead the entire time. They had committed suicide in the library at 12:08, forty-nine minutes after beginning the attack. The killing and the terror had been real. The standoff had not.

The SWAT teams discovered the truth around 3:15. They peered into the library and saw bodies scattered around the floor. No sign of movement. They cleared the entrance and prepared to enter. They took paramedic Troy Laman in with them. The SWAT team warned Laman to be cautious. Touch as little as possible, they said; anything could be booby-trapped. Be especially suspicious of backpacks.

It was horrible. The room was a shambles; blood spattered the furniture, and enormous pools soaked into the carpet. The tabletops were oddly undisturbed: books open, calculus problems under way, a college application half-completed. A lifeless boy still held a pencil. Another had collapsed beside a PC, which was still running, undisturbed.

Laman was tasked with determining whether anyone was alive. It didn't look like it. Most of the kids had been dead for nearly four hours, and it was obvious by sight. "If I couldn't get a look at somebody, at their face, to see if they were still alive, I tried to kind of touch them," Laman said. Twelve were cold. One was not. Laman touched a girl, felt the warmth, and rolled her over to get a look at her face. Her eyes were open, tears trickling out.

Lisa Kreutz was carried down the stairs and rushed to Denver Health Medical Center. A gun blast had shattered her left shoulder. One hand and both arms were also injured. She had lost a lot of blood. She survived.

Most of the bodies lay under tables. The victims had been attempting to hide. Two bodies were different. They lay out in the open, weapons by their sides. Suicides, clearly. The SWAT team had descriptions of Eric and Dylan. These two looked like a match. It was over.

The team discovered four women hiding in back rooms attached to the library. Patti Nielson, the art teacher from the 911 call, had crept into a cupboard in the break room. She had squatted in the cupboard for three more hours, knees aching, unaware the danger had passed. Three other faculty hid farther back. An officer instructed one to put her hand on his shoulder and follow him out, staring directly at his helmet, to minimize exposure to the horror.

It had been over how long? No one knew. With the fire alarm blaring, none of the staff had been close enough to hear.

Detectives would piece it together eventually—how long the attack had lasted, and how long Eric and Dylan had killed. Those would turn out to be very different answers. Something peculiar had transpired seventeen minutes into the attack.

———

The investigation outpaced the SWAT teams. Detectives were combing the park, the library, Leawood Elementary, and the surrounding community. They interviewed hundreds of students and staff—everyone they could find. When waves of fresh survivors outnumbered police officers, they conducted thirty- to sixty-second triage interviews: *Who are you? Where were you? What did you see?* Friends of the killers and witnesses to bloodshed were identified quickly, and detectives were waved over for lengthier interviews.

Lead investigator Kate Battan performed some interviews personally; she was briefed on the rest. Battan was intent on getting every detail right—and avoiding costly errors that might come back to haunt them later. "Everyone learned a lot from hearing about the O. J. Simpson case and JonBenét Ramsey," she said later. "We didn't need another situation like those."

Her team also ran a simple search on Jeffco computer files and found something stunning. The shooters were already in the system. Eric and Dylan had been arrested junior year. They got caught breaking into a van to steal electronic equipment. They had entered a twelve-month juvenile Diversion program, performing community service and attending counseling. They'd completed the program with glowing reviews exactly ten weeks before the massacre.

More disturbing was a complaint filed thirteen months earlier by Randy and Judy Brown, the parents of the shooters' friend Brooks. Eric had made death threats toward Brooks. Ten pages of murderous rants printed from his Web site had been compiled. Someone in Battan's department had known about this kid.

Battan organized the information and composed a single-spaced six-page search warrant for Eric's home and a duplicate for Dylan's. She dictated them over the phone. The warrants were typed up in Golden, the county seat, delivered to a judge, signed, driven out to the killers' homes, and exercised within four hours of the first shots—before the SWAT team reached the library and discovered the attack was over.

The warrants cited seven witnesses who'd identified Harris and/or Klebold as the gunmen.

———

Agent Fuselier heard about the bodies on the police radio at 3:20. He had just gotten word that his son Brian was OK. Mass murder meant a massive investigation. "How can I help?" Fuselier asked the Jeffco commanders. "Do you want federal agents?" Definitely, they said. Jeffco had a small detective team—there was no way it could handle the task. An hour later, eighteen evidence specialists began arriving. A dozen special agents would follow, along with half a dozen support staff.

At 4:00 P.M., Jeffco went public about the fatalities. Chief spokesman Steve Davis called a press conference in Clement Park, with Sheriff Stone by his side. The pair had been briefing reporters all afternoon. Most of the press had never heard of either man, but consensus about them emerged quickly. Sheriff Stone was a straight shooter; he had a deep, gruff voice and classic western mentality: no hedging, no bluster, no bullshit. What a contrast to the blow-dried spokesman affixed to his side. Steve Davis began the conference by reiterating warnings about rumors. Above all, he stressed caution on two subjects: the number of fatalities and the status of the suspects.

Davis opened the floor to questions. The first was directed to him by name. Sheriff Stone stepped forward, brushing Davis and his cautions aside. He held custody of the microphone through most of the press conference. The sheriff answered nearly every question directly, despite later evidence that he had little or no information on many of them. He winged it. The death count nearly doubled. "I've heard numbers as high as twenty-five," he said. He pronounced the killers unequivocally dead. He fed the myth of a third shooter. "Three—two dead [suspects] in the library," he said.

"Well, where is the third?"

"We're not sure if there is a third yet or not, or how many. The SWAT operation is still going on in there."

Stone repeated the erroneous death count several times. It led newscasts around the world. Newspaper headlines proclaimed it the next morning: TWENTY-FIVE DEAD IN COLORADO.

Stone said the three kids detained in the park appeared to be "associates of these gentlemen or good friends." He was wrong; they had never met the killers, and were soon cleared.

Stone made the first of an infamous string of accusations. "What are these parents doing that are letting their kids have automatic weapons?" he asked.

Reporters were surprised to hear the rumors about automatic weapons confirmed. They rushed in with follow-ups. "I don't know anything about the weapons," Stone admitted. "I assume there were probably automatic weapons just because of the mass casualties."

A reporter asked about motive. "Craziness," Stone said. Wrong again.

———

By now dozens of kids had fled the school with their friends. School officials herded them across Clement Park to meet school buses that would drive past police barricades to Leawood. The buses parked directly beside the site of the press conferences.

The kids trudged meekly toward the media throng. Many sobbed quietly. Others helped distraught students along, holding their hands or slinging an arm over their shoulders. Most of the kids stared at the ground. The crowd of reporters parted. These were not the faces of interview subjects.

But the students were eager to speak. Teachers hurried the kids, chiding them to keep quiet. They were having none of that. The bus windows started coming down, heads popped out, and kids recounted their ordeals. Kids piled off the buses.

The teachers tried to coax them back on. Not a chance. A tough-looking senior described his terror in the choir room with a sense of bravado and chivalry. But his voice cracked when a reporter asked how he felt. "Horrible," he said. "There were two kids lying on the pavement. I just—I started crying. I haven't cried for years, I just—I don't know what I'm going to do."

———

Attention focused on the students. Endless reunions with their parents played out on TV. A different group weathered the crisis in seclusion. More than a hundred teachers worked at Columbine, along with dozens of support staff. A hundred and fifty families feared for their husbands, wives, and parents. There was no rendezvous point where they could gather. Most drove home and waited by their phones. That's where Linda Lou Sanders kept vigil.

She had celebrated her mom's seventieth birthday with the family; then they'd headed up into the mountains for a pleasure drive. On the way, Linda's brother-in-law called her sister, Melody, on her cell.

"Where does Dave teach?"

"Columbine."

"You better head back down here."

Everyone gathered at Linda's house. Most of the news was good. Only one adult was reported injured, and it was a science teacher, which ruled out Dave. So why hadn't he called?

Those reports were nearly accurate. Only one adult had been hit, and Dave was still bleeding at that moment. The sense that afternoon was that gunfire had erupted all over the place. In fact, it had mostly been limited to the library and the west steps outside. Teachers had not been studying for tests or strolling outside to enjoy their lunch in the sunshine. If the bombs had gone off as planned, it would have wiped out a quarter of the faculty in the teachers' longue. But they had been spared by dumb luck. All but one.

Dave held on for hours in Science Room 3. Then the kids and teachers were evacuated, and none knew whether he'd made it. It would be a few days before the family would fully understand what had transpired in that room. It would take years to resolve why he'd lain there for over three hours, and who was to blame.

All Dave's family knew was that he had failed to call. He must be trapped inside the building, they thought. That wasn't good. Linda hoped he wasn't a hostage. She assumed he was hiding. He would be safe; he was not a risk taker.

The family monitored the TV and took turns answering calls. The phone rang incessantly, but it was never Dave. Linda called his business line repeatedly. Nobody picked up.

Linda was an athletic woman in her late forties, but she had a fragile psyche. Her smile was warm but tentative, as if she could shatter from a harsh word or gesture. Dave had found great satisfaction in protecting her. In his absence, her daughters and sister stepped in. Every call was fraught, so her family made sure to screen. In midafternoon, she got the urge to answer a call herself. "It was a woman," she said later. "And she said she was from the *Denver Post* and my husband had been shot—Do I have a comment? I screamed, I threw the phone. I have no idea what happened from then on."

Robyn Anderson was scared. Her prom date was a mass murderer. She had apparently armed him.

To her knowledge, only three people had known about the gun deal, and the other two were dead. Had they told anyone? Were guns traceable? She had not signed anything. Would the cops know? Should she keep her mouth shut?

The cops did not know. Robyn had been debriefed in Clement Park and had played it totally cool. She told the detective where she had been and what she had seen. She told the truth, but not the whole truth. She didn't know for sure who had been shooting, so she didn't mention that she knew them. She certainly didn't mention the guns. Should she? The guilt began eating her up.

Robyn talked to Zack Heckler on the phone that afternoon. She kept her mouth shut about the weapons. He didn't. He was clueless about the guns, thank God, but he knew the guys had been making pipe bombs. Bombs? Really? That astounded Robyn. Yes, really, Zack said. And he wasn't surprised at all. Zack didn't have quite the innocent picture of Dylan that Robyn did. It sounded just like those guys to run down the halls laughing while they killed people, he said.

Zack did not tell Robyn that he had helped Eric and Dylan make any pipe bombs. She wondered. Did he? Was he mixed up in this? More than her?

Zack was scared, too. They all were—anybody close to the killers. Zack wasn't volunteering information to the cops. He'd omitted mentioning the pipe bombs during his debriefing.

Chris Morris went the opposite route. He'd called the cops in the first hour, as soon as he suspected that his friends were involved. He was handcuffed in Clement Park and spirited away on national television. He kept talking at the police station. He described Eric's interest in Nazis, a crack about jocks, and some scary recent suggestions: cutting power to the school and setting PVC bombs at the exits with screws for shrapnel.

If Chris's story was legit, it suggested the killers had been leaking information about their plans—a classic characteristic of young assailants. If Eric and Dylan had leaked to Chris, chances were they had tipped off others as well.

Chris's dad was called. He contacted a lawyer. At 7:43 P.M., the three sat down with detectives for a formal interview. Chris and his father signed a form waiving their rights. The cops found Chris highly cooperative. He described the killers' obsessions with explosives and volunteered all sorts of details. Dylan had brought a pipe bomb to work once, but Chris ordered him to get it out of there. Chris knew the guys had gotten their hands on guns. It had been an open secret around Blackjack several months ago that Eric and Dylan were looking for hardware. They'd never told Chris directly, but he had heard it from several people.

Chris had a hunch who had come through for them: a kid named Phil Duran. Duran used to work at Blackjack, then moved to Chicago for a high-tech job. Before he'd left, Duran told Chris he had gone shooting with Eric and Dylan. Something about bowling pins and maybe an AK-47. Duran never said he had bought the guns, but Chris figured it was him.

It sounded staggering, how much Chris had known. He swore he had not taken it seriously. He agreed to turn over the clothes he was wearing and allow detectives to search his room. Everyone agreed to rendezvous at his house. Chris's mom met the cops at the front door, handed them his PC, and showed them upstairs. Then his brother arrived with Chris's clothes in a paper bag. He said Chris was afraid to come home. Mobs of media were already staking out the street.

The cops found nothing of obvious value, but gathered up piles of material. They left at 11:15.

———

Robyn needed company. She couldn't handle the stress alone. Her best friend, Kelli, came over around 7:30 on Tuesday evening. They went to Robyn's room. Kelli knew the boys well, too, especially Dylan. She had been part of the prom group. There was something Kelli didn't know, Robyn told her. *Remember that favor she had done Eric and Dylan last November?* Kelli remembered. It had been a big secret. Robyn had told Kelli repeatedly about this big favor she had done the guys, but she never would divulge what it was. Now she had to tell someone. It had been a gun show. The Tanner Gun Show in Denver. Eric and Dylan had called her on a Sunday, if she remembered right. They had checked the show out on Saturday, seen these sweet-looking shotguns. But they'd gotten carded; they were both underage then. They needed an eighteen-year-old with them. Robyn was eighteen. She really liked Dylan. So she went.

It was their money. Robyn made sure not to sign any papers. But she was the one who bought the three guns. The boys each got a shotgun. One had some kind of pump thing on it. Eric went for a rifle, too—a semi-automatic that looked like a giant paintball gun. Robyn felt so guilty, Kelli said later. How could she have imagined this?

Robyn didn't tell Kelli everything. She came clean with the main secret, but held back on a detail. She told Kelli she didn't know it was Eric and Dylan killing people until she heard it announced on TV that night. Kelli didn't buy it. Robyn had never received a B in high school—she could have put that mystery together. When she heard about the trench coats, she had to have known.

———

The Klebolds spent the afternoon and evening on their porch. Waiting. They were no longer allowed inside. At 8:10 P.M., a deputy arrived with instructions. Their home was now a crime scene. They had to go. Tom and Sue Klebold told friends they felt hit by a hurricane. Hurricanes don't hit the Rockies. They'd never seen it coming.

"We ran for our lives," Sue said later. "We didn't know what had happened. We couldn't grieve for our child."

Officers escorted Tom in to gather clothes for the next couple of days. Then Sue went in to take care of the pets. She fetched two cats, two birds, and their food bowls and litter boxes. At 9:00 P.M., they drove away.

They talked to a lawyer that night. He related a sobering thought. "Dylan isn't here anymore for people to hate," he said. "So people are going to hate you."

18. Last Bus

The buses kept arriving at Leawood Elementary, delivering discouragement as well as joy. It was great if your kid got off, but the odds kept dropping as the remaining parents dwindled. "I was getting envious of parents who were finding their kids and screaming out their names," Doreen Tomlin recalled. She found it harder and harder to get up. Her husband kept the faith, but hers played out. Buses arrived, and she stayed in her seat, silently chastising herself. "I thought, *Why aren't you getting up and looking? All these other parents are pinned to the stage, and you're just sitting here.*"

Brian Rohrbough had given up even earlier. By 2:00 P.M., while Leawood was packed with hopeful parents, Brian had accepted Danny's fate. "I knew he was gone," he said. "I assume it was God telling me, preparing me. I hoped I was wrong. We waited for busloads of kids, but I knew he wasn't going to be on it. I told Sue, 'You know he's gone.'"

But his ex-wife was hopeful. In the public library, Misty Bernall was, too. Her son, Chris, had turned up, but Cassie was still missing. *She is alive!* Misty told herself fiercely. Nothing could dampen Misty's resolve, or her perseverance.

"Her mom came up to me every two minutes and asked if I'd seen Cassie," a friend of her daughter said. "I told her, 'I'm sure there are a lot of people unaccounted for.'" Not what Misty wanted to hear.

Prayer helped. "Please, God, just give me my baby back," she prayed. "Please, God, where is she?"

Misty gave up on the public library. She made her way through Clement Park and discovered the buses being loaded. She scurried from one to the next. A friend of Cassie's reached out to grab her hand.

"Have you seen Cass?" Misty cried.

"No."

Misty returned to the library. Brad and Chris met her there. Then everyone was sent to Leawood. That was a huge relief for the parents waiting there: more families, better odds.

The buses kept coming, every ten to twenty minutes for a while. Then arrivals slowed. Around four o'clock, they stopped. One more bus was promised. Parents looked around. Whose kids would it be?

The wait went on endlessly. At five o'clock, it still wasn't there. Siblings wandered out to watch for it, hoping to run inside with the news. Doreen Tomlin had not gotten up in a long time, but she was still praying her boy would be on it. "We were clinging to that hope," she said.

At dinnertime, President Clinton held a press conference in the West Wing to discuss the attack. "Hillary and I are profoundly shocked and saddened by the tragedy today in Littleton," he said. He passed on the hope of a Jeffco official, who had just told him: "Perhaps now America would wake up to the dimensions of this challenge, if it could happen in a place like Littleton."

Clinton sent a federal crisis response team and urged reporters to resist jumping to conclusions. "What I would like to do is take a couple of days because we don't know what the facts are here," he said. "And keeping in mind, the community is an open wound right now."

At Leawood, even the resilient families were faltering. Nothing had changed: no buses, no word, for hours on end. District attorney Dave Thomas tried to comfort the families. He knew which ones would need it. He had thirteen names in his breast pocket. Ten students had been identified in the library, and two more outside, based on their clothing and appearance. One teacher lay in Science Room 3. All deceased. It was a solid list, but not definitive. Thomas kept it to himself. He told the parents not to worry.

At eight o'clock, they were moved to another room. Sheriff Stone introduced the coroner. She handed out forms asking for descriptions of their kids' clothing and other physical details. That's when John Tomlin realized the truth. The coroner asked them to retrieve their kids' dental records. That went over unevenly. Many took it gravely; others perked up. They had a task, finally, and hope for resolution.

A woman leapt up. "Where is that other bus!" she demanded.

There was no bus. "There was never another bus," Doreen Tomlin said later. "It was like a false hope they gave you." Many parents felt betrayed. Brian Rohrbough later accused the school officials of lying; Misty Bernall also felt deceived. "Not intentionally, perhaps, but deceived nonetheless," she wrote. "And so bitterly that it almost choked me."

Sheriff Stone told them that most of the dead kids had been in the library. "John always went to the library," Doreen said. "I felt like I was going to pass out. I felt sick."

She felt sadness but not surprise. Doreen was an Evangelical Christian, and believed the Lord had been preparing her for the news all afternoon. Most of the Evangelicals reacted differently than the other parents. The press had been cleared from the area, but Lynn Duff was assisting the families as a Red Cross volunteer. A liberal Jew from San Francisco, she was taken aback by what she saw.

"The way that those families reacted was markedly different," she said. "It was like a hundred and eighty degrees from where everybody else was. They were singing; they were praying; they were comforting the other parents, especially the parents of Isaiah Shoels [the only African American killed]. They were thinking a lot about the other parents, the other families, and responding a lot to other people's needs. They were definitely in pain, and you could see the pain in their eyes, but they were very confident of where their kids were. They were at peace with it. It was like they were a living example of their faith."

But not all the Evangelicals reacted the same way. Misty Bernall was defiant. She was sure Cassie was alive.

———

Mr. D stayed with the families. He was doing his best to console them, and waiting for word on a close friend. He had known Dave Sanders for twenty years. They had coached three sports together, shared hundreds of beers, and Frank had attended Dave's wedding. Frank had been hearing rumors about Dave all afternoon.

Sometime after the coroner's announcements, a teacher and a friend of both men, Rich Long, showed up at Leawood. He saw Frank and rushed up to hug him. "All I can remember was seeing blood on his pants and his shirt," Frank said later. "And I said, 'Rich, tell me. Is it true? Is Dave dead?' And he couldn't give me an answer."

Frank assured Rich he was strong enough to take the news. "Tell me!" he pleaded. "I need to know."

Rich couldn't help him. He was struggling with the same question.

———

Agent Fuselier had talked gunmen down and seen a few open fire right in front of him. He had struggled for weeks to release eighty-two people at Waco, then watched the gas tanks erupt and the buildings burn down. He'd known they were all dying inside Waco. Watching had been unbearable. This was worse.

Fuselier went home and gave Brian a hug. It had been a long time between hugs, and it was hard to let go. Then he sat down to watch the news reports with Mimi. He held her hand and choked back tears. "How could you go home and get dental records?" he asked. "Then what? You know your kid is lying there dead. How do you go to sleep?"

19. Vacuuming

Dave Sanders was one of the few teachers unaccounted for. He was still in Science Room 3. The SWAT team had reached him still alive, but hopeless. Several minutes later, before he was evacuated, Dave Sanders bled to death.

His family was not notified. Late in the afternoon, they got word he was injured and taken to Swedish Medical Center.

"I don't know who drove me," Linda Lou said. "I don't know how I got there. I don't remember the ride, I don't remember walking in there. I remember when we got there. They took us in a room. There was food, there was coffee, there were the sisters—the nuns." It was like a greeting committee, awaiting their arrival but, curiously, waiting for Dave, too. Linda found the head nurse reassuring. "She said, 'As soon as he gets here, you get to see him.' And he never got there. He never got there."

Eventually, they gave up and went to Leawood. They waited there awhile and then headed back home. Relief agencies dispatched victim's advocates. Several showed up at the house—a helpful but ominous sign. The phones rang constantly—five separate cells, laid out on the coffee table—but never with the call they wanted.

Linda retreated to her room. Every time someone used the bathroom downstairs, the exhaust fan clicked on, and Linda jumped up, believing it was the garage door opening.

"Finally, about ten-thirty, Mom and I got sick of waiting," Angie said. "We knew there had been a couple teachers with him, teachers who've known him for—since before I was born. And so we called them to find out what happened. And they informed us." Dave had been the teacher bleeding to death.

But had he bled out? Dave was alive when the SWAT team evacuated all the civilians. After that, no one seemed to know. Only the cops had seen it end, and they weren't ready to say.

"We still didn't know whether he was taken out of the school or not," Angie said. "But at least we knew a little more about what happened inside."

Linda tried to sleep. That was useless. She curled up with a pair of Dave's socks.

———

Linda spent the evening trying to blank out her mind. Odd thoughts slipped through. "All those people in my living room," she thought, "and I didn't have time to vacuum."

It was a common response. Survivors focused on mundane tasks—tiny victories they could still accomplish. Many were horrified by their thoughts.

Marjorie Lindholm had spent much of the afternoon with Dave Sanders. He kept getting whiter. Explosions kept erupting. When the SWAT team finally freed her, Marjorie ran past two bodies on the way out. She worried about how she had dressed. Her parents would find her in a tank top that suddenly felt sleazy. She borrowed a friend's shirt to cover herself up. A cop drove her to safety in Clement Park, and a paramedic stepped up to examine her. God, he was hot, she thought. "I felt ashamed," she wrote later. "I was thinking how this paramedic looked and people died."

A sophomore reproached herself for her survival instincts. She saw the killers and she took off running. Another girl was right by her side. The other girl went down. "Blood was everywhere," the sophomore said. "It was just terrible." She kept running. Later that day, she confessed her story to a *Rocky Mountain News* reporter. "Why didn't I stop to help that girl?" she asked. Her voice grew very soft. "I'm so mad," she said. "I was so selfish."

———

Brad and Misty Bernall got home around ten P.M. Brad climbed on top of the garden shed with a pair of binoculars to peer across the field. The library windows were blown out, and he could see men milling about inside. They were in blue jackets with big yellow letters: ATF. They had their heads down, but Brad couldn't quite make out what they were up to. "I guess they were stepping over bodies, looking for explosives," he said.

They were searching for live explosives and live gunmen. SWAT teams searched every broom closet. If third, fourth, or fifth shooters were still hiding out, they would be flushed out by morning.

Brad came back into the house. At 10:30, an explosion shook the neighborhood. Brad and Misty ran upstairs. They looked out Cassie's window, but nothing moved. Whatever it was, it had passed. Cassie's bed was empty. Misty feared she was still in the school. Had she been injured by the blast?

It was the bomb squad's one major mistake. They were moving bombs out of the area for controlled explosions. As they loaded one into a trailer, the strike-anywhere match Eric used for a detonator brushed the trailer wall and it blew. Bomb technicians fell backward as trained, and the blast shot straight up. No one was hurt, but it threw a big scare into the team. Everyone was exhausted. This was getting dangerous. They called it a night. Commanders instructed them to return at 6:30 A.M.

Brad and Misty kept watching. "I knew Cassie was in there somewhere," Brad said. "It was terrible to know that she was on the other side of the fence, and there was nothing we could do."

PART II

AFTER AND BEFORE

20. Vacant

There is a photograph. A blond girl lets out a wail. Her head is thrown back, caught in her own hands: palms against her temples, fingers burrowing into her scalp. Her mouth is wide open, eyes squeezed shut. She became the image of Columbine. Throughout Clement Park Tuesday afternoon, and in the photos that captured the experience, the pattern repeated: boy or girl, adult or child, nearly everyone was clenching something—a hand, her knees, his head, each other.

Before those pictures hit the newsstands, the survivors had changed. Kids drifted into Clement Park on Wednesday morning unclenched. Their eyes were dry, their faces slack. Their expressions had gone vacant.

Most of the parents were crying, but almost none of their kids were. They were so quiet it was unsettling. Hundreds of teenagers and not a whiff of nervous energy. Here and there a girl would sob and a boy would rush over to hug her—boys practically fought over who would provide the hugs—but those were brief exceptions.

They were aware of the blankness. Acutely. They didn't understand it, but they saw it and discussed it candidly. A vast number said they felt they were watching a movie.

The lack of bodies contributed to the problem—they were still inside the perimeter. None of the names had been released. The school was effectively gone. Nobody but police could get near it. It wasn't even visible from the line of police tape where everyone gathered.

Students had a pretty good idea of who had been killed. All the murders had been witnessed, and word spread quickly. But so many stories had turned out to be wrong. Doubt persisted. Everyone seemed to have at least a few people unaccounted for. "How can we cry when we don't know who we are crying for?" one girl asked. And yet she had cried. She had cried most of the night, she said. By morning, she had run out of tears.

———

No one from the sheriff's department called Brian Rohrbough. No officer appeared on the doorstep to inform him that his son had been killed. The phone woke Brian Wednesday. It was a friend calling to warn him, before he picked up the *Rocky Mountain News*. There was a picture.

Brian flipped past the huge HEARTBREAK headline, the dozens of stories and diagrams and pictures of clenched survivors, none of whom were his boy. He stopped at page 13. It was an overhead shot from a news chopper, but the photo filled half the page, so the subjects were large and unmistakable. Half a dozen students huddled behind a car in the parking lot with a policeman squeezed in beside them, squatting behind the wheel for cover, his rifle mounted across the trunk, eyes to the gun sight, finger on the trigger. A boy lay unprotected on the sidewalk nearby. He was out in the open, collapsed on his side, one knee curled up toward his chest, both arms splayed. "Motionless," the caption read. An enormous pool of blood, nearly the size of his body, stained the concrete a foot away and trickled down the crevice between two sidewalk squares. The victim was unidentified, his face blurry and almost completely obscured by the angle. But Brian Rohrbough knew. He never turned to page 14.

Brian was a tall man with the heavy build of a laborer. He had a long, puffy face with receding silver hair that accentuated his clenched brow: deep grooves stacked up across his forehead, over a pair of vertical gashes above the bridge of his nose. Danny looked remarkably similar, though he had yet to grow into all his features or develop the worry lines.

Danny was all Brian had. He and Sue had divorced when their son was four. Sue had remarried, but Brian had not. He had his custom audio business. It was successful, and he loved it, but the best part was that Danny did, too. He had been toddling around the workshop since he could walk. By seven, he was building wiring harnesses and running speaker wire. In junior high he started working for real weekdays after school. Brian and Sue had a friendly divorce and lived only a few blocks apart, but Danny could never get enough time with his father.

The shop was such a cool hangout for a high school boy: a big, greasy garage filled with power tools and hundred-thousand-dollar vintage cars up on blocks. Danny helped fit them with opera-caliber sound systems worth more than his wealthier friends' cars. Depending on the project, the place might reek of burnt rubber or prickly epoxy fumes. When Brian manned the buzz saw, the sweet smell of fresh-cut cherrywood wafted into the street.

Danny was a natural. He loved cars and he loved sound. He was great with the PC and had an ear for pitch. He liked to mess around with computer programs and was promising to take the business in a new direction. And he knew how to behave. Brian catered to some of the oldest and richest families in Colorado. Danny had grown up in their houses. He knew the drill. He was a charmer, and Brian reveled in showing him off.

A few months ago, Danny had come to a decision: college was not for him. He would go straight into the business from Columbine, make a career of it. Brian was ecstatic. In three years, he would make his son a partner. In four weeks, Danny was going to spend his first summer working at the shop full-time.

Wednesday morning, as soon as he saw the picture, Brian got in his car. He drove to Columbine. He stormed up to the perimeter and demanded his boy's body. The cops there said no.

Not only were they not turning Danny over, they had not brought him inside. Danny was still out there, lying on the sidewalk; he had weathered the elements all night. Too many bombs, the authorities said—the body could be booby-trapped.

Brian knew he wasn't getting a straight answer. Bomb squads had been clearing the school since Tuesday afternoon; Brian's son just wasn't a priority. Brian couldn't believe they were treating a victim's body so cavalierly.

Then it began to snow.

Danny lay out on that sidewalk for twenty-eight hours.

Misty Bernall started Wednesday at three A.M. She had slept a little, drifting in and out. Nightmares would jolt her awake: Cassie trapped in the building, huddled in the dark in some closet or lying on the cold tile floor. Her daughter needed her. She's over the fence a hundred yards away, Misty thought, and they won't let us get to her.

She gave up and took a shower. Brad did, too. They dressed and crossed the backyard to the perimeter.

A cop was standing guard. Brad told him Cassie was in there. He implored the cop give it to them straight. "We just want to know if there is anyone still alive in there."

The cop paused. "No," he said finally. "No one left alive."

They thanked him. "We appreciate your honesty," Misty said.

But Misty wasn't giving up. The cop could be wrong. Or Cassie might be lying in a hospital, unidentified. Misty kept trying the perimeter all morning. She was rebuffed each time.

Then the parents were alerted to return to Leawood. Brad and Misty headed right over. They waited for hours.

District attorney Dave Thomas arrived around 1:30. He still had the list of the deceased. It had not changed; nor had it been confirmed. The coroner required another twenty-four hours. So he decided to risk it. He informed the families one by one. "I don't know how to tell you this," he told Bob Curnow.

"You don't have to," Curnow said. "It's written on your face."

Misty took it hard, but she did not take it definitively. The DA said Cassie was dead, but he also said it was unofficial.

Hope gradually dissolved into anger. If Cassie were dead, Misty wanted her body out of that library and attended to.

———

Linda Sanders's family awaited the news at her home. By Wednesday afternoon, the house was packed with friends and relatives. Everyone knew what was coming. News crews set up a row of cameras to capture the moment of agony. "Be ready," a victim's advocate told Melody. "Be prepared to support your sister."

A patrol car pulled up just before three P.M. The deputy rang the bell, and Melody let him in. Linda was still not ready to hear it. "We have tentatively identified your husband as a victim at Columbine," he said.

Linda screamed. Then she threw up.

———

Frank DeAngelis didn't know if he was safe yet. He woke up at his brother's house on Wednesday, because he had been advised against staying at his own home. His car was sealed off inside the perimeter, so an assistant principal was on his way to pick Frank up before dawn. He was headed for meetings, to figure out what to do. What on earth were they going to do?

And what could he say? They were coming to hear him at ten A.M. Kids, parents, teachers—anyone aching—had been told to gather at Light of the World, a large Catholic church, one of the few venues large enough. They would look to him for answers. He had none.

Frank had lain awake much of the night grappling with it. "God, give me some guidance," he'd prayed.

Morning came, and he was no closer. He was consumed with guilt. "My job is to provide an environment that's safe," he said later. "I let so many people down."

Light of the World seats eight hundred and fifty and every pew was packed, with hundreds more students and parents standing against the walls. A parade of local officials took the podium in turn, trying to console the kids, who were inconsolable. The students applauded each speaker politely. Nobody was getting through.

Mr. D would settle for polite applause. He was hoping he wouldn't get lynched. Did he deserve to be? He had no speech prepared, no notes—he just planned to tell them what he felt.

His name was announced, he rose to approach the microphone, and the crowd leapt up from the pews. They were shouting, cheering, whistling, applauding—kids who hadn't registered a smile or a frown for hours were beating their palms together or pumping their fists, fighting back tears or letting them stream down their chins.

Mr. D. buckled at the waist. He clutched his stomach and staggered around, turning his back to the audience, sobbing uncontrollably. His torso was parallel to the floor, shaking so hard it was visible from the last row. He stood there for a full minute while the crowd refused to subside. He couldn't face them; he couldn't right himself. "It was so strange," he said later. "I just couldn't control it; my body just went into convulsions. The reason I turned my back is I was feeling guilt. I was feeling shameful. And when they started clapping and standing, knowing I had their approval and support, that's when I broke down."

He made it to the podium and began with an apology: "I am so sorry for what happened and for what you are feeling." He reassured them and promised to stand by them—"I will be there for you, whenever you need it"—but refused to sugarcoat what they were in for. "I'd like to take a wand

and wipe away what you are feeling, but I can't do that. I'd like to tell you those scars will heal, but they will not," he said.

His students were grateful for the candor. So many kids in Clement Park that morning would describe how tired they already were of hearing so many people tell them everything would be all right. They knew the truth; they just wanted to hear it.

Mr. D. ended his speech by telling them he loved them. Each and every one of them. They needed to hear that, too.

———

Kids were having trouble with their parents, especially their moms. "It's kind of hard for me to sit at home," a boy said. "Like when my mom comes home, I try to stay out of the house." Lots of other boys nodded; more and more told the same story. Their mothers were so scared, and the fear hadn't abated when they'd found their kids; now they just wanted to hug them. *Hug him/her forever*—that was the refrain Tuesday. Wednesday, it was *My mom doesn't understand*. Emotionally, their mothers were wildly out of synch. At first, the kids needed the hugs badly; now they needed them to stop.

———

Most of the student body wandered the park, desperate to unload their stories. They needed adults to hear them, and their parents would not do. They found their audience: the press. Students were wary at first, but let their guards down quickly. Reporters seemed so understanding. Clement Park felt like an enormous confessional Wednesday. The kids would regret it.

In the midst of it, a shriek pierced the media camp. Mourners froze, unsure of what to do. More screams: different voices, same direction. Hundreds ran toward them: students, journalists, everyone within hearing range. They found a dozen girls gathered around a single car that remained among the satellite trucks in a small lot on the edge of the park. It was Rachel Scott's car—the first girl shot dead. Rachel didn't have an assigned spot, so she had parked half a mile from the school on Tuesday. No one had come to claim the car. Now it was covered front to back with flowers and candles. Messages to Rachel in heaven had been soaped across the windows. Her girlfriends held hands in a semicircle around the back of the car, sobbing uncontrollably. One girl began to sing. Others followed.

The Harrises and Klebolds both hired attorneys. They had good reason: the presumption of guilt quickly landed on their shoulders. Investigators didn't expect to charge them, but the public did. National polls taken shortly after the attack would identify all sorts of culprits contributing to the tragedy: violent movies, video games, Goth culture, lax gun laws, bullies, and Satan. Eric did not make the list. Dylan didn't either. They were just kids. Something or someone must have led them astray. Wayne and Kathy and Tom and Sue were the chief suspects. They dwarfed all other causes, blamed by 85 percent of the population in a Gallup poll. They had the additional advantage of being alive, to be pursued.

Their attorneys warned them to keep quiet. Neither family spoke to the press. Both released statements on Wednesday. "We cannot begin to convey our overwhelming sense of sorrow for everyone affected by this tragedy," the Klebolds said. "Our thoughts, prayers and heartfelt apologies go out to the victims, their families, friends and the entire community. Like the rest of the country, we are struggling to understand why this happened, and ask that you please respect our privacy during this painful grieving period."

The Harrises were more brief: "We want to express our heartfelt sympathy to the families of all the victims and to all the community for this senseless tragedy," they wrote. "Please say prayers for everyone touched by these terrible events."

Dylan's brother stayed home from work for several days. Byron was nearly three years older than Dylan, but because of Dylan's early enrollment, just two years out of school. He was doing gofer work at an auto dealership: washing cars, shoveling snow, moving inventory around the lot. "It was an entry-level job, but man, he's good," a spokesman for the store told the *Rocky Mountain News*.

His employers understood the need for time away. "It's shocking for everyone," the spokesman said. "We're a family here and we look out for each other. Our hearts go out to Byron. This kid's great."

Supervisory Special Agent Fuselier's concern Wednesday morning was the conspiracy. Everyone assumed the Columbine massacre was a conspiracy, including the cops. It was just too big, too bold, and too complex for a couple of kids to have imagined, much less pulled off. This looked like the work of eight or ten people. Every attack of this magnitude spawns conspiracy theories, but this time they appeared sound. The legacy of those theories, and Jeffco's response to them, would haunt the Columbine recovery in peculiar ways.

Wednesday morning, Fuselier entered the ghastly crime scene. The hallways were scattered with shell casings, spent pipe bombs, and unexploded ordnance. Bullet holes and broken glass were everywhere. The library was soaked in blood; most of the bodies lay under tables. Fuselier had seen carnage, but still, it was awful. The sight that really stunned him was outside, on the sidewalk and the lawn. Danny Rohrbough and Rachel Scott were still out there. No one had even covered them. Years later, he shuddered at the memory.

Fuselier arrived at Columbine as an FBI agent, but he would play a more significant role as a clinical psychologist. Altogether, he had spent three decades in the field; he'd started in private practice, then worked for the air force. A hostage-negotiation course in Okinawa changed his life. He could read people. He could talk them down. In 1981, Fuselier joined the FBI. He took a $5,000-a-year pay cut for a detective job, just to get a shot at the Bureau's Special Operations and Research Unit (SOARU)—the leading center of hostage-negotiation study in the world.

Agent Fuselier worked his way up through standard casework and discovered he liked detective work, too. He got the assignment at SOARU, finally, and began a new career defusing gun battles. He would handle some of the nation's worst hostage crises, including the 1987 Atlanta prison siege and the Montana Freemen standoff. He was the FBI's last hope at Waco, and the final person to talk to David Koresh before the tanks rolled in. Fuselier spent most of his time at SOARU studying prior incidents and analyzing success rates. His team developed the fundamental tactics for hostage standoffs employed today. Fuselier became known for steadiness under pressure, but his heart was weakening, his temples were graying, and eventually he sought a quieter life. He moved his family to Colorado in 1991, and they settled into a tranquil neighborhood in Littleton.

Fuselier would play the leading role in understanding the Columbine killers, but it was luck that drove him to the case. If his son Brian had not been attending that high school, Fuselier would not have even been assigned to the investigation. In fact, it's unlikely that the FBI would have played a major role. But because Fuselier arrived on the scene, established a rapport with the commanders, and offered federal support, FBI agents would play a major role on the team. Fuselier was one of the senior supervisory agents in the region and already had a relationship with local commanders, so he was placed in command of the FBI team. Before April 20, Fuselier headed up the domestic terrorism unit for the FBI in the region. For the next year, he delegated most of that responsibility. This was more important.

Columbine was the crime of the century in Colorado, and the state assembled the largest team in its history to solve it. Nearly a hundred detectives gathered in Jeffco. More than a dozen agencies loaned out their best minds. The FBI contributed more than a dozen special agents, a remarkable number for a local investigation. Agent Fuselier, one of the senior psychologists in the entire Bureau, headed up the FBI team. Everyone else reported to Jeffco's Kate Battan, a brilliant detective, whose work unraveling complex white-collar crimes would serve her well. She reported to Division Chief John Kiekbusch, a rising star who had just been promoted to senior command. Kiekbusch and Fuselier each played an active daily role and consulted regularly about the overall progress of the case.

The team identified eleven likely conspirators. Brooks Brown had the most suspicious story, and Chris Morris had admitted to hearing about bombs. Two others matched the descriptions for third and fourth shooters. Those four perched atop the list, with Dylan's prom date, Robyn Anderson, close behind.

Bringing them to justice would require a Herculean effort. Detectives planned to question every student and teacher at Columbine and every friend, relative, and associate of the killers, past or present. They had five thousand interviews ahead of them in the next six months. They would snap thousands of photographs and compile more than 30,000 pages of evidence. The level of detail was exacting: every shell casing, bullet fragment, and shotgun pellet was inventoried—55 pages and 998 evidence ID numbers to distinguish every shard.

The Jeffco command team hastily reserved a spot for Fuselier in the Columbine band room. The killers had made a mess of the place without setting foot inside it. Abandoned books, backpacks, sheet music, drum kits, and instruments were strewn among the shrapnel. The door was missing—blown away by the SWAT team searching for gunmen.

Much of the school looked considerably worse. Pipe bombs and Molotov cocktails had burned through stretches of carpeting and set off the sprinkler system. The cafeteria was flooded, the library unspeakable. Veteran cops had staggered out in tears. "There were SWAT team people who were in Vietnam who were weeping over what they saw," District Attorney Dave Thomas said.

The detective team was moving in. Every scrap of wreckage was evidence. They had 250,000 square feet of crime scene—just on the inside. Footprints, fingerprints, stray hairs, or gun residue could be anywhere. Crucial DNA evidence might be floating through the cafeteria. And live explosives might still be present, too.

Detectives had stripped down Eric and Dylan's bedrooms, left the furniture, and hauled out much of the rest. The Klebold house yielded little—some yearbooks and a small stack of writings—but Dylan had wiped his hard drive clean. Eric's house provided a mother lode: journals, more computer rants, an audiotape, videotapes, budgets and diagrams and timelines...Eric had documented everything. He'd wanted us to know.

———

Adding to the sense of urgency—and conspiracy—was a cryptic message suggesting more possible violence to come. "We went scrambling for days trying to track that down," Fuselier said. They searched the school for explosives again. They raised the pressure on the probable conspirators.

The detectives conducted five hundred interviews in the first seventy-two hours. It was a great boost, but it got chaotic. Battan was worried about witnesses, who were growing more compromised by the hour from what they read and saw on TV. Investigators prioritized: students who had seen the shooters came first.

Other detectives headed to the suspects' childhood hometowns.

21. First Memories

It didn't start with a murder plot. Before he devised his massacre, Eric settled into a life of petty crime. Earlier still, even before adolescence, he was exhibiting telltale signs of a particular breed of killer. The symptoms were stark in retrospect, but subtle at the time—invisible to the untrained eye.

Eric wrote about his childhood frequently and fondly. His earliest memories were lost to him. Fireworks, he remembered. He sat down one day to record his first memory in a notebook and discovered he couldn't do it. "Hard to visualize," he wrote. "My mind tends to blend memories together. I do remember the 4th of July when I was 12." Explosions, thunderclaps, the whole sky on fire. "I remember running outside with a lot of other kids," he wrote. "It felt like an invasion."

Eric savored the idea—heroic opportunities to obliterate alien hordes. His dreams were riddled with gunfire and explosions. Eric relished the anticipation of the detonator engaging. He was always dazzled by fire. He could whiff the acrid fallout from the fireworks again just contemplating the memory. Later the night of the fireworks display, when he was twelve, Eric walked around and burned stuff.

Fire was beauty. The tiny eruption of a cardboard match igniting. A fuse sputtering down could drive Eric delirious with anticipation. Scaring the shit out of stupidass dickwads—it didn't get much better than that.

In the beginning, explosions scared Eric even as they exhilarated him. He ran for cover when the fireworks started in his "earliest memory" account. "I hid in a closet," he wrote. "I hid from everyone when I wanted to be alone."

———

Eric was a military brat. His father moved the family across five states in fifteen years. Wayne and Kathy gave birth to Eric David Harris in Wichita, Kansas, on April 9, 1981, eighteen years and eleven days before Eric attempted to blow up his high school. Wichita was the biggest town Eric would live in until junior high. He started school in Beavercreek, Ohio, and did stints in rural air force towns like Oscoda, Michigan, and Plattsburgh, New York. Eric enrolled in and was pulled out of five different schools along the way, often those on the fringes of military bases where friends came and went as fast as he did.

Wayne and Kathy worked hard to smooth over the disruptions. Kathy chose to be a stay-at-home mom to focus on her boys. She also performed her duties as an officer's wife. Kathy was attractive, but rather plain. She wore her wavy brown hair in a simple style: swept back behind her ears and curling in toward her shoulders in back.

Wayne had a solid build, a receding hairline, and very fair skin. He coached baseball and served as scoutmaster. In the evenings, he would shoot baskets on the driveway with Eric and his older brother, Kevin.

"I just remember they wanted the children to have a normal, off-base relationship in a normal community," said a minister who lived nearby. "They were just great neighbors—friendly, outgoing, caring."

Major Harris did not tolerate misbehavior in his home. Punishment was swift and harsh, but all inside the family. Wayne reacted to outside threats in classic military fashion: circle the wagons and protect the unit. He didn't like snap decisions. He preferred to consider punishment carefully, while the boys reflected on their deeds. After a day or two, Wayne would render his decision, and it would be final. It was typically grounding or loss of privileges—whatever they held dear. As Eric grew older, he would periodically have to relinquish his computer—that stung. Wayne considered a conflict concluded once he'd discussed it with Eric and they'd agreed on the facts and the punishment. Then Eric had to accept responsibility for his actions and complete his punishment.

Detectives discovered gross contradictions to Eric's insta-profile already cemented in the media. In Plattsburgh, friends described a sports enthusiast hanging out with minorities. Two of Eric's best friends turned out to be Asian and African American. The Asian boy was a jock to boot. Eric played soccer and Little League. He followed the Rockies even before the family moved to Colorado, frequently sporting their baseball cap. By junior high he had grown obsessed with computers, and eventually with popular video games.

In his childhood photos Eric looks wholesome, clean-cut, and confident—much more poised than Dylan. Both were painfully shy, though. Eric "was the shyest out of everybody," said a Little League teammate from Plattsburgh. He didn't talk much, and other kids described him as timid but popular.

At the plate, one of his core personality traits was already on display. "We had to kind of egg him on to swing, to hit the pitch sometimes," his coach said. "It wasn't that he was afraid of the ball, just that he didn't want to miss. He didn't want to fail."

Eric continued to dream. Major Harris inspired military fantasies, but Eric usually saw himself as a Marine. "Guns! Boy, I loved playing guns," he wrote later. The rustic towns he grew up in provided fields and forests and streams where he could play soldier. When Eric was eight, the family moved to Oscoda, Michigan, where the scenic Au Sable River meets Lake Huron in the rugged northern region of the state. Wayne and Kathy bought a house in town so the boys could grow up with civilians. Oscoda was dominated by the air force base; population 1,061 and dropping. Work for adults was sparse, but it offered a world of adventure for little boys.

The Harris house sat near the edge of Huron National Forest. It seemed vast, empty, and ancient to Eric's young eyes. The air was thick with the scent of musty white pines. This was early lumberjack territory. The state proclaimed it Paul Bunyan's home, and the Lumberman's Monument had been erected in bronze nearby. Eric, Kevin, and their friend Sonia would spend afternoons hunting down enemy troops and withstanding alien invasions. They built a little tree fort out of sticks and branches to use for a base camp.

"Fire!" Eric screamed in one of their enactments. The three young heroes rattled off machine-gun fire with their toy guns. Sonia was always fearless—she would charge straight into the imaginary rifle fire. Kevin yelled for air support; Eric tossed a stick grenade into the trees. The three defenders took cover and felt the earth shudder from the convulsion. Eric hurled another grenade, and another and another, taking wave after wave of enemy troops down. Eric was always the protagonist when he reminisced about those days in high school. Always the good guy, too.

When he was eleven, id Software released the video game Doom, and Eric found the perfect virtual playground to explore his fantasies. His adversaries had faces, bodies, and identities now. They made sounds and fought back. Eric could measure his skills and keep score. He could beat nearly everyone he knew. On the Internet, he could triumph over thousands of strangers he had never met. He almost always won, until later, when he met Dylan. They were an even match.

In 1993, Wayne retired. The family moved again, this time to Colorado, and settled down for good in Jeffco. Eric entered seventh grade, and Kevin started at Columbine. Wayne eventually took a job with a defense contractor that created electronic flight simulators. Kathy began part-time work at a catering company.

Three years later the Harrises upgraded to a $180,000 home in a nicer neighborhood just north of the beautiful Chatfield Reservoir and two miles south of Columbine High School. Kevin played tight end and was the kicker for the Rebels before heading off to the University of Colorado. The color gradually drained out of Major Harris's thinning hair. He grew a thick white mustache, put on a few pounds, but maintained his military bearing.

Eric loved a good explosion, but treasured his own tranquillity. Fishing trips with his dad were the best. He captured the serenity in a vivid essay called "Just a Day." The night before, he had to go to bed early, which would normally provoke "a barrage of arguments and pouting," but on these occasions he didn't mind. He'd wake up to black skies and rich ground coffee vapors wafting up to his room. Eric didn't like to drink the stuff, but he couldn't get enough of the smell. "My brother would already be up," he continued, "trying to impress our father by forcing down the coffee he hadn't grown to like yet. I always remember my brother trying to impress everyone, and myself thinking what a waste of time that would be."

Eric would scamper out to the garage to get his tackle together and help load the cooler into the back of their '73 Ram pickup. Then they headed into the hills. "The mountains were always peaceful, a certain halcyon hibernating within the tall peaks & the armies of pine trees. It seemed back then that when the world changed, these mountains would never move," he wrote. They would drive out to a mountain lake in the wilderness, almost deserted, except for "a few repulsive suburbanite a$$holes. They always seemed to ruin the serenity of the lake."

Eric loved the water. Just standing back on the bank and gazing at it: the waves dancing around the surface in peculiar patterns, getting caught suddenly by a burst of current, forming unexpected shapes and vanishing again—what a glorious escape. When his eye caught something interesting, Eric would cast into it, presuming the fish might have been attracted to it, too.

Then it was over. Back to shithead society, populated by automatons too dense to comprehend what was out there. "No regrets, though," he concluded. "Nature shared the secret serenity with someone who was actually observant enough to notice. Sucks for everyone else."

22. Rush to Closure

HEALING BEGINS, the *Denver Post* announced Thursday morning. The headline spanned the full width of page 1 thirty-six hours after the attack. Ministers, psychiatrists, and grief counselors cringed. It was an insanely premature assessment The paper was trying to be helpful, but its rush to closure did not go over well in Jeffco. With every passing week, more of the community would grumble that it was time to move on. The survivors had other ideas.

The bodies were finally returned to the victims' families on Thursday. Most of the parents were desperate to learn how their child had died. There were plenty of witnesses, but a few were tempted to inflate their accounts, and the more dramatic versions of their stories tended to travel.

A heroic version of Danny Rohrbough's death quickly gained currency and was widely reported in the media. "[He] held the school door open to let others escape and laid down his life for his friends," the *Rocky Mountain News* reported.

"You know, he might have lived," the Rohrboughs' pastor would tell fifteen hundred mourners at Danny's funeral. "He chose to stay there and hold the door for others so that they might go out before him and make their way to safety. They made it and Danny didn't."

The story was later disproved. Danny's father, Brian, said he never believed it. "I know that Dan and his friends wouldn't have been standing there if they had thought they were in danger," he said. Brian was irritated by the urge to juice the story to make Danny's death more tragic or meaningful. It was tragic enough, he said.

A hundred students in Clement Park crushed together in a throbbing teen prayer mosh. They stood on their toes, reached toward the heav-

116

ens, and pressed their arms together in a mass human steeple. The mood was rapturous, the faces serene. They sang sweet hymns, swayed as one body, and cried out to Jesus to pull them through. They named The Enemy. "We feel the presence of Satan operating in our midst!" a young girl declared.

The school set up a second official gathering for students on Thursday afternoon. The megachurches were among the only structures in the area big enough to accommodate a crowd that large, so the gathering was held at West Bowles Community Church. This session was to be informal, just a designated place for students who wanted to find each other in one place. Mr. D wasn't planning to speak, until a counselor interrupted his meeting with faculty down the hall. "Frank, they need you," he said. "You need to go out there."

Frank walked the hallway to the nave of the church, contemplating what to say. And again he faced the dilemma of how to act at the microphone. Several of his friends, and staff, too, had warned him not to cry again. "God, you're going to be in the national media," they said. "You can't show that, it's a sign of weakness." He had gotten away with it once, but the media would crucify him if they discovered he was buckling.

The trauma specialists disagreed. These kids had been raised in a western mentality, they argued: real men fend for themselves; tears are for weaklings; therapy is a joke. "Frank, you are the key," one counselor advised him. "You're an emotional person, you need to show those emotions. If you try to hold your emotions inside, you're going to set the image for other people." The boys, in particular, would be watching him, DeAngelis felt. They were already dangerously bottled up. "Frank, they need to know it's all right to show emotion," the counselor said. "Give them that permission."

The students were awaiting his appearance, and when he walked in, they started chanting the school's rallying cry, which he'd last heard at the assembly before the prom: "We are COL-um-*BINE!* We are COL-um-*BINE!*" Each time they yelled it more loudly, confidently, and aggressively. Mr. D hadn't realized until he heard them that he had been longing to draw strength from them, too. He'd thought he was there just to provide it. "I couldn't fake it," he said later. "I walked on that stage and I saw those kids cheering and the tears started coming down."

This time he decided to address the tears. "Guys, trust me, now is not the time to show your manliness," he told them. "Emotion is emotion, and keeping it inside doesn't mean you're strong."

That was the last time Mr. D worried about crying in public.

———

The big question facing the school was how to finish out the year. These kids needed to get back together fast. But the cops weren't going to open the building for months. The administration decided to restart classes a week later at nearby Chatfield High School, Columbine's traditional rival. Columbine would take over the school in the mornings, and Chatfield would resume use in the afternoons. Classes would be shortened for both groups until the end of the school year.

The long-term solution was trickier. Some people suggested that the building be demolished; some parents insisted that their kids would never set foot in that murder scene again. But others pointed out that the psychological blow of losing their high school entirely would be much worse. The *Rocky Mountain News* led its Thursday edition with a letter from the publisher stating, "If students, teachers and parents feel there is no way they can return to the classrooms of Columbine, the Denver *Rocky* will lead the charge to raise the funds to build a new school and urge legislators to help. If they decide that they do not want to be driven from their school, we will support the community in rebuilding the campus."

———

Reverend Bill Oudemolen began preparing two funerals. John Tomlin and Lauren Townsend had been faithful members of the Foothills Bible Church. The pastor walked through Clement Park and sniffed the air. Satan. The pastor could smell him wafting through the park. It was an acrid odor—had it been a little stronger, it might have singed his nose hairs. The Enemy had swept in with this madness on Tuesday, but the real battle was only now under way.

"I smell the presence of Satan," Reverend Oudemolen thundered from the pulpit Sunday morning. "What we saw Tuesday came from Satan's home office. Satan had a plan. Satan wants us to live in fear in Littleton. He wants us to see black trench coats or people in Goth attire and makeup and here's what he wants us to feel: *Look how powerful and scary Satan is!*"

He'd watched an ABC special examining the fallout in West Paducah,

Kentucky, thirteen months after its school shooting. West Paducah was still riven with hostility, Oudemolen told his congregation. "I know what Satan wants Littleton to look like in thirteen months," he said. "He wants us to be angry. Satan wants us to stay right here, with uncontrollable grief. He wants evil to be repaid by evil. He wants hatred to be repaid by hatred. Satan has plans for Littleton."

Cassie Bernall's pastor, George Kirsten, charged the same culprit. This was so much more than two boys with guns or even bombs, in their eyes. This was spiritual warfare. The Enemy had taken the battlefield in broad daylight in Jeffco, and Reverend George Kirsten was eager to see Christ reappear to smite him. When Kirsten addressed his congregation at West Bowles Community Church, he likened Cassie to the martyrs calling out to God at the onset of the Apocalypse in the book of Revelation: "How long? How long will it be until my blood is avenged?" he cried.

It's a pivotal scene Reverend Kirsten was invoking. Immediately after the appearance of the four horsemen, the fifth seal is broken and all the Christian martyrs since the beginning of time appear under the altar, pleading for enemy blood to be spilled in return. Shortly thereafter, all true believers are raptured and the Apocalypse commences.

Reverend Kirsten happened to be teaching Revelation—one chapter a week—to his Bible study group at West Bowles. He believed, as they did, that the great signs of the Apocalypse were already under way and the moment might be at hand.

———

Reverend Don Marxhausen disagreed with all the riffs on Satan. He saw two boys with hate in their hearts and assault weapons in their hands. He saw a society that needed to figure out how and why—fast. Blaming Satan was just letting them off easy, he felt, and copping out on our responsibility to investigate. The "end of days" fantasy was even more infuriating.

Marxhausen had managed to reach the kids at the Light of the World assembly. He led the large Lutheran congregation near Columbine, and for years he'd headed up a council of mainline Protestant clergy—*mainline* being the common term for the large, moderate denominations such as Presbyterians, Episcopalians, Methodists, and Baptists outside the Southern Baptist Convention. Marxhausen was only forty-five, but widely regarded on as the old wise man of the western suburbs. Mainliners were outnumbered by the Evangelicals, and probably even the Catholics, in Jeffco, but they maintained a strong presence, and Marxhausen's thousand-seat church was packed solid every Sunday.

Most of the mainliners and the Catholics were averse to pinning the Columbine tragedy on Satan, but they were determined not to fight about it. Local ministers agreed very quickly that they needed to pull together and put factional bickering aside.

Barb Lotze faced her first test barely twenty-four hours after the massacre. She arranged a huge prayer service for Wednesday evening at Light of the World Catholic Church, where she served as youth pastor. Students from all faiths had been invited, and every pew was packed. She wanted to make them all feel welcome.

Midway through the service, an excited youth minister from an Evangelical church approached Lotze about performing an "altar call"—the practice where new or renewed believers are summoned forward to be born again. It was a decidedly un-Catholic ritual, and it seemed like an inappropriate time, but Lotze was determined to establish some sort of reciprocity with the Evangelical churches.

She reluctantly agreed.

The young pastor rushed to the microphone and proclaimed the power of Jesus. Who was ready to accept Jesus Christ as their own personal savior? he cried.

No one moved. He was astonished.

"Nobody?" he asked.

He sat down, and the audience moved on. "They just want to be hugged," Lotze said. "They want to be loved, told that we're going to get through this together."

The kids kept pouring into the churches. What began Tuesday night as a means to escape from their parents and find each other quickly became a habit. Night after night they returned to the churches in vast numbers—kids who had not seen an altar in years. For some it was a conscious choice to look to God in desperation, but most said it was just a place to go.

The churches organized informal services at night. In the daytime, they just opened their doors and gave the kids the run of the place. A handful saw a recruiting opportunity. Anyone who drove to Clement Park and stayed a few hours would find several flyers stacked under their wiper blades: "WE'RE HERE TO LISTEN AND ASSIST YOU," "If you need: prayer, counseling, meals prepared...," "FREE!! HOT CHOCOLATE COFFEE COOKIES, COME BE WARM AT CALVARY CHAPEL." Boxes of pocket-sized Bibles were trucked to the park and distributed to passersby. Scientologists handed out *Way to Happiness* booklets to mourners filing past Rachel Scott's car—still abandoned in the parking lot where she'd left it.

Eventually, investigators would escort dozens of witnesses back through the school to help re-create the attack. Mr. D was the first. A few days after the massacre, detectives walked him down the main hallway. Dr. Fuselier was with them. They passed the remnants of the trophy case and DeAngelis described it exploding behind him. They proceeded down the corridor and he indicated where he'd intercepted the girls' gym class.

He re-created everything: the shouts, the screams, the acrid smell of the smoke. None of that fazed Frank DeAngelis. He was cried out by this time, as stoic as the boys he was hoping to open up.

They turned the corner, and Frank saw bloody smears on the carpet. He knew Dave Sanders had gone down there. He had not anticipated the stains. "You could see the knuckle prints," he said. "He actually was on all fours and there were his knuckle prints—he was struggling. It tore me up."

A trail of blood traced Dave's path around the corner and down the hall. Detectives led Frank DeAngelis to Science Room 3. Nothing had been disturbed.

"They took me into where Dave died," Frank recalled. "And there were sweatshirts there full of blood. That got to me." In the science room, Frank broke down again. He turned to Fuselier. "I was glad he was here," DeAngelis said later. "Most FBI guys wouldn't have done anything. Dwayne gave me a hug."

Aside from witnesses, the best hope for cracking the case seemed to lie in the physical evidence: the guns, first and foremost. Dylan was a minor; Eric had just turned eighteen. They had probably gotten help securing the weapons. Whoever turned up at the front end of those acquisitions would likely be co-conspirator number one.

Investigators worked parallel tracks hunting them down. ATF agents took the technical angle: they came up with a solid lifespan on the semiautomatics. Eric's carbine rifle was less than a year old; it had been sold originally in Selma, Alabama, and had made its way to a gun shop in Longmont, Colorado, less than an hour from Denver. They traced Dylan's TEC-9 through four different owners between 1997 and 1998, but then the records disappeared. The third owner said he'd sold it at the Tanner Gun Show but had not been required to keep sales records at that time. The shotguns were a bigger problem. They were three decades old, before serial numbers were required. They were impossible to trace.

The bomb squad disassembled and studied the big bombs. The centerpiece of Eric's performance was a complete mess. "They didn't understand explosive reactions," the deputy fire marshal said. "They didn't understand electrical circuitry."

Officials refused to be more specific, arguing that they didn't want to give copycatters any hints. The deputy marshal summarized the primary mistake as "defective fusing."

Detectives were having more luck working the suspects. Chris Morris had implicated Phil Duran the first day. If they could believe Morris, that could explain several guns, possibly all four. Duran was playing innocent, but they knew they could crack him. And then they heard from Robyn Anderson.

Unloading her secret to Kelli on Tuesday night had not appeased Robyn's conscience. Wednesday morning, she called Zack again. This time, she told him. And she told him another small lie—that he was the only one who knew. Then she told her mom.

———

Robyn's mom brought her down to the school. Jeffco had setup its Columbine Task Force inside the crime scene, headquartered in the band room. Detectives interviewed Robyn, with her mom by her side. Two detectives traded off questioning—one from the DA's office, one from a nearby suburb's police force. They videotaped the session. And they were harsh. The first time they asked about the guns, Robyn "visibly recoiled," according to the detective's synopsis of the videotape. And she looked to her mom for support. Did she buy the guns? they asked. *No, she did not. She went to the show with them, but they bought the weapons.* Why did they want them? *Dylan lived out in the country, so she assumed they wanted to hunt. No, they never talked about hunting people, not even as a joke.*

Detectives asked her about the prom, the Trench Coat Mafia, the killers' personalities, and then returned to the guns. It was a private dealer, she said. The boys paid cash. They didn't try to bargain, they just paid the asking price—somewhere around $250 to $300 apiece. No one signed anything, and she never showed an ID. The shotguns had very long barrels, but the dealer said they could cut them down.

The detectives began to press her harder: Dylan and Eric didn't really seem like hunters, did they? *Dylan lived in the mountains, there were deer all over the place. And her dad owned a gun—he never used it, but he had one. Lots of people have gun collections. Eric and Dylan were into that kind of stuff—why wouldn't they want one?* She'd actually asked the boys if they were going to do something stupid with the guns, she said. They'd assured her they would never hurt anyone.

Did Eric and Dylan tell you to keep the guns secret? the detectives asked. *Yes.* And that didn't raise your suspicions? *They were underage. It was illegal. They had to hide it from their parents.* And where did they hide them? *She didn't know about Eric. Dylan dropped him off first, and Eric put his guns in the trunk of his Honda. She assumed he stashed them in the house later. Dylan tried to hide his in his bottom dresser drawer, but it was too big. He stuck it in the closet, but he told her later that he cut the barrel down and made it fit in the drawer.*

And that didn't arouse her suspicions? *No, because the gun dealer had already suggested it.*

Robyn said she never saw the guns again. The detectives moved on. They asked about a wide range of subjects; eventually, they got to the explosives. Had she seen any, had she helped make any, had any of Eric and Dylan's friends assisted them? *No, no, and…maybe Zack Heckler.* Zack? Why Zack? *Zack had told her he knew more of what was going on.* She told them about the call with Zack, about his admission that he knew about the pipe bombs.

How strange, the detectives said—Eric and Dylan went bowling with her every week, Dylan called her every other night, they confided in her about the guns, and yet they never said a word about the pipe bombs. *They must not have wanted me to know.* Come on! the detectives said. You're lying! Over and over, they mocked her about the disparity—the boys told Zack about the pipe bombs, but they never told her? *No, no, never. That's what they*

*were like. When they wanted you to know something, you knew. When they wanted you
in the dark, you stayed there. They could get very secluded about it, very isolated.*

They kept on her. *The guns were an isolated incident,* she said. *And Zack—he
didn't know much either. He knew they were making bombs, but he had no idea what
they were up to.*

The interrogation went on for four hours. Robyn held her ground.

———

Bomb squads had been through the school several times and found nearly
a hundred bombs of varying sizes and composition—most exploded, some
not. Most were pipe bombs or crickets, but one in the cafeteria stood out: a
big white propane tank, standing upright, nearly two feet tall. It was wedged
against a one-gallon gasoline can. The most ominous part was the alarm
clock. There were remnants of an orange duffel bag, too, mostly burned
away. The car bombs were also discovered, with more faulty wiring. The
diversionary bomb in the field was disturbing for another reason. It had
blown shortly after being moved, suggesting booby traps. Trip wires could
be anywhere.

The FBI provided a group of crime scene specialists to assist in the massive effort of documenting the evidence. At 8:15 on Thursday morning, the
team slogged through the cafeteria debris. Hundreds of backpacks, lunch
trays, and half-eaten meals had been abandoned, many of them knocked
over, singed by fire, or scattered by explosions, and everything had been
soaked by the sprinkler system, which had run for hours. Muted pagers
buried inside the backpacks beeped methodically, alerting the kids to
phone home.

As they walked, an agent spotted a blue duffel bag ten feet from the
burned-out orange bag with the big bomb. It was bulging and sized to fit
the same contraption. They walked over. One of the agents pressed down
slowly on the top. Hard. Probably another tank. They called help over: a
couple of deputies and an FBI bomb technician. One of the officers was
Mike Guerra, the same man who had investigated Eric Harris a year earlier.
He sliced open the bag. They could see the end of a propane tank and an
alarm clock that matched the other. There were still active bombs in here.
How many more? They closed off the area immediately.

Had the propane bombs detonated, they would have incinerated most or
all of the inhabitants of the commons. They would have killed five hundred

people in the first few seconds. Four times the toll in Oklahoma City. More than the ten worst domestic terrorist attacks in U.S. history combined.

For investigators, the big bombs changed everything: the scale, the method, and the motive of the attack. Above all, it had been indiscriminate. Everyone was supposed to die. Columbine was fundamentally different from the other school shootings. It had not really been intended as a shooting at all. Primarily, it had been a bombing that failed.

That same day, officials announced the discovery of the big bombs, and their destructive power. It instigated a new media shock wave. But, curiously, journalists failed to grasp the implications. Detectives let go of the targeting theory immediately. It had been sketchy to begin with, and now it was completely disproved. The media never shook it off. They saw what happened at Columbine as a shooting and the killers as outcasts targeting jocks. They filtered every new development through that lens.

23. Gifted Boy

D ylan Bennet Klebold was born brilliant. He started school a year early, and by third grade was enrolled in the CHIPS program: Challenging High Intellectual Potential Students. Even among the brains, Dylan stood out as a math prodigy. The early start didn't impede him intellectually, but strained his shyness further.

The idealistic Klebolds named their two boys after Dylan Thomas and Lord Byron. Tom and Sue met at Ohio State University, studying art, Tom in sculpture. They moved to Wisconsin and earned more practical master's: Tom in geophysics, Sue in education, as a reading specialist. Tom took an oil job and moved the family to Jeffco, before the Denver metroplex stretched out to reach them.

Dylan was born there, five months after Eric, September 11, 1981. Both grew up as small-town boys. Dylan earned merit badges in the Cub Scouts and won a Pinewood Derby contest. Sports were always big. He was a driven competitor, hated to lose. When he pitched in Little League he liked to whiff hitters so badly they tossed their bats. He would idolize major leaguers until the day he died.

The Klebold house was orderly and intellectual. Sue Klebold was a stickler for cleanliness, but Dylan enjoyed getting dirty. A neighbor—the woman who would struggle so hard to stop Eric before the massacre—fed Dylan's early Huck Finn appetite. Judy Brown was the neighborhood mom, serving up treats, hosting sleepovers, and rounding up the boys for little adventures. Dylan met her son Brooks in the gifted program. Brooks had a long, egg-shaped face, like Dylan's, narrowing at the jaw. But where Dylan's eyes were animated, Brooks's drooped, leaving a perpetual weary, worried expression. Both boys grew faster than their classmates—Brooks would eventually reach six-five. They would hang out all afternoon at the Browns' house, munching Oreos on the sofa, asking Judy politely for another. Dylan was painfully shy with strangers, but he would run right up, plop down in her lap, and snuggle in there. He couldn't be more adorable, until you tripped his fragile ego. It didn't take much.

Judy first saw him blow when he was eight or nine. They had driven down to a creek bed for a typical adventure. Sue Klebold had come along—horrified by all the mud, but bearing it to bond with her boy. Officially, it was a crawdad hunt, but they were always on the lookout for frogs or tadpoles or anything that might slither by. Sue fretted about bacteria, hectoring the boys to behave and keep clean.

They'd brought a big bucket to haul the crawdads home, but came back up the hillside with nothing to show. Then one of the boys slogged out of the creek with a leech attached to his leg. The kids all went delirious. They plopped the leech into the frog jar—a mayonnaise bottle with holes punched in the lid—and watched it incessantly. They had a picnic lunch and then ran back for more fun in the creek. The water was only a foot deep, but too murky for them to see the bottom. Dylan's tennis shoes squished down into the glop. All the boys were slipping around, but Dylan took a nastier slide. He wheeled his arms wildly to catch himself, lost the battle, and smacked down on his butt. His shorts were soaked instantly; dank black water splashed his clean T-shirt. Brooks and his brother, Aaron, howled; Dylan went ballistic.

"Stop!" he screamed. "Stop laughing at me! Stop! *Stooooooooooooooooooooo oooop!*"

The laughing ended abruptly. Brooks and Aaron were a little alarmed. They had never seen a kid freak out like that. Judy rushed over to comfort Dylan, but he was inconsolable. Everybody was silent now, but Dylan kept screaming for them to stop.

Sue grabbed him by the wrist and whisked him away. It took her several minutes to calm him down.

Sue Klebold had come to expect the outbursts. Over time, Judy did, too.

"I would see Dylan get frustrated with himself and go crazy," she said. He would be docile for days or months, then the pain would boil over and some minor transgression would humiliate him. Judy figured he would grow out of it, but he never did.

Detectives assembled portraits of the killers that felt maddeningly similar and vanilla: youngest sons of comfortable, two-parent, two-child, quiet small-town families. The Klebolds had more money; the Harrises were more mobile. Each boy grew up in the shadow of a single older sibling: a bigger, taller, stronger brother. Eric and Dylan would eventually share the same hobbies, classes, job, friends, clothing choices, and clubs. But they had remarkably different interior lives. Dylan always saw himself as inferior. The anger and the loathing traveled inward. "He was taking it out on himself," Judy Brown said.

———

Dylan's mother was Jewish. Sue Klebold had been born Sue Yassenoff, part of a prominent Jewish family in Columbus. Her paternal grandfather, Leo Yassenoff, was a philanthropist and a bit of a local tycoon. The city's Leo Yassenoff Jewish Community Center was established by the foundation he funded. Classmates said Dylan never shared Eric's fascination with Hitler, Nazis, or Germany, and some suggested it bothered him. Tom was Lutheran, and the family practiced some of each religion. They celebrated Easter and Passover, with a traditional Seder. Most of the year they remained quietly spiritual, without much organized religion.

In the mid-1990s, they took a stab at a traditional church. They joined the parish of St. Philip Lutheran Church; the boys went to services along with their parents. Their pastor, Reverend Don Marxhausen, described them as "hardworking, very intelligent, sixties kind of people. They don't believe in violence or guns or racism and certainly aren't anti-Semitic." They liked Marxhausen, but formal church service just wasn't a good fit for them. They attended for a brief time and then dropped away.

Sue spent her career in higher education. She began as a tutor, then a lab assistant, and finally worked with disabled students. In 1997, she left a local community college for a position with the Colorado Community College System. She coordinated a program there to help vocational/rehab students get jobs and training.

Tom did reasonably well in the oil business, but better at renovating and renting out apartments. He was great with repairs and remodeling. A hobby became a business. Tom and Sue formed Fountain Real Estate Management to buy and administer the properties. Tom continued consulting to independent oil companies part-time.

The Klebolds were rising financially, but worried about spoiling their kids. Ethics were central in their household, and the boys needed to learn restraint. Tom and Sue settled on appropriate figures to spend on the boys and stuck to them. One Christmas, Dylan wanted an expensive baseball card that would have consumed his entire gift budget. Sue was torn. One tiny present in addition to the card for her boy? Maybe she could spend a little extra. Nope. Austerity was a gift, too, and Dylan got what he'd asked for and no more.

In 1990, as metro Denver encroached into Jeffco, the Klebolds retreated beyond the hogback, the first strip of foothills hundreds of feet high, which from the air looked like the bumps along a hog's back. The hogback functions like Denver's coastline—it feels like civilization ends there. Roads are scarce; homes are distant and highly exclusive. Shops and commerce and activity are almost nonexistent. The family moved into a run-down glass-and-cedar house on Deer Creek Mesa, inside a panoramic rock formation, a smaller version of the Red Rocks Amphitheatre, a few miles away. Tom gradually brought the house back into stunning shape. Dylan officially lived in the backcountry now—part-time country boy, riding over to the populated side every morning for school in suburbia.

In seventh grade, Dylan faced a frightening transition. He had been sheltered among the brainiacs in CHIPS. Ken Caryl Middle School was five times as big and it didn't have a gifted program. Tom described Dylan lurching from "cradle to reality."

24. Hour of Need

Reverend Marxhausen led a congregation of several thousand at St. Philip Lutheran Church. Quite a few attended Columbine. He spent much of the "hostage crisis" at Leawood, searching for students, calming parents. His parish appeared to be spared.

He organized a vigil that first evening, at St. Philip. He distributed communion, a task he found utterly soothing. The gently whispered interplay calmed him like a mantra: *The body of Christ...Amen.... The body of Christ... Amen....* It was a steady cadence: his softly commanding baritone punctuated by a brief, nearly inaudible response. A fluttering variety of tenors and sopranos colored his symphony, but the rhythm remained the same. As the communion line dwindled, a woman softly broke the spell. "The body of Christ..." he said.

"Klebold."

What? It startled him at first, but this happened occasionally: a parishioner lost herself in prayer on the slow march up the aisle, and the pastor's voice startled her out of it.

Reverend Marxhausen tried again: "The body of Christ..."

"Klebold."

This time he recognized the word—from the TV; he had forgotten his brief association with the family.

He looked up. The woman continued: "Don't forget them in their hour of need."

She accepted the host and moved on.

That night, Marxhausen checked the parish rolls. Tom and Sue Klebold and their two boys, Dylan and Byron, had registered five years ago. They had not stayed long, but that did not diminish his responsibility. If they had failed to find a spiritual home, they remained under his care.

He found a family close to Tom and Sue and sent word that he was available.

They called a few days later. "I need your help," Tom said. That was obvious; his voice was shaking. He needed a funeral for his boy. How embarrassing to ask after a five-year absence, but Tom was out of options.

He also had a requirement. "It has to be confidential," he said.

Of course, Marxhausen said—to both counts. He talked to Tom and then Sue, asked how they were doing. "They used the word 'devastated,' " he recalled later. "I didn't want to ask them any more."

Tom and Sue received the body on Thursday. The service was conducted on Saturday. It was done quietly, with just fifteen people, including friends, family, and clergy. Marxhausen brought another minister and both their wives. Dylan lay in an open casket, his face restored, no sign of the gaping head wound. He looked peaceful. His face was surrounded by a circle of Beanie Babies and other stuffed toys.

When Marxhausen arrived, Tom was in denial, Sue was falling apart. She crumpled into the pastor's arms. Marxhausen engulfed her. Her frail body quaked; she sobbed there for perhaps a minute and a half—"which is a long time," he said.

Tom just couldn't see his little boy as that killer. "This was not my son" is how Marxhausen paraphrased his statements the next day. "What you see in the papers was not my son."

The other mourners arrived, and the awkwardness only increased. A liturgy wasn't going to help them. Marxhausen felt a terrible need to scrap his service and let them speak. "Do you mind if we just talk for a while?" he suggested. "And then we'll worship."

He shut the door and asked who wanted to begin.

"There was this one couple, they just poured out their hearts," he recalled. "Their son used to play with Dylan when the boys were little. They loved Dylan."

Where did the guns come from? Tom asked. They had never had more than a BB gun. Where did the violence come from? What was this Nazi stuff?

And the anti-Semitism? Sue said. She's Jewish, Dylan was half Jewish, what kind of sense did this make?

They were such good parents, a friend said. Dylan was a great kid. "He was like our son!"

They went around and around—fewer than a dozen of them, but for forty-five minutes they spilled out anguish and confusion, and love for the awkward kid who'd had occasional outbursts.

Dylan's brother, Byron, mostly listened. He sat quietly between Tom and Sue and finally spoke up near the end. "I want to thank you all for being here today, for my parents and myself," he said. "I love my brother."

Then Marxhausen read from Scripture and offered some muted encouragement. "True enough, there will be those who do not know grace and will want to give only judgment," he said. But help would come in time and in surprising ways. "I have no idea how you are going to heal. But God still wants to reach out to you and will always reach out to you in some way."

He read the Old Testament story of Absalom, beloved son of King David. Absalom skillfully ingratiated himself to his father, the court, and all the kingdom but secretly plotted to seize the throne. Eventually, he thrust Israel into civil war. He appeared poised to vanquish his father, but David's generals prevailed. The king was informed first of the triumph, then of his son's death. "David's grief made the victory like a defeat, and the people stole silently into the city," Marxhausen read from 2 Samuel. David wept and cried out, "O my son Absalom, my son, my son Absalom! Would God I had died for thee, O Absalom, my son."

The Klebolds were afraid to bury Dylan. His grave would be defaced. It would become an anti-shrine. They cremated his body and kept the ashes in the house.

Marxhausen assumed the media would get wind of the service. He asked one of the Klebold attorneys how to handle the inquiries. The attorney said, "Just tell them what you've seen here tonight."

So he did. He told the *New York Times,* which featured the account on the front page. Tom and Sue were racked by grief, guilt, and utter confusion, he said: "They lost their son, but their son was also a killer." He told the story lovingly. He described Tom and Sue as "the loneliest people on the planet."

Don Marxhausen made some of his parish exceptionally proud. That was their pastor—a man who could find compassion in his heart for anyone. A man capable of consoling the couple who had unwittingly produced a monster. That's why they had packed the pews to hear him every Sunday.

Some of his parish, and much of the community, was appalled. Lonely? The Klebolds were lonely? Several of the victims were still awaiting burial. Survivors still faced surgery. It would be months before some would walk again, or talk again, or discover they never would. Some people had trouble rousing sympathy for the Klebolds. Their loneliness was not an especially popular concern.

———

Wayne and Kathy Harris presumably held some ceremony for Eric. But they have never once spoken to the press. Word never leaked.

25. Threesome

No one remembers for sure how Eric and Dylan met. Eric arrived at Ken Caryl Middle School in seventh grade. Dylan was already attending. The two boys met there at some point but didn't connect right away.

They both continued on to Columbine High. Brooks Brown reentered the school district there. His friendship with Dylan had fallen off after his parents moved him into private schools years earlier. But he returned to public school his freshman year and met Eric on the bus. Pretty soon all three were tight.

They played video games for hours. Sometimes they played in person, but they also stayed up late competing online. They went to Columbine Rebel football games together freshman year. Eric was practically a celebrity because his brother was a starter on the varsity team.

Eric, Brooks, and Dylan were three aspiring intellectuals. They took an interest in classical philosophers and Renaissance literature. All three boys were shy at that point, but Eric began breaking through his shell. It started with occasional rumblings. Just two months into high school, he asked a classmate to Homecoming. She remembered him as nervous and quiet, largely forgettable, until he faked his suicide a few days after the dance.

"He had his friend take me over to his house," she said later. "When I went there, he was lying with his head on a rock, and there was fake blood around him, and he was acting like he was dead." It wasn't an original stunt—probably ripped off from the 1970s classic movie *Harold and Maude*. But it weirded her out. She refused to date him again.

First semester freshman year, Eric turned in an "I Am" poem. His self-portrait informed the reader five times in eighteen lines how nice he was.

"I am a nice guy who hates when people open their pop can just a little," the poem began. Eric ended each stanza with that same line. He described himself flying above all the rest of us, bragged about his straight A's, and demonstrated his emotional depth: "I cry when I see or hear a dog die."

He kept much of the work he produced in high school. Apparently, he was proud of it. "I dream that I am the last person on earth," he wrote in "I Am."

Eric was always a dreamer, but he liked them ugly: bleak and morose, yet boring as hell. He saw beauty in the void. Eric dreamed of a world where nothing ever happened. A world where the rest of us had been removed.

Eric shared his dreams in Internet chat rooms. He described them vividly to online chicks. In one, he was suspended inside a small dank room, like the interior hull of a ship. Futuristic yet decaying old computer screens lined the walls, covered with dust and mold and vines. The moon provided the only light, trickling dimly in through the portals, shadows creeping all around. A vast sea rose and fell monotonously. Nothing happened. Eric was overjoyed.

He rarely encountered humans in his creations—just the occasional combatant to extinguish or a disembodied voice to drop an ironic bon mot. Dreamland Eric had snuffed us out. He invented a world of precise textures, vivid hues, and absolutely no payoff for himself. When he did linger on the destination, it was to revel in the banality of the gloom. He described one of his dreamworlds to a girl in a chat room.

"wow kind of gloomy," she responded.

"yeah. but its still nice. no people at all. kind of like, everyone is dead and has been for centuries."

Happiness for Eric was eliminating the likes of us.

The girl said she could go for it, but only with some people. Eric said he'd only want a couple, and that led him to the burning question he loved to pose online:

With only a few people left, would she repopulate or choose extinction?

Probably extinction, she said.

Good answer. That's what he was going for. That was the point of the entire conversation: "mmm," he said. "i just wish I could actually DO this instead of just DREAM about it."

Extinction fantasies cropped up regularly and would obsess Eric in his final years. But in his online chats, there was never a sense of him intending to do the deed. He had bold dreams for the world, but more modest ideas about himself. And he was pretty convinced that we would all take care of destroying the planet without his help anyway.

———

Zack Heckler had one class with Dylan freshman year—that was all it took. Finally, somebody understood him. Brooks and Eric were fun to hang with, but they never really got Dylan. Not the way Kibbie did. Zack did not care for that nickname, but it stuck. He was an insatiable snacker, so the kids had branded him "Kibble." Great. Nicknames could be a bitch—almost impossible to shake a wussy one. So Zack was smart about it. He quit fighting the tag and adapted it. Kibble, KiBBz, Lord Kibbz—the last one wasn't bad at all.

Zack and Dylan's teacher gave them a lot of free study time. Eric would wander from the adjoining room. At first he came around to chat with Dylan, but pretty soon all three were cutting up. They played Doom, bowled, did sleepovers, went to ball games and drag races at Bandimere Speedway. They made fun of dumb kids and ignorant adults. Computer illiterates were the worst, especially when some fool put them in front of a class. The boys watched a ton of movies: lots of action and horror and science fantasy. They cruised the mall to pick up chicks. Eric did the talking. Zack and Dylan hung back and followed his lead.

Dylan joined the theater group. He was too shy for the stage, but he worked lights and sound. Eric had no interest in that. They got close with Nate Dykeman and Chris Morris, too. Mostly they hung at Dylan's. "His parents were so nice to me," Nate said. "Either they'd get doughnuts for me or they'd be making crepes or omelets." Dylan also looked after his house-guests, worried about whether they were having a good time.

At Eric's, it was totally strict when the major got home, but until then Eric had free rein down in the basement, where he'd set up his bedroom. They had girls over, and showed off how they nailed garden crickets with the BB gun.

Friendships came and went, but the bond between Zack and Dylan grew stronger. They were snarky, clever, and seething with teenage anger, but way too timid to show it.

Dylan and Zack needed Eric. Someone had to do the talking. Eric needed an audience; he also craved excitement. He was cool and detached, tough to rattle. Nothing seemed to faze him. Dylan was an unlit fuse. Eric led the parade. Perfect fit.

They were a threesome now.

———

Eric kept improving his Doom skills. When he got bored with the images id Software provided, Eric invented his own, sketching a menagerie of heroes and villains on his notepads. He hacked into the software and created new characters, unique obstacles, higher levels, and increasingly elaborate adventures. He created muscle-bound mutants with aviator-sunglass eyes, and hulk-sized demons with ox horns, claws, and fangs. Many of his warriors were decked out in medieval armor and submachine guns; one was blessed with flamethrowers for forearms. Victims were frequently on fire or freshly decapitated; sometimes they held their own head in their hands. Eric's creations were unparalleled, in his view. "In this day and age it can be hard to find a skill that can be completely dominated and mastered," he wrote in one assignment. "But I believe that I will always be the best at Doom creativity."

Eric enjoyed the act of creation. "I often try to create new things," he wrote in a freshman English paper titled "Similarities Between Zeus and I." He hailed both of them as great leaders, finding no fault in their pettiness or malice but identifying common inclinations. "Zeus and I also get angry easily and punish people in unusual ways," he wrote.

26. Help Is on the Way

———— ⨳ ————

Dave Sanders's daughters were angry. Before they got confirmation that their dad was dead, they heard disturbing stories about his final hours.

"My concern is that my dad was left there," Angie Sanders told an Australian newspaper. "[He] was still alive and not helped."

The impression her family was getting was that twelve victims had been goners once the bullets left the chambers, but Dave Sanders had held on for well over three hours. From what Angie understood, her father could have been saved.

Dave's daughters began looking into the reports but kept their mouths shut around their mother. They had to keep the TV off when she was awake. They snatched newspapers off the doorstep and magazines out of the mailbox. They had to protect Linda. She was already a wreck.

Dave Sanders was just a few feet from safety when the first shot hit him. He saw the killers, spun around, and ran for the corner, trying to save a few more students on the way there. One bullet got him in the back. It tore through his rib cage and exited through his chest. The other bullet entered through the side of his neck and came out his mouth, lacerating his tongue and shattering several teeth. The neck wound opened up one of his carotid arteries, the major blood routes to the brain. The shot to his back clipped his subclavian vein, a major vessel back to the heart. There was a lot of blood.

Everyone had been guessing which way was the safest to run. Rich Long, who was head of the technology department and a good friend of Dave's, had chosen an opposite route. He first heard the shooting from the library, told students to get out, and directed a group down the main stairway right into the cafeteria, unaware that hundreds had just fled from that location. Toward the bottom of the stairs, they saw bullets flying outside the windows and reversed course. At the top of the stairs, they turned left, away from the library and into the science wing, which also included the music rooms. They arrived just in time to see Dave get shot.

Dave crashed into the lockers, then collapsed on the carpet. Rich and most of the students dove for the floor. Now Dave was really desperate.

"He was on his elbows trying to direct kids," one senior said.

Eric and Dylan were both firing. They were lobbing pipe bombs down the length of the hall.

"Dave, you've got to get up!" Rich yelled. "We've got to get out of here."

Dave pulled himself up, staggered a few feet around the corner. Rich hurried over. As soon as he was out of the line of fire, he ducked his shoulder under Dave's arm. Another teacher got Dave from the other side, and they dragged him to the science wing, just a dozen feet away.

"Rich, they shot me in the teeth," Dave said.

They moved past the first and second classrooms, then entered Science Room 3.

"The door opened, and Mr. Sanders [comes] in and starts coughing up blood," sophomore Marjorie Lindholm said. "It looked like part of his jaw was missing. He just poured blood."

The room was full of students. Their teacher had gone out to the hallway to investigate. When he came back, he told them to forget the test and ordered everybody up against the wall. The classroom door had a glass pane. To shooters who might be stalking through the halls, the room would appear empty if everyone huddled along the interior perimeter.

That's when Dave stumbled in with two teachers assisting. He collapsed again, face-first, in the front of the room. "He left a couple of teeth where he landed," a freshman girl said.

They got Dave into a chair. "Rich, I'm not doing so well," he said.

"You'll be OK. I'm going to go phone for help."

Several teachers had arrived, so Rich ran back out into the melee, searching for a phone. He learned that somebody was already calling for help. He went back.

"I need to go get you some help," Rich said. He went back into the smoky corridor and tried another lab. But the killers were getting closer, apparently right outside the lab's door this time. Rich finally took cover.

Dave had several adults with him, and plenty of calls had been made about the shooting. Rich had no doubt that help was on the way.

Kent Friesen, another teacher with Dave, went for immediate assistance. He ran into a nearby lab, where more students were huddled. "Who knows first aid?" he asked.

Aaron Hancey, a junior and an Eagle Scout, stepped up.

"Come with me," Friesen said. Then all hell seemed to break loose out in the hallway.

"I could feel it through the walls," Aaron said. "With each [blast], I could feel the walls move." He was scared to go out there. But Friesen checked for shooters, bolted down the corridor, and Aaron followed.

Aaron ran through a rapid inspection of Dave's condition: breathing steady, airway clear, skin warm, shoulder broken, gaping wounds, heavy blood loss. Aaron stripped off his own white Adidas T-shirt to stanch the flow. Other boys volunteered their shirts. He tore several into bandage strips and improvised a few tourniquets. He bundled others together into a pillow.

"I've got to go, I've got to go," Dave said. He tried to stand, but failed.

Teachers attended to the students. They flipped over tables to barricade the door. They opened a partition in back to an adjoining science lab, and several kids rushed to the center, farthest from the doors. The gunfire and explosions continued. A fire erupted in a nearby room and a teacher grabbed a fire extinguisher to put it out. Screams filtered down the hall from the library. It was nothing like screams Marjorie Lindholm had heard before—screams like "when people are being tortured," she said.

"It was like they were carrying out executions," another boy in the room said. "You would hear a shot. Then there would be quiet. Then another shot. Bam. Bam. Bam."

The screaming and gunfire both stopped. Silence, then more explosions. On and off and on again. The fire alarm began blaring. It was an earsplitting pitch designed to force people out of the building through sheer pain. The teachers and students could barely hear anything over the alarm's shriek, but could just make out the steady flap of helicopters outside.

Someone turned on the giant TV suspended from the ceiling. They kept the volume off but the subtitles on. It was their school, from the outside. Much of the class was transfixed at first, but their attention waned quickly. Nobody seemed to know anything.

Aaron called his father, who used another line to call 911, so that paramedics could ask questions and relay instructions. Several other students and teachers called the cops. The science room group remained linked to authorities via multiple channels throughout the afternoon.

Sophomore Kevin Starkey, also an Eagle Scout, assisted Aaron. "You're doing all right," the boys whispered to Dave. "They're coming. Just hold on. You can do it." They took turns applying pressure, digging their palms into his wounds.

"I need help," Dave said. "'I've got to get out of here."

"Help is on the way," Aaron assured him.

Aaron believed it was. Law enforcement was first alerted to Dave's predicament around 11:45. Dispatchers began responding that help was "on the way" and would arrive "in about ten minutes." The assurances were repeated for more than three hours, along with orders that no one leave the room under any circumstances. The 911 operator instructed the group to open the door briefly: they were to tie a red shirt around the doorknob in the hallway. The SWAT team would look for it to identify the room. There was a lot of dissent about that directive in Science Room 3. Wouldn't a red flag also attract the killers? And who was going to step out into that hallway? They decided to obey. Someone volunteered to tie the shirt to the doorknob. Around noon, teacher Doug Johnson wrote 1 BLEEDING TO DEATH on the whiteboard and moved it to the window, just to be sure.

Occasionally the TV coverage grabbed attention in the room. At one point, Marjorie Lindholm thought she spotted a huge mass of blood seeping out a door pictured on-screen. She was mistaken. Fear had taken control.

Each time Aaron and Kevin switched positions, they felt Dave's skin grow a little colder. He was losing color, taking on a bluish cast. *Where are the paramedics?* they wondered. *When will the ten minutes be up?* Dave's breathing began to slow. He drifted in and out. Aaron and Kevin rolled him gently on the tile floor to keep him conscious and to keep his airway clear. He couldn't remain on his back for very long or he would choke on his own blood.

They pulled out wool safety blankets from a first-aid closet and wrapped him up to keep him warm. They asked him about coaching, teaching, anything to keep him engaged and stave off shock. They slipped his wallet out and began showing him pictures.

"Is this your wife?"

"Yes."

"What's your wife's name?"

"Linda."

He had lots of pictures, and they used them all. They talked about his daughters and his grandchildren. "These people love you," the boys said. "This is why you need to live."

Aaron and Kevin grew desperate. The treatment had exceeded scouting instruction. "You're trained to deal with broken arms, broken limbs, cuts and scrapes—stuff you get on a camping trip," Aaron said. "You never train for gunshot wounds."

Eventually, Aaron and Kevin lost the struggle to keep Dave conscious. "I'm not going to make it," Dave said. "Tell my girls I love them."

———

It was relatively calm for a while. The alarm kept blaring, the choppers kept thumping, and gunfire or explosions would periodically rumble through the hallways, somewhere off in the distance. Nothing had sounded particularly close for a while; nothing seemed imminent. Dave's chest rose and fell, blood oozed out, but the boys could not rouse him. Aaron and Kevin kept trying.

Some of the kids gave up on police. Around 2:00 P.M., they informed the 911 operator they were going to hurl a chair through the window and get Dave out themselves. She insisted they abandon the plan, which she warned them might draw the attention of the killers.

At 2:38, the TV suddenly caught the room's attention again. Patrick Ireland was tumbling out the library window. "Oh my God!" some of the kids yelled. They'd hidden quietly for hours, but this was too much. Coach Sanders was not an isolated case. A kid was just as bloody just down the hall. They had assumed it was bad out there; now they had proof. Some kids closed their eyes, pictured loved ones, and silently said good-bye.

Just a few minutes later, the danger suddenly drew close again: screams erupted from the next room. Then everything went silent for a minute. All at once, the door burst open and men in black rushed in. The killers were dressed in black. The invaders toted submachine guns. They waved them at the students, shouting fiercely, trying to outscream the fire alarm. "I thought they were the gunmen," Marjorie Lindholm wrote later. "I thought that now I was going to die."

Some of the men turned and pointed to the huge block letters on their backs: *SWAT*.

"Be quiet!" an officer yelled. "Put your hands on your heads and follow us out."

"Someone's got to stay with Mr. Sanders," someone said.

"I will," Aaron volunteered.

"No!" an officer said. "Everyone out."

Then how about hauling Dave out with them, Kevin suggested. There were folded tables—they could improvise one as a stretcher.

No.

It seemed heartless, but the SWAT team was trained to make practical choices. Hundreds of students were trapped. The gunmen could reappear any moment. The team had to assume a battlefield mentality and evacuate the maximum number in the minimum time. They could send a medic back for the injured later.

The SWAT team led students single file down the stairs to the commons. They waded through three inches of water that had rained down from the sprinklers. Backpacks and pizza slices floated by. Don't touch them, the officers warned. *Don't touch anything.* A SWAT member held the door. He stopped each student, held them for two seconds, then tapped them on the shoulder and told them to run. That was a standard infantry maneuver. A single pipe bomb could take out an entire pack of children; a well-aimed machine-gun burst could do the same. Safer to space them.

Outside, the kids ran past two dead bodies: Danny Rohrbough and Rachel Scott. Marjorie Lindholm remembered "a weird look on their faces, and a weird color to their skin." The girl just ahead of her stopped suddenly when she saw the bodies, and Marjorie caught up. A SWAT officer screamed at them to keep moving. Marjorie saw their guns trained right on her. She gave the girl a push, and they both took off.

Two SWAT officers stayed with Dave, and another called for help. It fell to a Denver SWAT member outside the building to recruit a paramedic. He spotted Troy Laman, an EMT who had driven out from the city and was manning a triage station. "Troy, I need you to go in," the SWAT officer said. "Let's go."

Laman followed the officer through the flooded commons, up the stairway, past the rubble, and into Science Room 3. By that time, Dave had stopped breathing. According to emergency triage protocol, that qualified him as dead. "I knew there was nothing I could do for this guy," said Laman, who had no equipment. "But because I was stuck in a room with him by myself for fifteen minutes, I wanted to help him."

The SWAT officer eventually cleared Laman to keep moving. "There's nothing you can do," he said.

So Laman went on to the library. He was one of the first medics to go in.

Dave Sanders's story got out fast. Both local papers, the *Rocky Mountain News* and the *Denver Post,* described his ordeal on Wednesday. On Thursday the *Rocky,* as it's often called, ran a piece called POLICE DISPUTE CHARGES THEY WERE TOO SLOW. "A lot of people are angry," one student said. But the bulk of the story focused on the police response.

"We had 1,800 kids rushing from the school," said Jeffco sheriff's spokesman Steve Davis. "The officers had no idea which were victims and which were potential suspects."

The *Rocky* offered this summary of the SWAT response based on the department's claims: "Within twenty minutes of the first panicked call for help, a makeshift six-man SWAT team rushed into the sprawling school, and within an hour, dozens of heavily armed officers in body armor launched a methodical, room-by-room search of the building."

The department would eventually admit that it took more than twice that long, 47 minutes, for the first five-man team to enter. The other half of that team attended to wounded students on the lawn, but never proceeded in. A second team entered after nearly two hours. Until the killers' bodies were found, that was it.

The situation grew hotter on Friday when a veteran suburban cop laid down thirteen roses in Clement Park and then described the SWAT response as "pathetic."

"It pissed me off," he told reporters. "I'd have someone in there. We are trained to do that. We are trained to go in there."

The officer's statement was widely reported. He became an instant symbol. And his department foolishly extended the story by placing him on nondisciplinary leave and ordering a "fitness for duty" evaluation. They backpedaled a few days later.

Members of the SWAT teams began responding in the press. "It was just a nightmare," said a sergeant. "What parents need to understand is we wanted teams in there as quickly as we could. We were going into the situation blind. We had multiple explosions going off. We thought there could have been a band of terrorists in there."

Officers were nearly as confused as TV viewers. Outside, they could hear the blasts. But once they entered, they couldn't even hear one another. The fire alarm drowned out everything. Communication was limited to hand signals. "Had we heard gunfire and screaming, we would have gone right to that," a SWAT officer explained.

The barrage of noise and strobe lights beat down their psyches like psychological warfare. Officers could not locate anyone with the alarm code to shut it down. They found an assistant principal, but she was so frazzled she couldn't remember the digits. In desperation, officers tried to beat the alarm speakers off the walls. One tried to disable the control panel by smashing the glass cover with his rifle butt. The alarms and sprinklers continued until 4:04 P.M. The strobe light that flashed with the alarm continued for weeks.

Those were legitimate obstacles, the Sanders family acknowledged. But more than three hours after he was shot? Linda's sister Melody was designated family spokesperson. "Some of his daughters are angry," she told the *New York Times* a few days later. "They feel like, had they gone in and gotten Dave out sooner, he would have lived."

Melody said the Sanders family didn't hold the SWAT members responsible. But the system was a disaster. "It was utter chaos," Melody said.

The family expressed gratitude for the efforts that had been made. As a gesture of goodwill, they invited the full SWAT teams to Dave's funeral. All the officers attended.

27. Black

Eric was evolving inside. Sophomore year, the changes began to show. For his first fifteen years, Eric had concentrated on assimilation. Dylan had sought the same goal, with less success. Despite the upheavals of moving, Eric always made friends. Social status was important. "They were just like everybody else," a classmate said later. Eric's neighbor described him as nice, polite, preppy, and a dork. High school was full of dorks. Eric could live with that—for a while.

Sophomore year, he tried an edgier look: combat boots, all-black outfits, and grunge. He started shopping at a trendy shop called Hot Topic and the army surplus store. He liked the look. He liked the feeling. Their buddy Chris Morris began sporting a beret. That was a little much, Eric thought. He wanted to look different, not retarded. Eric was breaking out of his shell. He grew boisterous, moody, and aggressive. Sometimes he was playful, speaking in funny voices and flirting with girls. He had a lot of ideas and he began expressing them with confidence. Dylan never did.

Most of the girls who knew Eric described him as cute. He was aware of the consensus but didn't quite accept it. He responded candidly to one of those chain e-mail questionnaires asking for likes, dislikes, and personal attributes. Under "Looks," he wrote, "5' 10" 140. skinny but handsome, some say." The one thing he would like to change about himself was his weight. Such a freaking runt. He'd always hated his appearance—now at least he had a look.

Eric took some flack for the new getup—older kids and bigger guys razzed him sometimes, but nothing exceptional. And he was talking back now and provoking confrontations. He'd shaken off his silence along with the preppy uniform.

Dylan remained quiet right up until the end. He wasn't much for mouthing off, except in rare sudden bursts that freaked everyone out a little. He followed Eric's fashion lead but a less intense version, so he took a lot less ribbing. Eric could have silenced the taunts anytime by conforming again, but by this point, he got a kick out of standing out.

"The impression I always got from them was they kind of wanted to be outcasts," another classmate said. "It wasn't that they were labeled that way. It's what they chose to be."

"Outcast" was a matter of perception. Kids who slapped that label on Eric and Dylan meant the boys rejected the preppy model, but so did hundreds of other kids at the school. Eric and Dylan had very active social calendars, and far more friends than the average adolescent. They fit in with a whole thriving subculture. Their friends respected one another and ridiculed the conformity of the vanilla wafers looking down on them. They had no desire to emulate the jocks. Could there be a faster route to boredom?

For Dylan, different was difficult. For Eric, different was good.

For Halloween that year, Eric Dutro, a junior, wanted to go as Dracula. He needed a cool coat, something dramatic—he had a flair for theatrics—so his parents picked up a long black duster at Sam's Club. The kids referred to this as a trench coat.

The costume didn't work out, but the trench coat was cool. Eric Dutro hung on to it; he started wearing it to school. It made quite an impression. The trench coat turned a whole lot of heads, and Dutro loved turning heads.

He had a hard time at school. Kids at Columbine picked on him. Kids would ridicule him relentlessly, calling him a freak and a faggot. Eventually he fought back the only way he knew how: by upping the ante. If they were going to call him freak, he was going to give them one hell of a freak show. The trench coat made a nice little addition to his freakdrobe.

Not surprisingly, Dutro hung with a bunch of kids who liked turning heads, too. After a while, several of them were sporting trench coats. They would dress all in black and wear the long coats even in the summer. Somewhere along the line, someone referred to them as the Trench Coat Mafia, TCM for short. It stuck.

Eric Dutro, Chris Morris, and a handful of other boys were pretty much the core of the TCM, but a dozen more were often associated with the TCM as well, whether they sported trench coats or not.

Eric and Dylan were not among them. Each of them knew some of the TCM kids, and Eric, especially, would become buddies with Chris. That was as close as they came.

Eventually, after the TCM heyday was over, Eric got himself a trench coat. Dylan followed. They wore them to the massacre, for both fashion and functional considerations. The choice would cause tremendous confusion.

28. Media Crime

The Trench Coat Mafia was mythologized because it was colorful, memorable, and fit the existing myth of the school shooter as outcast loner. All the Columbine myths worked that way. And they all sprang to life incredibly fast—most of the notorious myths took root before the killers' bodies were found.

We remember Columbine as a pair of outcast Goths from the Trench Coat Mafia snapping and tearing through their high school hunting down jocks to settle a long-running feud. Almost none of that happened. No Goths, no outcasts, nobody snapping. No targets, no feud, and no Trench Coat Mafia. Most of those elements existed at Columbine—which is what gave them such currency. They just had nothing to do with the murders. The lesser myths are equally unsupported: no connection to Marilyn Manson, Hitler's birthday, minorities, or Christians.

Few people knowledgeable about the case believe those myths anymore. Not reporters, investigators, families of the victims, or their legal teams. And yet most of the public takes them for granted. Why?

Media defenders blame the chaos: two thousand witnesses, wildly conflicting reports—who could get all those facts straight? But facts were not the problem. Nor did time sort them out. The first print story arrived in an extra edition of the *Rocky Mountain News*. It went to press at three o'clock on Tuesday afternoon, before the bodies in the library were found. The *Rocky's* nine-hundred-word summary of the massacre was an extraordinary piece of journalism: gripping, empathetic, and astonishingly accurate. It nailed the details and the big picture: two ruthless killers picking off students indiscriminately. It was the first story published that spring to get the essence of the attack right—and one of the last.

It is an axiom of journalism that disaster stories begin in confusion and grow clearer over time. Facts rush in, the fog lifts, an accurate picture solidifies. The public accepts this. But the final portrait is often furthest from the truth.

One hour into the Columbine horror, news stations were informing the public that two or more gunmen were behind it. Two hours in, the Trench Coat Mafia were to blame. The TCM were portrayed as a cult of homosexual Goths in makeup, orchestrating a bizarre death pact for the year 2000.

Ludicrous or not, the TCM myth was the most defensible of the big media blunders. The killers did wear trench coats. A small group had named themselves after the garment a year earlier. A few kids put the two together, and it's hard to blame them. It seemed like a tidy fit. But the crucial detail unreported Tuesday afternoon was that most kids in Clement Park were *not* citing the TCM. Few were even naming Eric and Dylan. In a school of two thousand, most of the student body didn't even know the boys. Nor had many seen gunfire directly. Initially, most students told reporters they had no idea who attacked them.

That changed fast. Most of the two thousand got themselves to a television or kept a constant cell phone vigil with viewers. It took only a few TV mentions for the trench coat connection to take hold. It sounded so obvious. *Of course! Trench coats, Trench Coat Mafia!*

TV journalists were actually careful. They used attribution and disclaimers like "believed to be" or "described as." Some wondered out loud about the killers' identities and then described the TCM, leaving viewers to draw the link. Repetition was the problem. Only a handful of students mentioned the TCM during the first five hours of CNN coverage—virtually all fed from local news stations. But reporters homed in on the idea. They were responsible about *how* they addressed the rumors, but blind to the impact of how often.

Kids "knew" the TCM was involved because witnesses and news anchors had said so on TV. They confirmed it with friends watching similar reports. Word spread fast—conversation was the only teen activity in south Jeffco Tuesday afternoon. Pretty soon, most of the students had multiple independent confirmations. They believed they knew the TCM was behind the attack as a fact. From 1:00 to 8:00 P.M., the number of students in Clement Park citing the group went from almost none to nearly all. They weren't making it up, they were repeating it back.

The second problem was a failure to question. In those first five hours, not a single person on the CNN feeds asked a student *how* they knew the killers were part of the Trench Coat Mafia.

Print reporters, talk show hosts, and the rest of the media chain repeated those mistakes. "All over town, the ominous new phrase 'Trench Coat Mafia' was on everyone's lips," *USA Today* reported Wednesday morning. That was a fact. But who was telling whom? The writers assumed kids were informing the media. It was the other way around.

———

Most of the myths were in place by nightfall. By then, it was a given that the killers had been targeting jocks. The target myth was the most insidious, because it went straight to motive. The public believes Columbine was an act of retribution: a desperate reprisal for unspeakable jock-abuse. Like the other myths, it began with a kernel of truth.

In the first few hours, a shattered junior named Bree Pasquale became the marquee witness of the tragedy. She had escaped unharmed but splattered in blood. Bree described the library horror in convincing detail. Radio and television stations replayed her testimony relentlessly: "They were shooting anyone of color, wearing a white hat, or playing a sport," she said. "And they didn't care who it was and it was all at close range. Everyone around me got shot. And I begged him for ten minutes not to shoot me."

The problem with Bree Pasquale's account is the contradiction between facts and conclusion. That's typical of witnesses under extreme duress. If the killers were shooting "everyone," didn't that include jocks, minorities, and hat wearers? Four times in that brief statement, she described random killing. Yet reporters glommed on to the anomaly in her statement.

Bullying and racism? Those were known threats. Explaining it away was reassuring.

By evening, the target theory was dominating most broadcasts; nearly all the major papers featured it. The *Rocky* and the *Washington Post* refused to embrace the targeting theory all week, but they were lonely dissenters.

Initially, most witnesses refuted the emerging consensus. Nearly all described the killing as random. All the papers and the wire services produced a total of just four witnesses advancing the target theory Wednesday morning—each one contradicting his or her own description. Most of the papers advanced the theory with just one student who had actually seen it—some had zero. Reuters attributed the theory to "many witnesses" and *USA Today* to "students."

"Student" equaled "witness." Witness to everything that happened that day, and anything about the killers. It was a curious leap. Reporters would not make that mistake at a car wreck. *Did you see it?* If not, they move on. But journalists felt like foreigners stepping into teen culture. They knew kids can hide anything from adults—but not from each other. That was the mentality: *Something shocking happened here; we're baffled, but kids know.* So all two thousand were deputized as insiders. If students said targeting, that was surely it.

Police detectives rejected the universal-witness concept. And they relied on traumatized witnesses for observations, not conclusions. They never saw targeting as plausible. They were baffled by the media consensus.

———

Journalists were not relying exclusively on "students." The entire industry was depending on the *Denver Post*. The paper sent fifty-four reporters, eight photographers, and five artists into the field. They had the most resources and the best contacts. Day one, they were hours ahead of the national pack; the first week they were a day ahead on most developments. The *Rocky Mountain News* had a presence as well, but they had a smaller staff, and the national press trusted the *Post*. It did not single-handedly create any of the myths, but as the *Post* bought into one after another after another, each mistaken conclusion felt safe. The pack followed.

———

The Jeffco Parks and Recreation District began hauling truckloads of hay bales into Clement Park. It was a mess. Thousands of people gathered at the northeast corner of the park on Wednesday, and tens of thousands appeared on Thursday and Friday. The snow had begun fluttering down Wednesday, and the foot traffic tore the field to shreds. By Thursday it was an enormous mud pit. Nobody seemed to care much, but county workers scattered thick layers of hay in winding paths all along the makeshift memorials.

They didn't know it yet, they had no idea there was a name for it, but many of the survivors had entered the early stages of post-traumatic stress disorder. Many had not. It wasn't a matter of how close they had been to witnessing or experiencing the violence. Length and severity of exposure increased their odds of mental health trouble down the road, but long-term responses were highly varied, depending on each individual. Some kids who had been in the library during the shootings would turn out fine, while others who had been off to Wendy's would be traumatized for years.

Dr. Frank Ochberg, a professor in psychiatry at Michigan State University and a leading expert on PTSD, would be brought in by the FBI a few months later and would spend years advising mental health workers on the case. He and a group of psychiatrists had first developed the term in the 1970s. They had observed a phenomenon that was stress-induced but was qualitatively more severe, and brought on by a really traumatic experience. This was something that produced truly profound effects and lasted for years or, if untreated, even a lifetime.

————

A far milder and more common response was also under way: survivor's guilt. It began playing out almost immediately, in the hallways of the six local hospitals where the injured were recovering. At St. Anthony's, the first week, the waiting rooms were packed with students coming to see Patrick Ireland. Every seat in every room was taken. Dozens of students waited in the hallways.

Patrick spent the first days in ICU. Most visitors were refused, but the kids kept streaming into the hospital room anyway. They just needed to be there.

"You have to realize that this was part of their healing too," Kathy Ireland said.

All day, some of them stayed, and well into the evening. The staff started bringing food in once they realized some of the kids hadn't been eating.

————

Patrick's situation looked grim. His doctors were just hoping to keep him alive. They advised John and Kathy to keep expectations low: whatever condition they observed the first day or two would be the prognosis for the rest of his life. John and Kathy accepted this. And they saw a paralyzed boy, struggling mightily to speak gibberish.

The medical staff chose to not operate on Patrick's broken right foot. They cleaned out the wound and placed a brace around it. *Why?* his parents asked. There were more pressing concerns, they were told. And Patrick was never going to use that foot.

John and Kathy were devastated. But they had to be realists. They turned their attention to raising an invalid, and figuring out how to help him be happy that way.

Patrick was unaware of the prognosis. It never occurred to him that he might not walk. He viewed the injury like a broken bone: you wear a cast, you build the muscle back, you pick your life up where you left off. He knew it would be tougher than the time he broke his thumb. A lot tougher. It might take three or four times as long to recover. He assumed he would recover.

———

Patrick's friend Makai was released from St. Anthony's Friday. He had been shot in the knee alongside Patrick. Reporters were invited into the hospital library for a press conference, broadcast on CNN. Makai was in a wheelchair. It turned out that he'd known Dylan.

"I thought he was an all right guy," Makai said. "Decent, real smart."

They'd taken the same French class and worked together on school projects.

"He was a nice guy, never treated me bad," Makai said. "He wasn't the kind of person he's being portrayed as."

———

Patrick made improvement with his speech the first week, and his vitals began returning to normal. On Friday, he was moved out of the ICU and into a regular room. Once he had settled in, his parents decided it was time to ask him the burning question. Had he gone out the library window?

They knew. They just had to know if he did. Did he know why he was there? Was the trauma of the truth still ahead?

"Well, yeah!" he stammered. Were they just figuring that out?

He was incredulous, Kathy said later. "He looked at us like, 'How could you be so ignorant?'" She was OK with that. All she felt was relief.

———

That same week, Dr. Alan Weintraub, a neurologist from Craig Hospital, came to see Patrick. Craig is one of the leading rehab centers in the world, specializing in brain and spinal cord injuries. It's located in Jeffco, not far from the Irelands' home. Dr. Weintraub examined Patrick, reviewed his charts, and gave John and Kathy his assessment: "The first thing I can say to you is there's hope."

They were astounded, relieved, and perplexed. Later, the discrepancy made sense to them. The staffs had different expertise and different perspectives. St. Anthony's specialized in trauma. "Their goal is to save lives," Kathy said. "At Craig the goal is to rebuild them."

They began making arrangements to transfer Patrick to Craig.

———

By Thursday, students in Clement Park were angry. The killers were dead, so much of the anger was deflected: onto Goths, Marilyn Manson, the TCM, or anyone who looked, dressed, or acted like the killers—or the media's portrayal of them.

The killers were quickly cast as outcasts and "fags."

"They're freaks," said an angry sophomore from the soccer team. "Nobody really liked them, just 'cause they—" He paused, then plunged ahead. "The majority of them were gay. So everyone would make fun of them."

Several jocks reported having seen the killers and friends "touching" in the hallways, groping each other or holding hands. A football player captivated reporters with tales of group showering.

The gay rumor was almost invisible in the media, but rampant in Clement Park. The stories were vague. Everything was thirdhand. None of the storytellers even knew the killers. Everyone in Clement Park heard the rumors; most of the students saw through them. They were disgusted at the jocks for defaming the killers the same way in death as they had in life. Clearly, "gay" was one of the worst epithets one kid could hurl against another in Jeffco.

Eric and Dylan's friends generally shrugged off the stories. One of them was outraged. "The media's taken my friends and made them to be gay and neo-Nazis and all these hater stuff," he said. "They're portraying my friends as idiots." The angry boy was a brawny six-foot senior dressed in camouflage pants. He ranted for several hours, and he was soon all over the national press—sometimes looking a bit ridiculous. He stopped talking. His father began screening media calls.

A few papers mentioned the gay rumors in passing. Reverend Jerry Falwell described the killers as gay on *Rivera Live*. A notorious picketer of gay funerals issued a media alert saying, "Two filthy fags slaughtered 13 people at Columbine High." Most significantly, the Drudge Report quoted Internet postings claiming that the Trench Coat Mafia was a gay conspiracy to kill jocks. But most major media carefully sidestepped the gay rumor.

The press failed to show similar deference to Goths. Some of the most withering attacks were reserved for that group: a morose-acting subculture best known for powder-white face paint and black clothes, black lips, and black fingernails, accented by heavy, dripping mascara. They were mistakenly associated with the killers on Tuesday by students unfamiliar with the Goth concept. Equally clueless reporters amplified the rumor. One of the most egregious reports was an extended *20/20* segment ABC aired, just one night after the attack. Diane Sawyer introduced it by noting that unnamed police said "the boys may have been part of a dark, underground national phenomenon known as the Gothic movement and that some of these Goths may have killed before." It was true, Goths had killed before—as had members of every conceivable background and subculture.

Correspondent Brian Ross described a double murder committed by Goths and two ghastly attempts in graphic detail. He presented them as evidence of a pattern: a Goth crime wave poised to sweep through suburbia and threaten us all. "The so-called Gothic movement has helped fuel a new kind of teenage gang—white suburban gangs built around a fascination with the grotesque and with death," he said. He played other examples, as well as a horrifying 911 tape of a victim calling for help with a knife still protruding from his chest. "Hurry," he pleaded. "I'm not going to last too much longer." Ross described the killers in that case as "proud, self-proclaimed members of the Gothic movement, and like the students involved in yesterday's shootings, focused on white extremism and hate."

The only real problems with Ross's report were that Goths tended to be meek and pacifist; they had never been associated with violence, much less murder; and, aside from long black coats, they had almost nothing in common with Eric and Dylan.

Where it avoided snap conclusions, much of the reporting was first rate. The *Rocky* passed on most of the myths, and it, the *Post*, and the *Times* ran excellent bios on the killers. On TV, several correspondents helped survivors convey their stories with empathy, dignity, and insight. Katie Couric was a particular standout. And several papers tried to rein in the Goth scare. "Whatever the two young men in Colorado might have imagined themselves to be, they weren't Goths," a *USA Today* story began. "The morose community, much too diffuse to be called a movement, is at its heart quiet, introverted and pacifistic....Goths tend to be outcasts, not because they are violent or aggressive, but the opposite."

Thursday, a young Goth from a nearby school showed up in Clement Park. Andrew Mitchell was a striking sight, standing alone in a foot of snow. Black on black on white on white. Jet-black hair cut long on top, shaved on the sides, bare skin above his ears. A silver-and-blue support ribbon pinned to his black lapel. The densely packed crowd parted. A ten-foot perimeter opened up around him. Reporters rushed in.

"Why are you here!" one demanded.

"To pay my respects," Mitchell said. Then he offered a plea: "Picture these kids, for years being thrown around, treated horribly. After a while you can't stand it anymore. They were completely wrong. But there are reasons for why they did it."

Mitchell was wildly mistaken about the killers' lives and their intentions. But it was already the pervasive assumption. The massacre brought widespread tales of alienation out into the open. *Salon* published a fascinating piece called "Misfits Who Don't Kill." It consisted of first-person accounts from rational adults who had shared similar fantasies but lived to avoid them. "I remember sitting in biology class trying to figure out how much plastic explosive it might take to reduce the schoolhouse—my biggest source of fear and anxiety—to rubble," one man wrote. "I scowled at those who teased me, and I had fantasies of them begging me for mercy, maybe even with a gun in their mouths. Was I a sick person? I don't think so. I'm sure there were thousands of other students who had the same fantasies I did. We just never acted on them."

The more animosity reporters sensed, the deeper they probed. What was it like to be an outcast at Columbine? Pretty hard, most of the kids admitted. High school was rough. Most of the students in Clement Park were still speaking confessionally, and everyone had a brutal experience to share. The "bullying" idea began to pepper motive stories. The concept touched a national nerve, and soon the anti-bullying movement took on a force of its own. Everyone who had been to high school understood what a horrible problem it could be. Many believed that addressing it might be the one good thing to come out of the tragedy.

All the talk of bullying and alienation provided an easy motive. Forty-eight hours after the massacre, *USA Today* pulled the threads together in a stunning cover story that fused the myths of jock-hunting, bully-revenge, and the TCM. "Students are beginning to describe how a long-simmering rivalry between the sullen members of their clique [the TCM] and the school's athletes escalated and ultimately exploded in this week's deadly violence," it said. It described tension the previous spring, including daily fistfights. The details were accurate, the conclusions wrong. Most of the media followed. It was accepted as fact.

There's no evidence that bullying led to murder, but considerable evidence it was a problem at Columbine High. After the tragedy, Mr. D took a lot of flak for bullying, particularly since he insisted he was unaware it had gone on.

"I'm telling you, as long as I've been an administrator here, if I'm aware of a situation, then I deal with that situation," he said. "And I believe our teachers, and I believe our coaches. I turned my own son in. I believe that strongly in rules."

That may have been part of his downfall. Mr. D did believe that strongly in the rules. He held his staff to the same standard, and seemed to believe they would meet it. His unusual rapport with the kids also created a blind spot. It was all smiles when Mr. D strode down the corridor. They sincerely warmed at the sight of him, and sought to please him as well. Sometimes he mistook that joy for pervasive bliss in his high school.

Personal affinities also obscured the problem. Mr. D knew he was drawn to sports. He worked hard to offset that by attending debate tournaments, drama tryouts, and art shows. He conferred regularly with the student senate. But those were all success stories. Mr. D balanced athletics and academics better than overachievers and unders.

"I don't think he had a preference on purpose," a pierced-out girl in a buzz cut and red tartan boots said. "He's got a lot of school spirit, and I think he aims it in the direction he's most comfortable with, like school sports and student congress." She saw DeAngelis as a sincere man, making a tremendous effort to interact with students, unaware that his natural inclination toward happy, energetic students created a blind spot for the outsiders. "My Goth friends hated the school," she said.

———

The crowds in Clement Park kept growing, but the students among them dwindled. Wednesday afternoon they poured their hearts out to reporters. Wednesday evening they watched a grotesque portrait of their school on television. It was a charitable picture at first, but it grew steadily more sinister as the week wore on. The media grew fond of the adjective "toxic." Apparently, Columbine was a horrible place. It was terrorized by a band of reckless jock lords and ruled by an aristocracy of snotty rich white kids in the latest Abercrombie & Fitch line.

Some of that was true—which is to say, it was high school. But Columbine came to embody everything noxious about adolescence in America. A few students were happy to see some ugly truths about their high school exposed. Most were appalled. The media version was a gross caricature of how they saw it, and of what they thought they had described.

It made it difficult for social scientists or journalists to come to Littleton later, to study the community in-depth and see what was really going on. Heisenberg's uncertainty principle had played out in full force: by observing an entity, you alter it. How bad were the Columbine bullies? How horribly were the killers treated? Every scrap of testimony after day two is tainted. Heisenberg was a quantum physicist, observing electron behavior. But social scientists began applying his principle to humans. It was remarkable how similarly we behaved. During the third week of April, Littleton was observed beyond all recognition.

The bright side is that a tremendous amount of data was gathered in those first few days, while students were naive, before any developed an agenda. Hundreds of journalists were in the field, and nearly as many detectives were documenting their findings in police reports. Those reports would remain sealed for nineteen months. Virtually all the early news stories were infested with erroneous assumptions and comically wrong conclusions. But the data is there.

29. The Missions

Two years before he hauled the bombs into the Columbine cafeteria, Eric took a crucial step. He had always maintained an active fantasy life. His extinction fantasies progressed steadily, but reality held firm and was completely separate from his fantasy life. Then one day, midway through sophomore year, Eric began to take action. He wasn't angry, cruel, or particularly hateful. His campaign against the inferiors was comically banal. But it was real.

The mischief started as a threesome. Dylan and Zack were co-conspirators and squad mates. In his written accounts, Eric referred to the two by their code names, VoDKa and KiBBz. They launched the escapades in January 1997, second semester of their sophomore year. They would meet at Eric's house mostly, sneak out after midnight, and vandalize houses of kids he didn't like. Eric chose the targets, of course.

They had to be careful sneaking out. They couldn't wake his parents. Lots of rocks to navigate in Eric's backyard and a pesky neighbor's dog kept "barking its faulking head off," Eric wrote. Then they plunged into a field of tall grass he compared to Jurassic Park's Lost World. To Eric, it was one hell of an adventure. He had been role-playing Marine heroes on military maneuvers since grade school. Finally, he was in the field conducting them.

Eric dubbed his pranks "the missions." As they got under way, he ruminated about misfit geniuses in American society. He didn't like what he saw. Eric was a voracious reader, and he had just gobbled up John Steinbeck's *The Pastures of Heaven,* which includes a fable about the idiot savant Tularecito. The young boy had extraordinary gifts that allowed him to see a world his peers couldn't even imagine—exactly how Eric was coming to view himself, though without Tularecito's mental shortcomings. Tularecito's peers failed to see his gifts and treated him badly. Tularecito struck back violently, killing one of his antagonists. He was imprisoned for life in an insane asylum. Eric did not approve. "Tularecito did not deserve to be put away," he wrote in a book report. "He just needed to be taught to control his anger. Society needs to treat extremely talented people like Tularecito much better." All they needed was more time, Eric argued—gifted misfits could be taught what was right and wrong, what was acceptable to society. "Love and care is the only way," he said.

Love and care. Eric wrote this at the very moment he started moving against his peers. Sometimes he attacked their houses to retaliate for perceived slights, but most often for the offense of inferiority.

Between missions, the boys got into unscripted trouble. Eric got mad at Brooks Brown and stopped talking to him. Then he escalated a snowball fight by breaking a chunk of ice off a drainpipe. He hurled it at the car of a friend of Brooks's and dented the trunk. He grabbed another hunk and cracked the windshield of Brooks's Mercedes.

"Fuck you!" Brooks screamed. "You're going to pay for this!"

Eric laughed. "Kiss my ass, Brooks. I ain't paying for shit."

Brooks drove home and told his mom. Then he headed to Eric's. He was furious, but Kathy Harris remained calm. She invited Brooks in and gave him a seat in the living room. Brooks knew lots of Eric's secrets, and he spilled them all. "Your son's been sneaking out at night," he said. "He's going around vandalizing things." Kathy seemed incredulous. She tried to calm the kid down. Brooks kept ranting: "He's got liquor in his room. Search it! He's got spray-paint cans. Search it!" She wanted him to talk, but he felt that she was acting like a school counselor. He was out of there, he said—he was getting out before Eric got back.

Brooks went home and discovered his friend had grabbed Eric's backpack, taking it hostage, more or less. Brooks's mom, Judy, took control of the situation. She ordered everyone into her car and brought them to see Eric.

He was still enjoying the snowball fight. "Lock the doors!" Judy demanded. She rolled her window down a crack and yelled over to Eric: "I've got your backpack and I'm taking it to your mom's. Meet us over there."

Eric grabbed hold of the car and screamed ferociously. When she pulled away, he hung on, wailing harder. Eric reminded her of an escaped animal attacking a car at a wildlife theme park. Brooks's friend shifted to the other side of the back seat. Judy was terrified. They had never seen this side of Eric. They were used to Dylan's tirades, but he was all show. Eric looked like he meant it.

Judy got up enough speed, and Eric let go. At his house, Eric's mom greeted them in the driveway. Judy handed her the backpack and unloaded the story. Kathy began to cry. Judy felt bad. Kathy had always been so sweet.

Wayne came home and threw the fear of God into Eric. He interrogated him about the alcohol, but Eric had it hidden and played innocent convincingly. He wasn't taking any chances, though—as soon as he got a chance, he destroyed the stash. "I had to ditch every bottle I had and lie like a fuckin salesman to my parents," he wrote.

That night, he went with the confessional approach. He admitted a weakness to his dad: the truth was, he was afraid of Mrs. Brown. That explained a lot, Wayne thought.

Kathy wanted to hear more from the Browns; Wayne bitterly resented the interference. Who was this hysterical woman? Or her conniving little brat Brooks? Wayne was hard enough on the boys without outsiders telling him how to raise his sons.

Kathy called Judy that night. Judy felt she really wanted to listen, but Wayne was negative and dismissive in the background. It was kids' stuff, he insisted. It was all blown way out of proportion. He got on the line and told Judy that Eric had copped to the truth: he was afraid of her.

"Your son isn't afraid of me!" Judy said. "He came after me at my car!"

Wayne jotted notes about the exchange on a green steno pad. He outlined Eric's misdeeds, including getting in Judy Brown's face and "being a little bully." At the bottom of the page he summarized. He found Eric guilty of aggression, disrespect, property damage, and idle threats of physical harm. But he did not look kindly on the Browns. "Over-reaction to minor incident," he concluded. He dated it February 28, 1997.

At school the next day, Brooks heard Eric was making threats about him. He told his parents that night. They called the cops. A deputy came by to question them, then went to see the Harrises. Wayne called a few minutes later. He was bringing Eric over to apologize.

Judy told Brooks and his brother, Aaron, to hide. "I want you both in the back bedroom," she said. "And don't come out."

Wayne waited in the car. He refused to supply moral support—Eric had to walk up to the door and face Mr. and Mrs. Brown alone.

Eric had regained his normal composure. He was exceptionally contrite. "Mrs. Brown, I didn't mean any harm," he said. "And you know I would never do anything to hurt Brooks."

"You can pull the wool over your dad's eyes," she said, "but you can't pull the wool over my eyes."

Eric gaped. "Are you calling me a liar?"

"Yes, I am. And if you ever come up our street, or if you ever do anything to Brooks again, I'm calling the police."

Eric left in a huff. He went home and plotted revenge. He was wary now, but he wouldn't back down. The next mission target was the Browns' house. The team also hit "random houses." Mostly, they would set off fireworks, toilet paper the places, or trigger a house alarm; they also stuck Silly Putty to Brooks's Mercedes. Eric had been bragging about the missions on his Web site, and at this point, he posted Brooks's name, address, and phone number. He encouraged readers to harass "this asshole."

Brooks had betrayed Eric. Brooks had to be punished, but he was never significant. Eric had bigger ideas. He was experimenting with timers now, and those offered new opportunities. Eric wired a dozen firecrackers together and attached a long fuse. He was fastidiously analytical, but he had no way to assess his data, because he fled as soon as he lit the fuses.

Judy Brown viewed Eric as a criminal in bloom. She and Randy spoke to Eric's dad repeatedly. They kept calling the cops.

Wayne did not appreciate that. He would do anything to protect his sons' futures. Discipline was a no-brainer, but the boys' reputations were out of his control. Every kid was going to screw up now and then. The important thing was keeping it inside the family. One black mark could wipe out a lifetime of opportunities. What was the purpose of instilling discipline if one crazy family could ruin Eric's permanent record?

Wayne scrutinized Eric for a while, but ultimately he bought into his son's version. Eric was smart enough to cop to some bad behavior. His calm contrition made the Browns look hysterical.

Three days after the ice incident, Wayne was grappling with more parents and a Columbine dean. Wayne pulled out the six-by-nine-inch pad and labeled the cover "ERIC." He filled three more notebook pages over two days. Brooks knew about the missions and had gone to see a dean. The dean was concerned about alcohol consumption and damage to school property. He would get the police involved if necessary.

Eric played dumb. The word "denial" appears in large letters on two consecutive pages of Wayne's journal. Both times the word is circled, but the first entry is scribbled out. "Denial of even knowledge about alcohol subject between he & me," the second entry reads. "Didn't know what [Dean] Place was talking about." Wayne concluded that the issue was "Over & done—don't discuss with friends." He repeatedly stressed that silence was key. "Talked to Eric: Basically—finished," he wrote. "Leave each other alone don't talk about it. Agreed all discussion is over with."

Wayne Harris apparently breathed easier for a while. He didn't write in his journal for a month and a half. Then come four rapid entries documenting a slew of phone calls. First, Wayne talked to Zack's mom and another parent. The next day, two years and one day before the massacre, a deputy from the Jeffco sheriff's department called. Wayne put his guard up. "We feel victimized, too," he wrote. "We don't want to be accused every time something happens. Eric learned his lesson." He crossed out the last phrase and wrote "is not at fault."

The real problem was Brooks, Wayne was convinced. "Brooks Brown is out to get Eric," he wrote. "Brooks had problems with other boys. Manipulative & Con Artist."

If the problem continued, it might be time to hire a mediator. Or a lawyer. Wayne's last entry on the feud occurred a week later, on April 27, after a call with Judy Brown. "Eric hasn't broken promise to Mr. Place—the dean—about leaving each other alone," he wrote. At the bottom of the page he repeated his earlier sentiments: "We feel victimized, too. Manipulative, Con Artist."

———

Eric totally rocked on the missions. Dylan enjoyed them, too—he liked the camaraderie, especially. He fit in there, he had a role to play, he belonged. But the missions were brief diversions; they were not making him happy. In fact, Dylan was miserable.

30. Telling Us Why

J effco had a problem. Before Eric and Dylan shot themselves, officers
had discovered files on the boys. The cops had twelve pages from Eric's
Web site, spewing hate and threatening to kill. For detectives, a written
confession, discovered before the killers were captured, was a big break. It
certainly simplified the search warrant. But for commanders, a *public* confession, which they had sat on since 1997—that could be a PR disaster.

The Web pages had come from Randy and Judy Brown. They had warned
the sheriff's department repeatedly about Eric, for more than a year and a
half. Sometime around noon April 20, the file was shuttled to the command
center in a trailer set up in Clement Park. Jeffco officials quoted Eric's site
extensively in the search warrants executed that afternoon, but then denied
ever seeing it. (They would spend several years repeating those denials. They
suppressed the damning warrants as well.) Then Sheriff Stone fingered
Brooks as a suspect on *The Today Show.*

It was a rough time for the Brown family. The public got two conflicting
stories: Randy and Judy Brown had either labored to prevent Columbine or
raised one of its conspirators. Or both.

To the Browns it looked like retribution. Yes, their son had been close
to the killers—close enough to see it coming. The Browns had blown the
whistle on Eric Harris over a year earlier, and the cops had done nothing. After Eric went through with his threats, the Browns were fingered as
accomplices instead of heroes. They couldn't believe it. They told the *New
York Times* they had contacted the sheriff's department about Eric fifteen
times. Jeffco officials would insist for years that the Browns never met with
an investigator—despite holding a report indicating they had.

The officers knew they had a problem, and it was much worse than the
Browns realized. Thirteen months before the massacre, Sheriff's Investiga-

tors John Hicks and Mike Guerra had investigated one of the Browns' complaints. They'd discovered substantial evidence that Eric was building pipe bombs. Guerra had considered it serious enough to draft an affidavit for a search warrant against the Harris home. For some reason, the warrant was never taken before a judge. Guerra's affidavit was convincing. It spelled out all the key components: motive, means, and opportunity.

A few days after the massacre, about a dozen local officials slipped away from the Feds and gathered clandestinely in an innocuous office in the county Open Space Department building. It would come to be known as the Open Space meeting. The purpose was to discuss the affidavit for a search warrant. How bad was it? What should they tell the public?

Guerra was driven to the meeting, and told never to discuss it outside that group. He complied.

The meeting was kept secret, too. That held for five years. March 22, 2004, Guerra would finally confess it happened, to investigators from the Colorado attorney general. He described it as "one of those cover-your-ass meetings."

District Attorney Dave Thomas attended the meeting. He told the group he found no probable cause for the investigators to have executed the draft warrant—a finding ridiculed once it was released. He was formally contradicted by the Colorado attorney general in 2004.

At a notorious press conference ten days after the murders, Jeffco officials suppressed the affidavit and boldly lied about what they had known. They said they could not find Eric's Web pages, they found no evidence of pipe bombs matching Eric's descriptions, and had no record of the Browns meeting with Hicks. Guerra's affidavit plainly contradicted all three claims. Officials had just spent days reviewing it. They would repeat the lies for years.

Several days after the meeting, Investigator Guerra's file on his investigation of Eric disappeared for the first time.

———

The cover-your-ass meeting was a strictly Jeffco affair, limited mostly to senior officials. Most of the detectives on the case—including the Feds and cops from local jurisdictions—were unaware of the cover-up. They were trying to crack the case.

Police detectives continued fanning out across Littleton. They had two thousand students to interview—no telling where the truth might be tucked away. They all reported back to the leadership team in the Columbine band room. It was chaos. Guys were coming in with notes on scraps of paper and matchbook covers.

At the end of the week, Kate Battan took control of the situation. She called everyone into the band room for a massive four-hour debriefing and information exchange. At the end of the meeting, three crucial questions remained: How had the killers gotten all the guns? How had they gotten the bombs into the school? Who had conspired to help them?

Battan and her team had a good idea where the conspiracy lay. They had nearly a dozen chief suspects. They pitted two against each other. Chris Morris claimed he was innocent. Prove it, they said. Help us smoke out Duran.

Chris agreed to a wiretap. On Saturday afternoon, he called Phil Duran from FBI headquarters in Denver, while federal agents listened in.

They commiserated about how rough it had gotten. "It's pretty crazy, man," Phil said.

"Yeah. The media's going psycho."

Chris went for the kill too soon. He had heard Duran had gone out shooting with the killers, and someone videotaped it. He mentioned the tape, but Duran brushed it off. For fourteen minutes, they spoke. Chris kept circling back to it; Duran deflected as many times. "I have no clue, dude," he said.

Finally, Chris got an admission that Duran had been out shooting with Eric and Dylan. He got a name: the place was called Rampart Range.

It didn't sound like much. It was leverage.

———

On Sunday, an ATF agent paid Duran a visit. Duran told him everything. Eric and Dylan had approached him about a gun. He'd put them in touch with Mark Manes, who'd sold them the TEC-9. Duran admitted to relaying some of the money but said he'd earned nothing on the deal. Every bit of that was true.

Five days later, detectives hauled Manes into ATF headquarters in downtown Denver, with attorneys for defense and prosecution. Manes made a full confession. Duran had introduced him to Eric and Dylan on January 23 at the Tanner Gun Show—the same place the killers had bought the three other guns. Duran identified Eric as the buyer, and he did the talking. Manes agreed to sell the gun on credit. Eric would pay $300 now, $200 more when he could raise it.

It was Dylan who showed up at Manes's house that night. He handed over the down payment and picked up the gun. Duran delivered the $200 a couple of weeks later.

Detectives asked Manes repeatedly about the killers' ages. Eventually, he admitted that he'd assumed they were under eighteen.

Manes had bought the TEC-9 at the same show, about six months earlier. He'd used his debit card. Later, he produced a bank statement, showing he'd paid $491. He'd made nine dollars on the deal. It could cost him eighteen years.

Dr. Fuselier didn't think much about motive the first few days. It was kind of a moot point, and they had a conspiracy to rope in. Every minute, evidence could be vanishing, alibis arranged, cover stories coordinated. But curiosity soon intruded, and refused to be dented. His mind kept returning to the critical question of *why?*

With nearly a hundred detectives working the case, that central question largely fell to one. It began as a small part of Agent Fuselier's job. He was primarily concerned with leading the FBI team. He met daily with his team leaders: they briefed him, he asked questions, shot holes in their theories, suggested new questions, and challenged them to probe harder. He spent eight to ten hours a day leading that effort, and on Saturdays he drove into Denver to sort through his in-box at FBI headquarters. He had to get up to speed on the federal cases he had handed off, and offer insight and suggestions where he could.

But he began to carve out a little time every evening to assess the killers. He had teams of people to assemble the data, but no one else was qualified to analyze it. He was the only psychologist on the team. He had studied this very sort of killer for years for the FBI, and he knew what he was up against. Even if it meant a few hours of extra work each night, he was going to understand these boys. It pissed him off, watching them brag on video about the people they would maim. "You damn little jerks," he would hear himself mutter. But sometimes he felt a little sorry for them. Their point of view was indefensible, but he had to embrace it temporarily and empathize with them. If he refused to see the world through their lens, how would he ever understand how they could do it? They were high school kids. How did they get this way? Dylan, in particular—what a waste.

Fuselier's peers and subordinates were glad someone had taken on the informal role of chief psychologist. They had a lot of questions about the killers, and they needed someone to turn to: one person who deeply understood the perps. Fuselier quickly became known internally as the expert on the two boys. Kate Battan was leading the day-to-day investigation, and everyone deferred to her on logistical questions, like who'd been running down a particular hallway at a certain moment during the attack. But Fuselier understood the perpetrators. He returned to Eric's journal over and over, and then Dylan's, pouring over every line.

About a week after the murders, Fuselier was introduced to the Basement Tapes and earlier footage Eric and Dylan had shot of themselves. He took the tapes home and watched them repeatedly. He hit the Pause button frequently, advancing frame by frame, going back over revealing moments to dissect nuance. On the surface, much of the material was tedious and banal: little snippets of daily life, like the boys making dumb high school jokes with Chris Morris in the car, and bickering over the drive-thru order at Wendy's. Nothing even tangentially related to the murders appeared on most of the tapes, but Fuselier soaked up ordinary impressions of his murderers.

Fuselier watched or read every word from the killers dozens of times. His big break came just a few days after the murders, before he saw the Basement Tapes. Fuselier heard an ATF agent quoting a ghastly phrase Eric Harris had written.

"What you got there?" Fuselier asked.

A journal. For the last year of his life, Eric Harris had written down many of his plans in a journal.

Fuselier zipped over and read the opening line: "I hate the fucking world."

"When I read that first sentence, all the commotion in the band room ended," he said later. "I just zoned out. Everything else faded." Suddenly the big bombs began to make a lot more sense. *The fucking world.* "That's not Brooks Brown," Fuselier said. "That's not the jocks. That is an all-pervasive hate."

Fuselier read a bit further, then turned to the ATF agent. "Can I have a copy of this?"

The pages had been photocopied from a spiral notebook: sixteen handwritten pages and a dozen more of sketches and charts and diagrams. There were nineteen entries, all dated, running from April 10, 1998, to April 3, 1999, seventeen days before Columbine. They ran a page or two at the beginning, then shortened considerably, with the last five crammed into the last page and a half. They were dark and fuzzy from too many trips through the copier. Eric's scrawl was hard to decipher at first, but Fuselier was reading again while the pages made another pass through the copy machine. "It was mesmerizing," he said.

The journal told infinitely more than Eric's Web site had. The Web site—which predated the journal by at least a year—was mostly vented rage. It told us who he hated, what he wanted to do to the world, and what he had already done. It said very little about why. The journal was angry but deeply reflective. And infinitely more candid about the urges driving Eric to kill.

Fuselier read while the photocopies ran, he read on the walk back to the ATF agent's desk, and he stood there reading rather than return to his own chair. He didn't notice his back stiffening up for several minutes, until the pain finally interrupted. Then he took a seat. And kept reading. *Holy shit,* Fuselier thought. *He's telling us why he did it.*

Eric would prove the easier killer to understand. Eric always knew what he was up to. Dylan did not.

PART III

THE DOWNWARD SPIRAL

31. The Seeker

Dylan's mind raced night and day: analyzing, inventing, deconstructing. He was fifteen, he had tagged along on the missions, he was Eric's number one go-to guy, and none of that mattered. Dylan's head was bursting with ideas, sounds, impressions—he could never turn the racket off. That asshole in gym class, his family, the girls he liked, the girls he loved but could never get—why could he never get them?—he was never going to get them. A guy could still dream, right?

Dylan was in pain. Nobody got it. Vodka helped. The Internet did, too. Girls were hard to talk to; Instant Messaging made it easier. Dylan would IM alone in his room for hours at night. Vodka made the words flow but reduced his ability to spell them. When an Internet girl called him on it, he laughed and admitted he was sloshed. It was easy to hide from his parents—they never suspected. It all happened quietly in his room.

IMs were not enough. Too many secrets to hold on to; too many concepts zipping over their heads. Suicide was consuming him—no way Dylan was confessing that. He tried explaining some of the other ideas, but people were too thick to understand.

Shortly after the missions started, in the spring of sophomore year, March 31, 1997, Dylan got drunk, picked up a pen, and began the conversation with the one person who could understand. Himself. He imagined his journal as a stately old tome, with oversized covers extending just past the parchment, and a fine satin ribbon sewn into the binding, like in a Bible. All he had was a plain pad of notebook paper, college-ruled and three-hole punched. So he drew the imaginary cover on the cover. He titled his work "Existences: A Virtual Book."

There was no hint of murder that first day, not even violence. Only traces of anger seeped out, mostly aimed at himself. Dylan was on a spiritual quest. "I do shit to supposedly 'cleanse' myself in a spiritual, moral sort of way," he wrote. He had tried deleting the Doom files from his computer, tried staying sober, tried to stop making fun of kids—that was a tough one. Kids were so easy to ridicule.

The spiritual purge wasn't helping. "My existence is shit," he wrote. He described eternal suffering in infinite directions through infinite realities.

Loneliness was the crux of the problem, but it ran deeper than just finding a friend. Dylan felt cut off from humanity. Humans were trapped in a box of our own construction: mental prisons caging us from a universe of possibilities. God, people were annoying! What were they afraid of? Dylan could see an entire universe opening up in his mind. He was a seeker, he sought to explore it all, across time and space and who knew how many dimensions. The possibilities were breathtaking. Who could fail to behold the wonder of it all? Almost everyone, unfortunately. Humans loved their little boxes, so safe and warm and comfy and *boring!* They were zombies by choice.

Some of Dylan's ideas were hard to put into words. He drew squiggles in the margins and labeled them "thought pictures."

He was a profoundly religious young man. His family was not active in any congregation, yet Dylan's belief was unwavering. He believed in God without question, but constantly challenged His choices. Dylan would cry out, cursing God for making him a modern Job, demanding an explanation for the divine brutality of His faithful servant.

Dylan believed in morality, ethics, and an afterlife. He wrote intently about the separation of body and soul. The body was meaningless, but his soul would live forever. It would reside either in the peaceful serenity of heaven or in the blistering tortures of hell.

Dylan's anger would flare, then fizzle quickly into self-disgust. Dylan wasn't planning to kill anyone, except, God willing, himself. He craved death for at least two years. The first mention comes in the first entry: "Thinking of suicide gives me hope that i'll be in my place wherever i go after this life—that ill finally not be at war w. myself, the world, the universe—my mind, body, everywhere, everything at PEACE—me—my soul (existence)."

But suicide posed a problem. Dylan believed in a literal heaven and hell. He would be a believer right up until the end. When he murdered several people, he knew there would be consequences. He would refer to them in his final video message, recorded on the morning he called "Judgment Day."

Dylan was unique, that much he was sure of. He had been watching the kids at school. Some were good, some bad, but all so utterly different from him. Dylan exceeded even Eric in his belief in his own singularity. But Eric equated "unique" with "superior"—Dylan saw it mostly as bad. Unique meant lonely. What good were special talents when there was no one to share them with?

His moods came and went quickly. Dylan turned compassionate, then fatalistic. "I don't fit in here," he complained. But the road to the afterlife was just monstrous: "go to school, be scared & nervous, hoping that people can accept me."

———

Eric and Dylan both left journals behind. Dr. Fuselier would spend years studying them. At first glance, Dylan's looked more promising. Fuselier was hungry for data, and Dylan provided an impressive stack. His journal began a year earlier than Eric's, filled nearly five times as many pages, and remained active right up to the end. But Eric would begin his journal as a killer. He already knew where it would end. Every page pointed in the same direction. His purpose was not self-discovery but self-lionization. Dylan was just trying to grapple with existence. He had no idea where he was headed. His ideas were all over the map.

Dylan liked order. Each journal entry began with a three-line heading in the right margin: name, date, and title, all written out in half-sized letters. He then repeated the title—or sometimes adapted it—in double-sized characters centered above the main text. Most of the copy was printed, but occasionally he would veer into script. He wrote one entry a month, nearly every month, but hardly ever twice a month. He would fill two complete pages and then stop. If he ran out of ideas or interest, he would fill out the second page with huge lettering or sketches.

His second entry came early: just two weeks after the first. His ideas were beginning to cohere. "The battle between good & bad never ends," he wrote. Dylan would repeat this idea endlessly for the next two years. Good and evil, love and hate—always wrestling, never resolving. Pick your side, it's up to you—but you better pray it picks you back. Why would love never choose him?

"I dont know what i do wrong with people," he wrote, "it's like they are set out to hate & (insult) me, i never know what to say or do." He had tried. He had brought in Chips Ahoy cookies to win them over. What exactly would it take?

"My life is still fucked," he wrote, "in case you care." He had just lost $45, and before that it was his Zippo lighter and his knife. True, he had gotten the first two back, but still. "Why the fuck is he being such an ASS-HOLE??? (god i guess, whoever is the being which controls shit.) He's fucking me over big time & it pisses me off. Good god i HATE my life, i want to die really bad right now."

32. Jesus Jesus Jesus

Sunday morning, April 25, the Columbine churches were packed. Afterward, the crowds trekked down to the Bowles Crossing Shopping Center, across from Clement Park. Organizers had planned for up to thirty thousand mourners in the sprawling parking lot. Seventy thousand showed up. Vice President Al Gore was on the platform, along with the governor, most of Colorado's congressional delegation, and a whole lot of clergy. The TV networks broadcast the ceremony live.

"Put your faith and trust in the living son of God, the Lord Jesus Christ," Reverend Billy Graham's son Franklin instructed the crowd. "We must be willing to receive His son Jesus Christ."

"Genuine lasting comfort comes only through Jesus Christ," local pastor Jerry Nelson proclaimed. "We, your pastors, urge you: Seek Jesus!"

Jesus Jesus Jesus. There was a whole lot of Him that day. Reverend Graham dominated the ceremony with a long, impassioned appeal for returning prayer to public schools. He invoked the name of his personal savior seven times in a single forty-five-second flurry. "Do you believe in the Lord Jesus Christ?" he asked. He called upon God and Jesus nearly fifty times in course of the speech. Cassie had been ready, he said. She'd stood before a gunman who'd transported her immediately into the presence of Almighty God. "Are you ready?" he asked.

Christian pop star Amy Grant sang twice; a drum and bugle corps performed a stirring rendition of "Amazing Grace"; and a succession of thirteen white doves were released as Governor Bill Owens recited the names of the victims. Toward the end, it began to rain. A slow, steady shower. Nobody moved. Thousands of umbrellas went up, but tens of thousands of mourners just got wet.

For many, Cassie Bernall was the heroine of Columbine. Word spread quickly that her killer had held her at gunpoint and asked if she believed in God. "Yes," she'd answered. She'd professed her faith and had promptly been shot in the head. Vice President Gore recounted her story to the crowd and the cameras. He quoted liberally from Scripture throughout his speech.

"To the families of the victims, may you feel the embrace of the literally hundreds of millions of Americans who grieve with you," Vice President Gore said. "We hold your agony in the center of our prayers. You are not alone."

———

The country was transfixed. In the first ten days, newsmagazines on the four main broadcast networks devoted forty-three pieces to the attack. The shows dominated the ratings that week. CNN and Fox News charted the highest ratings in their history. A week afterward, *USA Today* was still running ten separate Columbine stories in a single edition. It would be nearly two weeks before the *New York Times* would print an issue without Columbine on page 1.

And Cassie Bernall's martyrdom was showing the most legs. "Millions have been touched by a martyr," Pastor Kirsten proclaimed to his congregation. He shared a vision his youth pastor had received while ministering to the Bernalls: "I saw Cassie, and I saw Jesus, hand in hand. And they had just gotten married. They had just celebrated their marriage ceremony. And Cassie kind of winked over at me, like, 'I'd like to talk, but I'm so much in love.' Her greatest prayer was to find the right guy. Don't you think she did?"

Kirsten consoled his grieving congregation, but he saw opportunity in the tragedy to unabashedly save more souls. "Pack that ark with as many people as possible," he said.

Down the road at the Foothills Bible Church, Pastor Oudemolen was sharing a similar enthusiasm. "Men and women, open your eyes!" he declared. "The kids are turning to God! They're going to churches!"

Much of the Denver clergy was appalled. The opportunism at the public service drew an outcry, particularly from mainline Protestant pastors. Reverend Marxhausen, the pastor who'd performed Dylan's funeral, told the *Denver Post* he'd felt "hit over the head with Jesus" at the service.

Evangelicals faced a profound moral dilemma: respect for others' beliefs versus an obligation to stand up for Jesus as the only way, every day. Eric and Dylan had terrorized the country, but they offered an invaluable opportunity as well. Evangelical clergy would answer to God if they wasted it. One thoughtful Evangelical pastor said he approved of using the massacre for recruitment, as long it was truly done for God. He bristled at "spiritual headhunters, just racking up another scalp. The Bible was never meant to be a club," he said. "If I'm using it as a weapon, that's really sad."

———

Craig Scott was a sophomore, sixteen years old, and exceptionally good looking, like his sister Rachel. He had hidden under a library table with Matthew Kechter and Isaiah Shoels. While he was down there, one of the gunmen yelled, "Get anyone with white hats!" Craig was wearing one. He yanked it off and stuffed it under his shirt. Both killers passed his table several times. They stopped there, eventually, and both of them fired. Matt slumped; so did Isaiah. Craig was spared. The shots were so loud Craig thought his ears were going to bleed. He spent much of his time in the fetal position, with his head down, silently praying for courage and strength. When he looked up to assess the damage, Matt and Isaiah had collapsed leaning against each other and moaning. Their blood had pooled around Scott—he couldn't tell whose it was that had soaked into his pants. Smoke or steam was rising up from the rupture in Matt's side.

Then the killers moved into the hallway. "I think they're gone," Craig called out. "Let's get out of here." Other kids were getting up slowly, heading for a side exit. Craig dropped his white hat on the floor by his table. On his way out, a girl under the computer desk said, "Please help me." Kacey Ruegsegger had a big hole in her right shoulder. Scott helped her up. He draped her good arm over his shoulder and led her out.

Outside, they ran for a police car parked on the side of the hill. Cops were there, pointing their guns at the library windows. Craig continued to pray. He asked other kids to join him. Craig had accepted Jesus Christ as his personal savior, and they needed Him badly now. He led a small prayer group.

The cops shuttled the wounded out first. When Craig's turn came, he heard more gunfire behind him. "They're shooting at us," one of the cops said.

The officers dropped the kids off at a cul-de-sac just off the school grounds. Craig joined hands with others in a group to pray. Then he got to a phone, called his mom, and asked her to pray for his sister. He had a bad feeling about her. He prayed that Rachel was not injured. Within an hour or two, he began accepting that she might be dead. She was. Rachel had been the first one killed, on the lawn outside. Matt and Isaiah were dead too. Kacey lived.

Craig took it hard. He had seen horrible things, but he'd heard something wonderful. In the worst of it in the library, he'd heard a girl profess her faith. Amazing. Craig began telling the story early that first afternoon. It spread like brushfire. Among Evangelicals, e-mails, faxes, and phone calls whipped across the country.

On Friday it hit the mainstream media. Both Denver papers featured it. The *Rocky*'s piece, "Martyr for Her Faith," opened with a play-by-play:

> A Columbine killer pointed his gun at Cassie Bernall and asked her the life-or-death question: "Do you believe in God?"
>
> She paused. The gun was still there. "Yes, I believe in God," she said.
>
> That was the last thing this 17-year-old Christian would ever say.
>
> The gunman asked her "Why?" She had no time to answer before she was shot to death.
>
> Bernall entered the Columbine High School library to study during lunch. She left a martyr.

The *Post* ran a similar account. The national press quickly jumped aboard. On Saturday, an Evangelical Teen Mania rally in Michigan "turned into a Cassie Bernall festival," according to *Weekly Standard* writer J. Bottum. He described 73,000 teens in the Silverdome "weeping along with sermon after sermon about her death." On Sunday morning, it was proclaimed from countless pulpits.

At first, her mother was unsure what to make of Cassie's martyrdom. But soon Misty was bursting with pride, and her husband, Brad, was, too. "This tragic incident has been thrown back into the face of Satan," Brad said in a statement. He called on teens to step forward while The Enemy was in retreat: "To all young people who hear this: Don't let my daughter's death be for nothing. Make your stand. If you're not in the local church's youth group, try it. They want you and will help support you."

On Monday, Brad and Misty were featured on a *20/20* segment titled "Portrait of an Angel." Stories were circulating that the killers had targeted Evangelicals as well as jocks and minorities. Brad's community presumed that Cassie's response had provoked the killer to shoot. "She knew where he was coming from," Brad said. "And she was saying that, 'You can't defeat me. You can't really kill me. You can take my body away, but you can't kill me. I'm going to live in heaven forever.'"

Initially, Brad seemed to draw a bit more strength from Cassie's bravery than Misty did. "You wake up crying," she said. "I hope one day I can wake up in the morning and not cry. But I said to Brad, I wondered how they could do this. Why did they kill our baby girl? Why did they do that? Why?"

A few days after the *20/20* segment, Brad and Misty appeared on *Oprah*. "Do you wish she had said 'No'?" Oprah asked.

"Knowing that a girl begged for her life and was released" made a big difference, Misty said. Eric had taunted Bree Pasquale for several minutes, repeatedly forcing her to beg, then finally dismissed her. "As a mom, you would have wanted her to beg," Misty said. "So on the one hand, you're like, 'Yeah, I'd have wanted her to beg.' But I can't think of a more honorable way to die than to profess your faith in God."

33. Good-bye

Two years before Cassie's murder, Dylan laid out his case for God. He enumerated the pros and cons of his existence. Good: a nice family, a beautiful house, food in the fridge, a few close good friends, and some decent possessions. The bad list went on and on: no girls—not even platonic, no other friends, nobody accepting him, doing badly in sports, looking ugly and acting shy, getting bad grades, having no ambition in life.

Dylan understood what God had chosen for him. Dylan was to be a seeker: "one man in search of answers, never finding them, yet in hopelessness understands things. He seeks knowledge of the unthinkable, of the undefinable, of the unknown. He explores the everything—using his mind, the most powerful tool known to him."

Dylan thrashed about madly, but clarity sometimes emerged: "death is passing through the doors," he wrote. "the ever-existant compulsion of everything is the curiosity to keep moving down the hall." Down the hall, exploring the rooms, finding the answers, raising new questions—at long last, Dylan the seeker would achieve the state he was searching for.

Dylan took to referring to humans as zombies. That was a rare similarity to Eric. But pitiful as we zombies were, Dylan didn't want to harm us. He found us interesting, like new toys. "I am <u>GOD</u> compared to some of these un-existable brainless zombies," he wrote.

That was Dylan's first brush with blasphemy. He immediately qualified it: he wasn't claiming godhood, just that he was *like* God compared to humans. It would be months before he'd try it again. Each time, he would push the idea further, but he never quite seemed to believe. As spring 1997 progressed, he filled page after page with aborted attempts.

He saw history as good vs. bad, love vs. hate, God vs. Satan—"The Everlasting Contrast." And he saw himself on the good side.

Eric had more practical concerns. Two months of heat from his dad taught Eric to cover his tracks better. The vandalism missions continued through spring and early summer, with no record of further detection. By mission 5 the boys were drinking again. Wayne appeared to have watched Eric closely for a while, then resumed trusting him. According to Eric, only one outing went alcohol-free.

The emphasis on larger explosives continued; some of the timing devices began to work. Eric discovered that he could light the tip of a cigarette and let it burn down toward the fuse for an added delay. The boys survived a few close calls, including near detection by a police officer in a squad car. On the sixth outing, they brought along Dylan's sawed-off BB gun and fired randomly into houses. "We probly didnt do any damage," Eric wrote, "but we arent sure." That same night, they stole some Rent-a-Fence signs from a construction site. Eric didn't make much of the swipe, but this appears to be the moment where they crossed the hazy boundary between petty vandalism and petty theft.

———

The missions had been satisfying for a couple of months. But sophomore year was over. Eric was hungry for more. In the summer of 1997, Zack Heckler went to Pennsylvania for two weeks. When he got back, Eric and Dylan had built a pipe bomb. Dylan was involved, but it was Eric's baby.

Eric would not begin his journal until the spring of 1998. But he was active with his Web site the previous year. By the summer of 1997, he had posted his hate lists:

YOU KNOW WHAT I HATE!!!?

—Cuuuuuuuuhntryyyyyyyyyy music!!!

YOU KNOW WHAT I HATE!!!?

—R rated movies on CABLE! My DOG can do a better damn editing job than those tards!!!...

YOU KNOW WHAT I REALLY HATE!!!?

—THE "W.B." network!!!! OH JESUS MARY MOTHER OF GOD ALMIGHTY I HATE THAT CHANNEL WITH ALL MY HEART AND SOUL.

The list went on for pages, fifty-odd entries about hating "fitness fuckheads," phony martial arts experts, and people who mispronounced "acrosT" or "eXspreso." At first, his targets seem preposterously random, but Fuselier divined the underlying theme: stupid, witless inferiors. It wasn't just the WB network Eric hated heart and soul, it was all the morons watching it.

Eric's briefer love lists backed Fuselier's analysis. Eric loved "Making fun of stupid people doing stupid things!" His greatest love was "Natural SELECTION!!!!!!!!!!! God damn it's the best thing that ever happened to the Earth. Getting rid of all the stupid and weak organisms. I wish the government would just take off every warning label. So then all the dumbasses would either severely hurt themselves or DIE!"

What the boy was really expressing was contempt.

―――

Eric's ideas began to fuse. He loved explosions, actively hated inferiors, and passively hoped for human extinction. He built his first bombs.

He started small: nothing that would kill anyone, just enough to injure people or their property. He went searching for instructions and found them readily available on the Web. During the summer of 1997, he built several explosives and began setting them off. Then he bragged about it on his Web site.

"If you havent made a CO_2 bomb today, I suggest you do so," he wrote. "Me and VoDkA detonated one yesterday and it was like a fucking dynomite stick. Just watch out for shrapnel."

That was an exaggeration. They had taken small carbon dioxide cartridges—which kids often called whip-its—and punctured them, then shoved gun powder inside. Eric called them crickets, and they were closer to a large firecracker than a bomb. Eric had also built pipe bombs, which were more powerful. He was still searching for a spot safe for detonation.

Eric realized his Web audience would doubt him. He backed his claims with specifications and an ingredient list. He wanted to make sure his readers understood that he was serious.

———

Someone sensed the danger. On August 7, 1997, a "concerned citizen"—apparently Randy Brown—read Eric's Web site and called the sheriff's department. On that day—one year, eight months, and thirteen days before Columbine—the killers' names permanently entered the law enforcement system.

Deputy Mark Burgess printed out Eric's pages. He read through them and wrote up a report. "This Web page refers to 'missions' where possible criminal mischiefs have occurred," he wrote. Curiously, Burgess made no mention of the pipe bombs, which seem far more serious.

Burgess sent his report to a superior, Investigator John Hicks, with eight Web site pages attached. They were filed.

———

Eric and Zack and Dylan were working age now. They all got jobs at Blackjack together. There were flour fights and water chases all the time. Eric plunged right in; Dylan watched from the sidelines. They made dry-ice eruptions out back in the parking lot, watched how high they could get a construction cone to sail. It was great. Then Zack met a girl. Bastard.

Dylan took it hard. Devon was her name, and she totally ripped the team apart. Zack was with her all the time now, and that squeezed his buddies out of the picture. Eric and Dylan were nobodies. The missions were suddenly over. Eric didn't seem to mind too much, but Dylan was a mess.

It wasn't good for him now, he confided to "Existences." "My best friend ever: the friend who shared, experimented, laughed, took chances with, & appreciated me, more than any friend ever did.... Ever since Devon (who i wouldn't mind killing) has loved him—that's the only place hes been!" They had done everything together: drinking, cigars, sabotaging houses. Since seventh grade, he had felt so lonely. Zack had changed all that. "hello I finally found someone who was like me! who appreciated me & shared very common interests. I finally felt happiness (sometimes)." But Zack had found a girlfriend and moved on. "i feel so lonely, w/o a friend."

Who he wouldn't mind killing? Dylan tossed out the comment in passing, and presumably it was just a figure of speech. Presumably. But he had verbalized the idea—a big step. And Dylan did not yet consider Eric his best friend. Dylan belabored the point that no one besides Zack had ever understood him; no one else appreciated him. That would include Eric.

———

Dylan was lonelier than ever. Conveniently, he stumbled into a solution: "My 1st love???"

"OH My God," his next entry began. "I am almost sure I am in love w, Harriet. hehehe. such a strange name, like mine." He loved everything about her, from her good body to her almost perfect face, her charm, her wit and cunning and *not* being popular. He just hoped she liked him as much as he *loved* her.

That was the wrinkle. Dylan had not actually spoken to Harriet. But he couldn't let that stop him. He thought of her every second of every day. "If soulmates exist," he wrote, "then I think I've found mine. I hope she likes Techno."

That was the other hurdle. He had not yet established whether she liked techno.

———

Dylan felt happiness sometimes. He got excited about his driver's license. But he couldn't stay happy. Shortly after falling for Harriet, he returned to his journal to complain. Such a desolate, lonely, unsalvageable life. "NOT FAIR!!!" He wanted to die. Zack and Devon looked at him like he was a stranger, but Harriet had played the meanest trick: Dylan had fallen for "fake love."

"She in reality doesn't give a good fuck about me," he said. She didn't even know him, he admitted. He had no happiness, no ambitions, no friends, and "no LOVE!!!"

Dylan wanted a gun. He had spoken to a friend about getting one. He planned to turn the weapon on himself. That was a big step in the long suicide process: from writing about it to action.

At this point, nearly two years before Columbine, Dylan saw the gun as his last resort. He continued his spiritual quest "i stopped the pornography," he said. "I try not to pick on people." But God seemed intent on punishing him. "A dark time, infinite sadness," he wrote. "I want to find love."

Love was the most common word in Dylan's journal. Eric was filling his Web site with hate.

———

When Fuselier examined a crime, one of his primary tactics was to begin ruling out motives. Dylan seemed like a classic depressive, but Fuselier had to be sure. With both Columbine killers, an obvious question loomed: Were they insane? Most mass murderers act deliberately—they just want to hurt people—but some truly can't help themselves. Fuselier would describe those killers as psychotic. A broad term, *psychotic* covers a spectrum of severe mental illnesses, including paranoia and schizophrenia. Psychotics can grow deeply disoriented and delusional, hearing voices and hallucinating. In severe cases, they lose all contact with reality. They sometimes act out of imaginary yet terrifying fear for their own safety, or according to instructions from imaginary beings. Fuselier saw no indication of any of that here.

Another possibility was psychopathy. In popular usage, any crazy killer is a called a psychopath, but in psychiatry, the term denotes a specific mental condition. Psychopaths appear charming and likable, but it's an act. They are coldhearted manipulators who will do anything for their own gain. The vast majority are nonviolent: they want your money, not your life. But the ones who turn sadistic can be monstrous. If murder amuses them, they will kill again and again. Ted Bundy, Gary Gilmore, and Jeffrey Dahmer were all psychopaths. Typically, murderous psychopaths are serial killers, but occasionally one will go on a spree. The Columbine massacre could have been the work of a psychopath, but Dylan showed none of the signs.

Fuselier continued ruling out profiles. None of the usual theories fit. Everything about Dylan screamed depressive—an extreme case, self-medicating with alcohol. The problem was how that had led to murder. Dylan's journal read like that of a boy on the road to suicide, not homicide.

Fuselier had seen murder arise from depression, but it rarely looked like this. There is usually a continuum of depressive reactions, ranging from lethargy to mass murder. Dylan seemed muddled on the languorous side. Depressives are inherently angry, though they rarely appear that way. They are angry at themselves. "Anger turned inward equals depression," Fuselier explained. Depression leads to murder when the anger is severe enough and then turns outward. Depressive outbursts tend to erupt after a debilitating loss: getting fired, dumped by a girlfriend, even a bad grade, if the depressive sees that as significant. "Most of us get angry, kick a trash can, drink a beer or two, and get over it," Fuselier explained. For 99.9 percent of the population, that's the end of it. But for a few, the anger festers.

Some depressives withdraw—from friends, family, schoolmates. Most of them get help or just get over it. A few spiral downward toward suicide. But for a tiny percentage, their own death is not enough. They perform a "vengeful suicide"—a common example is the angry husband who shoots himself in front of his wedding photo. He deliberately splatters his remains on the symbol of the marriage. The offense is directed straight at his conception of the guilty party. A tiny number of angry depressives decide to make the tormentor pay. Typically that's a wife, girlfriend, boss, or parent—someone close enough to matter. It's a rare depressive who resorts to murder, but when one does, it nearly always ends with a single person.

A few lash out in a wider circle: the wife and her friend who bad-mouthed him; the boss and some coworkers. The targets are specific. But the rarest of these angry depressives take the reasoning one step further: *everyone* was mean to them; *everyone* had a role in their misfortune. They want to lash out randomly and show us all, hurt us back and make sure we feel it. This is the gunman who opens fire on a random crowd.

Fuselier had seen each of those types several times over the course of his career. Dylan didn't look like a candidate. Murder or even suicide takes willpower as well as anger. Dylan fantasized about suicide for years without making an attempt. He had never spoken to the girls he dreamed of. Dylan Klebold was not a man of action. He was conscripted by a boy who was.

34. Picture-Perfect Marsupials

Patrick Ireland was trying to learn to talk again. So frustrating. The first couple of days he couldn't manage much of anything. He struggled to spit out a single sentence, word by word, and when he had finished, it often made no sense. In his best moments, Patrick spoke like the victim of a severe stroke: slow, labored attempts would produce a single guttural syllable, then a sudden burst of sound. He could form the words in his head, but few made the passage to his mouth. Where did all the rest go? Any chance distraction could hijack the thought as it made its way to his vocal chords. Random phrases often slipped in to replace the ideas. His mom would ask how he was feeling, and he'd answer in Spanish, or recite the capitals of South American countries. His brain was never aware of the mix-up. He was sure he had just described his mood or asked for a straw, and was confused by her confusion.

Patrick's brain tended to spit out whatever was in short-term memory. He had been studying the capitals just before the shooting, and recently returned from Spain. Often the memories were more immediate. Hospital intercom announcements were constantly echoing out of Patrick's mouth, in response to unrelated questions. He had no idea he had even heard the voices in the background. Other times it was complete nonsense. "Picture-perfect marsupials" kept popping out. No one knows where that came from.

It got frustrating, for everyone. One of Patrick's first meals out of the ICU was a juicy hamburger. He was so excited about it, and couldn't wait to slather the bun with...something. Kathy gently asked him to repeat. That was annoying, but he answered with fresh gibberish. Over and over he repeated himself, more angry with each new batch of nonsense. He tried miming it, shaking the bottle—he *really* wanted that condiment. Kathy's sister ran downstairs and got one of everything from the cafeteria: mustard, relish, salsa—big handfuls of packets. None of that. They never did figure out what he wanted.

———

Patrick understood that he'd been shot. He knew he had gone out the window. He didn't grasp the scale of the massacre. He didn't know he had been on TV—or that television shows were interested in him. He had no idea the networks had cast him as The Boy in the Window.

Now and then, Patrick would stammer out an intelligible answer. And it would make him extremely happy. His motor skills seemed fine on the left side. If his brain could control his left hand to work a fork, why not a pen? Someone fetched a pack of markers and a whiteboard.

"Oh boy, was that a mistake," Kathy recalled.

"*Big* mistake," John said. "It was just scribbles. Just scribbles, absolute."

It was one thing to hear Patrick struggle. Seeing his inability sketched out in black and white, that was a shocker. It was like a diagram of a brain malfunctioning: scads of tiny neurons, misfiring randomly into nowhere.

The Irelands were also confronted with the realization that the problem lay deeper than the control centers for Patrick's vocal cords: he couldn't organize the thoughts behind them. He could respond emotionally, but he could not translate that into language, regardless of the medium.

"It frustrated him; it scared the hell out of us," John said. "He can't speak and now he can't write, and how are we going to communicate with him?"

Sometimes, with a great struggle, Patrick formed the words out loud. Sometimes that posed bigger problems. The questions could be unsettling. Urgently, he begged them to tell him one thing: "How long is this going to be?"

This?

The hospital, the recovery—he didn't have time for all this. He had finals in three weeks, he had ski season and basketball to train for, he was totally coming into his own on the basketball court. He couldn't afford to get a B. He had gone three straight years without one; he had worked his ass off again all semester, and he was acing every class. The valedictorian thing was for real now, almost in reach. He wasn't about to screw it up with this hospital crap. He was *going* to graduate as valedictorian.

It had been an ambitious goal. Patrick was a bright kid, but no genius. And Columbine was competitive. Some kids could cruise to easy A's, but Patrick had to fight for some of his. Several students with unblemished records shared the valedictory title every year. He couldn't afford even one B.

The geniuses could cruise to A's without breaking a sweat. Patrick hated getting lumped in with them.

So Patrick made his parents a little uneasy when he announced his intention, freshman year, in the car, on the way to basketball practice. He didn't make a big deal out of it, and he didn't say he would try, he just said he was going to do it.

Two years later, in his hospital room, John and Kathy Ireland had let go of basketball, waterskiing, and academic honors. Walking and talking sounded ambitious.

The severity of his situation was more than Patrick could swallow. "I didn't comprehend, really," he said later.

Patrick Ireland did not see a television or a newspaper the first week. He didn't realize his family was protecting him or how big the Columbine tragedy was. He had no idea the whole country was watching. He didn't even know who had died.

The first indication of what he was involved in came when friends called to check on him from Europe. He had gone on a class trip a month earlier and stayed with a family near Madrid. Now they were worried about him. Patrick was taken aback. *They were hearing about this in Spain?*

Seven days out, he transferred to Craig Hospital. He began rehab and was quickly scooting around the hospital in a wheelchair. He returned from therapy one day and turned on the TV. It was the news, they were listing the people killed. They showed Corey DePooter's picture. Patrick was stunned. Corey was one of his best friends. They had started in the library together, but gotten separated when the noises first started outside and Corey went to investigate. Patrick had never seen him since.

"I started bawling," Patrick said later. "I think that was the first time I cried."

The staff at Craig was not pushing for a first step—just a little movement. If he could get control of that leg and lift it up off the mattress, there was hope. His leg was fine. All the neural pathways up and down his spinal cord were intact. Signals passed unimpeded to the muscles wrapped around his femur. Millions of tiny nerve endings continued transmitting sensory data along the length of his thigh.

Patrick knew, intellectually, that all that fine machinery was functional. But he couldn't reach it. There was just the tiniest little gap in the network inside his brain. Somewhere inside his head he could feel himself issue the command. He felt it moving in there, but then it got lost. He squeezed his eyes, squeezed his brain, tried to force it. Squeezing didn't help. The leg refused.

Something was missing. The makeshift memorials in Clement Park had grown enormous over the first few days. Hundreds of thousands of flowers were piled up with poems, drawings, and teddy bears. Letter jackets, jewelry, and wind chimes added sprinkles of individuality. The district rented several warehouses to store them.

It wasn't enough. The survivors didn't know what they needed, or where or why, exactly, but they needed something. They were searching for a symbol, and they knew it immediately when it came.

Seven days after the massacre, shortly before sunset, a row of fifteen wooden crosses rose up along the crest of Rebel Hill. They stood seven feet high, three feet wide, and were spaced evenly along the length of the mesa. Clement Park's floodlights lit up the low-hanging clouds behind them, and the crosses cast an eerie silhouette against the thunderheads. The tips seemed to glow. They were startling, too, for their imperfections. The dimensions seemed a little off: the crossbeams looked far too short, and were branched too close to the top. Some were planted poorly, leaning badly to one side. Within hours, the arms dangled beads, ribbons, rosaries, placards, flags, and so many blue and white balloons.

Over the next five days, 125,000 people trekked up the hill to reach the crosses. They trudged through the mud as a vicious storm pounded the hill. They tore away the grass. Many waited two hours in the rain just to begin the climb. It felt like a pilgrimage.

The crosses had come from Chicago. A short, pudgy carpenter built them out of pine he got at Home Depot. He drove them to Colorado in a pickup, planted them on the hill, and drove back. He'd taped a black-and-white photo of one victim or killer to each cross, and he left a pen dangling from each one to encourage graffiti.

"I couldn't believe how fast people came up and started putting stuff around them," an onlooker said. Soon each cross had sprouted a pile covering the base and making its way up to the arms. Christian dog tags were popular, with phrases like "God Is Awesome" and "Jesus Lives." Several crosses were wrapped head to foot in flowers, others dressed in shirts and jackets and pants.

On thirteen crosses, the messages were loving and uncontroversial. The killers' crosses hosted a bitter debate: "HATE BREEDS HATE." "How can anyone forgive you?"

"I forgive you," someone responded. Half the messages were conciliatory: "Sorry we all failed you." "No one is to blame."

It was exactly as Tom and Sue Klebold had feared. If they had buried Dylan, his grave would look like that.

A woman told a reporter she'd been spit on for grieving for the killers, then shoved into the mud. A woman with a baby wrote "Evil Bastard" on Dylan's cross. The crowd didn't like it. Then she wrote it again. Two teenage girls approached her; crying, they begged her to stop. Someone began singing "Amazing Grace." Soon much of the hillside was belting out the refrain. The woman left.

"The crosses ask an implicit question," *Rocky Mountain News* columnist Mike Littwin wrote. "Are you ready to forgive? When I first saw the crosses and understood what they meant, I wondered if it was too soon even to ask that question. Most people wouldn't have defaced the cross, but many would have been tempted. Do those crosses defile what has become sacred ground?"

Hell yes, Brian Rohrbough said. Just when he thought the pain couldn't get any worse, some jerk had raised a shrine to his son's murderer. Who could be that cruel?

Despite the flare-ups, controversy was the exception. One woman marveled at the forgiveness in her community. "How many other places would allow this and not have taken [Eric and Dylan's crosses] out of the ground already?" she asked.

Saturday's edition of the *Rocky* led with a three-word headline: DAD DESTROYS CROSSES. A haunting photo captured thirteen remaining tributes, with two stark gaps. Eric and Dylan's crosses had lasted three days.

"You don't cheapen what Christ did for us by honoring murderers with crosses," Brian said. "There's nowhere in the Bible that says to forgive an unrepentant murderer. Most Christians don't know that. These fools have come out saying 'Forgive everyone.' You don't repent, you don't forgive them—that's what the Bible says."

Rohrbough divided the community. Some people understood his anger. Others found his response a little harsh. "People need to learn to forgive," a woman on the hill told the *Rocky*. But then she thought for a moment. "I can understand his rage."

Brian's first response was not to destroy the two crosses. He initially affixed each one with a sign saying "Murderers burn in hell."

The park district took them down. Officials said they had also removed a teddy bear smeared with ketchup and were prohibiting anything obscene.

Brian conferred with his ex-wife, Sue, and her husband, Rich Petrone. They agreed to a united front on everything. Rich called several officials: Sheriff Stone; Dave Thomas, the DA; and the man in charge of the parks department.

"The three of them said those crosses shouldn't be there; we're going to take them down—give us until tomorrow at five and we promise you they'll be gone," Brian said. He and the Petrones went to the hill at five and nothing had happened. "So we decided, let's just go take care of this," Brian said. "We don't need to put up with this stuff."

Brian wanted those symbols out, and he wanted the world to see it. He called CNN and a crew filmed it. "It wasn't going be done in darkness," Brian said.

Brian and the Petrones hauled the crosses away, hacked them into little pieces, and then tossed the rubble into a Dumpster.

"We got back and we were sitting there talking about it, and the phone rings," Brian recalled. "It was Thomas: 'Just give us a little more time.' And Rich says, 'Nope, we've already taken care of it.'"

Brian took charge of his tragedy that day. He discovered the power of being Danny Rohrbough's dad. From that day forward, he would not hesitate to wield it.

But this particular battle was just getting under way. The carpenter drove back from Chicago and pulled out the thirteen remaining crosses. Now Brian Rohrbough was really fuming. The cruelest man of the aftermath had returned to tear down the monument to his son. Rohrbough also sensed opportunism. "I question his motives," he said.

Brian had good instincts. The carpenter had made a family business out of similar stunts. He returned with a new set of crosses, and a pack of media on his heels. The highlight was a joint appearance with Brian on *The Today Show*. The showman apologized profusely and offered a series of solemn vows: he would never build another cross for the killers, or for *any* killer, and he would drive around the country removing several he had erected in the past.

He broke every promise. He built fifteen new crosses and took them on a national tour. He milked his celebrity for years. Brian Rohrbough returned to cursing him: "The opportunist, the great [carpenter], the most hateful, despicable person who would come to someone else's tragedy."

The world forgot the carpenter. Few had noted his name. Most never knew what a huckster he was, or the lies he told, or the pain he inflicted. But they remember his crosses fondly. They recall the comfort that they found.

Eric was a thief now. He had a set of Rent-a-Fence signs. He liked the feeling, he wanted more. Junior year, the boys got right to work. Eric and Dylan and Zack hacked into the school computer and commandeered a list of locker combinations. They began breaking in. They got sloppy. On October 2, 1997, they got caught. They were sent to the dean, who suspended them for three days.

The Harris and Klebold parents responded the way they always did. Wayne Harris was a pragmatist. He would make Eric regret what he'd done. With outsiders he was focused on containment; Eric's future was at stake. He called the dean and argued that Eric was a minor. The dean was unmoved. What would show up on Eric's records? Wayne asked. He jotted down the answer in his journal: "In-house only because police were not involved. Destroyed upon graduation." Good. Eric had a promising future ahead.

The Klebolds addressed the situation intellectually. Dylan had demonstrated a shocking lapse of ethics, but Tom disagreed with suspensions on philosophical grounds. There were more effective ways to discipline a child. The dean had rarely met such a thoughtful, intelligent parent, but the judgment stood.

Eric and Dylan were each grounded for a month and were forbidden contact with each other or with Zack. Eric also lost his computer privileges. Eric and Dylan weathered the punishment and remained close. Zack began drifting away, particularly from Eric. The tight threesome was over. From that day forward, Eric and Dylan committed their crimes as a pair.

Fuselier considered Eric's psychological state at this point, a year and a half before the murders. Eric was not a depressive like Dylan, that was for sure.

And there were no signs of mental illness. No signs of anything to predict murder. Eric's Web site was obscenely angry, but anger and young men were practically synonymous. The instincts that would lead to Columbine were surely in place by now, but Eric had yet to reveal them.

———

Dylan fixated on Harriet. Fifty minutes a day, for one class period, Dylan lolled around in heaven. Harriet was in his class.

Sometimes she would laugh. What a darling little laugh she let out. So innocent, so pure. Innocence—what an angelic quality. Someday Dylan would speak to her.

One day Dylan saw his chance. He had a group project for the class, a report to work on together, and Harriet was on his team. Blessed day. This was it.

He did nothing.

Dylan described his trajectory as a downward spiral. He borrowed the phrase from Nine Inch Nails's gripping concept album, which documents a fictional man unraveling. It climaxes with him killing himself with a gun to the mouth.

Oliver Stone's satirical film *Natural Born Killers* would become the pop culture artifact most associated with the Columbine massacre. That was reasonable, since Eric and Dylan used "NBK" as shorthand for their own event, and the film bears considerable resemblances. It also captured the flavor of Eric's egotistical, empathy-free attitude, but it bore no relation to Dylan's psyche. It certainly wasn't where he saw his life headed, at least not until the final months. For the first eighteen to twenty months of his journal, Dylan identified with two powerful characters to convey his torment: the protagonists of *The Downward Spiral* and David Lynch's film *Lost Highway*.

After the murders, controversies raged about the role of violent films, music, and video games. Some columnists and talk-radio hosts saw an easy cause and effect. That seems simplistic for Eric—who was a gifted critical thinker with a voracious appetite for the classics—and absurd for his partner. Dylan identified with depressives on the brink of suicide. He focused on fictional characters mired in the hopelessness he already felt.

———

Eric got sloppy. He allowed the worst imaginable person to discover one of his pipe bombs: his dad.

Wayne Harris was beside himself. Firecrackers were one thing, but this was too much. He wasn't even sure what to do with it. Eric told several friends about the incident, and their accounts of Wayne's response varied. Zack Heckler said Wayne could not figure out how to defuse the bomb, so he went outside with Eric and detonated it. But Nate Dykeman said Wayne had merely confiscated the bomb. Sometime later, Eric took Nate into his parents' bedroom closet and showed it to him. Wayne Harris never referred to the incident in his journal on Eric, which was dormant at this time.

Eric swore up and down to his parents that he would never make a bomb again. They apparently believed him. They wanted to. Eric probably shut down production for a while, and he definitely covered his tracks better. Eventually, he got back to business. At some point, he showed Nate two or three of his later products, which he was storing in his own room.

———

Dylan felt abandoned. He was grounded for the locker scam, home alone, and lonelier than ever. Then his older brother, Byron, was kicked out for drugs. Tom and Sue understood the tough love would cause an upheaval, so they went to family counseling with Dylan. That didn't change their son's outlook. He got a new room out of it, and he put his own stamp on the place: two black walls and two red ones, posters of baseball heroes and rock bands: Lou Gehrig, Roger Clemens, and Nine Inch Nails. Also, some street signs and a woman in a leopard bikini.

"I get more depressed with each day," he complained. Why did friends keep deserting him? They did not, actually, but Dylan perceived it that way. He fretted about Eric dumping him, too. "wanna die," he repeated. Death equaled freedom now; death offered tranquillity. He began using the words interchangeably.

Then he weighed the other option: He named a friend and said he "will get me a gun, ill go on my killing spree against anyone I want."

It was Dylan's second allusion to murder. The first had been ambiguous; this was overt. And now it was a spree.

He changed the subject immediately. That was unusual. As a rule, Dylan hammered ideas relentlessly. He would drill for two straight pages on the "Everlasting Struggle" or his destiny as a seeker. Murder was different. For the second time, he tossed in a single line, at the peak of despair, and promptly returned to his own destruction.

The idea was germinating, a year and a half out. Dylan appeared to be exploring a spree. With Eric? Probably. But the details of this critical moment are lost. Neither boy ever mentions those conversations in the paper trail they left behind. Eric recorded his actions: he was building bigger bombs. Coincidence? Unlikely. Eric's thinking had been evolving steadily in one direction since freshman year.

Late in 1997, Eric took notice of school shooters. "Every day news broadcasts stories of students shooting students, or going on killing sprees," he wrote. He researched the possibilities for an English paper. Guns were cheap and readily available, he discovered. *Gun Digest* said you could get a Saturday night special for $69. And schools were easy targets. "It is just as easy to bring a loaded handgun to school as it is to bring a calculator," Eric wrote.

"Ouch!" his teacher responded in the margin. Overall, he rated it "thorough & logical. Nice job."

The last day of school before Christmas, something extraordinary happened. Dylan's true love waved at him. Finally! Dylan was ecstatic; then he began to wonder. Had she waved? At him? Maybe not. Probably not. Definitely not. Just delusional, he decided. Again.

He sat down and considered who loved him. He listed their names on a page in his journal. He drew little hearts beside three. Nineteen people. Nineteen failures.

A few weeks later, Eric made it with a real woman. Brenda was almost twenty-three. She had no idea he was sixteen. "He acted a lot older," she said. When he told her he was in school, she took it to mean college. They met at the mall, and he drove to her house. They started going out: bowling, drag racing, driving into the mountains to get drunk. He taught her about the computer, he told her how great she looked, and she could not have been more charmed. She described it to reporters later as "a friendship but more than a friendship."

Sometimes Dylan would hang out with them. He was too shy to speak.

Eric and Dylan got cockier. They stole more valuable merchandise and started testing their pipe bombs. Outwardly, they seemed like responsible kids. Teachers trusted them and granted them access to the computer closet. They helped themselves to expensive equipment. At some point, Eric may have started a credit card scam. In his notebook, he listed eight steps to complete the scam, though there's no evidence that he carried them out. He later claimed he had.

Dylan was no good at deception. He kept getting caught. Eric did not. Tom Klebold noticed Dylan had a new laptop. Eric could have weaseled out of that one without missing a beat—*it was a friend's...he'd checked it out of the computer lab.* Dylan just confessed. His dad made him turn himself in. Eric and Dylan both had a penchant for picking on underclassmen, but Dylan got caught. In January 1998, he got sent to the dean for scratching a slur about "fags" onto a freshman's locker. He got another suspension and paid $70 to get the locker fixed.

The boys were shooting off their pipe bombs by then, and man, were those things badass. They bragged to Nate Dykeman and then brought him along for a demo. Eric was in charge where bombs were concerned, so everything went according to plan. They waited until Super Bowl Sunday, when the streets of metro Denver were deserted. The Broncos were underdogs in their fifth shot at the championship, and everyone was watching the game. Eric took advantage of the lull. He brought Nate and Dylan out to a quiet spot near his house, dropped the bomb in a culvert, and let her rip. *Whoa!* Nate was appropriately impressed.

On January 30, three days after Dylan's meeting with the dean, a crime of opportunity presented itself. It was a Friday night, and the boys were restless.

Eric and Dylan drove out into the country, pulled onto a gravel strip, and got out to break stuff. There was a van parked there, with lots of electronic gizmos inside. How cool would it be to steal it? The boys had no idea what they might use the stuff for, but they were sure they could get away with it. No witnesses and no fingerprints. Eric had a pair of ski gloves to mask detection.

"Everything seemed so easy," he wrote later. "No way we would get caught." Eric took guard duty and gave Dylan the dirty work. Dylan put one ski glove on and tried to punch out a window. They had no idea how solid a car window was. He hit it again and again. Nothing. Eric took over.

Just as useless. Dylan went for a rock. He hauled up a boulder, hurled it into the glass, and even that was deflected. It took several blows before the rock crashed through. Dylan put the other glove on, reached in to unlock the door, and started digging through the pile like crazy. Eric again left Dylan to commit the act. He ran back to man the getaway car. Dylan grabbed anything that looked interesting. He flung everything else all over the van. By his count, he nabbed "one briefcase, one black pouch, one flashlight, a yellow thing, and a bucket of stuff."

Dylan ran armloads of loot back to the Honda. Eric continued to "guard." Another car approached. Dylan froze; the car passed. Unfazed, Dylan ran back to grab more. Eric had grown wary. "That's enough!" he ordered. "Let's go."

They drove deeper into the country, over the hogback, to Deer Creek Canyon Park, a vast preserve that ran for miles up into the mountains. The park was deserted; it closed an hour after nightfall, and the sun had set four hours ago. They pulled into the parking lot, killed the engine, and checked out the take.

They cranked some tunes to enjoy themselves, then flipped on the dome light to hunt for another CD. Dylan reached back and hauled out his favorite item: a $400 voltmeter, the yellow thing with buttons along the base and black and red probes hanging off it. Dylan poked at the buttons; Eric watched intently. When the meter lit up, the boys went wild. Cool! Dylan pulled out the flashlight and switched it on. "Wow!" Eric howled. "That is really bright!" Then he spotted something cooler: "Hey, we've got a Nintendo game pad!"

They rummaged a bit more before Eric realized they had grown sloppy: time to resume precautions. "We better put this stuff in the trunk," he said. He popped the latch and stepped out.

That's when Jeffco Sheriff's Deputy Timothy Walsh decided to make his presence known. He had been standing outside the car for several minutes, watching and listening to the entire exchange. You can see for miles out in the country; a lone vehicle in an empty lot in a closed state park just asked for intervention. The boys had been so immersed, they'd failed to see his car, hear his engine or his footsteps, or notice his tall frame looming right over the rear window.

When Eric stepped out, Deputy Walsh blinded him with a flashlight beam. What were they up to? the deputy asked. Whose property was all this? "Right then I realized what a damn fool I was," Eric wrote later. He would claim remorse, but he didn't show any, even then.

Eric thought fast but lied poorly. He was off his game that night. He said they had been messing around in a parking lot near town and had stumbled onto the equipment stacked neatly in the grass. He gave a precise location and described it vividly. Details were the key to a good lie. Good tactics, bad choice: he depicted the actual robbery location.

Walsh was incredulous. He asked to see the property. "Sure," Eric said. He kept playing it cool. He kept doing the talking. Dylan shut up and went along. Walsh had the boys stack the goods on the trunk and tried again: Where did you find this property? Dylan summoned up his nerve. He parroted Eric's story. Walsh said it looked suspicious. He would radio another deputy to check on any break-ins.

Eric was confident. He looked over at his partner. Dylan folded.

Wayne and Kathy Harris were waiting when Eric arrived at the police station. Tom and Sue Klebold were close behind. They couldn't believe their boys could do something like this. The boys could be charged with three felonies, including a Class V, which carried up to a $100,000 fine and one to three years in prison. Eric and Dylan were questioned separately. With their parents' consent, they waived their rights. Each boy gave oral and written statements. Eric blamed Dylan. "Dylan suggested that we should steal some of the objects in the white van," he wrote. "at first I was very uncomfortable and questioning with the thought." His verbal account was more adamant. He said Dylan looked into the van and asked, "Should we break into it and steal it? It would be nice to steal some stuff in there. Should we do it?" Eric claimed he responded, "Hell no." He said Dylan kept pestering him and eventually wore him down.

Dylan accepted joint blame. "Almost at the same time, we both got the idea of breaking into this white van," he said.

The boys were taken to county jail. They were fingerprinted, photographed, and booked. Then they were released into the custody of four furious parents.

36. Conspiracy

After the murders, the detective team sought convictions. It had three possible crimes to uncover: participation in the attack, participation in the planning, or guilty knowledge. At first it looked easy. The killers had been sloppy; they hadn't even tried to cover their tracks. And the primary living suspects were juveniles. Most of the friends had withheld something crucial: Robyn had helped purchase three of the guns, Chris and Nate had seen pipe bombs, and Chris and Zack had heard about napalm. They all broke quickly. They were kids; it was easy. But they broke only so far. They admitted to knowing details, but claimed to be clueless about the plan.

Detectives pushed harder. The suspects didn't push back; they just threw up their hands. Fuselier had several solid agents on the case. He knew they could sniff out a liar. *How are the suspects responding?* he asked. *Do they seem deceptive?* Not at all. His team leader described them as wide-eyed and understandably anxious. Most had begun by hiding something, and it had been painfully obvious. They were awful actors. But once they spilled it, they just seemed relieved. They were calm, peaceful—all the signs of someone coming clean. Most of the suspects agreed to polygraphs. That usually meant they had nothing left to hide.

Two friends, Robert Perry and Joe Stair, had been identified by witnesses as shooters or at least present at the scene. They were both tall and lanky—and therefore matched a common description for Dylan. Both boys produced alibis. Perry's was shaky: he had been sleeping downstairs until his grandmother woke him with news of the shooting. He said he walked upstairs, stumbled out onto the porch, and cried. Did anyone see him, other than his grandmother? No, he didn't think so. But Perry had been seen by others—he'd just been too upset to notice them. Within a week, a neighbor who was interviewed described driving up around noon and seeing Perry crying just the way he'd described.

The physical evidence was even less damning. All the friends' houses were searched. No weapons were found. No ammo, no ordnance, no refuse of any pipe bomb assembly. Zack had a copy of *The Anarchist Cookbook,* but there was no sign that he had used it to build anything. Fingerprints at the crime scene were all a bust. There was an extraordinary amount of material: guns, ammo, gear, unused pipe bombs, strips of duct tape, and dozens of components from the big bombs. All of it was covered with the killers' prints; nobody else's. The same was true at the killers' houses: nothing on the journals, videotapes, camcorders, or bomb-assembly gear. No one appeared in the killers' records. Eric had been a meticulous planner and recorder of dates, locations, and receipts. Detectives searched the stores' files and credit card records. All signs indicated that the killers had purchased everything.

For months, Sheriff Stone publicly espoused a conspiracy theory. Fuselier could feel the conspiracy slipping away the first week. Within two, he knew it was remote. The most telling evidence came from the killers themselves. In their journals and videos, they cop to everything. They never mention outside involvement, except, derisively, when they talk about hapless dupes. The killers leaked their plans in countless way, but there's no indication that anyone close to them ever breathed a word. Their friends' e-mails, IMs, day planners, and journals were searched, along with every paper the investigators could find; there was no sign that any of the friends had known.

Rumors about a third shooter have continued right up to the present day, but publicly, it didn't take long for investigators to put them to rest. Eric and Dylan were correctly identified by witnesses who knew them. No one else turned up on the surveillance videos or the 911 audio. Witnesses' accounts were remarkably consistent about a tall shooter and a short one—but there seemed to be two of each: two in T-shirts and two in trench coats. "As soon as I learned Eric's coat was left outside on the landing, I knew what had happened there," Fuselier said. Witnesses exchanged stories, and reports of two guys in T-shirts and two in trench coats quickly turned into four shooters. Dylan's decision to leave his coat on until he reached the library made for more combinations, and the number multiplied over the afternoon. The killers also lobbed pipe bombs in every direction. Their gunfire shattered windows and ricocheted off walls, ductwork, and stairs. Many kids heard crashes or explosions and positively identified the location as the source of activity rather than the destination. Several witnesses insisted that they had spotted a gunman on the roof. What they had seen was a maintenance man adjusting the air-conditioning unit.

So what accounted for all the confusion? "Eyewitness testimony, in general, is not very accurate," one investigator explained. "Put that together with gunshots going off and just the most terrifying situation in their life, what they remember now may not be anywhere near what really happened." Human memory can be erratic. We tend to record fragments: gunshots, explosions, trench coats, terror, sirens, screams. Images come back jumbled, but we crave coherence, so we trim them, adjust details, and assemble everything together in a story that makes sense. We record vivid details, like the scraggly ponytail flapping against the dirty blue T-shirt of the boy fleeing just ahead. All the way out of the building, a witness may focus on that swishing hair. Later, she remembers a glimpse of the killer: he was tall and lanky—did he have scraggly hair? It fits together, and she connects it. Soon the killer is wearing the dirty blue T-shirt as well. Moments later, and forever after, she is convinced that's exactly what she saw.

Investigators identified nearly a dozen common misperceptions among library survivors. Distortion of time was rampant, particularly chronology. Witnesses recalled less once the killers approached them, not more. Terror stops the brain from forming new memories. A staggering number insisted they were the last ones out of the library—once they were out, it was over. Similarly, most of those injured, even superficially, believed they were the last ones hit. Survivors also clung to reassuring concepts: that they were actually hiding by crouching under tables in plain sight.

Memory is notoriously unreliable. It happens even with the best witnesses. Six years later, Principal DeAngelis described the shooting as if he had just experienced it. He retraced his steps through the building, pausing at the exact spot where he first saw Dylan Klebold fire his shotgun. Mr. D pointed out Dylan's position and described everything Dylan was wearing: white T-shirt, military harness, ball cap turned around backward. But he has two entirely different versions of how he got there.

In one version, he learned of the shooting in his office. That was unusual: normally he would have been in the midst of the cafeteria hubbub. But Tuesday he was held up by an appointment. He had a meeting with a young teacher working on a one-year contract. Mr. D had been happy with the teacher's performance and was about to offer him a permanent position. They had just shaken hands and sat down when Frank's secretary's face slammed into the glass on the top half of his door. She had run to warn him so frantically that she'd failed to turn the knob completely and had hurtled right into the door. A moment later, she burst in shouting.

"Frank! They're shooting!"

"What?"

"Gunshots! Downstairs, there are gunshots!"

He bolted up. They ran out together—into the main foyer, just past the huge hanging trophy case. Dylan fired, and the case shattered behind Frank.

It was two or three years after the fact that Frank's secretary recounted that version for him. He told her she was nuts. He had no memory of that.

"In my version, I'm walking out calmly going to lunch," he said. "We've finished the meeting, I've offered him the job. He's happy."

DeAngelis had planned to offer the job. He liked the teacher and had pictured his joyful acceptance. Mentally, it had already happened. The actual events—gunfire in the hallway, his charge toward the girls' gym class, and the desperation to hide them—wiped out everything in his mental vicinity. His secretary's appearance was unimportant, and it conflicted with his "memory" of offering the job. One memory had to go.

Mr. D checked with the teacher. No job offer—they'd just sat down. Other witnesses had seen him run alongside his secretary. He came to accept that version of the truth, but he can't picture it. His visual brain insists that the false memory is real. Multiply that by nearly two thousand kids and over a hundred teachers and a precisely accurate picture was impossible to render.

———

Investigators went back to interview the killers' closest friends several times. Each new interview and lead would raise more questions about the killers' associates. Sometimes new evidence revealed lies.

An FBI agent interviewed Kristi Epling the day after the murders. Kristi was connected to both killers, particularly Eric. They were close, and she was dating his buddy Nate Dykeman. She didn't seem to know much, though. Her FBI report was brief and unremarkable. She said Nate was in shock, the TCM connection was silly, and Eric had probably been the leader. Kristi did not mention any of his notes in her possession.

Like most of the killers' friends, Kristi was exceptionally smart; she was headed to college on an academic scholarship. She played it cool about the notes during her FBI interview, then mailed them to a friend in St. Louis who was unconnected to Columbine and unlikely to be questioned. Kristi was careful: no return address on the envelope. The friend went to the police. She did not inform Kristi.

The pages included notes passed back and forth between Kristi and Eric in German class—a rambling conversation, conducted in German. They mentioned a hit list. That was old news to investigators—most of the school was on one of Eric's lists. But they had withheld that information from the public. Kristi had been hiding it; maybe she was hiding more. Detectives returned to question her. They asked about German class, and Kristi said she had exchanged notes with Eric but had thrown them away months ago. She assured them repeatedly that Eric had never made any threats. She would have told a teacher, she insisted. Kristi also said Nate had fled to Florida, to stay with his father and avoid the media hounds. They had talked on the phone that morning.

The detectives asked Kristi what should happen to someone who had helped the killers. "They should go to jail forever," she said. "It was a horrible thing." And what about someone who withheld information after the attack? "I don't know," Kristi said. "It would depend on what it was." They should probably get counseling, she suggested, but some sort of punishment, too.

They asked again: Did she know anything more? No. Had she destroyed any notes from Eric? No. They kept repeating the questions, assuring her that she could disclose anything now without repercussions. No, there was nothing. They continued questioning her, repeated that offer, and finally she went for it. OK, there were notes, she admitted. And Nate was not in Florida; he was staying with her. He was there in the house right now. She said the notes had been very painful to hold on to but she did not want to destroy them. If she could just get them somewhere far, far away, she hoped to retrieve them someday when everything was more clear.

Once she copped to the truth, Kristi was forthcoming. She agreed to turn over her PC and her e-mail accounts and to take a polygraph. Beyond that, she didn't know anything significant. She told them about some things

Nate had confessed to, but detectives knew about them already. Kristi had just been afraid. She'd thought she had something incriminating, and she'd panicked. No evidence of a conspiracy. Another dead end.

Nevertheless, Dr. Fuselier learned a great deal from the German conversation. It revolved around Kristi's new boyfriend; she'd had a short-lived romance with a sophomore named Dan. Eric couldn't believe she was going out with that little fuck. *Why, what was wrong with Dan?* she asked. For one thing, the prettyboy had punched him in the face last year, Eric said. Eric, in a fistfight? That surprised her. He always seemed so rational. He got mad when kids made fun of his black clothes or all his German crap, but he always kept his cool. He would calmly figure out how to get even.

Kristi worried about Eric getting even. She asked her boyfriend about it, and he said he was afraid Eric might kill him.

Kristi decided to play peace broker. She took it up with Eric in German class again. She told him straight out how scared Dan was. She used the phrase "kill him." That made Eric nervous. He was in the juvenile Diversion program because of the van break-in, and threats like that could get him in trouble. Kristi said she'd be careful about it. But how could Dan make it up to him?

How about if he let me punch him in the face, Eric suggested. *Seriously?* Seriously.

Dr. Fuselier was not surprised by the notes. Very cold-blooded. Any kid could get in a fight. Dan had gotten really angry, and in the heat of a fistfight had clocked Eric. Eric was planning his punch. He wanted Dan to stand there defenseless and let him do it. Complete power over the kid. That's what Eric craved.

As the conspiracy theory crumbled, far from the eyes of the public, a new motive emerged. The jock-feud theory was accepted as the underlying driver, but that had supposedly gone on for a year. What made the killers snap? Nine days after the murders, the media found yet another trigger. The Marines. The *New York Times* and the *Washington Post* broke the story on April 29. The rest of the media piled on quickly.

They learned that Eric had been talking to a Marine recruiter during the last few weeks of his life. They also discovered he'd been taking the prescription antidepressant Luvox—something that would typically disqualify him (because it implied depression). A Defense Department spokesman verified that the recruiter had learned about the medication and rejected Eric. The media was off to the races, again.

Luvox added an extra wrinkle, as it functioned as an anger suppressant. The *Times* cited unnamed friends of Eric's as saying that "they believe that he may have tried to stop taking the drug, perhaps because of his rejection by the Marines, five days before he and his best friend, Dylan Klebold, stormed onto the Columbine campus with guns and bombs."

The story added a bit of evidence that seemed to confirm it: "the coroner's office said no drugs or alcohol had been found in Mr. Harris's body in an autopsy, but it would not specify whether the body had been screened for Luvox." It was finally coming together: the Marines rejected Eric, he quit the Luvox to fuel his rage, he grabbed a gun and started killing. It all fit.

Fuselier read the stories. He shuddered. All the conclusions were reasonable—and wrong. Eric's body had not initially been screened for Luvox. Later it had: he'd remained on a full dose, right up to his death. And investigators had talked to the Marine recruiter the morning after the murders. He had determined Eric was ineligible. But Eric had never known.

By this time, Fuselier had already read Eric's journal and seen the Basement Tapes. He knew what the media did not. There had been no trigger.

———

April 30, officials met with the Klebolds and several attorneys to discuss ground rules for a series of interviews. Kate Battan was aggravated that she could not question the family directly. So she asked them to tell her about their son. They were still dumbfounded. They described a normal teenage boy: extraordinarily shy but happy. Dylan was coping well with adolescence and developing into a responsible young adult. They entrusted him with major decisions when he could articulate his rationale. Teachers loved him and so did other kids. He was gentle and sensitive until the day he died. Sue could recall seeing Dylan cry only once. He came home from school upset, and went up to his room. He pulled a box of stuffed animals out of the closet, dumped them out, burrowed under, and fell asleep surrounded. He never did reveal what disturbed him.

His parents granted Dylan a measure of privacy in his own room. The last time Tom recalled being in there was about two weeks before the murders, to turn off the computer Dylan left on. Otherwise, they monitored

Dylan's life aggressively, and forbade him from hanging out with bad influences.

Tom said he was extremely close to Dylan. They shared Rockies season tickets with three other families, and on his nights, Tom usually took one of his sons. Tom and Dylan hung out all the time together. They played a lot of sports until Tom developed arthritis in the mid-1990s. Now it was a lot of chess, computers, and working on Dylan's BMW. They built a set of custom speakers together. Dylan didn't like doing repair work with Tom, though, and sometimes he got testy and snapped off one-word responses. That was normal. Tom considered Dylan his best friend.

Dylan had a handful of tight buddies, his parents said: Zack and Nate, and of course Eric, who was definitely closest. Chris Morris seemed like more of an acquaintance. Dylan had fun with Robyn Anderson—a sweet girl—but definitely nothing romantic. He hadn't had a girlfriend yet, but had been kind of group dating. His friends seemed happy. They sure did laugh a lot. They were always polite and seemed laid back—pretty immune to social pressure, they said.

Eric was the quietest of the group. Tom and Sue never felt they knew what was going on in that head. Eric was always respectful, though. They were aware Judy Brown had a different opinion. "Judy doesn't like a lot of people," Sue said.

Tom and Sue didn't perceive Eric to be leading or following their son. But they did notice that he got angry at Dylan when he "screwed something up."

Before they left, detectives asked the Klebolds if they had any questions. Yes. They asked to read anything Dylan had written. Anything to understand.

Battan left frustrated. "I didn't get to ask any questions," she said later. "All I got was a fluff piece on their son." She documented the interview, which remained sealed for eighteen months. The series of interviews never occurred. Lawyers demanded immunity from prosecution before they would talk. Jeffco officials refused. The Harrises took the same position. Battan didn't even get a fluff piece from them.

———

While Battan interviewed the Klebolds, the National Rifle Association convened in Denver. It was a ghastly coincidence. Mayor Wellington Webb begged the group to cancel its annual convention, scheduled long before. Angry barbs had flown back and forth all week. "We don't want you here," Mayor Webb finally said.

Other promoters gave in to similar demands. Marilyn Manson had been incorrectly linked to the killers. He canceled his concert at Red Rocks and the remainder of his national tour. The NRA show went on. Four thousand attended. Three thousand protesters met them. They massed on the capitol steps, marched to the convention site, and formed a human chain around the Adam's Mark Hotel. Many waved "Shame on the NRA" signs. One placard was different. Tom Mauser's said "My son Daniel died at Columbine. He'd expect me to be here today."

Tom was a shy, quiet man. It had been a rough week, and friends weren't sure he was up to public confrontation. "He had a tough, tough day yesterday," one coworker said.

But Tom drew a deep breath, let it out, and addressed the crowd. "Something is wrong in this country when a child can grab a gun so easily and shoot a bullet into the middle of a child's face," he said. He urged them not to let Daniel's death be in vain.

Tom had been struck by another coincidence. In early April, Daniel had taken an interest in gun control and had come to his father with a question: Did Tom know there were loopholes in the Brady Bill? Gun shows were excluded from the mandatory background checks. Two weeks later, Daniel was murdered by a gun acquired at one of those shows.

"Clearly it was a sign to me," Tom explained later.

Critics had already blasted Tom for profiting off his son's murder, or getting duped by gun control activists. "I assure you, I am not being exploited," he told the crowd.

Inside the Adam's Mark, NRA president Charlton Heston opened the show. He went straight at Mayor Webb. The crowd booed. "Get out of our country, Wellington Webb!" someone yelled. Conventioneers were amused.

Heston charged on. "They say, 'Don't come here,'" he said. "I guess what saddens me most is how it suggests complicity. It implies that you and I and eighty million honest gun owners are somehow to blame, that we don't care as much as they, or that we don't deserve to be as shocked and horrified as every other soul in America mourning for the people of Littleton. 'Don't come here.' That's offensive. It's also absurd."

The group observed a moment of silence for the Columbine victims. It then proceeded with the welcome ceremony. Traditionally, the oldest and youngest attendees are officially recognized at that time. The youngest is typically a child. "Given the unusual circumstances," Heston announced that the tradition would be suspended this year.

———

When the conspiracy evaporated, it left a dangerous vacuum. Dr. Fuselier saw the danger early on. "Once we understood there was no third shooter, I realized that for everyone, it was going to be difficult to get closure," he said. The final act of the killers was among their cruelest: they deprived the survivors of a living perpetrator. They deprived the families of a focus for their anger, and their blame. There would be no cathartic trial for the victims. There was no killer to rebuke in a courtroom, no judge to implore to impose the maximum penalty. South Jeffco was seething with anger, and it would be deprived of a reasonable target. Displaced anger would riddle the community for years.

The crumbling conspiracy eliminated the primary mission of the task force. The all-star team was left to sort out logistical issues: exactly *what* had happened, and *how*. Those were massive investigations, easy to get lost inside. Investigators wanted to retrace every step, reconstruct each moment, place every witness and every buckshot fragment in place and time and context. It was a Herculean effort, and it drew the team's attention from the real objective: *Why?* The families wanted to know how their children died, of course, but that was nothing compared to the underlying question.

Early on, officials began to say the report would steer clear of conclusions. "We deal with facts," Division Chief Kiekbusch said. "We'll make a diligent effort not to include a bunch of conclusions. Here are the facts: You read it and make your own conclusions."

The families were incredulous. So was the press. *Make our own conclusions? How many civilians felt qualified to diagnose mass murderers? Isn't that what homicide detectives were for?* The public was under the impression that a hundred of them had been paid for months to perform that service.

Of course homicide teams draw conclusions. What Kiekbusch meant was that they avoid *discussing* those conclusions externally. That's the DA's role. The cops develop the case, but the DA presents it to the jury—and to the public, as necessary. But aside from the gun providers, there was no one to try for the Columbine killings.

———

Sheriff Stone kept talking up the conspiracy theory with the press. He was driving his team nuts. They had all but ruled it out. Every few days, Jeffco spokesmen corrected another misstatement by the sheriff. Several corrections were extreme: arrests were *not* imminent, deputies had not blocked the killers from escaping the school, and Stone's descriptions of the cafeteria videos had been pure conjecture—the tapes had not even been analyzed yet. They did not try to correct some of his mischaracterizations, like when he quoted Eric's journal out of context to give the impression that the killers had been planning to hijack a plane when they'd started their attack. He was quickly becoming a laughingstock, yet he was the ultimate ranking authority on the case.

His staff begged him to stop speaking to the press. But how would it look if subordinates spoke about the case while the head man was muzzled? A tacit understanding developed on the team: if Stone kept his mouth shut, they would, too. (Though they continued background interviews with the *Rocky*.) For the next five months, until an impromptu interview by lead investigator Kate Battan in September, law enforcement officers would divulge virtually nothing more publicly about their discoveries or conclusions. After that, it would be a slow trickle, and a fight for every scrap of information. Nine days after the shootings, the Jeffco blackout began.

———

Columbine coverage ended abruptly, too. A string of deadly tornadoes hit Oklahoma, and the national press corps left town in a single afternoon. The school would return periodically to national headlines over the years, but the narrative of what had happened was set.

37. Betrayed

Eric needed professional help. His father made that determination within forty-eight hours of his arrest. Wayne picked up the steno pad that had sat idle for nine months and began filling half a dozen pages: "See psychologist," he wrote. "See what's going on. Determine treatment." Wayne gathered names and numbers for several agencies and services and added bulleted items to them: anger management, life management, professional therapist, mental health center, school counselor, juvenile assessment center, and family adolescent team. Wayne documented several conversations with lawyers. He wrote "probation," circled it, and added, "take any chances for reformation or <u>diversion</u>."

Wayne checked out half a dozen candidates for therapist. Their rates varied from $100 to $150 per hour. He settled on Dr. Kevin Albert, a psychiatrist, and made an appointment for February 16.

Wayne logged page after page of calls to cops, lawyers, and prosecutors, working through their options. The juvenile Diversion program sounded ideal: a year of counseling and community service, along with fines, fees, and restitution. If Eric completed it successfully and kept clean for an additional year, the robbery would be expunged from his record. But the DA's office had to accept him.

Eric told Dr. Albert he had anger problems. Depression was an issue. He had contemplated suicide. He apparently did not mention the bombs he took to the park the previous evening. Dr. Albert started him on Zoloft, a prescription antidepressant. Eric continued meeting with him biweekly, and Wayne and Kathy began occasional sessions as well.

At home, the boys received similar punishments. Each was grounded for a month, and forbidden contact with the other. Eric also had his computer access revoked. He went to work on his pipe bombs. He lost one—or

214

perhaps left it as a warning or clue. On February 15, the day before Eric's first appointment with Dr. Albert, someone in the neighborhood stumbled upon his work: a duct-taped PVC pipe in the grass with a red fuse protruding. Kind of an odd sight for a suburban park in Jeffco. The Jeffco cops sent out an investigator from the bomb squad. Sure enough, it was a homemade pipe bomb. Officers didn't find a whole lot of those around here. The investigator defused the bomb and filed a report.

———

Eric and Dylan hid their arrest from friends. They made excuses about their restrictions. Finally they began to come clean. Eric fessed up to a girl at Blackjack, and word traveled to Nate Dykeman. Nate couldn't believe Dylan had been hiding it from him.

"Is this the reason you can't go out?" Nate asked. Dylan turned red.

"He didn't want to talk about it," Nate said later.

After word leaked, Eric told friends it was the most embarrassing moment of his life.

Both boys were humiliated. And Eric was raging mad. Dylan's response was more complex. Three days after his arrest, Dylan pictured himself on the road to happiness with Harriet. He sketched it out in his journal as a two-lane highway with a road sign off one shoulder and a dashed stripe down the center. His road led off to a majestic row of mountains, with a giant heart guiding him onward. "Its so great to love," he wrote. He was a felon now, but he was ecstatic. He filled half the page with drawings and exclamations: "I love her, & she loves me."

Anger boiled up with the ecstasy. Dylan was beginning to see it Eric's way: "the real people (gods) are slaves to the majority of zombies, but we know & love being superior.... either ill commit suicide, or ill get w Harriet & it will be NBK for us. My happiness. her happiness. <u>NOTHING</u> else matters."

Suicide or murder? The pattern solidified: homicidal thoughts occasionally, self-destruction on every page. "If, by love's choice, Harriet didn't love me id slit my wrist & blow up Atlanta strapped to my neck," he wrote. Eric had named one of his pipe bombs Atlanta.

———

Wayne Harris kept working the phones. By early March, he secured an evaluation with Andrea Sanchez, a counselor with the juvenile Diversion program. Sanchez placed calls to Eric and Dylan to prescreen them. They passed. She sent a dozen forms and set up appointments. Each boy would come to her office with a parent and the stack of paperwork. Both intake sessions would take place on March 19.

For two months, Wayne Harris worked to get his son into Diversion, to keep his record clean. Eric was busy, too. He was detonating his first pipe bombs. He boldly posted the breakthrough on his Web site: "Mother fucker blew BIG. Flipping thing was heart-pounding gut-wrenching brain-twitching ground-moving insanely cool! His brothers haven't found a target yet though."

This time, Eric was producing to kill. Contempt had been the undercurrent in his "I HATE" rants; now he made it explicit. Morons had nerve to judge him, he said. To call him crazy just for envisioning mass murder? Empty, vacuous morons standing in judgment? "if you got a problem with my thoughts, come tell me and ill kill you," he posted. "DEAD PEOPLE DON'T ARGUE! God DAMNIT I AM PISSED!!"

———

As Eric embraced murder, Dylan retreated. After the arrest, he had the one brief outburst in his journal, and then he dropped all mention of it for nearly a year. Dylan still fretted about "this toilet earth," but his focus shifted dramatically toward love. Love. It had been prominent from the first page of his journal, but now, a year in, it grew overwhelming. He emblazoned entire pages with ten-inch hearts, surrounded by choirs of smaller, fluttering hearts.

Eric had no use for love. Sex, maybe. He shared none of Dylan's desires for truth, beauty, or ethereal love. Eric's only internal struggle concerned which stupid bastard was more deserving of his wrath.

Eric's dreams changed after his arrest. Human extinction was still his aim, but for the first time he made the leap from observer to enforcer. "I will rig up explosives all over a town and detonate each one of them at will after I mow down a whole fucking area full of you snotty ass rich mother fucking high strung godlike attitude having worthless pieces of shit whores," he wrote. He posted this openly on his Web site. "i dont care if I live or die in the shootout," he wrote. "all I want to do is kill and injure as many of you pricks as I can!"

It was too much for Dylan. Kill? Everything? Apparently not. He made a stunning move behind Eric's back. He told. He told the worst possible person: Brooks Brown. Brooks knew about the petty vandalism, and his parents saw Eric as a young criminal, but they had no idea how serious it was.

On the way to class, Dylan handed Brooks a scrap of paper. Just one line was written on it: a Web address.

"I think you should take a look at this tonight," Dylan said.

"OK. Anything special?"

"It's Eric's Web site. You need to see it. And you can't tell Eric I gave it to you."

Brooks pulled up the site that night. Eric was threatening to kill people. He threatened to kill Brooks personally, in three different places.

Dylan leaked the URL to Brooks the day before their admission interviews for the Diversion program. If Brooks told his parents—and Dylan knew he told Judy *everything*—the Browns would go straight to the cops, and Eric would be rejected and imprisoned for a felony. Dylan probably would be, too. He took that chance.

Brooks did tell his mom. Randy and Judy called the cops. Jeffco investigators came out that night. They followed up, they filed reports, but they did not alert the DA's office. Eric and Dylan proceeded into Diversion.

Only one parent was required at the Diversion intake meeting. Tom and Sue Klebold both attended. They considered it important. They filled out an eight-page questionnaire about Dylan, he did the same, and then Andrea Sanchez walked them through the results. The Klebolds were in for a few surprises. Dylan copped to five or six drunken bouts, starting at age fifteen. "Was not aware of it <u>at all</u>—until Andrea Sanchez asked the question a few moments ago," his parents wrote. Apparently they were unaware his nickname was VoDKa.

Dylan claimed he had quit drinking. He didn't like the taste and said it "wasn't worth it." He had tried pot, too, and rejected it for the same reasons. His parents were stunned about marijuana, too.

Tom and Sue were candid; it was the only ethical course. "Dylan is introverted and has grown up isolated," they wrote. "He is often angry or sullen, and behaviors seem disrespectful to and intolerant of others." They wrote a line about disrespecting authority figures, crossed it out, and then said that teachers had reported that he didn't listen or take correction well.

Eric was more cautious. He revealed just enough to appear confessional. He said he had tasted alcohol three times, had never gotten drunk, and had given it up for good. Exactly what a parent wanted to hear. It was vintage Eric—more believable than abstinence and reassuring to boot: he had faced the temptation already and the danger had passed. He understood how his parents thought, and in no time he'd read Andrea Sanchez. In their first meeting, he turned an admission into a virtue. He lied about pot, too. He claimed he had no interest. The alcohol admission gave the claim credence.

Wayne and Kathy both attended their session as well. Their surprise came in the mental health section. On a checklist of thirty potential problem areas, they marked three boxes: anger, depression, and suicidal thoughts. Eric had told them about those three, and he discussed them with Dr. Albert. He was getting help. Everyone agreed the Zoloft was helping, too. It was common for an adolescent to check several boxes. Eric picked fourteen. He marked virtually everything related to distrust or aggression. He checked jealousy, anxiety, suspiciousness, authority figures, temper, racing thoughts, obsessive thoughts, mood swings, and disorganized thoughts. He skipped suicidal thoughts, but he checked homicidal thoughts.

Wayne and Kathy worried about Eric suppressing his anger. They admitted that he would blow up now and then—lashing out verbally or hitting an object. He never tried it in front of his dad, but they'd gotten reports back from work and school. It didn't happen often, but they were concerned. Eric responded well to discipline. They had controlled his behavior, but how could they contain his moods? When he really got mad, Eric said, he would punch a wall. He had thought about suicide, but never seriously, and mostly out of anger. He got angry all the time, he said, at almost anything he didn't like.

Eric was seething as he scrawled out his answers, and he practically told them so on the form. The nerve of these lowlifes judging him. He explained how he hated fools telling him what to do. In the interview, he apparently directed his anger at *other* fools. They fell for it.

Eric would howl about it later. The partial confession was his favorite con of all. He could turn over half his cards and still pull off the bluff.

He posted his actual thoughts about the legal system on his Web site at around this same time: "My belief is that if I say something, it goes. I am the law. If you don't like it, you die." He described going to some random downtown area in some big city and blowing up and shooting up everything he could. He assured us he would feel no remorse, no sorrow, no shame. Yet there he sat, submitting. He bent to their will; he filled out their degrading form. Laughing on the inside was insufficient. He would make them pay.

———

Sanchez worried about the boys' failure to accept full responsibility. Eric was sticking to his story that the break-in was Dylan's fault. Dylan thought the whole thing was a little overblown. Sanchez noted her reservations but recommended them for enrollment.

The final decision was up to the court. A week later, on March 25, Eric and Dylan stood before Jeffco Magistrate John DeVita during a joint hearing. Their fathers stood beside them. That impressed DeVita. Most of the juveniles appeared alone, or with just a mom. Dads were a good sign. And these dads appeared to be taking control of the situation. DeVita was also impressed by the punishments they had imposed. "Good for you, Dad," he said. "It sounds to me like you got the circumstances under control."

"This has been a rather traumatic experience," Tom Klebold told him. "I think it's probably good, a good experience, that they got caught the first time."

"He'd tell you if there were any more?"

"Yes, he would actually."

DeVita didn't buy it. "First time out of the box and you get caught?" he asked Eric. "I don't believe it. It's a real rare occurrence when somebody gets caught the first time."

But he was impressed by the way the boys presented themselves: dressed up, well behaved, deferential. *Yes, Your Honor* and *No, Your Honor.* They respected the court, and it showed.

DeVita pegged Dylan as well. The B's and C's on his report card were a joke. "I bet you're an A student," DeVita said. "If you put the brainpower to the paperwork."

DeVita gave them a lecture; then he approved them for Diversion. This pair was going to do just fine, he thought.

Fourteen months later, after the murders, DeVita lamented how convincing the boys had been. "What's mind-boggling is the amount of deception," he said. "The ease of their deception. The coolness of their deception."

———

Judy and Randy Brown kept calling the cops. They were sure Brooks was in danger. Their other son was so scared he slept with a baseball bat. After two weeks of their pestering, the case was bumped up to Investigator John Hicks, who met with Judy. On March 31, he sat down with two other investigators, Mike Guerra and Glenn Grove, to discuss it. The situation looked pretty bad—bad enough for Investigator Guerra to type out a two-page affidavit for a search warrant, "duly sworn upon oath."

Guerra did good work. In the affidavit, he dramatically outlined all the crucial elements of the case against this kid. He detailed the specificity of Eric's plans, his methods, and his ordnance. He quoted liberally from Eric's Web site to provide proof. But most important, Guerra drew the connection to physical evidence: a bomb matching those in Eric's descriptions had recently been discovered near his home. The Harris house was to be searched for any literature, notes, or physical material related to the construction of explosives, as well as all e-mail correspondence—presumably to include the Web site.

The affidavit was convincing. It was filed. It was not signed or taken before a judge. It was not acted upon in any way. A plausible explanation for inaction was never provided. Years later, one official said Guerra was drawn away to another case, and when he returned, the affidavit, as written, lacked the timeliness required to take it to a judge.

The Browns said that Investigator Hicks also knew about Eric's arrest for the van break-in. There was no indication that he or anyone from the sheriff's department ever relayed their damning evidence about Eric to the Diversion officers. Magistrate DeVita was provided no indication before he approved them for the program.

Senior officials from the sheriff's department, the DA's office, and the criminal court were unaware of one another's actions concerning Eric. But Eric apparently knew what they were all up to. Eric got wind that the Browns were on to him, so he took his Web site down for a while. There is no indication he ever learned of Dylan's betrayal. There is no sign that he suspected.

Eric was getting serious about his plans now, and he would not risk posting anything about them on the Web again. He pulled out a spiral notebook and began a journal. For the next year, he would record his progress toward the attack and thoroughly explain his motives.

38. Martyr

She's in the martyrs' hall of fame," Cassie's pastor proclaimed at her funeral. That was not hyperbole. A noted religious scholar predicted Cassie could become the first officially designated Protestant martyr since the sixteenth century. "This is really quite extraordinary," he said. "The flames of martyrdom are being fanned by these various preachers, who apparently have embellished the story as they have told it. It takes on a life of its own."

In the *Weekly Standard*, J. Bottum compared her to the third-century martyrs Perpetua and Felicity and "the tales of the thousands of early Christians who went joyously to their deaths in the Roman coliseums." And the response felt like the Great Awakening of the eighteenth century, Bottum said. He foresaw a generation of kids rising up to recast our cultural landscape. He later described a national change of heart, "trembling on the cusp of breaking forth.... It's an ever-widening faith that the whole pornographic, violent, anarchic disaster of popular American culture will soon be swept away."

It was a great story. It gave Brad and Misty tremendous relief. They were due. The Enemy had taken on their little girl before. And in the first round, The Enemy had won.

It had been possession, pure and simple; that's how Misty saw it. The Enemy had crept into her house a decade earlier, but remained hidden until the winter of 1996. She discovered his presence just before Christmas. She had just quit her job as a financial analyst at Lockheed Martin in order to be a better, full-time mom. It was a tough transition, and Misty went looking for a Bible for inspiration. She found one in Cassie's room, and she also discovered a stack of letters. They were disturbing.

The letters documented a vigorous correspondence between Cassie and a close friend. The friend bitched about a teacher and then suggested, "Want to help me murder her?" The pages were filled with hard-core sex talk, occult imagery, and magic spells. They hammered a persistent refrain: "Kill your parents!...Make those scumbags pay for your suffering....Murder is the answer to all of your problems."

Misty found only the friend's letters, but they suggested a receptive audience. Blood cocktails and vampires appeared throughout, in descriptions and illustrations. A teacher was shown stabbed with butcher knives, lying in her own blood. Figures labeled Ma and Pa were hung by their intestines. Bloody daggers were lodged in their chests. A gravestone was inscribed "Pa and Ma Bernall."

"My guts are hungry for that weird stuff," one letter said. "I fucking need to kill myself, we need to murder your parents. School is a fucking bitch, kill me with your parents, then kill yourself so you don't go to jail."

Misty called Brad, then the sheriff. They waited for Cassie to come home. First, Cassie tried to downplay the letters. Then she got angry. She hated them, she said. She admitted to writing letters in kind. She screamed. She said she would run away. She threatened to kill herself.

Rev. Dave McPherson, the youth pastor at West Bowles, counseled Brad and Misty to get tough. "Cut her phone, lock the door, pull her out of school," he said. "Don't let her out of the house without supervision." That's what they did. They transferred Cassie to a private school. They let her leave the house only for youth group at the church.

A bitter struggle followed. "She despised us at first," Reverend McPherson said. She would threaten to run away and launch into wild, graphic screaming fits.

"I'm going to kill myself!" Brad recalled her yelling. "Do you want to watch me? I'll do it, just watch. I'll kill myself. I'll put a knife right here, right through my chest."

Cassie cut her wrists and bludgeoned her skull. She would lock herself in the bathroom and bash her head against the sink counter. Alone in her bedroom, she beat it against the wall. With her family, she was sullen and spoke in monosyllables.

"There is no hope for that girl," Reverend McPherson thought. "Not our kind of hope."

Cassie described the ordeal in a notebook her parents found after her death:

I cannot explain in words how much I hurt. I didn't know how to deal with this hurt, so I physically hurt myself.... Thoughts of suicide obsessed me for days, but I was too frightened to actually do it, so I "compromised" by scratching my hands and wrists with a sharp metal file until I bled. It only hurt for the first couple minutes, then I went numb. Afterwards, however, it stung very badly, which I thought I deserved anyway.

Suddenly, one night three months later, Cassie shook The Enemy free. It was after sunset, at a youth group praise and worship service in the Rocky Mountains. Cassie got caught up in the music and suddenly broke down crying. She blubbered hysterically to a friend, who couldn't make out half of what she said. When Misty picked her up from the retreat, Cassie rushed up, hugged her, and said, "Mom, I've changed. I've totally changed."

Brad and Misty were skeptical, but the change took. "She left an angry, vengeful, bitter young girl and came back brand-new," Reverend Kirsten said.

After the conversion, Cassie attended youth ministry enthusiastically, sported a WWJD bracelet, and volunteered for a program that helped ex-convicts in Denver. The following fall, Brad and Misty allowed her to transfer to Columbine High. But she struggled with social pressures right up to her last days. She did not attend prom that last weekend. She did not believe that kids liked her. The day before Cassie was killed, the leaders of her youth group gathered for a staff meeting. One of the items on the agenda was "How do we get Cassie to fit in better?"

Brad and Misty Bernall were forthcoming about Cassie's history. A few weeks after the massacre, it was widely reported in the media. By then, two other martyr stories had surfaced. Valeen Schnurr's account was remarkably similar to Cassie's, except for the chronology and the outcome. Val was shot *before* her exchange about God. Dylan pointed his shotgun under her table and fired several rapid bursts, killing Lauren Townsend and injuring Val and another girl. Val was riddled with shotgun pellets up and down her arms and torso. Dylan walked away.

Val dropped to her knees, then her hands. Blood was streaming out of thirty-four separate wounds. "Oh my God, oh my God, don't let me die," she prayed.

Dylan turned around. This was too rich. "God? Do you believe in God?"

She wavered. Maybe she should keep her mouth shut. No. She would rather say it. "Yes. I believe in God."

"Why?"

"Because I believe. And my parents brought me up that way."

Dylan reloaded, but something distracted him. He walked off. Val crawled for shelter.

Once she made it out, Val was loaded into an ambulance, transported to St. Anthony's, and rushed into surgery. Her parents, Mark and Shari, were waiting for her when she came to. Val started blurting out what had happened almost immediately. She made a full recovery, and her story never varied. Numerous witnesses corroborated her account.

Val's story emerged at the same time as Cassie's—the afternoon of the attack. It took a week longer to reach the media. It never caused much of a ripple there.

If the timing had been different, Val might have been an Evangelical hero: the brave girl who felt the brunt of a shotgun blast and still stood up for her Redeemer. She proclaimed her faith, and He saved her. What a message of hope that would have been. And the hero would have been alive to spread the good news.

It didn't work out that way. Val was seen more often as a usurper. "People thought I was a copycat," she said. "They thought I was just following the bandwagon. A lot of people just didn't believe my story."

The bigger Cassie's fame grew, the more Val was rejected. An Evangelical youth rally was particularly disturbing. She told her story to a crowd gathered to honor Cassie and Rachel Scott. She got a very cold reception. "No one really comes out and says that never happened," she said. "They just skirt around the issue. Like they ask, 'Are you sure that's how it happened?' Or, 'Could your faith really be that strong?'"

Val's parents were supportive, but it wore on her. "You know, it gets frustrating," she said. "Because you know in your heart where you were and what you said, and then people doubt you. And that's what bothers me the most."

———

Cassie's fame grew. Reverend Kirsten embarked on a national speaking tour to spread the good news. "Pack as many onto the ark as possible," he said. By summer's end, the local youth group Revival Generation had blossomed from a few local chapters to an organization with offices in all fifty states. The organizer put on national touring shows with Columbine High survivors. Cassie's name sent teenage girls storming to the stage.

Fame could be intoxicating. Brad and Misty were already celebrities in their world—blessed parents of the martyr. They resisted the temptation and carried on as humbly as before. For some time, Brad Bernall had been a greeter at Sunday worship services at West Bowles. He returned to the volunteer role almost immediately after Cassie's funeral. He offered a smile with each handshake. The smiles looked sincere, but his pain bled through.

In early May, the church brought in a grief expert and conducted a group counseling session open to anyone in the struggling community.

Misty arrived first. Brad would be a little late, she said—he was having a really bad day. He had not gone into Cassie's room since she'd died, but tonight, he was going in there alone. Brad showed up, shaken. He downplayed his trouble and offered to help. Misty did the same.

———

Emily Wyant watched in disbelief as the story mushroomed. "Why are they saying that?" she asked her mother. Emily had been under the table with Cassie. They were facing each other. Emily was looking into Cassie's eyes when Eric fired his shotgun. Emily knew exactly what had happened.

Emily was supposed to be in science class when the shooting happened. But they had a test scheduled, and because she had missed class the day before, she wasn't ready. Her teacher sent her down to the library to look over her notes. She pulled up a seat by the window, at a table with just one girl—Cassie Bernall, who was studying *Macbeth*. They heard some commotion outside, and some kids came to the window to check it out, but it dissipated. Emily stood up for a look, saw a kid running across the soccer field, and sat down, returning to her notes.

A few minutes later, Patti Nielson ran in screaming and ordered everyone to get down. Cassie and Emily got under the table and tried to barricade themselves in by pulling some chairs around their tiny perimeter. That made them feel a little safer. Cassie crouched by the window side of the table, looking in toward the room, and Emily got down at the other end, facing Cassie two feet away. They could keep in contact with each other that way and collectively maintain a view of the whole room. The chairs created a lot of blind spots, but the girls were not about to move them. That was the only protection they had.

Emily heard shots coming from down the hallway—one at a time, not in bursts. They were getting closer. The doors opened; she heard them come in. They were shooting, talking back and forth, and shouting stuff like "Who wants to be killed next?" Emily looked over her shoulder to watch. She saw a kid near the counter jump or go down. The killers walked around a lot, taunting and shooting, and Emily got a good look at them. She had never noticed them before—she was a sophomore—but was sure she could pick them out again if she ever saw them again.

The girls whispered back and forth. "Dear God, dear God, why is this happening?" Cassie asked. "I just want to go home."

"I know," Emily answered. "We all want to get out of here."

Between exchanges, Cassie prayed very quietly. Eric and Dylan passed by several times, but Emily never expected one of them to "come under the table" and shoot.

Eric stopped at their table, at Cassie's end. Emily could see his legs and his boots, pointing directly at the right side of Cassie's face. Cassie didn't turn. Emily didn't have to—she was facing perpendicular to Eric's stance, so she could look straight at Cassie and see Eric just to her left at the same time. Eric slammed his hand on table, then squatted halfway down for a look. "Peekaboo," he said.

Eric poked his shotgun under the table rim as he came down. He didn't pause long, or even stoop down far enough for Emily to see his face. She saw the sawed-off gun barrel. The opening was huge. She looked into Cassie's brown eyes. Cassie was still praying. There was no time for words between them. Eric shot Cassie in the head.

Everything was muffled then. The blast was so loud, it temporarily blew out most of Emily's hearing. The fire alarm had been unbearably loud, but now she could barely hear it. She could see the light flashing out in the hallway. Eric's legs turned.

Bree Pasquale was sitting there, right out in the open a few steps away, beside the next table over. It had been jammed with kids when she got there—she couldn't fit, so she sat down next to it on the floor.

Bree was a bit farther from Cassie than Emily—the next closest person—but she had a wider view. She had also seen Eric walk up with the shotgun in his right hand, slap Cassie's tabletop twice with his left, and say, "Peekaboo." He squatted down, balancing on the balls of his feet, still holding on to the tabletop with his free hand. Cassie looked desperate, holding her hands up against the sides of her face. Eric poked the shotgun under and fired. Not a word.

Eric was sloppy with that shot: a one-hander, in an awkward half squat. The shotgun kicked back, and the butt nailed him in the face. He broke his nose sometime during the attack, and that's the moment investigators believe it happened. Eric had his back to Bree, so she couldn't see the gun hit his nose. But she watched him yank back on the pump handle and eject a red shell casing. It dropped to the floor. She looked under the table. Cassie was down, blood soaking into the shoulder of her light green shirt. Emily appeared unhurt.

Bree was exposed, just a few feet from Eric, but she couldn't take it anymore. She lay down and asked the boy beside her, who was just barely under the table, to hold her hand. He did. Bree was terrified. She did not take her eyes off Eric. He stood up after ejecting the round and turned to face her. He took a step or two toward her, squatted down again, and laid the shotgun across his thighs. Blood was pouring out of his nostrils. "I hit myself in the face!" he yelled. He was looking at her but calling out to Dylan.

Eric took hold of the gun again and pointed it in Bree's direction. He waved it back and forth in a sweeping motion—he could shoot anyone he wanted—and it came to rest on her.

That's when Dylan's gun went off. Bree heard him laugh and make a joke about what he had done. When she looked back at Eric, he was staring her straight in the face.

"Do you want to die?" Eric asked.

"No."

He asked once more.

"No no no no no." She pleaded for him to spare her, and Eric seemed to enjoy that: The exchange went on and on. He kept the gun right to her head the whole time.

"Don't shoot me," she said. "I don't want to die."

Finally, Eric let out a big laugh. "Everyone is going to die," he told her.

"Shoot her!" Dylan yelled.

"No," Eric replied. "We're going to blow up the school anyway."

Then something distracted him. He walked away and continued killing.

Bree looked back at Cassie's table. The other girl, Emily, was on her knees now, still facing Cassie's crumpled body, blood everywhere. She looked scared as hell.

How could she tell? an investigator asked Bree later.

The girl was biting her hands, she said.

Bree kept an eye on that girl. When the explosions moved out into the hallway, Bree figured the killers had gone, and she called out to the girl to come join her group. Emily couldn't hear much, so Bree started waving her hands. Emily saw her, finally, and crawled over. She was not about to stand up. She sat next to Bree and leaned against some bookshelves. Time got blurry for Emily then. Later, she couldn't recall how long she'd sat there.

———

Emily and Bree knew Cassie never got a chance to speak. They gave detailed accounts to investigators. Bree's ran fifteen pages, single-spaced, but their police reports would remain sealed for a year and a half. The 911 tape proved conclusively that they were correct. Audio of the murders was played for families, but withheld from the public as too gruesome.

Emily and Bree waited for the truth to come out.

———

Emily Wyant was sad. She went to counseling every day. April 20 had been horrible, and now she was saddled with a moral dilemma. She did not want to hurt the Bernalls; nor did she want to embarrass herself by shattering Cassie's myth. The whole thing had gotten so big so fast. But by keeping quiet, Emily felt she was contributing to a lie.

"She was in a tough position," her mother, Cindie, said later. Emily had told the cops, but they were not sharing much with the media anymore. Definitely not that bombshell.

Emily wanted to go public. Her parents were afraid. The martyrdom had turned into a religious movement—taking that on could be risky. "She didn't know the ramifications that could come afterwards," Cindie said. "She was just thinking about 'I want to tell the truth.'"

Her parents were torn, too. They wanted the truth to come out, but not at the expense of their daughter. Emily had already faced more than any child should. This might be too much. Don't do anything drastic, her parents advised. "It's a wonderful memory for [Cassie's] family," Cindie told her. "Let's not aggravate anything."

In early May, the phone rang. It was the *Rocky Mountain News*. Dan Luzadder was one of the best investigative reporters in the city, and he was sorting out exactly what happened in the library. They were tracking down all the library survivors, and most were cooperating. Emily's parents were wary. Her situation was different.

The reporters showed the Wyants some of the maps and timelines they were building. The family was impressed. The team seemed conscientious, and their work was thorough and detailed. The family agreed to talk. Emily would tell her story, and the *Rocky* could quote her but not identify her by name. "We didn't want her to be some national scoundrel," Cindie said.

After the interview, Emily was glad she had participated. What a relief to get that off her chest. She waited for the story.

The *Rocky* editors felt they needed more. This could get ugly. They wanted somebody on the record.

Emily kept waiting. Her frustration grew.

The *Rocky Mountain News* was waiting, too. They had conducted their investigation and had an incredible story to tell. Much of the public perception about Columbine was wrong. They had the truth. They were going to debunk all myths, including jocks, Goths, the TCM, and Cassie's murder. All they needed was a "news peg." The story would travel much farther if they timed it right.

They were waiting for Jeffco to finish its final report. A week or two before the release, the *Rocky* planned to stun the public with surprising revelations. It was a good strategy.

———

Misty Bernall had been hit hard. Telling Cassie's story made it more bearable. Someone suggested a book. Reverend McPherson introduced her to an editor at the tiny Christian publisher Plough. Plough had published the book Cassie had been reading before she died, and Misty liked what she had seen of the company.

Misty was apprehensive at first. Profiting off Cassie was the last thing on her mind. But she had two terrific stories to tell: Cassie's long fight for spiritual survival would be the primary focus, and her gunpoint proclamation would provide the hook.

A deal was struck in late May. It would be called *She Said Yes: The Unlikely Martyrdom of Cassie Bernall.*

The family had no idea the *Rocky* had discovered that title was untrue. Misty, who had gone back to work at Lockheed Martin as a statistician, would take a leave of absence to write the story. To reduce expenses, Misty agreed to forgo an advance in lieu of a higher royalty rate. Plough also agreed to set up a charity in Cassie's name for some of its proceeds.

Plough Publishing foresaw its first bestseller. It planned a first printing of 100,000 copies, more than seven times larger than its previous record.

———

On May 25, something unexpected happened. Police opened the school up so families of the library victims could walk through the scene. This served two functions: victims could face the crime scene with their loved ones, and revisiting the room might jar loose memories or clarify confusion. Three senior investigators stood by to answer questions and observe. Craig Scott, who had initiated the Cassie story, came through with several family members. He stopped where he had hidden, and retold his story to his dad. A senior detective listened. Craig had sat extremely close to Cassie, just one table away, facing hers. But when he described her murder, he pointed in the opposite direction. It happened at one of the two tables near the interior, he said—which was exactly where Val had been. When a detective said Cassie had not been in that area, Craig insisted. He pointed to the closest tables to Val's and said, "Well, she was up there then!" No, the detective said. Craig got agitated. "She was somewhere over there," he said. He pointed again toward Val's table. "I know that for a fact."

Detectives explained the mistake. Craig got sick. The detective walked him out and Craig sat down in the empty corridor to collect himself. He apologized for getting ill. He was OK now, but he would wait for his family out there. He was not going back into that library.

———

Friends of the Bernalls said Brad was struggling much more than his wife. It was visible in the way he carried himself into worship on Sunday mornings. Brad looked broken. Misty took great solace in the book she was writing. It gave her purpose. It gave meaning to Cassie's death. Misty had put herself in God's hands, and He had handed her a mission. She would bring His message to a whole new audience. Her book would glorify her daughter and her God.

Investigators heard about the book deal. They decided that they owed it to Misty to alert her to the truth. In June, lead investigator Kate Battan and another detective went to see her. Misty described the meeting this way: "They said, 'Don't stop doing the book. We just wanted to let you know that there are differing accounts coming out of the library.'"

Battan said she encouraged Misty to continue with the book, but without the martyr incident. Cassie's transformational story sounded wonderful. Battan said she made the details of Cassie's murder clear, and later played the 911 tape for Brad and Misty.

Misty and her Plough editor, Chris Zimmerman, were concerned. They went back to their witnesses. Three witnesses stuck by the story that it was Cassie. Good enough. The martyr scene was going to be a small part of the book anyway. Misty wanted to focus on Cassie overcoming her own demons. "We wanted people to know Cassie was an average teenager who struggled with her weight and worried about boys and wasn't ever a living saint," she said.

Misty lived up to her word. That was the book she wrote. She described Cassie as selfish and stubborn on occasion, known to behave "like a spoiled two-year-old." Misty also agreed to run a disclaimer opposite the table of contents. It referred to "varying recollections" and stated that "the precise chronology...including the exact details of Cassie's death...may never be known."

Emily Wyant was getting more apprehensive. Her parents continued urging caution.

They had a dinner with the Bernalls. Brad and Misty asked Emily if she'd heard the exchange. Emily was a bit sheepish about answering, but she said no. Cindie Wyant felt that Emily had made herself clear, but afterward the Bernalls recalled no revelation. Cindie later surmised that they'd taken Emily's response to mean she didn't remember anything.

Val Schnurr's family was uneasy, too. Investigators had briefed them on the evidence and told them about Craig Scott's discovery in the library. Val and her parents wondered which was worse: hurting the Bernalls or keeping quiet. They also went to dinner with the Bernalls. Everyone felt better after that. Brad and Misty seemed sincere, and utterly distraught with pain. "So much sadness," Mark Schnurr said. Clearly, the book was Misty's way of healing.

The Schnurrs were less understanding with the publisher. The editor attended the dinner, and Shari asked him to slow down. Her husband followed up with an e-mail. "If you go ahead and publish the book, just be careful," he wrote. "There's a lot of conflicting information out there." He suggested that Plough delay publication until the authorities issued their report. Plough declined.

———

In July, the *Wall Street Journal* ran a prominent story titled "Marketing a Columbine Martyr." The publishing house was obscure, but Zimmerman had called in a team of heavy hitters. For public relations, the firm hired the New York team that had handled Monica Lewinsky's book. Publication was two months away, and Misty had already been booked for *The Today Show* and *20/20*. The William Morris Agency was shopping the film rights around. (A movie was never made.) An agent there had sold book club rights to a unit of Random House. He said he was marketing "virtually everything you can exploit—and I mean that in a positive way."

39. The Book of God

The screws were tightening. Eric met with Andrea Sanchez to receive his Diversion contract. He looked ahead to senior year. It would be consumed writing an apology letter, providing restitution, working off fines, meeting a Diversion counselor twice a month, seeing his own shrink, attending bullshit classes like Mothers Against Drunk Driving, maintaining good grades, problem-free employment, and forty-five hours of community service. They would periodically hand him a Dixie cup and direct him to a urinal. No more alcohol. No more freedom.

Eric's first counseling session and his first drug screening would commence in eight days. He met with Sanchez on a Wednesday. Thursday, he stewed. Friday, April 10, 1998, he opened a letter-sized spiral notebook and scribbled, "I hate the fucking world." In one year and ten days, he would attack. Eric wrote furiously, filling two vicious pages: *people are STUPID, I'm not respected, everyone has their own god damn opinions on every god damn thing.*

At first glance, the journal sounds like the Web site, but Fuselier found answers in it. The Web site was pure rage, no explanation. The journal was explicit. Eric fleshed out his ideas on paper, as well as his personality. Eric had a preposterously grand superiority complex, a revulsion for authority, and an excruciating need for control.

"I feel like God," Eric announced. "I am higher than almost anyone in the fucking world in terms of universal intelligence." In time, his superiority would be revealed. In the interim, Eric dubbed his journal "The Book of God." The breadth of his hostility was equally melodramatic.

Humans were pathetic fuckheads too dense to perceive their lifeless existence. We frittered our lives away like automatons, following orders rather than realizing our potential: "ever wonder why we go to school?" he asked. "its not to obvious to most of you stupid fucks but for those who think a little more and deeper you should realize it is societies way of turning all the young people into good little robots." Human nature was smothered by society; healthy instincts were smothered by laws. They were training us to be assembly-line robots; that's why they lined the school desks up in rows and trained kids to respond to opening and closing bells. The monotonous human assembly line squelched the life out of individual experience. As Eric put it, "more of your human nature blown out your ass."

Philosophically, the robotic conception was a rare point of agreement between the killers. Dylan referred often to zombies, too. Both boys described their uniqueness as self-awareness. They could see through the human haze. But Dylan saw his distinction as a lonely curse. And he looked on the zombies compassionately; Dylan yearned for the poor little creatures to break out of their boxes.

The problem, as Eric saw it, was natural selection. He had alluded to the concept on his Web site; here he explained—relentlessly. Natural selection had failed. Man had intervened. Medicines, vaccines, and special ed programs had conspired to keep the rejects in the human herd. So Eric was surrounded by inferiors—who would not shut their freaking mouths! How could he tolerate all the miserable chatter?

He had lots of ideas. Nuclear holocaust, biological warfare, imprisoning the species in a giant Ultimate Doom game.

But Eric was also realistic. He couldn't restore the natural order, but he could impose some selection of his own. He would sacrifice himself to accomplish it. "I know I will die soon," he wrote; "so will you and everyone else."

By soon, he meant a year. Eric had a remarkably long time horizon for a seventeen-year-old contemplating his own death.

The lies jumped out at Fuselier. Eric took giddy pleasure in his deceptions. "I lie a lot," he wrote. "Almost constant. and to everybody. just to keep my own ass out of the water. lets see, what are some big lies I have told; 'yeah I stopped smoking' 'for doing it not for getting caught,' 'no I haven't been making more bombs.'"

Eric did not believe in God, but he enjoyed comparing himself to Him. Like Dylan, he did so frequently but not delusionally—they were *like* God: superior in insight, intelligence, and awareness. Like Zeus, Eric created new rules, angered easily, and punished people in unusual ways. Eric had conviction. Eric had a plan. Eric would get the guns and build the explosives and maim and kill and so much more. They would terrify way beyond their gun blasts. The ultimate weapon was TV. Eric saw past the Columbine commons. He might kill hundreds, but the dead and dismembered meant nothing to him. Bit players—who cared? The performance was not *about* them. Eric's one-day-only production was about the audience.

The irony was, his attack was too good for his victims—it would sail right over their heads. "the majority of the audience wont even understand," Eric lamented. Too bad. They would feel the power of his hand: "if we have figured out the art-of time bombs before hand, we will set hundreds of them around houses, roads, bridges, buildings and gas stations." "it'll be like the LA riots, the oklahoma bombing, WWII, vietnam, duke and doom all mixed together. maybe we will even start a little rebellion or revolution to fuck things up as much as we can. i want to leave a lasting impression on the world."

———

Dr. Fuselier set down the journal. It had taken him about an hour to read, that first time, in the noisy Columbine band room, two or three days after the murders. Now he had a pretty good hunch about what he was dealing with: a psychopath.

PART IV

TAKE BACK
THE SCHOOL

40. Psychopath

I will choose to kill," Eric wrote. Why? His explanations didn't add up. Because we were morons? How would that make a kid kill? To most readers, Eric's rants just sounded nuts.

Dr. Fuselier had the opposite reaction. Insanity was marked by mental confusion. Eric Harris expressed cold, rational calculation. Fuselier ticked off Eric's personality traits: charming, callous, cunning, manipulative, comically grandiose, and egocentric, with an appalling failure of empathy. It was like reciting the Psychopathy Checklist.

Fuselier spent the next twelve weeks contesting his theory. That's how he approached a problem: develop a hypothesis and then search for every scrap of evidence to refute it. Test it against alternate explanations, build the strongest possible case to support them, and see if the hypothesis fails. If it withstands that, it's solid. Psychopathy held.

Diagnosis didn't solve the crime, but it laid the foundation. Ten years afterward, Eric still baffled the public, which insisted on assessing his motives through a "normal" lens. Eric was neither normal nor insane. Psychopathy (si-COP-uh-thee) represents a third category. Psychopathic brains don't function like those in either of the other groups, but they are consistently similar to one another. Eric killed for two reasons: to demonstrate his superiority and to enjoy it.

To a psychopath, both motives make sense. "Psychopaths are capable of behavior that normal people find not only horrific but baffling," wrote Dr. Robert Hare, the leading authority on psychopaths. "They can torture and mutilate their victims with about the same sense of concern that we feel when we carve a turkey for Thanksgiving dinner."

Eric saw humans as chemical compounds with an inflated sense of their own worth. "its just all nature, chemistry, and math," he wrote. "you die. burn, melt, evaporate, decay."

Psychopaths have likely plagued mankind since the beginning, but they are still poorly understood. In the 1800s, as the fledgling field of psychology began classifying mental disorders, one group refused to fit. Every known psychosis was marked by a failure of reasoning or a debilitating ailment: paralyzing fear, hallucinations, voices, phobias, and so on. In 1885, the term *psychopath* was introduced to describe vicious human predators who were not deranged, delusional, or depressed. They just enjoyed being bad.

Psychopaths are distinguished by two characteristics. The first is a ruthless disregard for others: they will defraud, maim, or kill for the most trivial personal gain. The second is an astonishing gift for disguising the first. It's the deception that makes them so dangerous. You never see him coming. (It's usually a him—more than 80 percent are male.) Don't look for the oddball creeping you out. Psychopaths don't act like Hannibal Lecter or Norman Bates. They come off like Hugh Grant, in his most adorable role.

In 1941, Dr. Hervey Cleckley revolutionized the understanding of psychopathy with his book *The Mask of Sanity*. Egocentrism and failure of empathy were the underlying drivers, but Cleckley chose his title to reflect the element that trumped those. If psychopaths were merely evil, they would not be a major threat. They wreak so much havoc that they should be obvious. Yet the majority have consistently eluded the law.

Cleckley worried about his title metaphor: psychopathy is not a two-dimensional cover that can be lifted off the face like a Halloween mask. It permeates the offender's personality. Joy, grief, anxiety, or amusement—he can mimic any on cue. He knows the facial expressions, the voice modulation, and the body language. He's not just conning you with a scheme, he's conning you with his life. His entire personality is a fabrication, with the purpose of deceiving suckers like you.

Psychopaths take great personal pride in their deceptions and extract tremendous joy from them. Lies become the psychopath's occupation, and when the truth will work, they lie for sport. "I like to con people," one of Hare's subjects told a researcher during an extended interview. "I'm conning you right now."

Lying for amusement is so profound in psychopaths, it stands out as their signature characteristic. "Duping delight," psychologist Paul Ekman dubbed it.

Cleckley spent five decades refining his research and publishing four further editions of *The Mask of Sanity*. It wasn't until the 1970s that Robert Hare isolated twenty characteristics of the condition and created the Psychopathy Checklist, the basis for virtually all contemporary research. He also wrote the definitive book on the malady, *Without Conscience*.

The terminology got muckier. *Sociopath* was in introduced in the 1930s, initially as a broader term for antisocial behavior. Eventually, *psychopath* and *sociopath* became virtually synonymous. (Varying definitions for the latter have led to distinctions by some experts, but these are not uniformly accepted.) The primary reason for the competing terms is that each was adopted in different fields: criminologists and law enforcement personnel prefer *psychopath;* sociologists tend toward *sociopath.* Psychologists and psychiatrists are split, but most experts on the condition use *psychopath,* and the bulk of the research is based on Hare's checklist. A third term, *antisocial personality disorder,* or APD, was introduced in the 1970s and remains the only diagnosis included in the latest edition of the *Diagnostic and Statistical Manual of Mental Disorders (DSM-IV)*. However, it covers a much broader range of disorders than does *psychopath* and has been roundly rejected by leading researchers.

So where do psychopaths come from? Researchers are divided, with the majority suggesting a mixed role: nature leading, nurture following. Dr. Hare believes psychopaths are born with a powerful predisposition, which can be exacerbated by abuse or neglect. A correlation exists between psychopaths and unstable homes—and violent upbringings seem to turn fledgling psychopaths more vicious. But current data suggests those conditions do not cause the psychopathy; they only make a bad situation worse. It also appears that even the best parenting may be no match for a child born to be bad.

Symptoms appear so early, and so often in stable homes with normal siblings, that the condition seems to be inborn. Most parents report having been aware of disturbing signs before the child entered kindergarten. Dr. Hare described a five-year-old girl repeatedly attempting to flush her kitten down the toilet. "I caught her just as she was about to try again," the mother said. "She seemed quite unconcerned, maybe a bit angry—about being found out." When the woman told her husband, the girl calmly denied the whole thing. Shame did not register; neither did fear. Psychopaths are not individuals losing touch with those emotions. They never developed them from the start.

Hare created a separate screening device for juveniles and identified hallmarks that appear during the school years: gratuitous lying, indifference to the pain of others, defiance of authority figures, unresponsiveness to reprimands or threatened punishment, petty theft, persistent aggression, cutting classes and breaking curfew, cruelty to animals, early experimentation with sex, and vandalism and setting fires. Eric bragged about nine of the ten hallmarks in his journal and on his Web site—for most of them, relentlessly. Only animal cruelty is missing.

At some point—as either a cause or an effect of psychopathy—the psychopath's brain begins processing emotional responses differently. Early in his career, Dr. Hare recognized the anatomical difference. He submitted a paper analyzing the unusual brain waves of psychopaths to a scientific journal, which rejected it with a dismissive letter. "Those EEGs couldn't have come from real people," the editor wrote.

Exactly! Hare thought. Psychopaths are that different. Eric Harris baffled the public because we could not conceive of a human with his motives. Even Kate Battan would describe him as a teenager trying to act like an adult. But the angst we associate with teenagers was the least of Eric's drives. His brain was never scanned, but it probably would have shown activity unrecognizable as human to most neurologists.

The fundamental nature of a psychopath is a failure to feel. A psychopath's grasp of fear and suffering is particularly weak. Dr. Hare's research team spent decades studying psychopaths in prison populations. They asked one psychopath to describe fear. "When I rob a bank, I notice that the teller shakes or becomes tongue-tied," he said. "One barfed all over the money." He found that puzzling. The researcher pushed him to describe his own fear. How would he feel with the gun pointed at him? The convict said he might hand over the money, get the hell out, or find a way to turn the tables. Those were responses, the researcher said. How would you *feel*? Feel? Why would he feel?

Researchers often compare psychopaths to robots or rogue computers, like HAL from *2001: A Space Odyssey*—programmed only to satisfy their own objectives. That's the closest approximation of their behavior, but the metaphor lacks nuance. Psychopaths feel something; Eric seemed to show sadness when his dog was sick, and he occasionally felt twinges of regret toward humans. But the signals come through dimly.

Cleckley described this as a poverty of emotional range. That's a tricky concept, because psychopaths develop a handful of primitive emotions closely related to their own welfare. Three have been identified: anger, frustration, and rage. Psychopaths erupt with ferocious bouts of anger, which can get them labeled "emotional." Look more closely, Cleckley advised: "The conviction dawns on those who observe him carefully that here we deal with a readiness of expression rather than a strength of feeling." No love. No grief. Not even sorrow, really, or hope or despair about his own future. Psychopaths feel nothing deep, complex, or sustained. The psychopath was prone to "vexation, spite, quick and labile flashes of quasi-affection, peevish resentment, shallow moods of self-pity, puerile attitudes of vanity, absurd and showy poses of indignation."

Cleckley could have been describing Eric Harris's journal. "how dare you think that I and you are part of the same species when we are soooooooooo different," Eric wrote. "you arent human. you are a robot....and if you pissed me off in the past, you will die if I see you."

Indignation runs strong in the psychopath. It springs from a staggering ego and sense of superiority. Psychopaths do not feel much, but when they lose patience with inferiors, they can really let it rip. It doesn't go any deeper. Even an earthworm will recoil if you poke it with a stick. A squirrel will exhibit frustration if you tease it by offering a peanut, then repeatedly snatching it back. Psychopaths make it that far up the emotional ladder, but they fall far short of the average golden retriever, which will demonstrate affection, joy, compassion, and empathy for a human in pain.

Researchers are still just beginning to understand psychopaths, but they believe psychopaths crave the emotional responses they lack. They are nearly always thrill seekers. They love roller coasters and hang gliding, and they seek out high-anxiety occupations, like ER tech, bond trader, or Marine. Crime, danger, impoverishment, death—any sort of risk will help. They chase new sources of excitement because it is so difficult for them to sustain.

They rarely stick with a career; they get bored. Even as career criminals, psychopaths underperform. They "lack clear goals and objectives, getting involved in a wide variety of opportunistic offenses, rather than specializing the way typical career criminals do," Cleckley wrote. They make careless mistakes and pass up stunning opportunities, because they lose interest. They perform spectacularly in short bursts—a few weeks, a few months, a yearlong big con—then walk away.

Eric spent his young life that way: he should have been a 4.0 student, but collected A's, B's, and C's. He made one yearlong commitment, to NBK, but he had no ambition, zero plans for his life. He was one of the smartest kids in his high school, but apparently never bothered to apply to college. No job prospects either, beyond Blackjack. Despite a childhood of soldier fantasies, a military father, and a stated desire for a career in the Marines, Eric made no attempt to enlist. When a recruiter cold-called him during the last week of his life, he met the guy, but never returned the call to find out whether he had been accepted.

Rare killer psychopaths nearly always get bored with murder, too. When they slit a throat, their pulse races, but it falls just as fast. It stays down—no more joy from cutting throats for a while; that thrill has already been spent.

A second, less common approach to the banality of murder seems to be the dyad: murderous pairs who feed off each other. Criminologists have been aware of the dyad phenomenon for decades: Leopold and Loeb, Bonnie and Clyde, the Beltway snipers of 2002. Because dyads account for only a fraction of mass murderers, little research has been conducted on them. We know that the partnerships tend to be asymmetrical. An angry, erratic depressive and a sadistic psychopath make a combustible pair. The psychopath is in control, of course, but the hotheaded sidekick can sustain his excitement leading up to the big kill. "It takes heat and cold to make a tornado," Dr. Fuselier is fond of saying. Eric craved heat, but he couldn't sustain it. Dylan was a volcano. You could never tell when he might erupt.

Day after day, for more than a year, Dylan juiced Eric with erratic jolts of excitement. They played the killing out again and again: the cries, the screams, the smell of burning flesh...

Eric savored the anticipation.

Dr. Hare's EEGs suggested the psychopathic brain operates differently, but he could not be sure how or why. After Eric's death, a colleague advanced our understanding with a new technology. Functional magnetic resonance imaging tests (fMRIs) create a picture of the brain, with light indicating active regions. Dr. Kent Kiehl wired subjects up and showed them a series of flash cards. Half contained emotionally charged words like rape, murder, and cancer; the others were neutral, like *rock* or *doorknob*. Normal people found the disturbing words disturbing: the brain's emotional nerve center, called the amygdala, lit up. The psychopathic amygdalae were dark. The emotional flavors that color our days are invisible to psychopaths.

Dr. Kiehl repeated the experiment with pictures, including graphic shots of homicides. Again, psychopaths' amygdalae were unaffected; but the language center activated. They seemed to be *analyzing* the emotions instead of experiencing them.

"He responds to events that others find arousing, repulsive, or scary with the words *interesting* and *fascinating*," Dr. Hare said. For psychopaths, horror is purely intellectual. Their brains search for words to describe what the rest of us would feel. That fits the profile: psychopaths react to pain or tragedy by assessing how they can use the situation to manipulate others.

So what's the treatment for psychopathy? Dr. Hare summarized the research on a century of attempts in two words: *nothing works*. It is the only major mental affliction to elude treatment. And therapy often makes it worse. "Unfortunately, programs of this sort merely provide the psychopath with better ways of manipulating, deceiving, and using people," Hare wrote. Individual therapy can be a bonanza: one-on-one training, to perfect the performance. "These programs are like a finishing school," a psychopath boasted to Dr. Hare's team. "They teach you how to put the squeeze on people."

Eric was blessed with at least two unintentional coaches: Bob Kriegshauser, in the juvenile Diversion program, and his psychiatrist, Dr. Albert. Eric was a quick study. The notes in his Diversion file document a steady improvement, session by session.

Oddly, a large number of psychopaths spontaneously improve around middle age. The phenomenon has been observed for decades, but not explained. Otherwise, psychopaths appear to be lost causes. Within the psychiatric community, that has drawn stiff resistance to diagnosing minors with the condition. But clearly, many juveniles are well on their way.

Dr. Kiehl has a mobile fMRI lab and a research team funded by the University of New Mexico. He mapped about five hundred brains at three prison systems in 2008. Because of the skewed sample pool, about

20 percent met the criteria for psychopathy. He believes that answers about the causes and treatment of psychopathy are coming within reach.

While Eric was devising his attack, Dr. Hare was working on a regimen to address his kind. Hare began by reexamining the data on those spontaneous improvers. From adolescence to their fifties, psychopaths showed virtually no change in emotional characteristics but improved dramatically in antisocial behavior. The inner drives did not change, but their behavior did.

Hare believes that these psychopaths might simply be adapting. Fiercely rational, they figured out that prison was not working for them. So Hare proposed using their self-interest to the public advantage. The program he developed accepts that psychopaths will remain egocentric and uncaring for life but will adhere to rules if it's in their own interest. "Convincing them that there are ways they can get what they want without harming others" is the key, Hare said. "You say to them, 'Most people think with their hearts, not with their heads, and your problem is you think too much with your head. So let's change the problem into an asset.' They understand that."

While Eric was in high school, a juvenile treatment center in Wisconsin began a program developed independently but based on that approach. It also addressed the psychopathic drives for instant gratification and control: subjects were rated every night on adherence to rules and rewarded with extended privileges the next day. The program was not designed specifically for fledgling psychopaths, but it produced significant improvements in that population. A four-year study published in 2006 concluded that they were 2.7 times less likely to become violent than kids with similar psychopathy scores in other programs.

For the first time in the history of psychopathy, a treatment appears to have worked. It awaits replication.

Psychopathy experts are cautiously optimistic about coming advances. "I believe that within ten years we will have a much better perspective on psychopathy than we do now," Dr. Kiehl said. "Ideally we will be able to help effectively manage the condition. I would not say that there is a cure on the horizon, but I do hope that we can implement effective management strategies."

41. The Parents Group

Fuselier was sure Eric was a psychopath. But the kid had been sixteen when he'd hatched the plot, seventeen for most of the planning, and barely eighteen when he opened fire. There would be resistance to writing Eric off at those ages.

Three months after Columbine, the FBI organized a major summit on school shooters in Leesburg, Virginia. The Bureau assembled some of the world's leading psychologists, including Dr. Hare. Near the end of the conference, Dr. Fuselier stepped up to the microphone and gave a thorough briefing on the minds of the two killers. "It looks like Eric Harris was a budding young psychopath," he concluded.

The room stirred. A renowned psychiatrist in the front row moved to speak. *Here it comes,* Fuselier thought. *This guy is going to nitpick the assessment to death.*

"I don't think he was a budding young psychopath," the psychiatrist said.

"What's your objection?"

"I think he was a full-blown psychopath."

His colleagues agreed. Eric Harris was textbook.

Several of the experts continued studying the Columbine shooters after the summit. Michigan State University psychiatrist Frank Ochberg flew in several times to help guide the mental health team, and every trip doubled as a fact-finding mission. Dr. Ochberg interviewed an assortment of people close to the killers and studied the boys' writings.

The problem for the community, and ultimately for Jeffco officials, too, was that Fuselier was not permitted to talk to the public. Early on, both local and federal officials were concerned about Jeffco getting overshadowed by the FBI. The Bureau firmly prohibited any of its agents from discussing the case with the media. Jeffco commanders had decided the killers' motives should not be discussed, and the FBI respected that decision.

Failure to address the obvious intensified suspicion toward Jeffco. It exacerbated a credibility problem already hovering over the sheriff's department. In addition to *why*, the public had two pressing questions: Should authorities have seen Columbine coming? And should they have stopped it sooner once the gunfire began? On both those controversial questions, Jeffco had obvious conflicts of interest. And yet they charged ahead.

It was a staggering lapse of judgment. Jeffco could have simply isolated the two explosive issues into an independent investigation. It would have been easy enough; they had nearly a hundred detectives at their disposal, few of whom worked for Jeffco.

The independent investigation didn't seem so obvious in 1999. The commanders were essentially honest men. Not one had a reputation as a dirty cop. John Kiekbusch was deeply respected inside and outside the force. They believed they were innocent, and that the public would see that. And many of them were. Stone and his undersheriff had been sworn in only three months earlier—they bore no responsibility for missing any warning signs from Eric Harris. Most of the team had no role in command decisions on April 20. Kate Battan was running the day-to-day operations; she was clean.

But some good cops made really bad decisions after April 20. Survivors were right to suspect a cover-up. Jeffco commanders were lying about the Browns' warnings about Eric, and Randy and Judy made sure everyone knew. Inside the department, someone was attempting to destroy the Browns' paper trail. Shortly after the massacre, Investigator Mike Guerra noticed that the physical copy of the file he had put together on Eric a year earlier disappeared from his desk. A few days later, it reappeared just as mysteriously. Later that summer, he tried to call up the computer record and found it had been purged.

The physical file again disappeared and has never been recovered.

Over the next several months, division chief John Kiekbusch's assistant took part in several activities she later found disturbing.

———

Each day Patrick tried to lift his leg again. Concentrate, they instructed him. Each time Patrick concentrated, electrons dispersed through the gray matter of his brain. Each time, those electrons sought fresh routes through the lacerated left hemisphere. Once they established a signal—faint, almost imperceptible—they laid the mental equivalent of fresh power lines. The signal grew stronger.

People were always in and out of his room. In the first week of May, a friend from waterskiing and some aunts and uncles were visiting. Patrick lay on his bed, the useless leg up on a pillow. The brace was wrapped around it, so it was extra heavy, but he bore down anyway. Slowly, barely, the thigh rose. "Hey!" he shouted. "Check out what I can do!"

They couldn't see anything. He had raised it just enough to expand the pillow below his brace. But he could feel it. The pillow wasn't supporting it, he was.

Patrick made steady progress once he reestablished contact with his limbs. Every morning, he could feel some change. The strength returned to the center of his body first, beginning in his torso, then radiating out through his hips and his shoulders and down toward his right elbow and knee. In a few more weeks, they had him on his feet. They started him off standing between a set of hip-high parallel bars. He had sort of a towrope around his waist that a therapist held on to, to steady him and guide him the short distance through the bars. That was a good day. The bars were tough, because his right arm was as feeble as his leg. But together, he gathered the strength for each step.

Later, he progressed to a walker and then a forearm crutch with a cuff that straps over the arm below the elbow. The wheelchair was always there for long trips, or any time he grew tired. Dexterity with his fingers and his toes would be the hardest thing to regain completely. It would take him months to hold a pen without shaking. His walk would be hindered by all sorts of fine adjustments we never notice our toes making.

————

Anne Marie Hochhalter progressed more slowly. She had barely made it through the attack. Her spinal cord was ruptured, causing unbearable nerve pain. She spent weeks lying delirious on morphine, with a ventilator and a feeding tube keeping her alive. She couldn't talk with the tubes, and through the fog, she didn't understand what had happened or what was ahead.

Eventually, she grew more lucid and asked whether she would walk again.

"Well, no," a nurse told her.

"I just cried," she said later. "The nurse had to go get my parents because I was crying so hard."

After six weeks, she joined Patrick at Craig. Danny Rohrbough's friend Sean Graves was there, too, partially paralyzed below the spine. He managed a few steps with braces over the summer. Lance Kirklin's face was reconstructed with titanium implants and skin grafts. Scarring was severe, but he made light of it. "It's cool being five percent metal," he said.

————

In the weeks just after the murders, nearly all the families of the library victims walked the crime scene with investigators. They needed to see it. It might be horrible—they had to find out. Dawn Anna stopped at the spot where her daughter Lauren Townsend had been killed. First table on the left. Nothing had been changed, except for the removal of the backpacks and personal effects, which had been photographed, inventoried, and returned to the families. "The emotional impact, I don't even know that I can adequately describe it," Anna said. But she could not avoid it. "I needed that connection, as did all of us, to get back and identify, in part, with what had happened there."

The thought of sending any schoolkid back inside was unthinkable. The library had to go. Independently, and collectively, most of the thirteen families came to that conclusion quickly.

Students reached the opposite consensus. They spent the spring battling for the *idea* of Columbine, as well as the proper noun: the name of a high school, not a tragedy. They were repulsed by phrases bandied about like "since Columbine" or "prevent another Columbine." That was one day in the life of Columbine High School, they insisted.

Then the tourists arrived. Just weeks after the tragedy, even before students returned, tour buses started rolling up to the school. Columbine High had leapt to second place, behind the Rocky Mountains, as Colorado's most famous landmark, and tour operators were quick to capitalize. The buses would pull up in front of the school, and tourists would pile out and start snapping pictures: the school, the grounds, the kids practicing on the athletic fields or milling about in the park. They captured a lot of angry expressions. The students felt like zoo specimens. Everyone still needed to know constantly, *How do you feel?*

Brian Fuselier was heading into his sophomore year at Columbine. Weeks under the microscope had been miserable; the tourists were too much. "I just want to walk up and punch them in the nose!" he told his dad.

On June 2, most of the student body finally reconnected with the physical Columbine. It was an emotional day. Students had two hours to go back inside and retrieve their backpacks and cell phones and everything else they had abandoned when they ran for it. Their parents were allowed in as well. It gave everyone a chance to face their fears. Hundreds of kids stumbled out in tears. Useful tears. Most found the experience stressful but cathartic.

They were kicked out again for two months, while construction crews renovated the interior. The students had mixed feelings about anything changing, but they were taking that one on faith. The district had open enrollment, so everyone expected a big drop in Columbine's student body the next fall. Students reacted the opposite way: transfers out were minimal. Fall enrollment actually went up. Students felt they had lost so much already, that surrendering an inch of corridor or a single classroom would feel like defeat. They wanted their school back. All of it!

Mr. D and the faculty were focused on the kids: getting them into therapy and watching out for trauma symptoms. School officials formed a design review board to address the library. It included students, parents, and faculty. Consensus came readily: gut the room and rebuild it. Redesign the layout, replace and reconfigure the furniture, change the wall color, the carpet, even the ceiling tiles. It was a drastic version of the plan put together for the entire school. Trauma experts advised the board to balance two objectives: make the kids feel their school had survived and surround them with changes too subtle to identify. The library was the exception: it would feel completely different.

Renovation of the school would cost $1.2 million, and would be tough to complete before school resumed in August. The design board moved quickly, and the school board adopted its proposal in early June. The parents of the murdered kids were aghast. Rearrange the furniture? Slap on some paint and recarpet? The design team saw their plan as a complete overhaul. Their adversaries called it "cosmetic."

Initially, the students and the victims' families assumed they were all in this together. It took them several weeks to realize they were about to battle each other. Parents of the Thirteen saw that they were outnumbered; they formed the Parents Group to fight back. On May 27, just as they were organizing, a notorious lawyer and media hound flew to Denver for a boisterous press conference. Geoffrey Fieger had become a cable news staple via splashy media trials, like that of Dr. Kevorkian, the assisted-suicide doctor. Fieger teamed with Isaiah Shoels's family to make an ostentatious demand sure to return Columbine to national headlines in the worst possible light: a wrongful death suit against the killers' parents, for a quarter of a billion dollars.

"This is not about money!" Isaiah's stepfather declared. "This lawsuit is about change! That's the only way you get change, if you go rattling their pocketbooks." He was right, but the public was skeptical about motives. Fieger insisted he would spend more money mounting the case than he could hope to recover. Colorado law limited awards from individuals to $250,000, and governmental entities were capped at $150,000. "This lawsuit is a symbol," he said. "There will be cynics who would chalk the lawsuit up to greed."

Lawsuits had been anticipated, but nobody had foreseen one so garish, or so soon. Colorado law gave victims a year to file and six months to declare intent. It had only been five weeks. Families had been talking about lawsuits as means of leverage, and a last resort.

The lawsuit served as a trial balloon that sank. The survivors were particularly repulsed. Many of them had dedicated the next phase of their lives to some form of justice: anti-bullying, gun control, prayer in schools, SWAT protocols, warning signs, or just reclaiming their school or destroying the library. Lawsuits threatened to taint all that. They also shed a bad light on the next big battle, which was already developing when the Shoelses conducted their press conference. That fight revolved around money, too. The public donations had been astonishing, but the good fortune came at a price.

More than $2 million rolled in the first month. A month later, the total was $3.5 million. Forty different funds sprouted up. The local United Way set up the Healing Fund to coordinate the distribution of monies. Robin Finegan was a veteran therapist and victim's advocate who had worked closely with Oklahoma City survivors. "It is predictable that this will become a very difficult, painful process," she told NPR. There were too many competing interests. "We're going to leave people, some people, not feeling great about this." That was an understatement.

When a pair of teachers were collectively granted $5,000 for anxiety treatment, Brian Rohrbough blew his stack. "That's criminal," he said. He wanted the money divided equally between the families of the injured and the dead. But was equality fair? Lance Kirklin's father estimated his medical bills at $1 to $2 million; the family was uninsured. Mark Taylor needed surgery for four gunshots to the chest; his mom couldn't afford groceries or pay the rent. The process was humiliating, she said. She felt like a beggar. "My son's in the hospital. I can't work. We're broke and they have millions of dollars in donations. I'm disgusted."

The attorney for the Taylors and Kirklins suggested that some families needed compensation more than others. Brian Rohrbough erupted again. That implied that Danny's life had no value, he told the *Rocky Mountain News*. For Brian, the money was symbolic: the ultimate valuation of each life. For others it was purely practical.

In early July, the Healing Fund announced its distribution plan: 40 percent of the $3.8 million would go to direct victims. A clever compromise was reached for that money: the four kids with critical injuries got $150,000 each; $50,000 went to each of the Thirteen. That totaled $650,000 for the dead versus $600,000 for the critically injured, giving the Thirteen the appearance of preeminence. Twenty-one injured students got $10,000 each, a fraction of the medical bills for many. Most of the remainder went to trauma counseling and tolerance programs. Roughly $750,000 was earmarked for contingencies, a compromise to cover unpaid medical bills without appearing to favor the injured over the dead.

Brian Rohrbough backed off once he felt heard.

———

Tom Klebold was dealing with a lot of anger. "Who gave my son these guns?" he asked Reverend Marxhausen. He also felt betrayed by the school culture that picked on kids outside the mainstream.

Tom did his best to shut out the angry world. His job allowed him to hunker down at home, and he took full advantage. Sue was not wired that way. "She has to get out," Marxhausen said.

May 28, Kathy Harris wrote condolence letters to the Thirteen. Many of the addresses were unpublished, so she sealed each one in an envelope with the family's name, put them all in a manila envelope, and mailed it to an address the school district had set up as a clearinghouse for correspondence to victims. A week later, Kathy sent a second batch for the families of twenty-three injured. The school district turned them all over to the sheriff's department as potential evidence. It sat on them. Officials decided not to read them or deliver them.

In mid-July, the media discovered the snafu. "It's really not our job" to distribute them, Sergeant Randy West said. The letters had no postage or addresses, so commanders decided to return to sender. West complained about the family's refusal to meet without immunity, and said his team had trouble reaching their attorneys. "They're busy, we're busy and we can't seem to connect with them," Sergeant West said. "I guess if you want to make things easier you could just talk to us."

The Harrises broke their three-month silence to issue a statement disputing "misstatements" on the letters. Their attorney insisted Jeffco had never tried to contact him about them.

The letters were eventually returned.

Sue Klebold also wrote apologies in May. She mailed them directly to the Thirteen. Brad and Misty received this handwritten card:

Dear Bernall family,

It is with great difficulty and humility that we write to express our profound sorrow over the loss of your beautiful daughter, Cassie. She brought joy and love to the world, and she was taken in a moment of madness. We wish we had had the opportunity to know her and be uplifted by her loving spirit.

We will never understand why this tragedy happened, or what we might have done to prevent it. We apologize for the role our son had in your Cassie's death. We never saw anger or hatred in Dylan until the last moments of his life when we watched in helpless horror with the rest of the world. The reality that our son shared in the responsibility for this tragedy is still incredibly difficult for us to comprehend.

May God comfort you and your loved ones. May He bring peace and understanding to all of our wounded hearts.

Sincerely,
Sue and Tom Klebold

Misty was moved—enough to publish the full text in the memoir she was drafting. She generously described the act as courageous. Tom and Sue lost a son in the same disaster, she wrote. At least Cassie had died nobly. What comfort did the Klebolds have? Misty also addressed the charges against the killers' parents. Should they have known? Were they negligent? "How do we know?"

42. Diversion

A year before the attack, the boys settled on the time and place: April 1999, in the commons. That gave Eric time to plan, build his arsenal, and convince his partner it was for real.

Shortly after starting Diversion, Eric and Dylan received their junior yearbooks. They swapped and filled page after page with drawings, descriptions, and rants. "We, the gods, will have <u>so</u> much fun w NBK!!" Dylan wrote in Eric's. "My wrath for january's incident will be godlike. Not to mention our revenge in the commons."

January's incident was their arrest. Eric was pissed about it, too. "Jan 31 sux," he wrote in Dylan's. "I hate white vans!!"

The arrest was a critical moment—the yearbooks confirmed Fuselier's tentative conclusion on that score. Eventually, Fuselier would see it as the single most important event in Eric's progression to murder. The arrest was followed, in rapid succession, by Eric detonating his first pipe bombs, threatening mass murder on his Web site, confiding worse visions to his journal, and settling on the outlines of his attack. But Eric was already headed that way. He did not "snap." Fuselier saw fallout from the crime as accelerant to murder rather than cause.

Eric was an injustice collector. The cops, judge, and Diversion officers were merely the latest additions to a comically comprehensive enemies list, which included Tiger Woods, every girl who had rejected him, all of Western culture, and the human species. What was different about the arrest, in Fuselier's eyes, was that it was the first dramatic rein-in on the boys' ability to control their own lives—"the screws are tightening," as Dylan put it. They were juniors in high school now, a time when personal freedom expanded faster than ever before. They had just gotten their driver's licenses, they had jobs with paychecks and their first rush of disposable income, their curfews were getting later, parental oversight was easing, Eric was dating…their universe of possibilities was expanding. They had suffered setbacks before, but those were mild and short-lived. This time, it was a felony. A felony, for the smallest trifle: some moron's van—so what? All freedom was lost. Eric's twenty-three-year-old was dumping him because he was grounded all the time and could never see her. He kept working Brenda, but it didn't look good.

Eric filled Dylan's yearbook with drawings: swastikas, robokillers, and splattered bodies. The dead outnumbered the living. An illustration in the margin suggested hundreds of tiny corpses piling up to the horizon, until they all blended together in an ocean of human waste.

Eric went through his own book, marking up the faces of kids he didn't like. He labeled them "worthless," said they would die, or just made an X over their pictures. Eric had two thousand photos to deface, and eventually he got to almost all of them.

Eric had it in for a couple of traitorous assholes: "God I cant wait till they die," he wrote in Dylan's book. "I can taste the blood now."

Psychopaths want to enjoy their exploits. That's why the sadistic ones tend to choose serial killing: they enjoy the cruelty as it plays out. Eric went a different route: the big kill, which he would relish in anticipation for a full year. He loved control—he couldn't wait to hold lives in his hand. When his day finally arrived, he took his time in the library and enjoyed every minute of it. He killed some kids on a whim, let others go just as easily.

He also used his Web site to enjoy a certain notoriety in his lifetime. He loved the irony of his online world, where all the other kids were posing but his fantasy was real.

One contradiction to Eric's control fetish is apparent in his willingness to entrust power to Dylan. The yearbook exchange represented a huge leap of faith for each of them. They had been talking about murder for months now, and corresponding catchphrases in both journals suggest they had been riffing on these ideas regularly. Eric had gone semipublic with his threats already, posting them on his Web site, but no one seemed to notice or take it seriously. This time, he scrawled out incriminating evidence of his plot in his own handwriting and turned it over to Dylan.

They hinted about plans in a few friends' yearbooks, but it all sounded like jokes. Dylan said he would like to kill Puff Daddy or Hanson, while Eric went with irony: don't follow your dreams, follow your animal instincts—"if it moves kill it, if it doesn't, burn it. kein mitleid!!!" *Kein mitleid* is German for "no mercy," and a common shorthand for his favorite band, KMFDM. This was just the kind of move that delighted Eric: warn the world, in writing, to show us how stupid we all are.

In each other's books, they took a real gamble, particularly Dylan. He wrote page after page of specific murder plans. They were at each other's mercy now. Exposure of the yearbooks could end their participation in Diversion and bring them back on felony charges. For the final year, each boy knew his buddy could get him imprisoned at any time, though they would both go down together. Mutually assured destruction.

———

Dr. Fuselier considered the yearbook passages. Both boys fantasized about murder, but Dylan focused on the single attack. Eric had a grander vision. All his writing alluded to a wider slaughter: killing everything, destroying the human race. In a passionate journal entry a month later, he would cite the Nazis' Final Solution: "kill them all. well in case you haven't figured it out yet, I say 'KILL MANKIND.'"

It's unclear whether Eric and Dylan were aware of the discrepancy—neither one addressed it in writing. It's hard to imagine that Eric failed to notice Dylan's focus on a more limited attack. Was he including Dylan in the full dream? Perhaps Dylan just didn't find it plausible. Blowing up the high school, that could actually happen—killing mankind…maybe that just sounded like science fiction to Dylan.

Despite the press's obsession with bullying and misfits, that's not how the boys presented themselves. Dylan laughed about picking on the new freshmen and "fags." Neither one complained about bullies picking on them—they boasted about doing it themselves.

———

The boys changed dramatically after they began Diversion—in reverse directions, once again. Eric launched a new charm offensive. Andrea Sanchez became the second most important person in his life. Snowing her was the best way to appease the first, his dad. It also kept the program from diverting Eric from his goal. Eric had a plan now. He was on a mission and he was revved. His grades dropped briefly after the arrest, but they rebounded to his best ever once he had his attack plan. It was a lot of work, which he complained bitterly about in his journal; but he worked his ass off to excel.

Dylan didn't even try to impress Andrea. He missed appointments, fell behind in community service, and let his grades plummet. He was actually getting two D's.

NBK was nothing but a diversion to Dylan—fantasy chats with his buddy about what they would like to do. Dylan didn't believe it; he didn't plan to go through with it. All he knew was that he was a felon now. His miserable life had grown pathetically worse.

Eric was the star performer in the program, at work and at school. He even earned a raise, and when school let out for his last summer, he got a second job at Tortilla Wraps, where his buddy Nate Dykeman worked. Eric started putting away more money to build his arsenal. His cover story was that he was saving up for a new computer. He worked both jobs, in addition to the forty-five hours of community service the judge had ordered for the summer. That was boring, menial crap, like sweeping and picking up trash at a rec center. He despised it but pasted on a smile. It was all for a good cause.

Dylan did not appear to contribute much to the attack, financially or otherwise. He quit Blackjack and didn't bother with a regular job over the summer; he just did some yard work for a neighbor.

Eric kept both his employers and the rec supervisors satisfied. "He was a real nice kid," his Tortilla boss said. "He would come in every day with nice T-shirts, khaki shorts, sandals. He was kind of quiet but everyone got along with him." Nate liked to wear his trench coat to work, but Eric didn't feel that was professional.

The boys were required to write apology letters to the van owner. Eric's exuded contrition. He acknowledged he was writing partly because he'd been ordered to "but mostly because I strongly feel that I owe you an apology." Eric said he was sorry repeatedly, and outlined his legal and parental punishments so the victim would understand that he was paying a price for his actions.

Eric knew exactly what empathy looked like. His most convincing moment in the letter came when he put himself in the owner's position. If his car had been robbed, he said, the sense of invasion would have haunted him. It would have been hard for him to drive it again. Every time he got in the car, he would have pictured someone rummaging through it. God, he felt violated just imagining it. He was so disappointed in himself. "I realized very soon afterwards what I had done and how utterly stupid it was," Eric wrote. "I let the stupid side of me take over."

"But he wrote that strictly for effect," Fuselier said. "That was complete manipulation. At almost the exact same time, he wrote down his real feelings in his journal: 'Isnt America supposed to be the land of the free? how come if im free, I cant deprive a stupid fucking dumbshit from his possessions. If he leaves them sitting in the front seat of his fucking van out in plain sight and in the middle of fucking nowhere on a Frifucking day night. NATURAL SELECTION. fucker should be shot.'"

Eric betrayed no signs of contempt to Andrea Sanchez. In her notes, she remarked on Eric's deep remorse.

Few angry boys can hide their feelings or sling the bullshit so convincingly. Habitual liars hate sucking up like that. Not psychopaths. That was the best part of the performance: Eric's joy came from watching Andrea and the van owner and Wayne Harris and everyone who caught sight of the letter fall for his ridiculous con.

Eric never complained about those lies. He bragged about them.

Eric could be a procrastinator—a common affliction among psychopaths—and Andrea suggested he work on time management. So Eric bought a Rebel Pride day planner, filled a week in, and brought it to his biweekly counseling session to show off. He gushed about what a great idea it was. It was really helping, he said. Andrea was impressed. She praised him for it in his file. Then he quit. He used the book to vent his real feelings. It had come packed with motivational slogans and tips for better living. Eric went through hundreds of pages rewriting selected words and phrases: "A person's mind is always *splattered*....Cut old *people* and other *losers* into rags....Ninth graders are required to *burn and die*." He altered the Denver entry on a population chart to show forty-seven inhabitants once he was through.

Andrea Sanchez was delighted with Eric. She worked with the boys directly for a few months and then transitioned them over to a new counselor. In Eric's file, Andrea ended her last entry with "Muy facile hombre"—very easy man.

Dylan got no affectionate sign-off. And why wouldn't Andrea Sanchez like Eric more? Everyone did. He was funny and clever, and that smile, man—he knew just when to flash it, too; just how long to hang back, tease you with it, make you work for it, and then lay it on.

Dylan was a gloom factory. The misery was self-fulfilling: who wanted to hang around under that cloud all day?

Inside, he was a dynamo of wild energy, hurtling in eight directions at once, jamming music in his head, thinking clever thoughts, bursting with joy and sadness and regret and hope and excitement...but he was scared to show it. Dylan kept it behind a veneer—you could see him silently simmering sometimes, but he mostly came across as sheepish and embarrassed. Anger was the one thing that would boil over sometimes. The loving part, that stuff could be singing inside from the highest mountain, only he wasn't about to let it show. The anger would just erupt. That would freak people out. You never would have expected it out of that kid.

———

Eric complained about his medication. Before he transitioned from Andrea Sanchez, he told her the Zoloft wasn't doing enough. He felt restless and couldn't concentrate. Dr. Albert switched him to Luvox. The change required two weeks unmedicated, to metabolize the Zoloft out of his system. Eric told Andrea he was worried about going without. He told a different story in his journal. Dr. Albert wanted to medicate him to eradicate bad thoughts and quell his anger, he wrote. *That* was craziness. He would not accept the human assembly line. "NO, NO NO God Fucking damit NO!" he wrote. "I will sooner <u>die</u> than betray my own thoughts. but before I leave this <u>worthless</u> place, I will kill whoever I deem unfit."

It's not clear exactly what Eric was up to with Dr. Albert. He might have actually complained about the Zoloft because it was *too* effective. Every patient reacts differently. The maneuver definitely solidified the facade of Eric working to control his anger.

"I would be very surprised if Eric was being honest and straightforward with his doctor," Fuselier said. "Psychopaths attempt to, and often succeed, in manipulating mental health professionals, too."

———

Wayne Harris was the hardest person for Eric to fool. He had seen Eric's boy scout act. It never lasted. Wayne made one undated entry in his journal sometime after the orientation meeting for Diversion in April. He was frustrated. He listed bulleted points for a lecture for Eric:

- Unwilling to control sleep habits.
- Unwilling to control study habits.
- Unmotivated to succeed in school.
- We can deal with 1 and 2: TV, phone, computer, lights out, job, social.
- You must deal with 3.
- Prove to us your desire to succeed by succeeding, showing good judgment, giving extra effort, pursuing interests, seeking help, advice.

He put Eric on restriction again: a 10:00 P.M. curfew except for studying, no phone during study time, and possibly another four weeks away from his computer.

The crackdown was the last entry Wayne Harris would record—and nearly the last words the public would get from him. The search warrant exercised on his home a year later was specific to Eric's writings. Nothing else from Wayne or Kathy or Eric's brother was confiscated. In the ten years since the attack, they have issued a few brief statements through attorneys, met with police briefly, and with parents of the victims once. They have never spoken to the press. The outlines of Eric's relationship to his father came through in their journals, and from testimony of outsiders. Kathy Harris is murkier, and a full picture of the family dynamic remains elusive.

———

With Eric, Dylan paid lip service to NBK. Privately, he was juggling two options: suicide or true love. He wrote Harriet a love letter, confessing all. "You don't consciously know who I am," he started, bluntly. "I, who write this, love you beyond infinince." He thought about her all the time, he said. "Fate put me in need of you, yet this earth blocked that with uncertainties." He was actually a lot like her: pensive, quiet, an observer. Like him, she seemed uninterested in the physical world. Life, school, it was all meaningless—how wonderful that she understood. Dylan caught a glimpse of sadness in her: she was lonely, just like him.

He wondered if she had a boyfriend. Odd that he'd never checked that out. He hardly saw her anymore. He realized this might be a bit much: "I know what you're thinking: '(some psycho wrote me this harassing letter.)'" But he had to take the chance. He was sure she had noticed him a few times—none of her gazes had gone unnoticed. Dylan confessed his scariest intentions—just like Zack, who had found a soul mate in whom to confide his suicidal desires. At first Dylan was a little coy: "I will go away soon...please don't feel any guilt about my soon-to-be 'absence' of this world." Finally he conceded that she would hate him if she knew the whole truth, but he confessed it anyway: "I am a criminal, I have done things that almost nobody would even think about condoning." He had been caught for most of his crimes, he said, and wanted a new existence. He was confident she knew what he meant. "Suicide? I have nothing to live for, & I won't be able to survive in this world after this legal conviction." But if she loved him as strongly as he loved her, he would find a way to survive.

If she thought he was crazy, please don't tell anyone, he pleaded. Please accept his apologies. But if she felt something for him, too, she should leave a note in his locker—No. 837, near the library.

He signed his name. He did not deliver it. Did he ever intend to? Or was it just for him?

Eric, meanwhile, was upset. He lashed out at Brooks Brown by e-mail. "I know you're an enemy of Eric's," it said. "I know where you live and what cars you drive."

Psychopaths do not attempt to fool everyone. They save their performances for people with power over them or with something they need. If you saw the ugly side of Eric Harris, you meant nothing to him.

Brooks told his mom; Judy called the cops. A deputy wrote up yet another suspicious incident report and added it to the ongoing investigation of Eric. It said the Browns were worried. They'd requested an extra patrol for the night.

———

The threesome was over. Zack was not included in NBK, and Eric froze him out completely. Eric went cold on him that summer, Zack said—he never figured out why. Open hostilities erupted that fall. Dylan kept clear of it. He stayed close to Zack, away from Eric, chatting away by phone every night.

Randy Brown called the cops again. Somebody had tagged his garage with a paintball gun. He was sure it was that same old little criminal,

Eric Harris. A deputy interviewed Randy and wrote up a report. "No suspects—no leads," he wrote.

"Eric is doing well," his new counselor, Bob Kriegshauser, wrote in Eric's file at that time. Eric was exceeding expectations and covering his mistakes. He got into a bit of a procrastination jam on his last four hours of community service. He waited until the last day, and he wasn't going to get to complete his full forty-five hours. So he sweet-talked the stranger in charge at the rec center that day, who was impressed enough to lie for him. As far as Bob Kriegshauser knew, Eric completed his service on time. Eric used the work for brownie points with a teacher that fall. He boasted about the summer he'd dedicated to the community.

The boys continued diverging philosophically: Eric held mastery over man and nature; Dylan was a slave to fate. And Dylan had a big surprise. He had no intention of inflicting Eric's massacre. He enjoyed the banter, but privately said good-bye. He expected his August 10 entry to be his last. Dylan was planning to kill himself long before NBK.

———

Senior year started for the killers. Eric and Dylan began a video production class. That was fun. They got to make movies. The fictional vignettes were mostly variations on a formula: aloof tough guys protecting misfits from hulking jocks. Eric and Dylan outwitted the bullies, but saved the real contempt for their clients. They bled the losers financially, then killed them just because they could. The victims deserved it; they were inferior. The story lines spilled right out of Eric's journal.

What an opportunity. Eric was guiding his unsteady partner: fantasy to reality, one step at a time. Dylan ate it up. He came alive on camera. His eyes bulged. You could sense true rage smoldering beneath his skin. The boys had riffed on NBK for months, but now they were acting out bits on film. They were celluloid heroes, screening their exploits for classmates and adults. Eric loved that. Hilarious to reveal his plans that way. He was right in the open, and they still couldn't guess. And he had Dylan out there with him.

———

Eric was gobbling up literature: *Macbeth, King Lear, Tess of the d'Urbervilles*. He could never get enough Nietzsche or Hobbes. Once a week, he wrote a short essay for English class on one of the stories or sometimes on a random topic. These essays reached Dr. Fuselier weeks after the murders. He found them revealing, particularly for what they omitted.

In September, Eric titled one of his short essays, "Is Murder or Breaking the Law Ever Justified?" Yes, he responded—in extreme situations. He described holding pets and humans hostage, threatening to blow up busloads of people. The irony of masking grisly murder fantasies in moralistic essays amused him. A police sniper could save many by killing one, Eric argued. The law must bend. Eric made the same case in his journal but took it a step further: moral imperatives are situational, absolutes are imaginary; therefore, he could kill anyone he wanted.

It's revealing that Eric took on a provocative issue and gauged exactly how far he could run with it. Fuselier saw no moral confusion, clearly no mental illness—Eric demonstrated his sanity by his ability to navigate such tricky terrain. He got the satisfaction of warning us in yet another way without giving himself away.

———

Dylan expected to be dead soon. What was the point of school? He had a light schedule and was still pulling two D's. He was sleeping in class. He missed the first calculus test and didn't bother making it up. Those grades are not acceptable, Bob Kriegshauser, his Diversion officer, said. He could get them up ASAP or do his homework at the Diversion office every afternoon. Kriegshauser was thrilled with Eric's progress. Eric was working on a speech about foreign music and memorizing "Der Erlkönig," Goethe's darkly operatic poem. He'd taken a road trip to Boulder to catch a University of Colorado football game. He was making a batch of doughnuts for Octoberfest, and soaking up everything he could find on the Nazis. He pored through books such as *The Nazi Party, Secrets of the SS,* and *The Ideological Origins of Nazi Imperialism.* He cited a dozen scholarly books for his paper "The Nazi Culture." It was a strong piece of work: vivid, comprehensive, and detailed.

The paper let Eric indulge in depravity right in the open. It began by asking the reader to imagine a stadium packed with murdered men, women, and children—not just filling the seats but piled high into the air above it. That would still represent just a fraction of the people exterminated by the Nazis, he said. Six million Jews they did away with, and five million others besides. Eleven million—now, there was a body count. Eric fantasized about topping it.

He described Nazi officers lining up prisoners and firing into the first man to see how many rib cages the bullet would penetrate. "Wow," his teacher responded in the margin. "This is scary.... Incredible."

Eric photocopied a passage from Heinrich Himmler's infamous speech to SS group leaders and kept it in his room. "Whether or not 10,000 Russian women collapse from exhaustion while digging a tank ditch interests me only in so far as the tank ditch is completed for Germany," Himmler said. "[Germans] will also adopt a decent attitude to these human animals, but it is a crime against our own blood to worry about them and to bring them ideals." Here was someone who got it! The Nazis used human animals for labor; Eric only needed his to explode. Five or six hundred dismemberments ought to be enough for one awesome afternoon of TV.

Eric was feeling rambunctious. He started wearing T-shirts with German phrases, he littered his papers with swastikas, and he yelled "Sieg Heil" when he landed a strike at Rock 'n' Bowl. For Eric's buddy Chris Morris, all the damn Nazi shit was wearing a little thin. Eric was quoting Hitler, spouting off about concentration camps...enough.

In October, Eric faced a setback. A speeding ticket. His parents were strict, and it cost him: they made him pay the fine, attend Defensive Driving, cover any increase in insurance premiums; plus, he was grounded for three weeks.

All the open Nazi lust was beginning to paint Eric into a corner. Four days after turning his paper in, Eric confided to his journal that he was showing too much. "I might need to put on one helluva mask here to fool you all some more," he wrote. "fuck fuck fuck. it'll be hard to hold out until April."

He tried a new tactic: recast what he had already revealed. He wrote a deeply personal essay for government class and turned it in to Mr. Tonelli—they called him T-dog. Eric admitted he was a felon. He had faced the horror of the police station as a criminal. But he was a changed man. He'd spent four hours in custody, and it had been a nightmare. When they put him in a prison-style bathroom, he had broken down. "I cried, I hurt, and I felt like hell," he wrote.

He was still trying to earn back the respect of his parents, he said. That was the biggest blow. Thank God he and Dylan never drank or did any drugs. In the closing lines, he made a classic psychopathic move: "Personally, I think that whole entire night was enough punishment for me," he wrote, explaining that it forced him to face a whole new world of experiences. "So all in all," he concluded, "I guess it was a worth while punishment after all."

T-dog fell for every move. What chance did he have against a clever young psychopath? Few teachers even know the meaning of the term. Tonelli typed up a response to Eric: "Wow what a way to learn a lesson. I agree that night was enough punishment for you. Still, I am proud of you and the way you have reacted....You have really learned from this and it has changed the way you think....I would trust you in a heartbeat. Thanks for letting me read this and for being in my class."

Fuselier compared the dates of the public and private confessions: just two days between them. It was remarkable how often Eric addressed the same ideas in both venues, and how craftily he obscured his true intent.

Months after the attack, following a briefing on the killers, Tonelli went to see Fuselier.

"I have to talk to you," he said. Fuselier sat down with him. Tonelli was racked with guilt. "What did I miss here?" he asked.

Nothing, Fuselier said. Eric was convincing. He told you exactly what you wanted to hear. He didn't play innocent; he confessed to guilt and pleaded for forgiveness. Civilians always believe a good psychopath.

Eric bragged about his performances again in his journal, and then took a turn: "goddammit I would have been a fucking great marine, It would have given me a reason to be good." That was unusual for Eric. He usually reveled in his "bad" choice, but just for a moment there he toyed with the other road: "and I would never drink and drive, either," he added. "It will be weird when we actually go on the rampage."

Dr. Fuselier read the passage with only mild surprise. Even extreme psychopaths show flickers of empathy now and then. Eric was extreme but not absolute. This was the closest he would come to betraying reservations, and it was a logical pass. The plan was becoming real now. Eric finally had the means to kill. He felt the power; he had to make a decision—keep it fantasy or make it real?

Eric's reflection lasted two lines. The sentences run together as if he was writing rapidly, and the next one envisioned a massive attack. A jumbo ammo cartridge would be great: "just think, 100 rounds without reloading, hell yeah!"

43. Who Owns the Tragedy

There is a house, outside of Laramie. It's a rugged Wyoming town on the fringe of the Rockies. That's where Dave and Linda Sanders were going to retire. A quiet college town, Laramie may appear desolate to most eyes, but it teems with youthful energy and is the intellectual capital of the state. Dave's Ford Escort could get them there in under three hours, and they made several trips a year.

They were closing in on it now—two years away, maybe three. They were looking forward to it. They called it retirement, but it was a work addict's version: off with one career, on to the next. Dave would move up to a college position; Linda had her eye on an antiques store. After twenty-five years at Columbine, Dave had qualified for his teaching pension. It was just a matter of an opening. University of Wyoming was a good bet: he had been scouting for them for years and coaching the summer camp, and was great friends with the head basketball coach.

They would watch their retirement home glide by from the highway every time they approached town. It was a gray ranch house with a wide porch running all the way around. They would add rocking chairs, and a porch swing for the grandkids.

Linda Sanders thought about that house in Laramie a lot after Dave died. She thought about how different her struggle was from all the other victims. All the attention was on the students and their parents.

Kathy Ireland had wanted to save her boy. Now she wanted to get her hands on the kids who did this to him. She looked into Patrick's eyes. Serene. Like hers, before this horror struck. Kathy had breathed tranquillity into her family, but it took all of her effort to stay calm around Patrick.

Kathy stood by Patrick's bed and asked if he understood who'd done this to him.

It didn't matter, he said. They were confused. Just forgive them. Please forgive them.

"It took my breath away," Kathy said later. At first she assumed Patrick was confused. He was not. He had too much work to do. He was going to walk again, and talk again, like a normal person. And he insisted he would still be valedictorian. Anger would eat him up inside. He couldn't afford that.

OK, Kathy said. She had been praying incessantly that Patrick would come through this with a sense of happiness—that in time he would find a way to let it go. This, she had not expected. She feared that it was more than she could do, but she would try to forgive, too. It would take her years to let go, and she never shook the anger completely, but she kept looking to Patrick leading the way.

———

Patrick Ireland was struggling. His days at Craig Hospital that first summer were exhausting. Speech therapy, muscle therapy, testing, prodding, poking, and the endless efforts just to communicate. Retrieving the right word often eluded him. At night Patrick would lie quietly in his room, winding down before settling off to sleep. John or Kathy would stay with him. They took turns each night; one of them would sleep on a fold-out chair beside his bed. Just in case.

They would turn the lights off around eleven or twelve and just sit there in the dark with him, quietly at first; then he would begin to ask questions. He needed to know everything. What exactly happened in the library? How did he respond? What was going to happen now? Patrick wanted to know about the other victims, too, and the killers sometimes—what could make them do something like that?

"There were certainly times that I was mad," Patrick said later. "But I think a lot of those were more for realizations of what was taken from me, rather than actually what transpired. My life was going be completely changed." Patrick tried not to stay angry on the basketball court. Make a mistake, brush it off. "Keep your eye on the ball," he could hear his dad say. Patrick focused on the present.

His speech was returning slowly. Short-term memory was a struggle.

There were exercises for everything. A therapist would recite a list of twenty things, and he'd have to repeat them in the same order. It was hard.

Patrick shed his anger toward the killers early, but his condition could be infuriating. Outbursts are typical with head wounds. Anger and frustration commonly last several months. The blue period, they call it. His therapists were tracking that as well. When Patrick shook his fist at them, they would note it in his chart.

———

Patrick stayed at Craig Hospital for nine and a half weeks. He walked out on July 2, using a forearm crutch to support himself. He wore a plastic brace on his right leg. His doctors sent him home with a wheelchair for when he needed to cover long distances. A banner signed by friends welcomed him back.

The summer went quickly. Patrick wasn't ready for school to start. He was overbooked already: occupational, physical, and speech therapy, and neuropsychology. They were exhausting days. But he was walking more steadily. His speech was pretty intelligible, and the extended pauses while he searched for words grew briefer. A sentence might be interrupted only once now, or sometimes not at all. The blue period passed.

As he continued working, Patrick thought more about the lake. He knew he couldn't get on the water. He could hear the buzz of the boat, smell the water lapping the pier. Eventually, Patrick convinced his father to take him out to watch his sister make some practice runs. He loved waterskiing. John started the boat. As the engine sputtered, Patrick smelled the fumes, closed his eyes, and he was out there riding the surface again. He sat on the dock reliving it all. Then he began to cry. He shook violently. He swore. John rushed over to comfort him. He was inconsolable. He wasn't angry at his parents or himself or Eric or Dylan—he was just angry. He wanted his life back. He was never going to get it. John assured him they would get through this. Then he held on to Patrick and let him cry.

———

Four months after the police tape went up, Columbine was set to reopen. August 16 was the target date. The atmosphere that morning would mean everything. If students came home feeling like they had made a clean break over the summer and moved on, then they would have. The first few minutes of that morning would set the tone for the entire year. Administrators had gathered students, faculty, victims, and other stakeholders and brainstormed all summer. They'd consulted psychologists and cultural anthropologists and grief experts and had come up with an elaborate ritual. It would be called Take Back the School.

For the ceremony to have impact, they needed an adversary to overcome. And the more tangible and odious the adversary, the better. It was an easy choice: the media. The *Denver Post* and the *Rocky Mountain News* were still running Columbine stories every day—several a day. As the fall semester beckoned, coverage shot back up: ten stories a day between the two papers. And the national outlets were back. *How do you feel?* everyone constantly wanted to know. Students started sporting BITE ME T-shirts, and quite a few faculty members did, too.

The media had made their lives hell. And reporters could be counted on to appear in record numbers. The rally would include speeches and cheers and rock music and a ribbon cutting, but the heart of the event was a public rebuke of the media and a ceremonial reclaiming of the school—from them. Thousands of parents and neighbors would be recruited to form a human shield to rebuke the press. The shield would function both symbolically and practically. It would prevent reporters from performing their despicable job. They literally would not be able to see what was going on. The rally could have easily been planned for inside—virtually every school rally was. This event would be held outside specifically to stick it to the media. No doors or locks or walls would keep out the media; they would be blocked by a human wall of shame. And the school would dare them to try to cross it.

———

Reporters were kept in the dark about the agenda until seven days before the rally. On August 9, the school convened a Media Guidelines Summit. Forty news organizations attended, local and national. The invitation was filled with conciliatory phrases like "exchange ideas" and "balance the interests." The district lined up a group of trauma experts. A professor outlined bereavement: these kids were still in the early stages, and many were suffering from PTSD. Mental repetition of the trauma trapped them there. The TV stations kept recycling the same stock footage: SWAT teams, bloody victims, hugging survivors, kids running out with hands on their heads.

Reporters did not like where this was going. Then victim's advocate Robin

Finegan introduced the larger idea: kids felt as if their identities had been stolen. "Columbine" was the name of a tragedy now. Their school was a symbol of mass murder. They had been cast as bullies or snotty rich brats. "There comes a point where victims need to have ownership of their tragedy," Finegan said. So far, the media owned the Columbine tragedy. That was about to change, the district said—or good luck getting your precious "Columbine returns" stories. Administrators outlined the gist of the ceremony.

"What's the human chain for?" a reporter asked.

"To shield the students from you folk," district spokesman Rick Kaufman said.

Most media would be excluded. A small pool would be escorted in. Reporters were incredulous. One print reporter? The White House didn't limit its pool that tightly. Reporters for the big national papers huddled in the back of the room, discussing options to "lawyer up."

The district wouldn't back down, Kaufman said. In fact, the pool would come only with major concessions: no helicopters, no rooftop photographers, and no breach of school grounds. "If we can't get agreement, then there's no pool," he said.

Try it, reporters threatened; it will backfire. "As long as parents understand that by saying no to everything, again it's going to be a situation where we're coming out of rocks and stuff in order to get sound and pictures," a TV executive said. "And I wonder if the parents really understand, if they think they control us by just saying no, they're really not; they're forcing us to go in other directions."

Kaufman said his back was to the wall. Angry parents had objected to any pool at all. "Parents and faculty, they have really hit the wall with you folks. They're saying, 'We're done! Enough is enough.'"

Later that week, a compromise was reached. The pool was expanded slightly, and a "bullpen" was added within the shield, where interested students could approach cordoned-off reporters. The press agreed to all previous demands and two new ones: no kid would be approached on the way to school that morning, and no photographs of any of the injured survivors would be used. The kids finally felt a sense of victory.

———

Mr. D was excited about the rally. But he was also worried about the new kids. It was a principal's thing—the incoming freshmen always commanded his thoughts this time of year. Kids would either assimilate quickly or spend four years struggling to fit in. The first two weeks were crucial.

Mr. D chose to combat the chasm by highlighting it. He met with the academic and sports teams and the student senate over the summer, and he gave every kid and every teacher the same mission: *These kids will never understand you. They will never endure your pain, never bridge the gap between social classes that you did. So help them.*

By and large, they went for it. Kids thought they were overwhelmed by their own struggle, but what they really needed was someone else to look out for. They had to salve a different sort of pain to comprehend how to heal their own.

Mr. D's team brainstormed up a slew of activities to grease the transition. The wall tile project seemed like an easy one. For three years, kids had been painting four-inch ceramic tiles in art class. Five hundred had been plastered above the lockers to brighten the Columbine corridors. Fifteen hundred new tiles would be added before school resumed, representing the single most noticeable change to the interior. For one morning, kids could express their grief or hope or desires visually and abstractly, without the intervention of words that wouldn't come.

———

Brian Fuselier didn't want his parents standing in the human shield. "The more you do that, the more you make it unnatural," he told his dad. Brian was doing OK with the trauma; he just wanted his life back, and his school back, the way it had been.

"That's just not going to happen," his father said.

Agent Fuselier took Monday morning off from the investigation to join the chain. Mimi stood beside him. By seven A.M. kids were streaming in with their parents. By 7:30, the shield was five hundred strong. It would grow much larger. The parents applauded each student's arrival.

Most of the kids wore matching white T-shirts emblazoned with their rallying cry: WE ARE on the front and COLUMBINE on the back. Small contingents had opted for their own messages: YES, I BELIEVE IN GOD or VICTORS NOT VICTIMS.

Frank DeAngelis took the microphone and a group of kids screamed, "We love you, Mr. D!"

He teared up at the welcome, then delivered a touching speech. "You may be feeling a little anxious," he said. "But you need to know that you are not in this alone."

The school's American flags were raised from half-mast for the first time since April 20, symbolically ending the period of mourning. A ribbon across the entrance was cut, and Patrick Ireland led the student body in.

44. Bombs Are Hard

Eric was counting on a slow recovery. He was less concerned about killing hundreds of people on April 20 than about tormenting millions for years. His audience was the target. He wanted everyone to agonize: the student body, residents of Jeffco, the American public, the human race.

Eric amused himself with the idea of coming back as a ghost to haunt survivors. He would make noises to trigger flashbacks, and drive them all insane. Anticipation satiated Eric for months. Then it was time to act.

Senior year, just before Halloween, he began assembling his arsenal. Eric sat down in his room with a stack of fireworks, split each one down the side, and tapped the shiny black powder into a coffee can. Once he had a sufficient volume, he tipped the can and guided a fine little trickle into a carbon dioxide cartridge. He measured it out carefully, almost to the rim. Then he applied a wick, sealed it off, and set it aside. One cricket, ready for detonation. He was pleased with his work. He assembled nine more.

The pipe bombs required a lot more gunpowder, as well as a PVC pipe to house each one. Eric assembled four of those that day. The first three he designated the Alpha batch. Not bad, but he could do better. He set them aside and tried a different approach. He built just one bomb for the Beta batch. Better. Still room for improvement. That was enough for one day.

Eric drew up a chart to record his production data. He set up columns to log each batch by name, size, quantity, shrapnel content, and power load. Then he rated his work. Six of his eight batches would earn an "excellent" assessment. His worst performance was "O.K."

The next day, Eric got right back to it, producing six more pipe bombs—the rest of the Beta batch. Later, he would create Charlie, Delta, Echo, and Foxtrot, using military lingo for all of the batches, except that soldiers use *Bravo,* not *Beta.*

Eric penned nearly a dozen new journal entries in the next two months. "I have a goal to destroy as much as possible," he wrote, "so I must not be sidetracked by my feelings of sympathy, mercy, or any of that."

It was a mark of Eric's ruthlessness that he comprehended the pain and consciously fought the urge to spare it. "I will force myself to believe that everyone is just another monster from Doom," he wrote. "I have to turn off my feelings."

Keep one thing in mind, he said: he wanted to burn the world. That would be hard. He had begun producing the explosives, and it was a lot of work. Ten pipe bombs and ten puny crickets after two days' effort. Those would not destroy much. "God I want to torch and level everything in this whole fucking area," he said, "but bombs of that size are hard to make."

Eric took a few moments to enjoy the dream. He envisioned half of Denver on fire: napalm streams eating the skin off skyscrapers, explosive gas tanks ripping through residential garages. Napalm recipes were available online. The ingredients were readily attainable. But he had to be realistic. "It will be very tricky getting all of our supplies, explosives, weaponry, ammo, and then hiding it all and then actually planting it all," he said. A lot could go wrong in the next six months, and if they did get busted, "we start killing then and there. I aint going out without a fight."

Eric repeated that last line almost verbatim in an English essay. The assignment was to react to a quote from literature, and Eric had chosen this line from Euripides' tragedy *Medea:* "No, like some yellow-eyed beast that has killed its hunters let me lie down on the hounds' bodies and the broken spears." Medea was declaring that she would die fighting, Eric wrote. They would never take her without a struggle. He repeated that sentiment seven times in a page and a quarter. He described Medea as brave and courageous, tough and strong and hard as stone. It is one of the most impassioned public essays Eric left behind.

For years after his death, Eric would be seen as a bundle of contradictions. But the threads come together in "I aint going out without a fight." Eric dreamed big but settled for reality. Unfortunately, that passage remained hidden from the public for years. Scattered quotes from his writings would leak out, and viewed as fragments, they could seem contradictory. Was Eric planning a gun battle or a plane crash or a terrorist attack bigger than Oklahoma City's? If he was so intent on mass murder, why did he kill only thirteen? Trying to understand Eric from the information available was like reading every fifth page of a novel and concluding that none of it made sense.

Dr. Fuselier had the advantage of reading Eric's journal from start to finish. Without the holes, the thrust was obvious: humans meant nothing; Eric was superior and determined to prove it. Watching us suffer would be enjoyable. Every week he devised colorful new scenarios: crashing planes into buildings, igniting blocks of skyscrapers, ejecting people into outer space. But the objective never wavered: kill as many as possible, as dramatically as imaginable.

In a perfect world, Eric would extinguish the species. Eric was a practical kid, though. The planet was beyond him; even a block of Denver highrises was out of reach. But he could pull off a high school.

———

A high school was pragmatic, but the choice was not arbitrary. If jocks had been his target, he would not just have hit the gym. He could have killed the few thousand packing the bleachers at a Columbine football game. If he'd been after the social elites, he could have taken out prom just three days before. Eric attacked the symbol of his oppression: the robot factory and the hub of adolescent existence.

For Eric, Columbine was a performance. Homicidal art. He actually referred to his audience in his journal: "the majority of the audience wont even understand my motives," he complained. He scripted Columbine as made-for-TV murder, and his chief concern was that we would be too stupid to see the point. Fear was Eric's ultimate weapon. He wanted to maximize the terror. He didn't want kids to fear isolated events like a sporting event or a dance; he wanted them to fear their daily lives. It worked. Parents across the country were afraid to send their kids to school.

Eric didn't have the political agenda of a terrorist, but he had adopted terrorist tactics. Sociology professor Mark Juergensmeyer identified the central characteristic of terrorism as "performance violence." Terrorists design events "to be spectacular in their viciousness and awesome in their destructive power. Such instances of exaggerated violence are constructed events: they are mind-numbing, mesmerizing theater."

The audience—for Timothy McVeigh, Eric Harris, or the Palestine Liberation Organization—was always miles away, watching on TV. Terrorists rarely settle for just shooting; that limits the damage to individuals. They prefer to blow up things—buildings, usually, and the smart ones choose carefully.

"During that brief dramatic moment when a terrorist act levels a building or damages some entity that a society regards as central to its existence, the perpetrators of the act assert that they—and not the secular government—have ultimate control over that entity and its centrality," Juergensmeyer wrote. He pointed out that during the same day as the first attack on the World Trade Center, in 1993, a deadlier attack was leveled against a coffee shop in Cairo. The attacks were presumably coordinated by the same group. The body count was worse in Egypt, yet the explosion was barely reported outside that country. "A coffeehouse is not the World Trade Center," he explained.

Most terrorists target symbols of the system they abhor—generally, iconic government buildings. Eric followed the same logic. He understood that the cornerstone of his plan was the explosives. When all his bombs fizzled, everything about his attack was misread. He didn't just fail to top Timothy McVeigh's record—he wasn't even recognized for trying. He was never categorized with his peer group. We lumped him in with the pathetic loners who shot people.

———

Eric miscalculated again. It was about drinking this time. He and Dylan talked a friend's mom into buying lots of liquor. She took requests. Eric ordered tequila and Baileys Irish Cream. Dylan asked for vodka, of course. There was also beer, whiskey, schnapps, and Scotch. The group had a little boozefest that weekend. Eric made off with the leftovers and stashed them in the spare-tire compartment of his car. He was pretty proud of himself. He had all the booze he needed for a long time. He bought himself a flask and loaded it up with smooth, potent Scotch. Eric didn't actually like alcohol, but he loved the idea. He took only three sips in the month he owned the flask, but he could sip Scotch whenever he wanted—how cool was that? He got a little cocky and bragged to a friend. The jerk ratted him out to Eric's dad.

There was one hell of a fight at the Harris house that night. Wayne was livid. *When are you going to get on track? What are you going to do with your life?*

Eric spun a fresh batch of lies. He had been keeping up his grades just to maintain his cover story, setting the stage for a fresh round of bullshit. Man, he was good that night. He even quoted lines out of his favorite movies and delivered them like he was totally in the moment. "I should have won a freaking Oscar," he wrote in his journal.

Despite the fighting, Eric convinced his Diversion officer that everything was great with his parents. Kriegshauser noted the happy home life in his notes for every session from that period. Eric had an instinct for when the truth would placate an adult, how much to reveal, and to whom. When he attended anger management class for Diversion, he wrote the required response paper, dutifully sucking up about how helpful it was. In person, he sensed Bob Kriegshauser would respond to a different tack. Eric admitted that the class was a waste of time. Bob was proud of him for coming clean. In his session notes, he praised Eric's honesty.

Dr. Fuselier found Eric's paper interesting for another reason. Eric really had learned something from the session. He'd listed the four stages of anger and several triggers: quick breathing, tunnel vision, tightened muscles, and clenched teeth. The triggers served as warning signs or symptoms of anger, Eric wrote. Just the kind of information he could use. Eric was a prodigy at masking his true emotions and simulating the desired effect, but prodigy was a long way from pro. Clarifying tiny giveaways where an expert might see through his act—that kind of data was invaluable. Eric described himself as a sponge, and mimicry of agreeable behavior was his number one skill.

———

Eric's grades were up, and his teachers were happy. He would end the fall semester with glowing comments on his report card about a positive attitude and cooperation. Dylan was still tanking. On November 3, he brought Kriegshauser another progress report. Calculus was no better, and now he had a D in gym, too. It was just tardiness, he explained.

You will get there on time, meaning not one minute late, Kriegshauser demanded. That better be a passing grade by next session.

By their next session, the grade had dropped to an F. Kriegshauser confronted Dylan on the situation, and Dylan tried to weasel out. There was a pattern, Kriegshauser said. Dylan wasn't even trying. The comments from his calculus teacher showed a bad attitude. He wasn't making use of his class time effectively. What was going on there? Dylan said he'd been reading a book in class. Kriegshauser was incredulous. Dylan wasn't much of a smooth talker. Listen to yourself, Kriegshauser told him. Think about what you're saying. You are minimizing everything. You're full of excuses. You sound like you think you're the victim.

Kriegshauser said there would be consequences if Dylan's efforts didn't change. That could include termination. Termination would translate to multiple felony convictions. Dylan could find himself in prison.

———

Eric manufactured three more pipe bombs: the Charlie batch. Then he halted production until December. What he needed was guns. And that was becoming a problem.

Eric had been looking into the Brady Bill. Congress had passed the law restricting the purchase of most popular semiautomatic machine guns in 1993. A federal system of instant background checks would soon go into effect. Eric was going to have a hard time getting around that.

"Fuck you Brady!" Eric wrote in his journal. All he wanted was a couple of guns—"and thanks to your fucking bill I will probably not get any!" He wanted them only for personal protection, he joked: "Its not like I'm some psycho who would go on a shooting spree. fuckers."

Eric frequently made his research do double duty for both schoolwork and his master plan. He wrote up a short research assignment on the Brady Bill that week. It was a good idea in theory, he said, aside from the loopholes. The biggest problem was that checks applied only to licensed dealers, not private dealers. So two-thirds of the licensed dealers had just gone private. "The FBI just shot themselves in the foot," he concluded.

Eric was rational about his firepower. "As of this date I have enough explosives to kill about 100 people," he wrote. With axes, bayonets, and assorted blades, he could maybe take out ten more. That was as far as hand-to-hand combat would get him. A hundred and ten people. "that just isn't enough!"

"Guns!" the entry concluded. "I _need_ guns! Give me some fucking firearms!"

45. Aftershocks

Milestones were hard. First day of school, first snowfall, first Christmas, first anything. All the ugly memories, all the feelings of helplessness swelled back to the surface.

The six-month anniversary was unnerving. Surveillance video of the killers roaming the cafeteria had just been leaked to CBS. The network led its national news broadcast with the first of footage inside the building during the attack. Eric and Dylan strolled around brandishing their weapons. They picked up abandoned cups from the tables and casually enjoyed a few sips. They shot at the big bombs, and terrified kids scurried away.

"It's one thing to hear or read about it, and another thing to see it," Sean Graves's mother said. She cried while she watched. She made herself sit through it—she needed to know. She was coming to terms with inevitability. "I wish it wasn't out," she said. "But I knew that it was going to come out. It was just a matter of time."

Her son took a pass. Sean did his homework in the other room.

Sean was semiparalyzed—one of the critically injured kids. Everyone was watching their progress. Anne Marie Hochhalter was struggling. She went to school for physics class, and a tutor taught her the rest at home. Her family had just moved into a new house, outfitted by volunteers to accommodate her wheelchair. Anne Marie was fighting her way toward walking again. A few days before the six-month anniversary, she finally moved her legs—one at a time, three to four inches high. It was "a tremendous, tremendous achievement," her dad, Ted, said. But the pain was still excruciating.

The six-month anniversary jitters made it harder. Rumors were rampant: *Eric and Dylan couldn't have done it alone. The TCM is still active—they could strike again at any moment.*

October 20, the six-month mark, seemed like the perfect moment. On October 18, a fresh rumor surfaced: a friend of Eric and Dylan's who had worked on their school videos told someone he was going to "finish the job."

The next day, police raided his house, searched the premises, and arrested him. His parents cooperated. He was charged with a felony and held on a $500,000 bond. He was put on suicide watch. He was seventeen.

The kid made a brief appearance in juvenile court on Wednesday, in leg shackles and a green prison uniform. He faced Magistrate John DeVita, the same man who'd sentenced Eric and Dylan a year and a half earlier. Because the suspect was a minor, his name was withheld and the record sealed. But DeVita confirmed the police had found an incriminating journal. "That was the basis for the allegation," he said. A diagram of the school was also recovered, but no signs of activity to carry anything out. In the twelve-page diary, the boy lamented his failure to help Eric and Dylan with their troubles. He contemplated suicide. He wrote about it. He talked about it when they came to arrest him.

That same day, the six-month anniversary, 450 kids called in sick. Why set foot in that deadly school? More drifted out all day. By the closing bell, half the student body was gone. Three of the critically injured kids, Richard Castaldo, Anne Marie Hochhalter, and Patrick Ireland, stuck it out. Sean Graves stayed home and baked chocolate chip cookies with friends. "I didn't want to risk it," he said.

Thursday, 14 percent were still out. The normal absentee rate was 5 percent.

The tension subsided. On Friday, attendance was back near normal. Anne Marie Hochhalter and her dad went to Leawood Elementary that morning to thank fund-raisers and accept donations raised on her behalf. Around ten A.M., Anne Marie's mother walked into an Alpha Pawn Shop south of Denver. She asked to see a handgun. The clerk offered several options; she looked at them through the glass case. She settled on a .38-caliber revolver. *That one.* While he got started on the background check, she turned her back to the counter and loaded. She had brought the ammo with her. First she fired at the wall. The second shot entered through her right temple.

Paramedics rushed Carla June to Swedish Medical Center, the same hospital that had treated Anne Marie. Carla June died a few minutes later. A counselor who had worked with the family came by the house to notify the family. Anne Marie answered the door, and the counselor asked to talk to Ted. "I started to breathe really fast," Anne Marie said later. "I just had an ominous feeling."

"I hate to be the bearer of bad news," the counselor said. "Carla's dead."

Ted Hochhalter crumpled.

"No!" Anne Marie said. "No! No! No!" Her dad pulled up and hugged her. It took him a few minutes to compose himself, and the counselor explained how it had happened.

"We just broke down again," Anne Marie said. "The look on my dad's face will be etched in my memory forever. It was just a look of sorrow and horror."

———

Columbine's mental health hotline was flooded with calls on Saturday. Several distraught messages were cued up on the machine when counselors arrived. They added an extra weekend shift. "It's been a hard week," a Jeffco official said. "They're sad and depressed and they want to talk."

Parents had watched their kids sputtering on the brink for months. Especially this month. Other parents had no idea what their kids were thinking. Were they getting that desperate, too? Would Carla's choice seem like a way out? Some kids fought the same thoughts about their parents.

"I just can't take it," Steve Cohn told the Associated Press. "I can't believe someone killed themselves over those idiots."

Steve's boy Aaron had made it out of the library unscathed physically, but the stress was wrenching the family apart. "I drive by the school and I'm looking behind every tree," Steve said. "I feel like a cop. I want to prevent it before it happens again."

Steve and his son had both gone to counseling, but that was useless while Aaron was shut down. "Until he opens up, there's nothing we can do," his dad said.

Connie Michalik was especially rattled. She'd spent months beside Carla at Swedish Medical Center, watching their children recover. Connie was Richard Castaldo's mom. Neither child was expected to walk again. "This just destroyed her," Connie said. "You'd look in her eyes and see she was lost. It didn't seem like she was there anymore. She was sweet and loving and kind, but it was too much for her."

Connie had felt herself waver, too. "When it first happened, [Carla] was just like any other parent," she said. "We were all depressed and devastated. There was a time where I thought I had nothing to live for. She was no different from us."

Connie worked past it; Carla could not. "We kind of saw her slipping," Connie said. "I saw her slide downhill." But Connie never foresaw that deep a plunge. She assumed Carla would pull out of it, especially when Anne Marie moved her legs.

What most people in the community did not know was that Carla was at the end of a long struggle with mental illness.

The Hochhalter family wanted the public to understand that. After her death, they released a statement saying she had been battling clinical depression for three years. She had been suicidal in the past. She had been on medication. A month earlier, Ted had called the authorities at three A.M. to report her missing. She walked into a local emergency room the next day, seeking treatment for depression. She was hospitalized for a month. Eight days before her suicide, she was transferred to an outpatient program.

The family later revealed that Carla had been diagnosed as bipolar. Columbine aggravated Carla's depression horribly. She may or may not have gone over the edge without it, but the Columbine tragedy was not the underlying cause.

———

The school suspended the boy who'd made the anniversary threat, pending expulsion. That made eight expulsion proceedings in Jeffco since April, for a variety of gun threats and bomb scares. Everything was zero tolerance now. No one was taking chances.

The boy spent seven weeks in jail, through Thanksgiving. It was during this period that the community learned of his plan. He'd intended to fill his car with gasoline canisters and plow into the school as a suicide bomber. In December, he pleaded down to two minor charges and was sentenced to a one-year juvenile Diversion program, just as Eric and Dylan had been. Other charges were dropped, including theft. He had stolen a hundred dollars from the video store he worked at, to run away to Texas. He had begun seeing a psychiatrist and taking medication. The sentence required both to continue. "This is a troubled young man, and he will be getting the help he needs," the prosecutor said.

The half-year anniversary also brought a deadline. Colorado law requires that anyone who wants to sue a government agency for negligence must file an intent notice within 180 days. Twenty families filed. Notices came from families of the dead, families of the injured, and the Klebolds.

Tom and Sue Klebold charged Stone's department with "reckless, willful and wanton" misconduct for failing to alert them about its 1998 investigation into Eric's behavior, particularly his death threats. That warning "would more likely than not have caused the Klebolds to become aware of dangers of which they were not aware and demand that their son, Dylan, be excluded from all contacts with Eric Harris," the filing read. The failure "caused the Klebolds to be subject to substantial damage claims, vilification, grief and loss of enjoyment of life." The notice said the family expected to be sued by victims, and sought damages from Jeffco equal to those eventual settlements.

The Klebolds had cause for concern. The two families still topped most blame lists.

The filing took the community by surprise. No one had heard from the Harrises or Klebolds in months.

The harshest rebuke came from Sheriff Stone. "I think it's outrageous," he said. "It's their parenting thing, not our fault for their kid doing this thing."

He also lamented the tragedy degenerating to "an ugly stage."

Brian Rohrbough took the Klebolds' move in stride. It surprised him at first, he said, but on reflection, "it seems reasonable." He directed his outrage at Sheriff Stone's response. "We felt that it was really ugly April 20th," Brian said.

Wayne and Kathy finally agreed to meet with investigators without immunity, October 25. It was a brief session led by Sheriff Stone. There is no record of it being documented in a police report.

Only two people would be charged with a crime: Mark Manes, who'd sold the TEC-9, and Phil Duran, who'd brokered the deal. Months earlier, Agent Fuselier had predicted that the two would be savaged—with both legitimate and displaced anger.

"Those two guys stepped in front of a freight train," he said.

He was right. Manes was up first. He copped to a plea agreement and was sentenced on November 11. It was ugly. Nine families spoke at the hearing. Every one of them demanded the maximum.

"I ask you clearly to make a statement," Tom Mauser, one of the Thirteen, implored.

"If we had our way, the defendant would never be allowed on the streets again," the Shoels family said.

The testimony lasted for two hours. Manes hung his head. Videos made by two families hit especially hard. The court reporter passed boxes of Kleenex around the gallery.

Manes's lawyer described a rough childhood: his client had gotten in trouble, then mended his ways. Manes had gotten off drugs, gone to college, and obtained a steady job in the computer field. "His character today is exemplary," he said.

That infuriated the relatives. "Having that attorney talk about how wonderful Mark Manes is, that was tough," Dave Sanders's daughter Coni said. "He wasn't misunderstood. He was in the wrong."

Manes spoke last. He faced the judge and assured him that he'd had no idea what Eric and Dylan were planning. "I was horrified," he said. "I told my parents I never want to see a gun for the rest of my life. There is no way I can adequately explain my sorrow to the families. It is something I will regret for the rest of my life."

Manes was eligible for eighteen years in prison, but his plea agreement knocked that down to a maximum of nine. Judge Henry Nieto said he had no choice. "The conduct of this defendant was the first step in what became an earthquake. All of us have a moral duty when we see the potential for harm to intervene." Nine years. But he would assign them concurrently, so Manes would serve only six—with parole, maybe as little as three. Nieto warned the families not to expect comfort from the sentence.

Manes looked calm, but he took it hard. His lawyer put his hand on Manes's neck and whispered that he loved him. Manes was led away in handcuffs. The families applauded.

Manes's lawyer described his client as a scapegoat. "There's no one else to be angry at," he told NBC. "These people have all this understandable anger. It has to go somewhere."

Christian martyr Cassie Bernall offered hope. In September, Misty went on a national book tour. *She Said Yes* leapt onto the *New York Times* best-seller list in its first week. The *Rocky Mountain News* editors had a dilemma. They knew Cassie had never said yes. They had expected to shatter the myth by now, but they were still waiting for the sheriff's report. They had to cover the book's release. The editors decided to run two pieces on publication day, affirming Cassie's myth.

A few weeks later, another publication broke the news. The *Rocky* followed up with Emily Wyant's testimony. With the story out, Emily agreed to allow her name to be used. The Bernalls' publisher lashed out at Emily. The news made front pages as far away as London. Brad and Misty were caught by surprise. They felt humiliated and betrayed—by Emily, by the cops, and by the secular press.

The evidence against martyrdom was overwhelming, but Cassie's youth pastor saw stronger forces at play. "You will never change the story of Cassie," Reverend Dave McPherson said. "The church is going to stick to the martyr story. You can say it didn't happen that way, but the church won't accept it."

He didn't mean just his church. He meant the vast Evangelical community worldwide. And to a large extent, he was right. Book sales continued briskly. A vast array of Web sites sprang up to defend the story. Others just repeated it, without even mentioning that it had been debunked.

Jeffco also faced a series of embarrassing leaks. Investigators had let the video get loose to CBS and had revealed the truth about Cassie Bernall; lead investigator Kate Battan had broken her silence and spoken to one reporter; and the first passages from Eric's journal had slipped out. And yet the department maintained its official silence. It delayed the report again.

The victims' families were furious. The sheriff's department's credibility plummeted. Its officers had done a thorough job of detective work on the case, but the public had no way to see that. Jeffco expressed shock and bewilderment at the leaks; officials offered flimsy excuses and assurances. A spokesman insisted that only two copies of Eric's journal existed, when in fact it had been run through photocopiers repeatedly, and no one had a clue how many copies were floating around.

Then the undersheriff let a *Time* reporter watch the Basement Tapes. He had assured the families repeatedly they would be the first to see the videos.

The magazine ran an exposé cover story shortly before Christmas. Stone and Undersheriff John Dunaway posed in their dress blues with white gloves, armed with the killers' semiautomatics.

Many families were aghast. Several called for Stone to resign. Charges of cowardice against the SWAT teams resurfaced. Prominent law enforcement officials joined the chorus. Stone insisted that his department would be exonerated by the final report—which was delayed again.

————

Turbulence was expected that fall. Everyone knew they would face anniversaries and hearings. No one foresaw the string of aftershocks. The school was sued over a craft project gone awry—the Rohrboughs charged infringement of their religious expression. Brian Rohrbough repeated the crosses incident at a memorial garden created at Cassie's church: his group picketed Sunday services and then chopped down two of the fifteen trees in front of the horrified youth group that had planted them. They inadvertently chose the tree symbolizing Cassie.

Bomb threats were a regular occurrence, but one gained traction in the wake of the *Time* story. The school was shut down until after Christmas. Finals were canceled. Legal battles over the Basement Tapes began.

"When will it end?" a local pastor asked. "Why us? What is happening in our community?"

The new year began, and it got worse. A young boy was found dead in a Dumpster a few blocks from Columbine High. On Valentine's Day, two students were shot dead in a Subway shop two blocks from the school. The star of the basketball team committed suicide.

"Two weeks ago they found the kid in the Dumpster," a friend of the Subway victims told reporters. "Now—I kind of want to move. This is worse than Columbine." Students had grudgingly come to adopt their school's name as the title of a tragedy.

Some events were unrelated to the massacre or even the school. But much of the community had lost the ability to distinguish. Perspective was impossible. A fight with your girlfriend, a car crash, a drought…it was all "Columbine." It was a curse. Kids were calling it the Columbine Curse.

Appointments at the mental health facility set up for Columbine survivors rose sharply through the fall. "Many come in after they've tried everything they know how to do," a psychologist on the team said. Utilization peaked about nine months after the tragedy and held steady until a year and a half out. At any given time during that period, case managers were following about fifteen kids on suicide watch. Gradually, each one came down from the brink, but another took that kid's place. Substance abuse spiked. The area experienced a marked increase in traffic accidents and DUIs.

"By definition, PTSD is a triad of change for the worse, lasting at least a month, occurring anytime after a genuine trauma," wrote PTSD pioneer Dr. Frank Ochberg. "The triad of disabling responses is: 1) recurring intrusive recollections; 2) emotional numbing and a constriction of life activity; and 3) a physiological shift in the fear threshold, affecting sleep, concentration, and sense of security."

Response to PTSD varies dramatically. Some people feel too much, others too little. The over-feelers often suffer flashbacks. Nothing can drive away the terror. They awake each morning knowing it may be April 20 all over again. They can go hours, weeks, or months without an episode and then a trigger—often a sight, sound, or smell—will take them right back. It's not like a bad memory of the event; it feels like it is the event. Others protect themselves by shutting down altogether. Pleasant feelings and joy get eliminated with the bad. They often describe feeling numb.

———

It was a rough year. The football team offered a respite. Matthew Kechter had been a sophomore when he was killed in the library. He had played JV on the defensive line in the 1998 season and had hoped to make varsity this fall. At his parents' request the team dedicated the season to Matt. Each player wore Matt's number on his helmet and Matt's initials, MJK, on his cap. They finished the season 12–1. They came from 17 behind in the fourth quarter to win the first playoff game. The players wept on the field. They chanted *MJK! MJK!*

They were heavy underdogs for the state championship. Denver powerhouse Cherry Creek High had taken five of the last ten titles. Columbine had made it to the big game only once: a loss two decades back.

Supporters flew in from around the world. Eight thousand people packed the stadium. The media were everywhere. The *New York Times* covered the game. The temperature dropped below freezing. Patrick Ireland sat in the front row, trying to keep warm.

Cherry Creek went ahead early. Columbine tied it up at the half, and then their defense came on strong. They allowed just two first downs in the second half, and a third touchdown put it away. Columbine won 21–14. Fans rushed the field. The familiar chant thundered through the stands. We are...COL-um-*BINE!* We are...COL-um-*BINE!*

The school held a victory rally. A highlight reel of the game was projected, ending with a picture of Matt. "This one's for you," it said. A moment of silence was held for all thirteen.

———

Some kids seemed immune to the gloom. Others fought private battles on completely different chronologies. Patrick Ireland made steady improvements, kept his 4.0 average that fall, and made sure valedictorian was still in sight. But a more significant problem loomed.

Patrick had had his life pretty well figured out junior year. Before he got shot, he was going to be an architect. His grandfather had been a builder, and Patrick had taken to drawing in his junior high drafting class. He lined up that T-square against the drafting table and he could feel it. He liked the precision. He enjoyed the artistry. At Columbine, he worked with sophisticated computer-aided design software. While Eric and Dylan finalized their plot, Patrick was deep into research on college programs and had started investigating internships.

He was still going to be an architect. Patrick clung to the dream straight through outpatient therapy. He took breaks for three out-of-state campus visits, at schools with leading architecture programs. They all accepted him. But they stressed how rigorous the work would be. Architecture programs are known for their massive workloads: five years of relentless all-nighters. All night was not an option for Patrick. He could cheat himself out of a couple hours' sleep, but his brain would take years to recover. He would slow his progress by taxing it too hard, and possibly even bring on seizures.

In March, he took a school trip to England. The jet lag was tough.

Kathy went with him, and Friday night she noticed his face went blank and his eyeball fluttered for a few seconds. "Did you do that on purpose?" she asked.

"Do what?"

Kathy believes it was a precursor to the event two days later. Patrick was walking through London and collapsed in the middle of a street. He shook violently, made it almost to the curb, and called out to a friend for help.

A London doctor prescribed antiseizure medication. The family confirmed the treatment back home, and Patrick will be on it for life.

Architecture school wasn't going to work. John and Kathy understood that from the start, but they waited for Patrick to accept the situation. He opted for Colorado State, just over an hour away. He would try business school for a year. CSU had an architecture program, too. If, a year later, he felt he could handle it, he could transfer.

Despite the cloud over his future, Patrick regained his bearing through the year. Socially, he was having the time of his life. Patrick had always been a catch. He'd been bright, charming, handsome, and athletic. He had been a little short on confidence, from time to time. Laura would have given anything to go to the prom with Patrick. She might have become his girlfriend if he had asked. The shotgun blasts had robbed him of some of his best assets, but he was a star. He was the most celebrated figure to live through the tragedy. And he had put up an incredible fight. Girls flirted unabashedly.

But Patrick wanted Laura. That first summer, he told her how much he wanted her—how deeply and how long.

God, me too, she said.

What a relief. Finally, after all this time, it was out in the open.

Laura confessed everything: all those nights flirting on the phone, hinting her heart out for him to ask. If only he had asked her to the prom.

OK, Patrick said: *I like you, you like me, let's do something about it.* Too late. She was dating the prom dude.

That didn't seem like an obstacle. Do you want to be with me? Yes. Then break up with him. She said she would do it.

He gave her time. He asked again. When are you going to do it? She said it would be soon. But nothing happened.

Girls were fighting for the chance to date him, so he got tired of waiting and asked one out. Then he asked another one. And another—this was fun!

Things grew strained with Laura. They never went out. They began avoiding each other. It was fourth grade all over again.

46. Guns

Eric named his shotgun Arlene. He acquired her on November 22, 1998, and declared it an important date in the history of Reb. "we.......have........GUNS!" he wrote. "We fucking got em you sons of bitches! HA!!"

Eric and Dylan had driven into Denver for the Tanner Gun Show the day before. They'd found some sweet-ass weapons. A 9mm carbine rifle and a pair of 12-gauge shotguns: one double-barreled and one pump-action single. They'd tried to buy them, and that was a great big no-go. Eric's charm was not getting them over this hurdle. No ID, no guns. They drove back to the suburbs.

Eric would be eighteen shortly before their attack date in April. They could have just waited, but Eric wanted real firepower to keep the plan on track. There was one more day in the gun show. Who did they know who was eighteen? Plenty of people. Who would do it for them, who could they trust? Robyn! Sweet little church girl Robyn. She was nuts about Dylan; she would do anything for him. Wouldn't she?

The following day, it was done.

In his journal, Eric labeled this "the point of no return." Then he waxed nostalgic about his dad. He'd had a lot of fun at the gun show, he wrote: "I would have loved it if you were there, dad. we would have done some major bonding. would have been great. Oh wait. But, alas, I fucked up and told [my friend] about the flask." That had been the end of good relations with Wayne for a while. Now his parents were on his ass more than ever about his future. *What do you want to do with your life?* That was easy. NBK. "THIS is what I am motivated for," he wrote. "THIS is my goal. THIS 'is what I want to do with my life.'"

———

Eric and Dylan sawed the barrels off their new shotguns—cut them way below the legal limit. The first week in December, they took the rifle out and fired it. A bullet erupted in the chamber, and the butt slammed into Eric's bony shoulder. Wow! That thing packed a lot of power. This wasn't a pipe bomb in his hands. This could kill somebody.

———

Psychopaths generally turn to murder only when their callousness combines with a powerful sadistic streak. Psychologist Theodore Millon identified ten basic subtypes of the psychopath. Only two are characterized by brutality or murder: the malevolent psychopath and the tyrannical. In these rare subtypes, the psychopath is driven less by a greed for material gain than by desire for his own aggrandizement and the brutal punishment of inferiors.

Eric fit both categories. His sadistic streak permeated the journal, but a late-autumn entry suggests the life Eric might have led had Columbine not ended it. He described tricking girls to come to his room, raping them, and then proceeding to the real fun.

"I want to tear a throat out with my own teeth like a pop can," he wrote. "I want to grab some weak little freshman and just tear them apart like a fucking wolf. strangle them, squish their head, rip off their jaw, break their arms in half, show them who is god."

———

Eric had not given up on the twenty-three-year-old. For months, he kept calling Brenda. She told him she had a new boyfriend, but he persisted. Late in the year, she met him at a Macaroni Grill. "He was really bummed out," she said. She thought he was bummed because she'd dumped him. He denied it, but offered no explanation. She never saw him again.

———

Just before Christmas, Eric celebrated his last final, ever. He laughed at his classmates, who assumed they had another batch ahead.

The next day, Eric ordered several ten-round magazines for his carbine rifle. Those would do some damage. He could peel off 130 rounds in rapid succession.

There was a problem. Eric gave Green Mountain Guns his home number. They called just before New Year's, and his dad answered.

"Your clips are in," the clerk told him.

Clips? He didn't order any gun clips.

Eric overheard the conversation. Oh God. He described the incident in his journal: "jesus Christ that was fucking close. fucking shitheads at the gunshop almost dropped the whole project." Luckily, Wayne never stopped to ask the guy if he had the right number. And the guy never asked any questions either. That could have been the end of it right there. If either one of them had handled that phone call a little differently, the entire plan might have come crashing down, Eric said. But they didn't.

But Wayne was suspicious.

"thank god I can BS so fucking well," Eric wrote.

———

Once they got the guns, Eric lost interest in "The Book of God." It was on to implementation. After New Year's, he would leave just one final installment, a few weeks before they did the deed.

Eric was raring to go; Dylan continued to waver. "Existences" had been silent for five months, since he said good-bye. But on January 20, Bob Kriegshauser called Dylan in for an important meeting. Dylan resumed his journal the same day.

"This shit again," he began. He didn't want to be writing this again, he wanted to be "free," meaning dead. "I thought it would have been time by now," he wrote. "The pain multiplies infinitely. never stops." Eric's plan offered the solace of suicide: "maybe Going 'NBK' (gawd) w. eric is the best way to be free. i hate this." Then more hearts and love. He hardly seemed committed to the plan. But he appeared to be putting up a good front to Eric. Neither boy ever recorded a suggestion of Dylan's resistance, but Eric seemed to be doing most of the work.

Eric was also working hard to get laid. He made a final stab with Brenda, leaving a string of messages on her answering machine. "I'm sorry I lied to you," he said. "There's something we need to talk about. I'm seventeen." He was through lying, he said—he wanted to take their relationship to the next level. And she could keep the Rammstein CDs he'd left at her house. He wouldn't be needing them anymore.

The last part made her nervous. She called back to make sure he was all right. And she reiterated one more time that they were just friends.

Eric wasn't bothered. He was working another chick. Kristi was the girl he had passed notes with in German class. Lately she seemed interested in more. So they tried a sort of informal group date to Rock 'n' Bowl night at Belleview Lanes.

Kristi liked him, but she was conflicted. There was this other guy, a friend of Eric's, Nate Dykeman. Bastard!

Eric turned on the charm, and Kristi went for it—just not enough. It was sex he really wanted; he had no interest in a real relationship, and maybe Kristi picked up on that.

Nate moved in on Kristi fast. They started dating, got serious, and Eric turned on Nate.

———

As Eric wrapped up plans for April 20, Dylan was laying into his journal in a frenzy. They were short entries and erratic, tossing aside all his conventions. Several ran half a page or less. He was expressing himself more and more in pictures, all his old icons returning, linked together in wild, feverish strokes. Fluttering hearts were everywhere, filling up entire pages, blasting out the road to happiness, bursting with stars and powered by an engine shaped like the symbol for infinity. Dylan was focused on one topic now: love. Up until his final week, Dylan wrote privately of almost nothing else.

47. Lawsuits

Ten days before the first anniversary, Brian Rohrbough threw a Hail Mary. The cops had been stonewalling, and litigation looked like the only answer. Families could sue for negligence or wrongful death, and use the process to force out information. The verdict would be less important than discovery.

Should they sue? How could they know? It all rested on Jeffco's final report. If Jeffco released all the evidence, most families would be satisfied. If Jeffco held back, they were going to court. No one had anticipated that the report would take this long. Way back in the summer of 1999, Jeffco had said its report was six to eight weeks away. It was April now, and officials were still saying they had six to eight weeks to go.

The investigators had wrapped up most of their work in the first four months, but Jeffco was skittish about presenting the information. Yet the longer they waited, the more leaks they risked, the more rebukes, and the higher the stakes to get every sentence right.

Even the school administration was frustrated. "We keep getting ready," Mr. D told a magazine in April. "I keep telling the community, 'OK, we're about two weeks away, we're two weeks away.' There's only so many times you can get so wound up saying, 'Oh, I'm ready now, I'm ready,' and then all of a sudden, 'No!' There's a level of frustration."

The delays were maddening, but a practical problem was also arising. The first anniversary coincided with the statute of limitations. By delaying the report past April 20, 2000, Jeffco forced the families to trust them or sue. That was an easy choice. On April 10, the Rohrboughs and the Flemings filed an open records request demanding to see the report immediately—one last option to avoid a lawsuit. Since they were filing, they asked for everything, including the Basement Tapes, the killers' journals, the 911 calls, and surveillance videos. Rohrbough wanted to compare the raw data to the narrative under construction by Jeffco. He predicted a chasm.

"They lie as a practice," he said.

District Judge R. Brooke Jackson read the request. He said yes. Over furious objections from Jeffco, three days before the anniversary, he allowed the plaintiffs to read the draft report. He also granted them access to hundreds of hours of 911 tapes and some video footage. He agreed to begin reading the two hundred binders of evidence himself, but noted that would take months.

The ruling stunned everyone. But it was too little, too late. Fifteen families filed suits against the sheriff's department that week. They would add additional defendants later.

The Klebolds chose not to sue. Instead they issued another apology letter. The Harrises did the same.

The lawsuits were expected to fail. The legal thresholds were too high. In federal court, negligence was insufficient; families needed to prove officers had actually made the students worse off. And that was only the first hurdle. But the main strategy was to flush out information.

The one suit with a plausible chance came from Dave Sanders's daughter Angela. She was represented by Peter Grenier, a powerhouse Washington, D.C., lawyer. They charged that Jeffco officials went beyond neglecting Dave Sanders for three hours: they impeded his movement and prohibited others from getting him out of there. They deceived volunteer rescuers with false claims about an imminent arrival, to discourage them from busting out a window or taking him down the stairs. By doing so, the suit argued, Jeffco accepted responsibility for Dave and then let him die. In legal terms, they'd denied his civil rights by cutting off all opportunities to save him when they were not prepared to do it themselves.

The Rohrboughs and others followed similar logic. The library kids could have escaped easily, they said, unencumbered by police "help." It looked ugly. But legal analysts were skeptical about any case holding up. "It's going to be tough to ask a jury to say we know better than a SWAT team how to handle this situation," said Sam Kamin, law professor at the University of Denver.

In legal circles, the lawsuits had been expected, but their ferocity shook the community. The anniversary was overwhelmed by animosity again, and media were everywhere. Many of the Thirteen left town. The school closed for the day and conducted a private memorial. A public service was held in Clement Park.

———

A few days after the anniversary, Judge Jackson ordered the sheriff's department to release its report to the public by May 15. He also released more evidence, including a video that drew a lot of heat. For months, Jeffco had referred to it as a "training video" created by the Littleton Fire Department. It was based on footage shot in the library shortly after the bodies were removed. It would be the families' first look at the gruesome scene. It would be "difficult" to watch, Jackson's ruling stated, but that was no reason to suppress it.

"There is no compelling public interest consideration that requires that the video or any part of it not be disclosed under the Open Records Act," Jackson wrote.

The next day, Jeffco began duplicating the tape and selling copies for $25. Spokesmen said the fee was to defray copying costs. The families were aghast. Then they saw the tape. There was no instruction, no narration, no attempt at "training." It was someone's ghastly attempt at commemoration: grisly crime scene footage set to pop music, Sarah McLachlan's "I Will Remember You." McLachlan's record company threatened to sue for copyright infringement. Jeffco removed the music. Sales remained strong.

———

Brian Rohrbough had broken through Jeffco's armor. Judge Jackson kept ordering releases. In May, he unleashed all the 911 tapes and a ballistics report. For a while, everything he read, he released. The killers' families tried to stop him. On May 1, they filed a joint motion to keep materials seized from their homes private. That would include the most vital evidence: the journals and the Basement Tapes.

Jeffco released its report on May 15, as ordered. The focus of the package was a minute-by-minute timeline of April 20, 1999, in great detail. It dramatically illustrated how fast everything happened: just seven and a half minutes in the library, all the deaths and injuries in the first sixteen minutes. How convenient, critics said. The cops' report was dedicated to illustrating that the cops had never had a chance.

As expected, the report ducked the central question of *why*. Instead, it provided about seven hundred pages of *what, how,* and *when.* The logistics were useful, but they were hardly what people had been waiting for.

There were three paragraphs about advance warning by the Browns: one paragraph summarizing and two defending. The department claimed it had been unable to access Eric's Web site, despite the fact that officials had printed the pages, filed them, and retrieved them within minutes of the attack on April 20, and had cited them at length in the search warrants issued before the bodies were found. But a year after the murders, Jeffco was still suppressing the file and the search warrants. So the families suspected a lie, but they couldn't prove it.

Jeffco was ridiculed for its report. Officials seemed truly bewildered by the response. Privately, they insisted they were just acting the way they always did: building a case internally, keeping their conclusions to themselves. Communicating the results was the prosecutors' role. It wasn't their job. They still couldn't grasp that this was not any normal case.

As the battles intensified, compassion fatigue set in. Hardly anyone said it out loud.

Chuck Green, a *Denver Post* columnist and one of Denver's nastier personalities, broke the ice. He stunned the families with a pair of columns, charging them with "milking" the tragedy.

They had gotten millions, he wrote. "It has been an avalanche of anguish never before witnessed, yet the Columbine victims still have their hands out for more."

The Parents Group was caught unaware. They'd had no idea. They were more stunned by the support for Green's ideas. "All of us are sick and tired of the continued whining," a reader responded. Another said those sentiments had been circulating for quite a while—"whispering in small circles, amongst clouds of guilt."

It was out in the open now.

The anniversary also offered a window of political opportunity. Tom Mauser had been energized at the NRA protest and devoted himself to the cause. "I am not a natural leader, but speaking out helps me because it carries on Daniel's life," he said. Tom took a one-year leave of absence to serve as chief lobbyist for SAFE Colorado (Sane Alternatives to the Firearms Epidemic). They supported several bills in the Colorado legislature to limit access to guns for minors and criminals. Prospects looked good, especially for the flagship proposal to close the gun-show loophole. It was narrowly defeated in February. A similar measure bogged down in Congress.

So a week before the anniversary, President Clinton returned to Denver to encourage survivors and support SAFE's new strategy: to pass the same measure in Colorado with a ballot initiative.

Colorado Republican leaders rebuked the president and refused to appear with him. Republican Governor Bill Owens supported the ballot initiative but refused to attend an MSNBC town hall meeting hosted by Tom Brokaw until President Clinton left the stage, midway through the show.

The visit appeared to force a little movement in Washington. Just before the meeting with Brokaw, House leaders announced a bipartisan compromise on gun-show legislation. But it had been a year already, and there was still a long way to go.

Tom Mauser kept fighting. At a rally the same week, SAFE spread 4,223 pairs of shoes across the state capitol steps—one for each minor killed by a gun in 1997. Tom took the sneakers off his feet and held them up to the crowd. They had been Daniel's. Tom took to wearing them to rallies. He needed a tangible link to his son. And they helped the shy man connect Daniel to his audience.

May 2, the governor and attorney general—the state's most prominent Republican and Democrat—put the first two signatures on the petition for the Colorado ballot initiative. It required 62,438 signatures. They gathered nearly twice that many.

The measure would pass by a two-to-one margin. The gun-show loophole was closed in Colorado.

It was defeated in Congress. No significant national gun-control legislation was enacted in response to Columbine.

———

The season ended well. On May 20, the second class of survivors graduated. Nine of the injured crossed the stage, two in wheelchairs. Patrick Ireland limped to the podium to give the valedictory address.

It had been a rough year, he said. "The shooting made the country aware of the unexpected level of hate and rage that had been hidden in high schools." But he was convinced the world was inherently good at heart. He had spent the year thinking about what had gotten him across the library floor. At first he assumed hope—not quite; it was trust. "When I fell out the window, I knew somebody would catch me," he said. "That's what I need to tell you: that I knew the loving world was there all the time."

PART V

—∞∞∞—

JUDGMENT DAY

48. An Emotion of God

Eric had work to do. Napalm was hard. It's an inherently unstable substance. Eric found lots of recipes online, but they never seemed to produce what the instructions predicted. The first batch was awful. He tried again. Just as bad. He kept varying the ingredients and the heating process, but it was one failure after another. Multiple batches were no easy feat, either. Eric didn't specify how or when he conducted his experiments; presumably he carried them out in the same place he did everything else: his house, when his parents were out. Each batch was a chore, time-consuming and risky. It involved mixing gasoline with other substances and then heating it on the stove, trying to make it congeal into a slushy syrup that would ignite with just a spark but burn continuously for some time when shot with force through a projectile tube.

Eric had to construct the flamethrowers, too. He drew out detailed sketches of his weaponry in the back of his journal notebook; some were quite practical, others pure fantasy. Dylan seemed to be no help with any of it. Each killer left hundreds of pages of writings and drawings and schedules in their day planners, and Eric's are riddled with plans, logs, and results of experiments; Dylan shows virtually no effort. Eric acquired the guns, the ammo, and apparently the material for the bombs, and did the planning and construction.

Figuring out how to sneak the huge bombs into the crowded cafeteria was another big problem. Each contraption would bulge out of a three-foot duffel bag and weigh about fifty pounds. They couldn't just trot them into the middle of the lunchroom, plop them down in front of six hundred people, and walk out without notice. Or could they? At some point, the boys gave up scheming. They decided to just walk right in with the bombs. It was a bold move, but textbook psychopath. Perpetrators of complex attacks tend to focus on weak links and minimize risk. Psychopaths are reckless. They have supreme confidence in their work. Eric planned meticulously for a year, only to open with a blunder that neutralized 95 percent of the attack. He showed no hint that he had even considered the gaping flaw.

Now he had to concentrate on getting Dylan a second gun. And Eric had a whole lot of production work. If only he had a little more cash, he could move the experiments along. Oh well. You could fund only so many bombs at a pizza factory. And he needed his brakes checked, and he'd just had to buy winter wiper blades, and he had a whole bunch of new CDs to pick up.

———

They also had Diversion to put behind them. Eric was a star in the program. His sterling performance earned him a rare early release—something only 5 percent of kids achieve. Kriegshauser decided to let Dylan out with him, despite Dylan's failure to raise his D in calculus. Kriegshauser advised Dylan to be careful about his future choices. His exit report said Dylan struggled with motivation in school, but the summary was all rosy: "Prognosis: Good. Dylan is a bright young man who has a great deal of potential. If he is able to tap his potential and become self-motivated he should do well in life.... Recommendations: Successful Termination. Dylan has earned the right for an early termination. He needs to strive to self-motivate himself so he can remain on a positive path. He is intelligent enough to make any dream a reality, but he needs to understand hard work is part of it."

Dylan responded with a bleak "Existences" entry. This was the meeting that drove him back to the journal. He wrote the same day, but failed to mention the good news. He insisted life was getting worse. In one sense it was. Release from Diversion was a painful sign. Dylan had not planned on leaving the program alive.

Eric earned a glowing report, start to finish: "Prognosis: Good. Eric is a very bright young man who is likely to succeed in life. He is intelligent enough to achieve lofty goals as long as he stays on task and remains motivated.... Recommendations: Successful Termination. Eric should seek out more education at higher levels. He impressed me as being very articulate and intelligent. These are skills that he should grow and use as frequently as possible."

Both boys arrived at murder gradually, but one event pushed each of them over the hump. Eric's occurred January 30, 1998, when Deputy Walsh shackled his wrists. From that night on, the boy was set on murder. Dylan's turn came a full year later and was more gradual, but the turning point seems clear. It was February 1999. They had agreed on April a year in advance, and it was almost here. Eric was serious. He was really going through with it. Dylan was conflicted, as always, still leaning against, heavily against. Dylan wanted to be a good boy. He had three choices: give in, back out, or perform a hasty suicide.

Those three choices had been hanging there for a year or more. He could not decide.

Then Dylan wrote a short story. It revolved around an angry man in black methodically gunning down a dozen "preps." The man did it for vengeance and amusement, and to demonstrate he could.

Dylan lifted most of the details right out of the NBK plan. He armed and outfitted his killer the way they planned to dress themselves. The story included a duffel bag, the diversion bombs, and reconnoitering the victims' habits. The smallest details match. The killer is a blend. His height matches Dylan's, but he behaves exactly like Eric: callous and methodical, viciously angry yet detached.

It was easy to imagine how Eric would react to pulling the trigger on April 20, but Dylan seemed baffled about his own response. He set Eric in motion on paper, with himself as narrator to observe. *How would murder feel?*

It felt wonderful. "If I could face an emotion of god, it would have looked like the man," he wrote. "I not only saw in his face, but also felt eminating from him power, complacence, closure, and godliness. The man smiled, and in that instant, thru no endeavor of my own, I understood his actions."

The story ended there: not with the murders but with the impact on the man behind them.

Nobody observed Dylan typing the story, but he appears to have spilled it all onto the screen in one great rush. He didn't stop to spell-check or fix errors or hit Return. It's all run together in a single paragraph that would have filled five pages in a normal font.

Dylan turned the story in as a creative writing assignment on February 7. His instructor, Judy Kelly, read it and shuddered. It was an astounding piece of writing for a seventeen-year-old, but she was deeply disturbed. Dylan wasn't the first kid to write a violent story—Eric had been writing combat scenes about heroic Marines all semester. Eric was obsessed with warfare; he mimed machine-gun fire in class all the time. But war stories were different; Dylan's protagonist was killing civilians, ruthlessly, and enjoying it. Kelly wrote a note at the bottom instructing Dylan to come see her. She wanted to talk to him before assigning a grade. "You are an excellent writer and storyteller, but I have rocky problems with this one," she wrote.

Dylan came to see her. The story was grossly violent and offensive, she said—unacceptable.

Submitting the story was probably an intentional leak. Dylan chickened out. "It's just a story," he said. This was creative writing class. He had been creative.

Creative was fine, Kelly said, but where was all this cruelty coming from? Just reading the thing was unnerving.

Dylan maintained it was just a story.

Kelly didn't buy it. She called Tom and Sue Klebold and discussed it with them at length. They did not seem too worried, she told police later. They made a comment about how understanding kids could be a real challenge.

Even after the murders, one of Dylan's classmates agreed. "It's a creative-writing class," she told the *Rocky Mountain News*. "You write about what you want. Shakespeare wrote all about death." The girl was not a friend of the killers'.

But Kelly knew she had picked up on something different. She had seen boys captivated by violence. She had read innumerable accounts of murder. She had never been confronted with a story this sadistic. It was not just a question of the events in the story but the attitude of the author conveying them. Dylan had a gift for bringing a scene to life: he conveyed action, thought, and feeling. A creepy, merciless feeling. Kelly described the story as "literary and ghastly—the most vicious story I ever read."

Kelly brought it to Dylan's school counselor, Brad Butts. He talked to Dylan, who downplayed it again. Good enough.

Kelly had done the right thing: she'd contacted the three people most likely to have other information about Dylan: his guidance counselor and his parents. If the counselor or parents knew Dylan had been setting off pipe bombs and showing them around at Blackjack Pizza, they could have connected fantasy with reality and NBK might have come to an end. They did not. Jeffco investigators had most of the pieces. Most of the adults close to the killers were in the dark.

———

In his journal, Dylan returned to his love obsession. He wanted to get to godliness, but he had been seeking for two horrible years now and none of his dreams had come true. Eric offered hope. Eric offered the very feelings Dylan was searching for. Eric offered reality, of all things.

Maybe seeking was a sham.

Dylan wasn't quite ready to embrace murder. He would fight it almost until the end. But from here on, he was close.

He would take the short story with him on April 20. It was found in Dylan's car, alongside the failed explosives, to be torn to bits in his final act. The car was slated for destruction, so Dylan didn't bring the story for our benefit. Perhaps he needed a little courage that day. Perhaps he wanted to read it one last time.

———

It was time for target practice. They picked a beautiful spot. The place was called Rampart Range: a winding network of unpaved roads through rugged national forest in the Rockies, not too far from Dylan's house. For their first extended gunplay, they picked an area set aside for dirt bikers and joyriding on ATVs. An off-roading Web site urged readers to experience the vistas slowly: "let your imagination run wild as the boulders take on everchanging faces."

Three friends went with them on March 6: Mark Manes and Phil Duran, who had teamed up to get Dylan the TEC-9, and Mark's girlfriend, Jessica. They brought the guns acquired for the attack, and their friends had a couple more. They packed bowling pins stolen from Belleview Lanes to use as targets. And they took a camcorder. It was important to document historic events.

It was cold up there, still plenty of snow on the ground. They dressed sensibly, in layers. Eric and Dylan started with their trench coats on, but worked up a sweat and shed them. They had ear protection and eye gear. Some of the time they wore it.

They shot a bowling pin full of lead, and then Eric had another idea. He aimed his shotgun at an imposing pine five feet away. He missed. And it hurt. The gun had a vicious recoil, which his arm had to absorb. Every inch you cut a shotgun back magnifies the kick. Eric and Dylan had cut theirs back ridiculously short, almost to the chamber, and now they were going to pay.

He directed Dylan to follow. "Try to hit a tree," he said. "I want to see what a slug does to the tree."

Dylan punched a two-inch-wide hole in the trunk. They rushed forward to inspect the damage. Eric dug his finger around and produced a pellet.

"That's a fucking slug!" Dylan squealed.

Eric's voice was subdued. "Imagine that in someone's fucking brain."

"It hurt my wrist, the son of a bitch!" Dylan said.

"I bet so."

Dylan was laughing now. "Look at that! I've got blood now!" He loved it.

Eric kept working the human metaphor. He picked up a bowling pin with a small hole drilled through the front and a crater out the back. He showed off each side to the camera: "Entry wound, exit wound." His buddy laughed, but he didn't understand. He got the little joke, missed the big one. The battle was already under way around him. Eric loved foreshadowing. Everyone there was implicated. Only two could see.

Most of the time they worked methodically to improve their skills. One kid would fire while another stood beside him, calling out results to make real-time adjustments: "High to the right…low to the left…left again…"

Single-barrel shotguns require a reload every round, and that would seriously impact the body count. Eric prepared by drilling himself in a rapid shoot-and-load technique. Every shot was punishing. The blast would tear the barrel out of his left hand and whip his gun arm back like a rubber band. But he learned quickly. Soon he was riding out the recoil to catch the barrel-stub as it swung around, snap it open, feed a shell, lock it down, squeeze a round, and repeat the process in one fluid, continuous motion. He pounded out four shots in five seconds. He was pleased.

It had all been theoretical up to that point: How much damage could they really do with that gun? They had their answer now. Eric was a killing machine.

Eric and Dylan approached the camera to show off their war wounds:

large patches of skin scraped off between thumb and forefinger, where they needed to work on tightening their grip.

"When high school kids use guns," somebody said. Everybody laughed.

Manes tried Eric's gun, and winced at that handgrip. "You should round that out," he advised.

"Yeah," Eric said. "I'm gonna work on that."

They fired more and showed the wounds again: bloodier, more severe. "Guns are bad," Manes said. "When you saw them off and make them illegal, bad things happen to you." That got lots more laughs. "Just say no to sawed-off shotguns."

They were on a roll now. Eric grabbed hold of his gun barrel and mugged for the camera. He spanked the firing assembly several times. "Bad!"

Dylan waved his index finger at it. "No! No! No!"

Dr. Fuselier watched the Rampart video a few days after the massacre. It showed the final progression from fantasy to fact. It had been a two-year evolution from frivolous prankster missions to a series of esclating thefts. Eric was turning into a professional criminal. He had crossed the mental hurdle from imagining crimes to committing them. This was how it would feel.

The boys continued training. They made three target-practice trips with Manes.

Dylan leaked again. He had been excited about his weapons, and sometime in February, he told Zack he had gotten something "really cool."

Like what?

Something in *Desperado,* Dylan said—a violent film they thought Quentin Tarantino directed.

Zack confronted him: It was a gun, wasn't it?

Yeah, a double-barreled shotgun, Dylan said, just like the piece in *Desperado.* Eric had gotten one, too. And they had fired them. Freaking wild!

They never spoke about it again, Zack told the FBI later.

49. Ready to Be Done

M r. D knew the date his mission would wrap: May 18, 2002. He had one objective after the massacre: to shepherd nearly two thousand kids to emotional high ground. The last class of freshmen would graduate that May.

Frank had no idea what he might do afterward. He could not plan yet—his hands were full. He had three school years to get through. He had seriously underestimated the turmoil of the first. Nobody had foreseen that torrent of aftershocks. He would not make that mistake again. The second summer offered a respite, just like the first, but when the doors reopened in August 2000, the faculty braced for the next onslaught. It never came. There was never a year like that first one—never anything close.

The second school year got off on a high note. An addition had been constructed over the summer, with a new library. The old one was demolished, converting the commons into a two-story atrium. Most of the Parents Group attended the opening. Sue Petrone glowed. For the past sixteen months, she had felt physically weak every time she'd stepped inside the school. "Like you're underwater and can't breathe," she'd said. All that was lifted away. She had been fighting for more than a year, and she was done. Nearly all the parents were.

Sue's ex-husband was the exception. Brian Rohrbough and Frank DeAngelis dominated the ceremony, standing thirty feet apart in the cafeteria with a cluster of reporters around each, talking about each other. Mr. D was diplomatic and tried to avoid the feud altogether. But reporters kept shuttling over from Rohrbough, with fresh accusations for Mr. D to respond to. Brian was brutal and direct. The school caused these murders, he said. The administration must pay.

———

Mr. D developed a heart condition. It appeared the first autumn after the shootings. Stress, the doctors said. No kidding.

Frank was riddled with symptoms of PTSD: numbness, anxiety attacks, inability to concentrate, and reclusiveness. Therapy helped him sort them out. Immediately after the murders, he had trouble making eye contact. It got worse. What was that about? "Guilt," he discovered. "I had never heard of survivor guilt. I felt guilty that Dave and the kids died and I lived."

His wife wanted to help. It was eating him up, but he couldn't express it to her. He was just like his students. "Don't shut your parents out," he begged them. He could cry in front of them. But his wife…she didn't understand. And he didn't particularly want her to. He just wanted solace at home.

The years after the tragedy were tumultuous. He got to Columbine at 6 A.M., left at 8 or 9 in the evening. Weekends he came in for shorter stints—quiet time to catch up. At any given time he had a dozen kids on suicide watch. Breakdowns were a daily occurrence among the students and the staff. He got tremendous satisfaction out of helping the kids, but it was a terrible drain. He had a couple of hours every night to forget it all. "I needed that time to regenerate," he said. "The last thing I wanted to do when I got home was talk about it."

His wife implored him to open up. His son and daughter were concerned. His parents and siblings seemed to call constantly. *Are you eating? Should you be driving?* "I think I know when to eat," he would say. Everyone had to know how he was feeling. *How are you doing? How are you doing?* "Enough!" he would say. "Please stop!"

Mr. D struggled with some of the staff, too. A therapist complained that she spent years in his school after the tragedy and he never learned her name. He could name all two thousand students. He had a strong team of administrators who were great at heading off problems, but some of them needed support themselves. One was brilliant but chatty—she had to talk out all her pain. Frank wouldn't do it. He confessed to his staff that he knew he wasn't there for them. He just didn't have the juice. He had so much in him, and it was all going to the kids. It got the kids through.

Frank sought out avenues for relaxation. He joined a Sunday night bowling league with his wife. Strangers would approach every frame. *How are you doing? How are the students?* "Once again, it was Columbine," he said. Out to dinner, same thing. "People would come right up to the booth. It got to the point where I didn't want to do anything. I just wanted to stay home."

Home was just as bad. "I would go down to my basement, to avoid my wife and kids," he said. His golden retriever followed. That was nice.

His family resented him. "They could not understand why I was acting that way," he said. He felt awful, too. "I wasn't the person I wanted to be."

He started counseling immediately after the attack, and he credits it with saving him. If he could do one thing over, it would be to include his family in the therapy. "They had no idea what PTSD was," he said. "If they had just understood what I was going through, it would have been all right."

His marriage didn't make it. Early in 2002, he and his wife agreed to divorce. He said Columbine had not been the sole reason, but it was a big part.

As he prepared to move out, Frank came upon four thousand letters he'd received in 1999. Most were supportive, some angry, a few threatened his life. He had tried to read twenty-five a day; that proved traumatic. Now he was ready to face them. He read through a big stack, and one name caught him off guard. Diane Meyer had been his old high school sweetheart. They had broken up before graduation and lost touch for thirty years. He looked her up. Her mom was in the same house. He called Diane and she was so understanding. They spoke several times, never in person, but long comforting chats. She helped him through the divorce and the emotional upheaval ahead of him in May. He had one more thing he had to do.

Columbine was a cathartic experience for much of the faculty. They reevaluated their lives. Many started over on new careers. By the spring of 2002, most of them had moved on. Every other administrator but Frank was gone. As May approached, Mr. D considered what had made him happiest. How did he *really* want to invest his remaining years?

No compromises, he decided; he would follow his dream. He chose to remain principal at Columbine. He loved that job. Some of the families hated him; they were disgusted by his announcement. Others were pleased. His kids were ecstatic.

Rohrbough was furious. But he was having success with the cops. His Hail Mary pass had broken the dam: Judge Jackson continued releasing evidence.

Eventually, Jeffco was ordered to release almost everything, except the supposedly incendiary items: the killers' journals and the Basement Tapes. The mother lode came in November 2000: 11,000 pages of police reports, including virtually every witness account. Jeffco said that was everything.

It was still hiding more than half. Reporters and families kept chipping away, demanding known items. Jeffco acted comically in its attempts to suppress. It numbered all the pages and *then* eliminated thousands, releasing the documents with numbered gaps. One release indicated nearly 3,000 missing pages.

Jeffco was forced to cough up half a dozen more releases over the next year; in November 2001, officials described a huge stack as "the last batch." More than 5,000 pages more came by the end of 2002, and 10,000 in 2003—in January, February, March, June, and three separate times in October.

Halfway through all that, in April 2001, district attorney Dave Thomas inadvertently mentioned the smoking gun: the affidavit to search Eric's house more than a year before the massacre. Jeffco had vigorously denied its existence for two years. Judge Jackson ordered it released.

The affidavit was more damning than expected. Investigator Guerra had astutely pulled together the threads of Eric's early plotting, and had documented mass murder threats and the bomb production to begin realizing them. The purpose of the cover-up was out in the open. Yet it continued for several more years.

Finally, in June 2003, the search warrant Kate Battan had composed on the afternoon of the massacre came out. It demonstrated conclusively that Jeffco officials had been lying about the Browns all along—that they knew about the warnings from the beginning, and the "missing" Web pages were so accessible they'd found them in the first minutes of the attack.

Anger and contempt kept rising. A federal judge finally had enough. He ruled that Jeffco could not be trusted even to warehouse valuable evidence. He ordered the county to hand over key material such as the Basement Tapes to be secured in the federal courthouse in Denver.

———

Agent Fuselier beat Mr. D to retirement. Six months after the massacre, the investigation was largely complete. Fuselier continued studying the killers, but he transitioned back to his role as head of domestic terrorism for the Colorado-Wyoming region. Few Americans had heard of Osama bin Laden, but a life-sized WANTED poster of him greeted visitors to the FBI branch office. Fuselier saw enemy number one's picture every morning as he got off the elevator on the eighteenth floor.

"He's a dangerous man," Fuselier told a visitor. The Bureau was determined to stop him.

Fuselier also resumed training hostage negotiators and went back on call for serious incidents. Two years later, he concluded one of the most notorious prison breaks in recent history. The Texas Seven had escaped a maximum-security facility and embarked on a crime spree. The ringleader was serving eighteen life sentences—he had nothing left to lose. On Christmas Eve 2000, they stole a cache of guns from a sporting goods store and ambushed a police officer. They shot him eleven times and ran him over on the way out, to be sure he was dead. He was. A reward was posted: $500,000.

The gang kept moving. On January 20, 2001, they were spotted in a trailer park near Colorado Springs. A SWAT team captured four of them, and a fifth killed himself to avoid recapture. The two holdouts barricaded themselves in a Holiday Inn. It took Agent Fuselier's team five hours to talk them out. They were fixated on corruption in the penal system, so Fuselier arranged a live interview on a local TV station at 2:30 A.M. A cameraman came inside the room so the holdouts could see they were actually broadcast live. Both convicts then surrendered and were sentenced to death. All six survivors await lethal injection in Texas.

The stress wore Fuselier down. He would have twenty years at the Bureau that October and be eligible for his pension. He announced his retirement for that date. He would be fifty-four.

On September 11, 2001, the country was attacked. Bin Laden was behind it. Fuselier postponed his retirement and spent most of the next eleven months on the case. By the summer of 2002, the United States had taken over Afghanistan, bin Laden had fled into hiding, and the urgency had abated.

Fuselier's son Brian graduated from Columbine High that May—the last class Mr. D had been waiting for. Brian was leaving for college in July. Dwayne scheduled his retirement for the week afterward, so Brian wouldn't see his dad lazing about jobless.

"I could see a change the next day," Brian told his dad when he returned home for a visit. "You had mellowed out more than I had ever seen."

Fuselier missed the work, though. Within months, he was consulting for the State Department. It sent him to conduct antiterrorism training in Third World countries. He spent a quarter of the year in sketchy sections of Pakistan, Tanzania, Malaysia, Macedonia—anywhere terrorists were active.

Mimi worried. Dwayne didn't think about it much, and Brian didn't hear the tension return to his voice. Fear wasn't the problem at the FBI; it was the responsibility.

"It was getting harder going to work knowing someone's life might depend on me not making any mistakes that day," he said.

———

Shortly before Brian left Columbine, Michael Moore's *Bowling for Columbine* drew raves at Cannes. It became the top-grossing documentary in U.S. history. It wasn't really much about Columbine, and the title featured a minor myth—that Eric and Dylan went bowling on April 20—but it included a dramatic scene where Moore and a victim went to Kmart and asked to return the bullets still inside the guy. The stunt and/or publicity around it shamed Kmart into discontinuing ammunition sales nationwide.

Marilyn Manson was interviewed in the film. Moore asked Manson what he would say to the killers, if he had a chance to talk to them: "I wouldn't say a single word to them," he said. "I would listen to what they have to say, and that's what no one did." That was the story the media had told.

The connection to KMFDM, the nihilistic band Eric *did* idolize and quote frequently, was ignored by the major media. Fans got word, however, and the band issued a statement of deep remorse: "We are sick and appalled, as is the rest of the nation, by what took place in Colorado...none of us condone any Nazi beliefs whatsoever."

———

The killers' parents remained silent. They never spoke to the press. Pastor Don Marxhausen stayed close to Tom and Sue Klebold. He was a great comfort. Sue went back to training disabled students at the community college. That helped her cope.

"It's amazing how long it took me to get up and say my name at a meeting, to say, 'I'm Dylan Klebold's mother,'" she said later. "Dylan could have killed any number of the kids of people that I work with."

Shopping could be intimidating—anticipating that moment of recognition as a salesperson examined her credit card. It was a distinctive name. Sometimes they noticed.

"Boy, you're a survivor," one clerk said.

Tom worked from home, so he had a choice about when to go out. He stayed in all the time. Pastor Don worried about him.

Reverend Marxhausen paid for that compassion. Much of his parish loved him for it; others were outraged. The church council split. That was untenable. A year after the massacre, he was forced out.

Marxhausen had been one of the most revered ministers in the Denver area, but now he could not find a job. After a bout of unemployment, he left the state to head up a small parish. He missed Colorado, and eventually moved back. He got a job as a chaplain at a county jail. His primary function was to advise inmates when loved ones had died. He was born for the job, ministering to the desperate. He empathized with each one, and it sucked the life out of him.

———

The lawsuits sputtered on for years. They got messier. A rash of new defendants was added, including school officials, the killers' parents, the manufacturer of Luvox, and anyone who had come in contact with the guns. The suits were consolidated in federal court. Judge Lewis Babcock accepted the county's two major arguments: that it was not responsible for stopping the killers in advance, and that cops should not be punished for decisions under fire. Babcock said the authorities *should* have headed off the massacre months earlier but were not legally bound.

In November 2001, he dismissed most of the charges against the sheriff and the school. The families appealed, and the county settled the next year: $15,000 each—a fraction of their legal fees. The discovery process never brought much to light; it didn't need to. The Rohrboughs' initial offensive had set the legal process in motion, and it continued under its own power.

Judge Babcock refused to dismiss the Sanders case. He balked at the contention that Dave's rescue involved split-second decisions.

"They had time in the third hour!" Babcock boomed.

The cops had hundreds of people to rescue, their attorney responded. They'd had to allocate resources.

More then 750 cops had been on the scene, the judge reminded him. "It's not as though they were a little shorthanded out there that day," he said.

In August 2002, Jeffco paid Angela Sanders $1.5 million. It admitted to no wrongdoing. The last Jeffco case to close was Patrick Ireland's. He got $117,500.

After years of wrangling, most of the fringe cases were dismissed. Luvox was pulled from the market. That left the killers' families. They wanted to settle. They didn't have a lot of money, but they had insurance. It turned out their home owner's policies covered murder by their children. About $1.6 million was divided between thirty-one families. Most of it came from the Klebolds' policy. Similar agreements were reached with Mark Manes, Phillip Duran, and Robyn Anderson, for an estimated total of approximately $1.3 million.

Five families rebuffed the Harrises and Klebolds: no buyout without information. It really wasn't about the money for the Rohrboughs and four others. They were battling for information, and they proved it.

But they were caught in a stalemate: the killers' parents would talk if the victims dropped the lawsuits; the victims would drop the suits if the parents spoke.

For two more years, it continued. Then the judge brokered a deal. The holdouts would dismiss their suits if the killers' parents answered all their questions—privately, but under oath. It was a bitter compromise. The holdouts wanted answers for the public as well as themselves. They settled for themselves.

In July 2003, the four parents were deposed for several days. Media came to photograph them. They had remained so private that few reporters even knew what they looked like. Two weeks after the depositions, an agreement was announced. It appeared to be over.

But Dawn Anna called for the depositions to be made public: understanding the warning signs could prevent the next Columbine. A chorus gathered behind her. A magistrate ruled that the transcripts would be destroyed, per the agreement. That set off a public outcry and a wave of open records requests. Judge Babcock agreed to consider arguments.

It had taken four years to reach this point. They were only halfway there.

In April 2007, Judge Babcock finally ruled. "There is a legitimate public interest in these materials so that similar tragedies may hopefully be prevented," he wrote. "I conclude, however, that the balance of interests still strikes in favor of maintaining strict confidentiality."

He settled on a compromise. The transcripts would be sealed at the national archives for twenty years. The truth would come out in 2027, twenty-eight years after the massacre.

———

Though he was retired, Fuselier hoped to see the depositions, too. Optimally, he would like to question the parents himself. He knew where the boys ended, psychologically, but their origins were a mystery, particularly Eric's. Only two people had an eighteen-year perspective on his path to psychopathy. When did Eric start exhibiting the early hallmarks, and how were they visible? Wayne had adopted a stern parenting style—how had that worked? Eric wrote little about interaction with his mother—what had Kathy's approach been? Were there any successes? Anything that could help the next parent?

Fuselier understood their refusal to talk.

"I have the utmost sympathy for the Harris and Klebold parents," he said. "They have been vilified without information. No one has sufficient objective information to draw any conclusions."

Fuselier said he had raised two sons, and either one could have emerged with traits beyond his comprehension. Eric documented his parents' frustration with his behavior, as well as their attempts to force him to conform. Their tactics might have been all wrong for a budding young psychopath, but how do parents even know what that is?

"I believe they have been unjustifiably criticized for what their sons did," Fuselier said. "They are probably asking themselves the same questions that we in the profession are asking."

———

Patrick Ireland left home for Colorado State in fall 2000. He did fine. He really took to campus life. And he was surprised by how much he enjoyed business school. Letting go of architecture turned out to be easy. He had been forced into something he liked more.

He still fought memory battles, struggled a bit to find words, and would probably remain on antiseizure medication for life. He met a girl his first night. Kacie Lancaster. She was clever, attractive, and a little shy. They clicked immediately and became close friends.

In May 2004, he graduated magna cum laude. Armed with a BS in business administration, he accepted a job as a financial planner at Northwestern Mutual Financial Network. He loved it.

One finger troubled him a little. His right pinkie jutted out away from the others, which caused a minor issue when he shook hands. It could poke the other person in the palm a little—just enough to signal that something was off. You could catch him glancing down there nervously, if you knew what to look for. It was not the first impression he wanted to make. But he had such a commanding presence once he spoke. Clients trusted him. His bosses were happy. He was becoming a star.

Patrick had retired the wheelchair and the crutch in high school. The foot brace remained. His right leg lagged behind a little: noticeable, but not debilitating. Running was out of the question, but water skis were not.

Balance, strength, and agility were all hurdles Patrick could overcome. But he would never regain the dexterity in his right foot to grip the ski. So he worked with an engineering friend to build a custom boot he could slip on as he tried to rise up on the water. They spent months working on prototypes and experimenting with them at the lake. John went with them for encouragement. Every time, the boat dragged Patrick uselessly behind.

They tried stripping the shell off a Rollerblade and adhering it to the ski. Nope. They refined it, and returned to the lake. Useless. Patrick tried over and over. He had made about ten runs that evening, and it was getting late. John was sure Patrick was exhausted, and thought it was time to break. *No, I can do this,* Patrick said.

John agreed. He sat in the passenger seat facing backward. The driver throttled the engine, and John watched his boy rise up onto the surface of the lake. Wow.

Patrick felt the spray pelt his face. The sun danced on the waves. The towrope jerked his arms. He dug in for a turn. A sheet of water shot up and sliced into his calf. It hurt, just a little. Ahhhhhh. The pain of competition. It felt great.

Everyone expected copycats. The country braced for a new level of horror. School shooting deaths actually dropped 25 percent over the next three years. But Eric and Dylan gave young eyes a fresh approach: terrorist tactics for personal aggrandizement. In 2001, a pair of ninth graders at a Fort Collins, Colorado, middle school procured a similar arsenal: TEC-9, shotgun, rifles, and propane bombs. They planned to reverse Eric's chronology: seal off exits, mow down students, and save the bombs for stragglers. They would finish by taking ten hostages, holding them in the counseling office for fun, then killing the kids and themselves.

But they leaked. Kids nearly always leak. The bigger the plot, the wider the leakage. The Fort Collins pair went recruiting for gunmen to cover all the exits. One of the plotters told at least seven people that he planned to "redo Columbine." He bragged to four girls that they would be the first to die. They went straight to the police.

Teen peers were different after 1999. "Jokes" scared the crap out of kids. Two more grandiose plots—in Malcolm, Nebraska, and Oaklyn, New Jersey—were foiled in the first five years.

School administrators around the country responded with "zero tolerance"—meaning every idle threat was treated like a cocked gun. That drove everyone crazy. Nearly all supposed killers turned out to be kids blowing off steam. It wasn't working for anyone.

A pair of government how-to guides helped. The FBI and the Secret Service each published reports in the first three years, guiding faculty to identify serious threats. The central recommendations contradicted prevailing post-Columbine behavior. They said identifying outcasts as threats is not healthy. It demonizes innocent kids who are already struggling.

It is also unproductive. Oddballs are not the problem. They do not fit the profile. *There is no profile.*

All the recent school shooters shared exactly one trait: 100 percent male. (Since the study a few have been female.) Aside from personal experience, no other characteristic hit 50 percent, not even close. "There is no accurate or useful 'profile' of attackers," the Secret Service said. Attackers came from all ethnic, economic, and social classes. The bulk came from solid two-parent homes. Most had no criminal record or history of violence.

The two biggest myths were that shooters were loners and that they "snapped." A staggering 93 percent planned their attack in advance. "The path toward violence is an evolutionary one, with signposts along the way," the FBI report said.

Cultural influences also appeared weak. Only a quarter were interested in violent movies, half that number in video games—probably below average for teen boys.

Most perps shared a crucial experience: 98 percent had suffered a loss or failure they perceived as serious—anything from getting fired to blowing a test or getting dumped. Of course, everyone suffers loss and failure, but for these kids, the trauma seemed to set anger in motion. This was certainly true in Columbine: Dylan viewed his entire life as failure, and Eric's arrest accelerated his anger.

So what should adults look for? First and foremost, advance confessions: 81 percent of shooters had confided their intentions. More than half told at least two people. Most threats are idle, though; the key is specificity. Vague, implied, and implausible threats are low-risk. The danger skyrockets when threats are direct and specific, identify a motive, and indicate work performed to carry it out. Melodramatic outbursts do *not* increase the risk.

A subtler form of leakage is preoccupation with death, destruction, and violence. A graphic mutilation story might be an early warning sign—or a vivid imagination. Add malice, brutality, and an unrepentant hero, and concern should rise. Don't overreact to a single story or drawing, the FBI warned. Normal teen boys enjoy violence and are fascinated with the macabre. "Writings and drawings on these themes can be a reflection of a harmless but rich and creative fantasy life," the report said. The key was repetition leading to obsession. The Bureau described a boy who'd worked guns and violence into every assignment. In home ec class he'd baked a cake in the shape of a gun.

The FBI compiled a specific list of warning signs, including symptoms of both psychopathy and depression: manipulation, intolerance, superiority, narcissism, alienation, rigidity, lethargy, dehumanization of others, and externalizing blame. It was a daunting list—that's a small excerpt. Few teachers were going to master it. The FBI recommended against trying. It suggested one person per school be trained intensely, for all faculty and administrators to turn to.

The FBI added one final caution: a kid matching most of its warning signs was more likely to be suffering from depression or mental illness than planning an attack. Most kids matching the criteria needed help, not incarceration.

———

Columbine also changed police response to attacks. No more perimeters. A national task force was organized to develop a new plan. In 2003, it released "The Active Shooter Protocol." The gist was simple: If the shooter seems active, storm the building. Move toward the sound of gunfire. Disregard even victims. There is one objective: Neutralize the shooters. Stop them or kill them.

The concept had been around for years but had been rejected. Pre-Columbine, cops had been exhorted to proceed cautiously: secure the perimeter, get the gunman talking, wait for the SWAT team.

The key to the new protocol was *active*. Most shootings—the vast majority—were labeled passive: the gunman was alive but not firing. Those cases reverted to the old protocol. Success depended on accurately determining the threat in the first moments.

Officers face a second decision point when they reach the shooters. If the killer is holed up in a classroom, holding kids but not firing, responders may need to stop there and use traditional hostage techniques. Storming the classroom could provoke the gunman. But if the shooter is firing, even just periodically, move in.

The active shooter protocol gained quick and widespread acceptance. In a series of shootings over the next decade, including the worst disaster, at Virginia Tech, cops or guards rushed in, stopped shooters, and saved lives.

———

Sue Petrone asked for and received the two sidewalk blocks her son Danny died on. They were jackhammered out of the ground and installed in her backyard, in the shadow of a fragrant spruce tree. Around the slab, she created a rock garden, with two big wooden tubs overflowing with petunias. She had a sturdy oak truss constructed over the slab, and a porch swing suspended from the crossbeam. She and Rich and their shaggy little dog can nestle comfortably into the generous swing.

Linda Sanders kept the Advil tablet found near Dave's body. He had trouble with knee swelling, so he always carried one in his pocket. Just one.

She took his bloody clothes, a swath of carpet from under his head, a little fragment of tooth that chipped off when he fell, and his glasses.

She would never let those glasses go. She snapped them into an eyeglass case and placed them on the nightstand by her bed. She intends to leave them that way forever.

The lawsuit on behalf of Dave Sanders outlived all the others, but his widow chose not to take part. She was not angry at the police, or the school, or the parents. She was angry at her situation. She was lonely.

50. The Basement Tapes

Eric wanted to be remembered. He spent a year on "The Book of God," but five weeks before Judgment Day, he decided that wasn't good enough. He wanted a starring role on-camera. So on March 15, he and Dylan began the Basement Tapes. It would be a tight shooting schedule, with no time for editing or postproduction. They filmed with a Sony 8mm camcorder, checked out from the Columbine High video lab.

The first installment was a basic talk-show setup: a stationary camera in the family room in Eric's basement, outside his bedroom. He continued making camera adjustments after he was rolling—perhaps as a sneaky way to ensure his audience would be clear on the director. The video project was entirely about his audience. Ultimately, the attack was, too.

Eric joined Dylan on-set. They kicked back in plush velvet recliners, bantering about the big event. Eric had a bottle of Jack Daniel's in one hand and Arlene laid across his lap. He took a swig and tried not to grimace. He hated the stuff. Dylan munched on a toothpick and took little sips of Jack as well.

They ranted for more than an hour. Dylan was wild and animated and angry, obsessively hurling his fingers through his long, ratty hair. Eric was mostly calm and controlled. They spoke with one voice: Eric's.

Eric introduced most ideas; Dylan riffed along. They insulted the usual inferiors: blacks, Latinos, gays, and women. "Yes, moms, stay home," Eric said. "Fucking make me dinner, bitch!"

Sometimes, Eric got kind of loud. That made Dylan nervous. It was after 1:00 A.M., and Eric's parents were upstairs, snoozing away. Careful, Dylan warned.

They rattled off a list of kids who'd pissed them off. Eric had been dragged across the country: the scrawny little white guy, constantly starting over, always at the bottom of the food chain. People kept making fun of him—"my face, my hair, my shirts." He enumerated every girl who had refused his advances.

Dylan got fired up just listening. He faced the camera and addressed his tormenters. "If you could see all the anger I've stored over the past four fucking years," he said. He described a sophomore who didn't deserve the jaw evolution gave him. "Look for his jaw," Dylan said. "It won't be on his body."

Eric named one guy he planned to shoot in the balls, another in the face. "I imagine I will be shot in the head by a fucking cop," he said.

No one they named would be killed.

It went back so much further than high school. From prekindergarten, at Foothills Day Care center, Dylan could remember them: all the stuck-up toddlers sneering at him. "Being shy didn't help," he said. At home it was just as bad. Except for his parents, his whole extended family looked down on him, treated him like the runt of the litter. His brother was always ripping on him; Byron's friends, too. "You made me what I am," Dylan said. "You added to the rage."

"More rage, more rage!" Eric demanded. He motioned with his arms. "Keep building it."

Dylan hurled another Ericism: "I've narrowed it down. It's humans I hate."

Eric raised Arlene, and aimed her at the camera. "You guys will all die, and it will be fucking soon," he said. "You all need to die. We need to die, too."

The boys made it clear, repeatedly, that they planned to die in battle. Their legacy would live. "We're going to kick-start a revolution," Eric said. "I declared war on the human race and war is what it is."

He apologized to his mom. "I really am sorry about this, but war's war," he told her. "My mother, she's so thoughtful. She helps out in so many ways." She brought him candy when he was sad, and sometimes Slim Jims. He said his dad was great, too.

Eric grew quiet. He said his parents had probably noticed him withdrawing. That was intentional—he was doing it to help them. "I don't want to spend any more time with them," he said. "I wish they were out of town so I didn't have to look at them and bond more."

Dylan was less generous. "I'm sorry I have so much rage, but you put it in me," he said. He got around to thanking them for self-awareness and self-reliance. "I appreciate that," he said.

The boys insisted their parents were not to blame. "They gave me my fucking life," Dylan said. "It's up to me what I do with it."

Dylan bemoaned the guilt they would feel, but then ridiculed it. He pitched his voice to mimic his mom: "If only we could have reached them sooner. Or found this tape."

Eric loved that. "If only we would have asked the right questions," he added.

Oh, they were wily, the boys agreed. Parents were easy to fool. Teachers, cops, bosses, judges, shrinks, Diversion officers, and anyone in authority were pathetic. "I could convince them that I'm going to climb Mount Everest," Eric said, "or that I have a twin brother growing out of my back. I can make you believe anything."

Eventually, they got tired of the talk show and moved on to a tour of their arsenal.

———

Eric outdid Dylan with the apologies. To the untrained eye, he seemed sincere. The psychologists on the case found Eric less convincing. They saw a psychopath. Classic. He even pulled the stunt of self-diagnosing to dismiss it. "I wish I was a fucking sociopath so I didn't have any remorse," Eric said. "But I do."

Watching that made Dr. Fuselier angry. Remorse meant a deep desire to correct a mistake. Eric hadn't done it yet. He excused his actions several times on the tapes. Fuselier was tough to rattle, but that got to him.

"Those are the most worthless apologies I've ever heard in my life," he said. It got more ludicrous later, when Eric willed some of his stuff to two buddies, "if you guys live."

"If you live?" Fuselier repeated. "They are going to go in there and quite possibly kill their friends. If they were the least bit sorry, they would not do it!"

This is exactly the sort of false apology Dr. Cleckley identified in 1941. He described phony emotional outbursts and dazzling simulations of love for friends, relatives, and their own children—shortly before devastating them. Psychopaths mimic remorse so convincingly that victims often believe their apologies, even from a state of ruin. Consider Eric Harris: months after his massacre, a group of experienced journalists from the top papers in the country watched him perform on the Basement Tapes. Most reported Eric apologizing and showing remorse. They marveled at his repentance.

———

The boys got the camera rolling again three nights later. Same place, same setup, same time frame.

They laughed about how easy it was to build all the stuff. Instructions for everything were right there on the Internet—"bombs, poison, napalm, and how to buy guns if you're underage."

In between the logistics, they tossed in more bits of philosophy: "World Peace is an impossible thing.... Religions are gay."

"Directors will be fighting over this story," Dylan gushed. They pondered whom they should trust with their material: Steven Spielberg or Quentin Tarantino?

———

Agent Fuselier watched the tapes dozens of times. In one respect, they were a revelation. While the journals explained motive, the tapes conveyed personality. There was ample testimony about them from friends, but there's nothing like meeting a killer in person. The tapes offered the best approximation.

Fuselier understood that the Basement Tapes had been shot for an audience. They were partially performance—for the public, for the cops, and for each other. Dylan, in particular, was working his heart out to show Eric how invested he was. To laymen, Dylan appeared dominant. He was louder, brasher, and had much more personality. Eric preferred directing. He was often behind the lens. But he was always in charge. Fuselier saw Dylan gave himself away with his eyes. He would shout like a madman, then glance at his partner for approval. *How was that?*

The Basement Tapes were a fusion of invented characters with the real killers. But the characters the killers chose were revealing, too.

———

Eric had a new idea. Columbine would remain the centerpiece of his apocalypse, but maybe he could make it bolder. Trip bombs and land mines? Nothing fancy, just simple explosives.

Expansion would require additional manpower. Eric began recruitment plans.

Around the end of March, Eric approached Chris Morris. *What if they strung up a trip bomb right there behind Blackjack? That hole in the fence would be perfect—kids crawled through there all the time.*

Chris was unenthusiastic. A bomb for pesky kids? Sounds a little extreme, he said.

Eric backpedaled. The bomb would not actually hit the kids, just scare the shit out of them.

No, Chris said. Definitely not.

Chris was starting to worry. Eric and Dylan were making a lot of bombs. They had blown a bunch off. And he was hearing stories from all kinds of kids about them getting guns.

Chris noticed a change in Eric. He was acting aggressive all of a sudden, picking fights with people for no good reason. Nate Dykeman saw something, too, in both Eric and Dylan: cutting classes more, sleeping in class, acting secretive. No one said anything.

Eric made at least three attempts to recruit Chris Morris, though Chris did not grasp that at the time. Some of the overtures came in the form of "jokes."

"Wouldn't it be fun to kill all the jocks?" he asked in bowling class. Why stop there, why not blow up the whole school? How hard would it be, really? Chris assumed Eric was joking, but still.

Come on, Eric said. They could put bombs on the power generators— that ought to take out the school.

Chris had enough. He turned to talk to someone else.

That is a standard recruitment technique for aspiring mass murderers, Fuselier explained. They toss out the idea, and if it's shunned it's a "joke"; if the person lights up, the recruiter proceeds to the next step.

When news of Eric's crack about killing the jocks was reported, many took it as confirmation of the target motive. Eric was a much wilier recruiter than that. He always played to the audience in front of him. He nearly always gauged their desires correctly. Suggesting the jocks didn't mean *he* wanted to single them out, it indicated he thought the idea would appeal to Chris.

Of course Eric would enjoy killing jocks, too, along with niggers, spics, fags, and every other group he railed against.

Dylan was leaking indiscriminately now. He made several public displays of the pipe bombs. These grew far more frequent as NBK came within sight. A lot of people knew about the guns. And the pipe bombs. Eric and Dylan were setting off more and more of them, getting bolder with whom they let in on it.

In February or March, Eric spilled something even scarier: napalm. It happened at a party at Robyn's house. Eric had not been friends with Zack since their falling out the past summer, but Eric needed something. He could not get the napalm recipes off the Web to work. Zack was good with that kind of thing. Eric had a pretty good idea that Zack was the man to help him.

Eric walked up to Zack good-naturedly, asked him how he was doing, chatted him up awhile. They talked about their futures.

Zack and Eric left the party at the same time, and drove separately to a supermarket, King Soopers. Zack bought a soda and a candy bar, and waited for Eric back in the parking lot. Eric came out and showed him a soda and a box of bleach. Bleach? What was the bleach for? Zack asked.

Eric said he was "going to try it."

Try what?

Napalm. Eric said he was going to try napalm. Did Zack know how to make it?

No.

Zack told the story to the investigators after the murders, but he lied the first time. He described Robyn's party, but edited out the napalm. He agreed to a polygraph, and just before they strapped him in, he confessed to the rest. He said the conversation went no further, and he never discussed napalm or the shotguns again—with Eric, Dylan, or anyone else. The results of his polygraph were inconclusive.

Eric also asked Chris to store napalm at his house. Eric and Dylan joked about it on the Basement Tapes: "Napalm better not freeze at that certain person's house." They disguised his identity at first, but then referred to "Chris Pizza's house." Crafty. (Chris Morris later testified that it was indeed him, and that he'd refused.)

No time. Less than a month to go. Eric had a lot of shit left to do. He organized it into a list labeled "shit left to do." He had to figure out napalm, acquire more ammo, find a laser-aiming device, practice gear-ups, prepare final explosives, and determine the peak killing moment. One item was apparently not accomplished: "get laid."

———

April 2, Staff Sergeant Mark Gonzales cold-called Eric about enlisting in the Marines. Eric said maybe. They talked several times.

That same month, he returned to "The Book of God." Months had passed; a whole lot had happened. He had thirty-nine crickets ready, twenty-four pipe bombs, and all four guns. Eric closed up the journal. That was done.

———

Eric met Sergeant Gonzales. He wore a black Rammstein T-shirt, black pants, and black combat boots. He took a screening test and got an average score. The sergeant asked Eric to describe himself by selecting among tabs labeled with personal attributes. He chose "physical fitness," "leadership and self-reliance," and "self-discipline and self-direction." He would think about enlisting, and talk it over with his parents. He agreed to a home visit, with his parents.

It's not clear what Eric was getting out of the exercise. He probably had multiple motives. He had always pictured himself as a Marine—he might enjoy a last-minute taste. And he needed information: he was still struggling with the time bombs and the napalm. He told Gonzales he was interested in weapons and demolitions training, and he asked a lot of questions. But his parents were probably the key motive. They kept hounding Eric about his future. This would get them off his back. Two weeks of tranquillity. Breathing room to maneuver.

———

Eric shot the next video scene on his own, in his car, driving, with the camera facing him from the dash. He had the music blaring, so much of what he said is unclear. He talked about the Blackjack crew, and apologized for what was ahead: "Sorry dudes, I had to do what I had to do." He was going to miss them. He was really going to miss Bob, his old boss who'd gotten drunk on the roof with them.

Eric still couldn't decide on the timing of the attack: before prom or after? "It is a weird feeling knowing you're going to be dead in two and a half weeks," he said.

———

April 9 was Eric's birthday. Eighteen years old—officially an adult. He got together with a bunch of friends at a local hangout.

A couple of days before or after, a friend saw Eric and Dylan in the cafeteria, huddled over a piece of paper. What was going on? she asked. They tried to hide it. She played it cool, then snatched the paper away. It was a hand-drawn diagram of the cafeteria, showing details like the location of surveillance cameras. That was weird.

Eric made several more diagrams. He conducted his inventory of cafeteria traffic. He did not allow that to be seen.

———

The boys shot more tapes. NBK would make for one hell of a graduation, they said. Lots of people crying, probably a candlelight vigil. Too bad they wouldn't see it. They congratulated themselves for documenting all this. But the cops would get the tapes first. Do you think they'll let people see them? Dylan asked. Probably not. The cops would chop up all their footage and show the public how they wanted it to look. That could be a problem. They resolved to copy the videos and distribute them to four news stations. Eric would scan his journal and e-mail it with maps and blueprints.

They never got around to that.

On Sunday, the boys headed into Denver for supplies. Of course they brought the camcorder. This was history. They picked up fuel containers and propane bottles. Dylan got his army pants. Eric seems to have been funding most of the operation, but Dylan paid his share this time. He brought $200 in cash; Eric had a check for $150.

The next shot was in Eric's bedroom, alone. He sat on his bed, pointing the camera at his face from a few inches away, producing an eerie fish-eye effect. Eric talked about his "best parents" again—and the cops making them pay.

"It fucking sucks to do this to them," he said. "They're going to be put through hell."

They could not have stopped him, Eric assured them. He quoted Shakespeare: "Good wombs have borne bad sons."

He wrote the same line in his day planner on the page for Mother's Day. That was revealing, Fuselier thought. Dylan wanted to be a good boy, but Eric understood he was evil.

It was funny, Eric told the television audience: all that razzing from his parents about goals and he was working his ass off. "It's kinda hard on me, these last few days," he said. "This is my last week on earth and they don't know."

The payoff would be worth it. "The apocalypse is coming and it's starting in eight days," he said. He licked his lips. "Oh yeah. It's coming, all right."

Then he held up his masterpiece: "This is 'The Book of God,'" he said. "This is the thought process"—if you want to understand why, read this. He flipped through to show off his best work. "Somehow, I'll publish these."

He stopped at a sketch in the back, of himself or Dylan in battle gear. The soldier was outfitted with a huge tank to be strapped to his back. It was labeled "napalm." He pointed to it and said, "This is the suicide plan."

———

Five days before Judgment, Dylan finally accepted that he was enacting it. "Time to die," he wrote. "We are in wait of our reward, each other."

We. The word dominates the entry, but does not include Eric. Dylan was addressing Harriet. He was grateful to Eric for providing the exit, but was uninterested in spending eternity with him.

———

Thursday evening, the Marine recruiter showed up for the home visit at 6:00 P.M. Wayne and Kathy had lots of questions about job opportunities in the corps. Kathy asked whether antidepressants would affect Eric's eligibility. She fetched the prescription bottle, and Sergeant Gonzales wrote down "Luvox." He said he would check and call back.

Like Eric cared. He had been invoking the Marines in his war fantasies all his life, but all he really wanted out of the corps was the prestige of its patch on his shoulder. Eric never depicted himself supporting a squadron, and certainly not taking orders. It was always an army of one or two, and the mission was about him, not country or his corps.

Gonzales phoned on Friday or Saturday and left a message to call him back. Eric never bothered.

———

Mr. D provided a dose of irony. He wrapped up Friday's assembly talking about everyone coming back alive. Perfect.

The boys picked up more propane that day. Eric hounded Mark Manes for ammo. The delay probably pushed NBK from April 19 to April 20.

Eric spent the night at Dylan's. That surprised Tom and Sue Klebold— they had not seen Eric in six months. The boys came in after 10:00 P.M. Dylan was nervous—Tom could hear it in his voice. His pitch was a little off; Tom described it later as "tight." He made a mental note to talk to Dylan about it. He never got to it.

Eric came with a great big duffel bag, stuffed with something. It was oversized and bulky and he was having trouble carrying it. Tom assumed it was a computer. It was a weapons cache, for a final fashion show. They filmed it, of course—the only scene from the Basement Tapes shot at Dylan's. Eric directed, as usual. Dylan strapped on gear: harness, ammo pouches... when he got to the knives, he joked about a certain sophomore's head impaled on one. He slung the TEC-9 over his shoulder and slid the shotgun into the cargo pocket on his pants. Then he strapped it in with the webbing to secure it into place.

He needed his backpack. Dylan went digging for it in the closet and ran into his tux, hanging up for prom tomorrow night. Whatever. He turned to the camera to rub it in: "Robyn. I didn't really want to go to prom. But since I'm going to be dying, I thought I might do something cool." Plus, he said his parents were paying for it.

Dylan pulled his trench coat on, struck a pose in the mirror. This was his entrance outfit—it was going to be so badass. It looked lumpy. "I'm fat on this side," he complained.

The whole point was impressing people. Details mattered. Wardrobe, staging, atmospherics, audio, pyrotechnics, action, suspense, timing, irony, foreshadowing—all the cinematic elements were important. And for the local audience, they were adding aroma: sulfur, burning flesh, and fear.

Dylan tried his next pose, and that was a problem, too. His very first move, once the scene got rolling, was to snatch the TEC out of its sling and toss it to his firing hand in a single dramatic motion. His trench coat got in the way. He tried it again. Lame. *Faster,* Eric said. He was visibly annoyed. He had practiced every move to perfection. Dylan was trying all this shit for the first time.

_____

Eric left around 9:00 A.M., without the duffel bag. The boys may have stayed up all night. Tom and Sue noticed that Dylan's bed didn't look slept in.

_____

Saturday was all about prom. Dylan came home at 3:00 A.M., and Sue was up to greet him. How was it? she asked. Dylan showed her a schnapps flask. He told her he'd only drunk a little. The rest of the group was going to breakfast, he said. He was tired. He was done.

He slept it off most of the next day.

_____

Monday morning, around 9 o'clock, Dylan grabbed his spiral notebook and drew the top of a giant numeral 1. He drew the bottom of it at the foot of the page, with a big gap in between for copy: "1. One day. One is the beginning or the end. Hahaha, rescued, yet there. About 26.5 hours from now the judgment will begin. Difficult, but not impossible, necessary, nervewracking & fun."

It was interesting, he said, knowing he was going to die. Everything had a touch of triviality. Calculus really did turn out to have no practical application in his life.

The last word is hard to read, but it appears to be "Fickt," German slang for "fucked."

_____

In his last twenty-four hours, Dylan got active. He drew up full-page sketches of himself in body armor: front and back displays geared up with explosives. One of the last pages included a brief schedule for NBK, now pushed back to Tuesday. It ended like this: "When first bombs go off, attack. have fun!"

Monday night, the boys went out to dinner with friends. They went to Outback Steakhouse, Eric's favorite restaurant. Dylan had some coupons, so they could economize. His mom asked how it was when he got home. Good, he said. They'd had a nice time. He'd had himself a nice steak.

Eric got the final two boxes of ammo from Mark Manes, and said he might go shooting tomorrow. He didn't get a lot of sleep that night, if any. He was still awake past 2:00 A.M., three hours before his wake-up call. He had a few reflections to add to his audio memoirs. He spoke into a microcassette recorder, indicating that there were fewer than nine hours to go. "People will die because of me," Eric said. "It will be a day that will be remembered forever."

Tuesday morning, the boys rose early. Tom and Sue heard Dylan leave around 5:15. They assumed he was on his way to bowling class. They did not see him.

"Bye," he called out.

Then they heard the door shut.

Eric left his microcassette on the kitchen counter. It was an old tape, reused, and someone had labeled it "Nixon" somewhere along the line. The meaning of that label perplexed observers for years to come. It meant nothing.

51. Two Hurdles

The fifth-anniversary commemoration drew a smaller audience than expected. The crowds had grown progressively smaller each year, but the school foresaw a bigger bump for this milestone. Nearly everyone was pleased by the light turnout. It meant people had moved on.

Many survivors began to think in terms of how many events were left to slog through. Only two remained now: the ten-year and the dedication of the memorial. Surely they wouldn't have to come back in twenty.

There were always a lot of the same faces, but Anne Marie Hochhalter showed up for the first time this year.

It had been a rough road there.

After her mother's suicide, Anne Marie finished out senior year and made a go at community college. She didn't like it much. She traveled to North Carolina for electrical stimulation therapy. Doctors hoped it might lead her to walk again. It failed.

The commotion over Columbine never seemed to end. Two years out, her dad moved the family way out to the country to get some peace. They went stir-crazy out there.

Anne Marie dropped out of school. She had no job. She was miserable. Doctors kept trying fresh approaches on her spine. Nothing worked. She wallowed in it for a while, then she had enough.

She went back to school—a four-year college, majoring in business. She bought a house with donations and equipped it for her wheelchair. Life began to feel good.

"I wish I could tell you I had an epiphany, but it was gradual," she said. The turnaround came when she let go of the dream of walking again. "I finally accepted that I was confined to a wheelchair. Once I did that, I was free to move on with my life. It was very liberating."

Her dad remarried and Anne Marie forgave her mother. She had struggled so long, and mental illness was so debilitating. "In her mind, she thought it was the best thing she could have done," she said.

Anne Marie let go of her anger at the killers, too. "That's counterproductive," she said. "If you don't forgive, you can't move on."

On the fifth anniversary, she returned to Columbine to share her hope.

———

Funding for the Clement Park memorial met unforeseen resistance. It was budgeted at $2.5 million, less than the library project, which the families had raised in four months. This one looked easy.

But by the time they started fund-raising in 2000, goodwill had been tapped out. They scaled back the project by a million in 2005. Still, they were not even close.

Bill Clinton had taken a personal interest in the massacre as president. He returned to Jeffco in July 2004 to rev up support. He brought in $300,000. That was a big boost, but momentum fizzled again.

———

Before he retired, Supervisory Special Agent Fuselier requested permission from the head of his branch to share his analysis. His boss agreed. Other experts brought in by the FBI cooperated as well, including Dr. Hare, Dr. Frank Ochberg, and others who spoke off the record. On the fifth anniversary of the massacre, a summary of their analysis was published.

New York Times columnist David Brooks devoted an op-ed piece to the team's conclusions. Tom Klebold read it. He didn't like it. He sent David Brooks an e-mail saying so. Brooks was struck by how loyal Tom still felt toward Dylan. After several exchanges, Tom and Sue agreed to sit down with Brooks to discuss their boy and his tragedy—the first and only media interview any of the four parents has ever given.

It turned out that they were kind of angry, too. Sue recounted an incident where she was offered absolution. "I forgive you for what you've done," the person said. That infuriated Sue. "I haven't done anything for which I need forgiveness," she told Brooks.

But mostly Tom and Sue were bewildered. They were convinced that jocks and bullying had been behind it, but jocks and bullies are everywhere and few kids are trying to blow up their high school. They were bright people, and they knew they weren't qualified to offer an explanation for their son's crimes. "I'm a quantitative person," Tom said. He was a scientist and a businessman. "We're not qualified to sort this out," he said.

They had run it over and over in their heads; they had tried to be objective, and they could honestly say they could rule one cause out. "Dylan did not do this because of the way he was raised," Susan said. They were emphatic about that. "He did it in contradiction to the way he was raised."

They were aware the public had reached a different verdict: the primary culprits were them. When Brooks met them, Tom had a stack of news stories documenting their poll numbers: 83 percent blamed the two of them and Eric's parents. In five years, the figure had barely budged. For the Klebolds, judgment was the price of silence. And it stung.

The public condemned them, but those close to the family did not. "Most people have been good-hearted," Tom said.

He and Sue accepted responsibility for one tragic mistake. Dylan was in agony; they'd thought he would be just fine. "He was hopeless," Tom said now. "We didn't realize it until after the end." They had not induced Dylan's homicide, they believed, but failed to prevent his suicide. They failed to see it coming. "I think he suffered horribly before he died," Sue said. "For not seeing that, I will never forgive myself."

Tom and Sue preferred to talk about Columbine as a suicide. "They acknowledge but do not emphasize the murders their son committed," Brooks wrote. What they really yearned for was an authoritative study that would explain why Eric and Dylan did it. Yet they had just read the analysis by some of the top experts in North America; they had dismissed it for providing the wrong explanation. They complained that Dr. Fuselier had assessed their son without interviewing them. Fuselier was dying to.

Mostly, the four parents remain a mystery. They have chosen that path. But David Brooks spent enough time with the Klebolds to form a distinct impression, and he has proven himself a good judge of character. He concluded his column with this assessment: Dylan left Tom and Sue to face terrible consequences. "I'd say they are facing them bravely and honorably."

The Klebolds wanted to understand what happened. They wanted to help other parents like them. They did not feel safe talking to the press, but they talked to a pair of child psychologists, under the condition that they not cite them directly. They were writing a book about teen violence. The problem was that at the time they published, the authors had no access to the crucial evidence.

———

Patrick Ireland slips his right foot into a hard plastic brace every morning as he gets dressed. He twists open a prescription bottle and swallows a dose of antiseizure meds. He walks with a limp. His mind is sharp, but he hesitates occasionally to find the words. His friends don't notice. He knows. It's not quite like before.

Patrick rarely thinks about before. Life is different than he imagined before. Better. Shoes are an issue, because of the brace. And his big toe is crooked inward, scrunches the others over. The little toe on his right foot sticks way out—nobody makes a shoe that wide. The doctors never set his foot right. "My dad's pretty pissed off," he said.

He still hangs out with many of his high school buddies. They don't talk about the massacre much, which is what many of the survivors report. It isn't emotional anymore, just boring. They're done.

He is tired of interviews, too. Occasionally he agrees to one. Reporters generally approach the library ordeal gingerly, but Patrick just plunges in, describing it unemotionally, as if recapping a movie. When he did Oprah's show, she played a clip of him going out the window.

"Whoa!" she said. "So is it difficult for you to see that video?"

"No."

"It's not? OK."

He felt good watching it, actually. He felt a sense of accomplishment.

Patrick got a perplexing voice mail one morning in the spring of 2005. It was an old friend he hadn't heard from in a while, wishing him well "today," hoping he was all right. *Huh. Now, what could that mean?*

That afternoon, Patrick dated a document at work: April 20. *Was it anniversary time already again?*

———

Linda Sanders felt every anniversary. Her mood began to sour each April; she got jittery, she could feel it coming.

She tried dating; that was impossible. Dave lingered, and men resented his presence. He was a national hero—who could compete with that?

"It's, like, *Top Dave Sanders*," she said. "It's not fair to another man to be compared to the man I've built. He's so high on a pedestal he's in heaven."

She knew Dave would have wanted her to find someone. She pictured him up there saying, "Linda, I want somebody to hug you."

"It's impossible," Linda said. "There's nobody coming. I'm destined to be alone because of the way he left."

Linda withdrew. She stopped answering the door, stopped answering the phone. For two years she hardly spoke at all. She sedated herself with Valium and alcohol. "I was like a vacant person," she said, "going through the motions of life. I'd go to the store, I was going places, but I was empty."

Her father worried. What could he do?

"I want my Linda back," he said.

Linda never went back to work. She walks every day, and she looks after her parents. She does not go near the Columbine Lounge—too many memories, and too close to alcohol. She can't watch movies with guns in them or read thrillers.

One of those Aprils, years after getting sober, she felt a sudden, desperate need for help. "I ran out the front door and I looked for any neighbor that was home," she said. "I needed a hug, you know, I needed a hug. So I knocked on my neighbor's door, she wasn't home, so I went to my next neighbor, she was home. I walked in and she was reading a book. 'You're it,' I said. And I can't remember her name. I said I needed a hug. She looked at me and I was crying and she said OK. She gave me a hug."

Linda still gets letters now and then from strangers who hear Dave's story or hers and sense immediately how it was for Linda. Most people don't. Most people see kids and they see parents. Every once in a while, someone gets how it was for the wife. A woman wrote to tell Linda she understood. "That letter came on a real bad day," Linda said. "And it carried me. I hold that letter every night. That woman has no idea what she did for me."

————

Several survivors published memoirs, and Brooks Brown wrote his take on the killers and his ordeal. None garnered a fraction of the attention of Misty Bernall's book.

In September 2003, the last known layer of the cover-up finally came out. It had unraveled over the course of a full year. It started when someone in the sheriff's department found some paperwork in a three-ring binder unrelated to the Columbine case. It was a brief police report on Eric Harris. Eight pages from his Web site were attached. They included the "I HATE" rants, boasts about the missions, and descriptions of the first pipe bombs. Eric bragged about detonating one. The report was dated August 7, 1997, more than six months earlier than reports uncovered to date.

The report was brought to the new Jeffco sheriff, Ted Mink. He called a press conference. "This discovery and its implications are upsetting," he said. "The obvious implication...is that the sheriff's office had some knowledge of Eric Harris's and Dylan Klebold's activities in the years prior to the Columbine shootings." He released the documents and asked Colorado Attorney General Ken Salazar to conduct an outside investigation.

Salazar assigned a team, which discovered that more crucial documents were missing. Much of Mike Guerra's file related to his premassacre investigation had disappeared—both the physical and electronic copies. In February 2004, the attorney general issued a report stating that Jeffco was not negligent, but should have followed through with the warrant and searched Eric's house more than a year before Columbine. It also said files were still missing.

His team continued investigating. Some people refused to cooperate. The interview report on former sheriff John Stone stated that he was visibly angry and considered the investigation politically motivated. "We were unable to ask Stone any questions or have any meaningful dialogue regarding our investigation due his apparent state of agitation," it concluded.

The breakthrough came a month later, when investigators went back for a third interview with Guerra. This time, he was more forthcoming. He spilled the one secret Jeffco officials had been good at keeping: the existence of the Open Space meeting. Investigators quietly began confronting other officials who had attended. They got some colorful responses. Former undersheriff John Dunaway said he believed Guerra was upset that "he might be viewed as some kind of blithering idiot. That he, you know, was sitting on top of all of this."

In August 2004, the Colorado attorney general called a grand jury to flush the file out and consider indictments. The panel swore in eleven witnesses. The file was never recovered, though investigators were able to reconstruct most of it.

The probe turned up other startling discoveries. According to the grand jury report, Division Chief John Kiekbusch's assistant, Judy Searle, testified that in September 1999, he asked her to find the Guerra file. He told her to search the computer network and the physical files, and to do it in secret. He instructed her specifically not to tell the officers involved. Searle testified under oath that she found that suspicious. She normally would have started her search by talking to those officers. Searle searched, and discovered nothing. She gave Kiekbusch the news: there seemed to be no record anywhere, no sign the file ever existed. She watched his reaction. She testified that he appeared "somewhat relieved."

According to that same report, in 2000, Kiekbusch instructed her to shred a large pile of Columbine reports. Searle testified that she did not find the request unusual at the time, because Kiekbusch was preparing to leave the office, and Searle assumed he was purging duplicates. She complied.

The grand jury released its report on September 16, 2004. It found that the Guerra file should have been stored in three separate locations, both physical and electronic. All three were destroyed, it concluded— apparently during the summer of 1999. It described that as "troubling."

It was also disturbed by attempts to suppress the information— specifically, the Open Space meeting, attended by Stone, Dunaway, Kiekbusch, Thomas, Guerra, and the county attorney, among others. "The topic of the Open Space meeting, the press conference omissions and the actions of Lt. Kiekbusch raise suspicions to the grand jury about the potential that the files were deliberately destroyed," its report stated.

But every witness denied involvement in the destruction, the report said. Given that, the grand jury could not determine whether the suspicious activity "is tied to a particular person or the result of a particular crime." Accordingly, it concluded that there was insufficient evidence to indict.

Kiekbusch filed a formal objection. He said the shredding was limited to drafts or copies. His assistant's perception of his relief was a mystery to him.

He said the grand jury implied that he had attempted to cover up, hide, or destroy documents. He unequivocally denied all of it.

———

Brian Rohrbough got most of what he sought: nearly all the evidence came out, and the national response protocol changed. But he never felt like he'd won. He gave up on justice. No one would pay; nothing would change.

Most of the top officials left the Jeffco sheriff's department. Stone survived the recall petition drive, but did not run for reelection. The one county official to come out of Columbine glowing was DA Dave Thomas. Many victims had perceived him as their champion. In 2004, he gave up his position to run for Congress. Polls indicated a toss-up, and the race gained national prominence and funding. The Open Space scandal broke less than two months before Election Day. Thomas's poll numbers plunged. Money dried up. He lost big. In 2007, he ran for school board. He now helps oversee 150 Jefferson county schools, including Columbine High.

Brian Rohrbough hurled himself into a different passion. He picketed abortion clinics and rose to president of Colorado Right to Life. There, he butted heads with the conservative parent organization, which he considered far too liberal. The last straw came when Rohrbough signed an open letter berating Christian conservative leader James Dobson as soft on abortion. It was published as a full-page newspaper ad. National Right to Life expelled his chapter. Dobson's organization, Focus on the Family, issued a news release calling it "a rogue and divisive group."

Later, Brian ran for office. He joined an obscure third party that got itself on the ballot in three states. It nominated Brian for vice president of the United States.

Brian wasn't always mad. He remarried and adopted two children, who gave him great comfort. At work, he could be surprisingly tranquil. He continued to run his custom audio business, doing most of the labor himself. He loved the precision work: tweaking the acoustic gauges, setting time delays for the front speakers just a fraction of an instant long, so the chords struck the driver's eardrum at precisely the same moment as the sound waves rolling in from the rear. Exquisite harmony. Brian could get lost for hours in his workshop. When a customer stopped by for a consultation, he was as gentle as Mr. Rogers buttoning up his cardigan.

Then he would think about Danny. Or a stray thought would lead him back to Columbine. The scowl returned.

Brad and Misty Bernall got out of Colorado. They moved to a hamlet called Blowing Rock, just off the Blue Ridge Parkway in the heart of the North Carolina mountains. They hated it out there. More isolation than they'd bargained for. Their marriage was shaky sometimes, but they held on. Nearly all the parents of the Thirteen stayed together.

Brad had struggled mightily in the early days, but as time wore on friends said he came to terms with Cassie's death. Misty smoldered. Nearly a decade later, friends described her as getting angry and frustrated at the mention of the martyr controversy. Misty felt she had been robbed, twice. Eric and Dylan took her daughter; journalists and detectives snatched away the miracle.

Mr. D found new ways to amuse his kids at school. For each homecoming assembly, he impersonated a celebrity. One year, the homecoming theme was Copacabana, and Mr. D strode out dressed as Barry Manilow, in a fluffy blond wig, white leisure suit, and Day-Glo Hawaiian shirt.

"Hey, Mr. D, nice shoes!" a girl yelled. He kicked his leg up to show off his four-inch platform heels. The kids ate it up. The assembly was standard high school: cheers, awards, a hands-free cake-eating contest, and a blindfolded obstacle course. Typical raucous confusion ruled the corridors before and after.

Every now and then, on a nice day, Mr. D wandered outside for serenity. The heavy door swung shut behind him, the bolt caught, and the frenzy of nervous energy ceased. It was so still. Each step, he could hear the grass squish beneath his shoes. A teacher strolled to her car in the distance. Her keys tingled—they could be dangling from his own hand. He made the short hike up Rebel Hill. The crosses were gone, their holes filled, but the grass had not grown back along the path.

At the top of the mesa, the back side of Rebel Hill was deserted. When he stopped there long enough, he would see the prairie dogs. At first there was no sign of them, no movement whatsoever, save the overgrown grasses bending softly to the breeze. After fifteen minutes of silence, they began to scurry about the clumps of mountain aster, foraging for food, socializing, grooming each other, fattening up for the winter. Six months after the tragedy, Mr. D had run into a Japanese film crew up there, enraptured by the charming rodents. The crew had come to shoot a documentary about the massacre; they had expected teen angst and American social Darwinism. They were seduced by the tranquillity—less than a hundred yards from the school. They shot hours of footage of the twelve-inch prairie dogs.

The Japanese crew saw this place somewhat differently than Americans did. Their depiction was by turns tumultuous, brutal, explosive, and serene.

———

School shooters faded as a national fear for a while. They worsened in Europe. They returned to the States in an uglier form in the fall of 2006, when a spate of adult killers realized that a school setting would reap attention. There were four shootings in a three-week span, beginning in late August 2006. The shooters used various tactics to resemble the Columbine killers, including trench coats and Web sites mentioning them by name. They appeared to see Eric and Dylan's legacy as a marketing opportunity. National attention focused on five girls killed in a one-room Amish school in Pennsylvania. But in Denver, the Platte Canyon shooting was particularly tough.

Platte Canyon High School was just one county over, and the police force so small that the Jeffco sheriff commanded the response team. It was a big national story for a few hours; then it was over. In Jeffco, it hit much harder. The Denver TV stations stayed live with the story all afternoon. Everyone was transfixed. This time it was a hostage standoff, and the SWAT team did rush the building. The gunman had only two girls left at that point. When the cops rushed in, he shot one in the head, then took care of himself. He died instantly, but the victim was medevaced out. The city watched her helicopter take off and land on the rooftop of St. Anthony's; then viewers waited, hoping, for two hours. Doctors held a press conference early in the evening. She'd never had a chance.

The next morning's *Rocky Mountain News* was filled with photos eerily like April 20: survivors sobbing, praying, holding on tight.

Bomb scares at Columbine spiked. The school was evacuated a few days later. Moms felt their muscles clench, bracing for the terrifying news. Some had almost forgotten Columbine, but their bodies remembered. In an instant, it was April 20 again. The danger passed in a few hours—it was only a prank. The anxiety lingered.

In the ten years after Columbine, more than eighty school shootings took place in the United States. The principals who survived — many were targeted — invariably found themselves in over their heads. Mr. D made himself available to all of them. Many accepted his offer. He spent hours every semester sharing what he had learned.

Those calls were hard. An e-mail he received that fall was worse. "Dear Principal," it said. "In a few hours you will probably hear about a school shooting in North Carolina. I am responsible for it. I remember Columbine. It is time the world remembered it. I am sorry. Goodbye."

It had been sent in the morning, but Mr. D didn't check e-mail for several hours. He called the cops immediately, and they sent word to the boy's high school. Too late. The nineteen-year-old had driven past his school and fired eight shots, injuring two superficially. Then police raided his home and found his father dead.

The shooter was apprehended and taken into court. He was asked why he was obsessed with Columbine. He said he didn't know.

School shooters were starting to feel like a threat again. But the real shocker came the following spring, at Virginia Tech. Seung-Hui Cho killed thirty-two people, plus himself, and injured seventeen. The press proclaimed it a new American record. They shuddered at the idea of turning school shootings into a competition, then awarded Cho the title.

Cho left a manifesto explaining his attack. It cited Eric and Dylan at least twice as inspiration. He'd looked up to them. He did not resemble them. Cho did not appear to enjoy his rampage. He did not expect to. He emptied his guns with a blank expression. He shared none of Eric or Dylan's bloodlust. The videos Cho left described *himself* as raped, crucified, impaled, and slashed ear to ear. Cho appears to have been severely mentally ill, fighting a powerful psychosis, possibly schizophrenia. Unlike the Columbine killers, he did not seem to be in touch with reality or comprehend what he was doing. He understood only that Eric and Dylan left an impression.

52. Quiet

The morning of the attack, Eric and Dylan shot a brief farewell video in Eric's basement. Eric directed. "Say it now," he said.

"Hey, Mom," Dylan said. "I gotta go. It's about a half an hour till Judgment Day. I just wanted to apologize to you guys for any crap this might instigate. Just know I'm going to a better place. I didn't like life too much, and I know I'll be happy wherever the fuck I go. So I'm gone. Good-bye. Reb…"

Eric handed him the camera. "Yeah.…Everyone I love, I'm really sorry about all this," Eric said. "I know my mom and dad will be just like…just fucking shocked beyond belief. I'm sorry, all right. I can't help it."

Dylan interrupted him from behind the camera. "It's what we had to do," he said.

Eric had one more thought, for the girl from prom night. "Susan, sorry. Under different circumstances it would've been a lot different. I want you to have that fly CD." Dylan got restless and snapped his fingers. Eric flashed an angry look. That shut him up. Eric had something profound to deliver. Dylan couldn't care less. Eric lost his big moment. "That's it," he said. "Sorry. Good-bye."

Dylan turned the camera to face himself. "Good-bye."

Eric and Dylan spent just five minutes firing outside. They killed two people and advanced into the school. For five minutes, they fended off deputies, shot Dave Sanders, and roamed the halls looking for targets. They began tossing pipe bombs over the railing, down into the commons, which appeared deserted. It was not. Several students hiding under tables made a run for it and fled out the cafeteria doors. They all made it out safely. Others stayed put.

Along the way, the boys passed the library windows, and ignored all the kids huddled there. Then they circled back. That room offered the highest concentration of fodder they had seen. They found fifty-six people inside. They killed ten, injured twelve. The remaining thirty-four were easy pickings. But Eric and Dylan got bored. They walked out seven and a half minutes later, at 11:36, seventeen minutes into the attack. Aside from themselves and the cops, they would not shoot another human again.

The boys wandered into the science wing. They walked past Science Room 3, where the Eagle Scouts were just getting started on Dave Sanders. They looked through the windowpanes in several classroom doors. Kids were inside most of them. At least two or three hundred kids remained in the school. The killers knew they were there. Many witnesses made eye contact. Eric and Dylan walked by. They chose empty classrooms to open fire.

They roamed aimlessly upstairs. To civilians, it seems odd that they stopped shooting and entered this "quiet period." It's actually pretty normal for a psychopath. They enjoy their exploits, but murder gets boring, too. Even serial killers lose interest for a few days. Eric was likely proud and inflated, but tired of it already. Dylan was less predictable, but probably resembled a bipolar experiencing a mixed episode: depressed and manic at once—indifferent to his actions; remorseless but not sadistic. He was ready to die, fused with Eric and following his lead.

Eric had a few thrills left to savor. Killing had turned tedious, but he was still up for an explosion. The biggest explosion of his life. He could still perform his primary feat: blow up the school and burn down the rubble.

He headed down the staircase into the commons at 11:44. Dylan followed closely behind. Eric stopped on the landing halfway down. He knelt and placed his rifle barrel on the railing to improve his accuracy. Backpacks were scattered everywhere, but Eric knew which duffel bag was his. He fired. The boys were easily within the blast area, and they were well aware of that fact. Twenty-five minutes into the massacre, Eric made his second attempt to initiate the main event, and his first attempt at suicide. He failed again.

Eric gave up. He walked directly to the bomb, with Dylan behind him. Dylan tried to fiddle with it. That failed, too. Kids were visible under some of the tables. The killers ignored them. Lots of drinks had been left on the tables, and the killers tipped back a few. "Today the world's going to come to an end," one of them said. "Today's the day we die."

The surveillance cameras picked up their movements in the commons. Their body language was vastly different than what witnesses in the library described. Their shoulders drooped, and they walked slowly. The excitement had drained out of them; the bravado was gone. Eric had also broken his nose. He was in severe pain.

They left the cafeteria after two and a half minutes. On the way out, Dylan tossed a Molotov cocktail at the big bombs—one last attempt to set them off. Another failure. Several kids felt the blast and ran.

The boys drifted about the school: upstairs and down again. They surveyed the damage in the commons. It was pathetic. The Molotov started a small fire that burned the duffel bag off one of the bombs and ignited some of the fuel strapped to it, but the propane tank was impervious. The fire set off the sprinkler system across the room. The boys had been going for an inferno; they caused a flood.

The killers were apparently out of ideas. They'd expected to be dead by now, but never planned how. The cops were supposed to take care of that. Eric predicted he'd be shot in the head. No one had obliged.

They had two essential choices: suicide or surrender. Eric would sooner die. He idolized Medea for going down in flames, but couldn't ignite his fire.

A cornered psychopath will often attempt "suicide by cop": an aggressive provocation to force the police to shoot. Eric and Dylan could have ended it dramatically by charging the perimeter. It would have been glorious. But it would take tremendous courage.

Eric craved self-determination. Dylan just wanted a way out. Alone, he might well have been talked down. He had been promising suicide for two years and never brought himself near it. He never had a partner to guide him out.

At noon, they returned to the library. Why end it there? Act III was about to commence. The car bombs were set to blow. Ambulances had massed around Dylan's BMW as planned. A triage unit was busy nearby. Limbs would fill the air, just like Eric's drawings. The library windows were set up like skyboxes. Eric and Dylan most likely chose the library, not just because of the carnage there already, but for a better view.

They found the room quite different than they'd left it twenty-four minutes before. Human decay begins rapidly. The first thing to assault them was probably smell. Blood is rich in iron, so large volumes emit a strong metallic smell. The average body contains five quarts. Several gallons had pooled on the carpet, coagulating into a reddish brown gelatin, with irregular black speckles. Aerosolized droplets dry quickly, so the spatters were black and crusty. Stray globs of brain matter would soon be solid as concrete. They would be scraped off with putty knives and the stubborn chunks melted down with steam-injection machines.

The killers had left the library in turmoil: shots, screams, explosions, and forty-two teens moaning, gasping, and praying. The commotion had ceased, replaced by the piercing fire alarm. The smoke cleared; a warm breeze floated through the blown-out windows. Twelve bodies shared the room with them. Two were breathing: Patrick Ireland and Lisa Kreutz had been fading in and out of consciousness, unable to move. Four staff hid in rooms farther back. Ten corpses had passed through pallor mortis, and livor mortis was setting in. The skin had gone white and purplish splotches were now appearing as the remaining blood settled.

The boys may have been oblivious. Mass murderers often shift into an altered state, dissociated and indifferent to the horror. Some barely notice, others take a clinical curiosity in variations like eyes either bulging or retracting, the whites clouding up or mottling with red clumps. If Eric or Dylan touched their victims, they would have found the bodies cooling noticeably, but still warm and pliable.

They walked on. Eric advanced toward a center window, among the heaviest carnage. He walked past the worst of it to get there. Dylan broke away and chose a spot closer to the entrance, half a dozen window panels down. If he took a direct route, he followed one of the cleanest pathways left.

The boys inspected the army surrounding them outside. Paramedics were just then breaching the perimeter to rescue Sean, Lance, and Anne Marie. Eric opened fire. Dylan did the same. Two deputies shot back, mostly suppressive fire. The medics gave up, the boys quit. This was their only fire on humans during the thirty-two-minute quiet period. It was a classic attempt at suicide by cop: heroically dying in battle, but at a time, place, and manner of their own choosing. That failed, too.

A minute or two later, at 12:06, the first SWAT team finally entered Columbine High School, on the opposite end of the building. Eric and Dylan could not have known. They apparently waited for their cars to explode, weathered a final disappointment, and then called it a day.

Eric turned his back on the mess. He retreated to the southwest corner, one of the few unspoiled areas in the room. Dylan joined him there. It was a cozy spot near the windows, nestled between walls and bookshelves on three sides, with a mountain view. One body lay nearby. It was Patrick Ireland, gently breathing, unconscious. The boys sat down on the floor facing out at the windows. They seemed to be staying low to avoid police fire. That may seem odd given their intentions, but it's all about control. Eric propped himself against a bookshelf, just a shoulder-width to the right of Dylan and a few feet behind, watching his back.

One of them lit the rag used as a fuse on a Molotov cocktail. He set it on the table right above Patrick. Eric raised the shotgun barrel to his mouth, like the antihero of *The Downward Spiral*. Dylan pointed the TEC-9 at his left temple. The Molotov rag burned down.

Eric fired through the roof of his mouth, causing "evacuation of the brain." He collapsed against the books, and his torso slumped to the side. He ended that way, with his arms curled forward, as if hugging an invisible pillow. Dylan's blast knocked him flat on his back and strewed brain matter across Eric's left knee. Dylan's head came to rest just beside it.

A lot of blood spilled, but less than their victims'. Eric and Dylan blew out their medullas, the brain center that controls involuntary functions. Their hearts stopped almost instantly. Medically, "bleeding" ceased. Gravity took over and they leaked. Dylan's blood soaked into Eric's pant leg.

The Molotov blew. It started a small fire. It also spilled Eric's crude napalm over the tabletop and sealed a lump of his brain underneath. That detail would prove the boys died just before the eruption. The alarm system detected the fire and recorded the time as 12:08.

The sprinklers put it out and drenched the boys. Blood drained from their skulls and oxidized like blackened halos.

Three hours later, police found Eric crumpled, Dylan sprawled leisurely. His legs flopped over to the side, one knee atop the other, ankles crossed. One arm draped across his stomach, underlining the word emblazoned on his black T-shirt. His head lay back, mouth open, jaw slack. Blood trickled out the corners, toward his ears. He looked serene. The red letters on his chest screamed WRATH.

53. At the Broken Places

It took eight and a half years to erect the permanent memorial. In 2006, the fund hit 70 percent of its reduced budget, permitting construction to begin. An event was planned for the groundbreaking in June—to honor the dead, and to publicize the $300,000 outstanding. Bill Clinton flew in. Two thousand mourners turned out.

Dawn Anna read the thirteen names. "We're here because we love them," she said. "We're here as a family and as a community that's been through the darkest of days and is coming through to the light."

Thunderheads rolled in and opened up on the crowd. Scattered umbrellas popped up, but most people were caught unaware. Nobody moved. They didn't care.

This was Republican country, but Clinton's introduction drew wild applause. These people were proud to host an American president.

"I am here today because millions of Americans were changed by Columbine," he said. "It was one of the darkest days Hillary and I had in the White House. We wept, we prayed."

Right before his appearance, she'd called from the Senate, he said— "Just to remind me of what we did that day. This was a momentous event in the history of the country. And every parent [was] left feeling helpless, even the president."

He had watched the survivors evolve, Clinton said. He compared them to his colleague, Max Cleland, who'd left both legs and one arm in Vietnam. It was a struggle for Max to dress every morning. He could have resented the thousands who came back unscathed or who'd avoided the draft, like him, Clinton said. What a waste that would be. Cleland ran for the Senate and represented Georgia for six years. He was fond of quoting Ernest

Hemingway, and Clinton recited his favorite passage: "The world breaks everyone and afterward many are strong at the broken places."

"Every day, from now on, the world will break someone," Clinton added. "These magnificent families, in memory of their children, and their teacher, can help them always to be strong."

———

Patrick Ireland proposed to Kacie, the girl he'd met his first night at CSU. They would never have met, he pointed out, if he had not been shot.

They married on an August afternoon. Six bridesmaids in rose red gowns walked the aisle of an ornate Catholic church.

Mr. D came. He was struck by the sight of Patrick standing at the altar with no physical support. He was also taken aback by the number of classmates involved. It was a familiar pattern. For twenty years, he had watched alumni drift away from their high school buds, but the two thousand survivors stuck close.

Patrick walked out gracefully and composed. Mr. D wiped off a tear. Patrick's doctor from Craig was there, still incredulous. So was Laura, the girl Patrick had been afraid to ask to prom.

The wedding party took a month of ballroom dance lessons to prepare for the reception. Patrick spun Kacie across the floor. They waltzed and two-stepped and did the fox-trot. They closed out the first dance with a deep dip. Patrick joined his mother for "Because You Loved Me." Diane Warren wrote the song to her father for encouraging her when no one else believed. Kathy teared up quietly in her son's arms.

———

Former agent Dwayne Fuselier was still being asked to address law enforcement groups and teachers' conventions. They still wanted to know *why?* Fuselier kept agreeing to speak, insisting each presentation would be the last.

He continues to teach hostage negotiators in the Third World. He finds a lot more time for golf, and his mind wanders occasionally to Eric and Dylan—with no satisfaction, because the ending never changes.

Both his sons graduated from college and launched successful careers.

He still hopes to interview Eric and Dylan's parents.

Brad and Misty Bernall resettled nearby in New Mexico. They are much happier there.

She Said Yes was reissued in two paperback formats, a library edition, and an audiobook. It has sold over a million copies. The Web is loaded with sites unabashedly recounting the myth. Cassie's youth pastor was right: the church stuck with the story.

Local churches felt a surge following Columbine. Attendance spiked, fervor was unprecedented. It faded. Pastors reported no long-term impact.

The Harrises and Klebolds remained secluded. The Harrises eventually sold their house, but remained in the area. The Klebolds have not moved. In July of 2006, Dylan's older brother, Byron, got married.

Kids at Columbine stopped using the word as the name of a massacre. It became just a high school again. Smokers returned to chatting up adult strangers who strolled through Clement Park near their pit. It did not occur to them to be afraid.

When a journalist stopped by to assess the return to normalcy, they were puzzled. Why would anyone be interested in their boring school? They really didn't know. Their faces lit up when they discovered he was from the city. *What were the clubs like? Had he been to Colfax Avenue? Were there really strip clubs and winos and hookers there?*

Of course they remembered the tragedy. What an awful day. Their grade schools were locked down, everyone was scared. Several had had older siblings trapped in the high school. Their parents had been upset for months. *So what was Denver like?*

Mr. D had two grandchildren. His son settled into a career and his daughter got engaged. Frank didn't let Diane Meyer get away the second time. After his divorce, they reunited in person. She was just as funny as in high school. Same blue eyes, same insightful mind and selflessness. "Someone to lean on," Frank said. They began dating again. On Christmas Eve 2003, Frank asked her to marry him. She said yes. They remain engaged.

Mr. D informed his students he planned to retire. He will stay through graduation in 2012, or 2013. He will be fifty-seven or fifty-eight. He's not sure what he'll do then. Golf, travel, enjoy.

———

Linda Sanders pulled out of her depression. She still has rough days, but not so often. By 2008, she was dating again.

———

The memorial felt like the final step. One last controversy marred its completion. In the spring of 2007, as bulldozers carved out the site on the back slope of Rebel Hill, Brian Rohrbough went to battle with the memorial committee. An inner Ring of Remembrance honored the Thirteen in a special way. The larger Ring of Healing that surrounded it would bear quotes from students, teachers, friends, neighbors—everyone touched by the tragedy, whether or not a bullet actually pierced their skin. Each of the thirteen families was allocated a space on the inner ring for a large inscription in the brown marble to remember their child, father, or spouse. They were asked to keep it tasteful and respectful.

Twelve and a half families agreed. Sue Petrone and Brian Rohrbough submitted separate inscriptions for Danny, to be run side by side. Sue described her boy's blue eyes, engaging smile, and infectious laugh. Brian submitted an angry rant blaming Columbine on a godless school system in a nation that legalized abortion where authorities lied and covered up their crimes. He ended with a biblical quote, declaring, *There is no peace for the wicked*.

The committee asked Brian to tone it down. He refused. Both sides agreed to keep the wording confidential, but the gist of the dispute leaked. It caused yet another firestorm in Colorado. The public was split. A standoff ensued. Nobody wanted an angry tirade inside the Ring of Remembrance. The committee had the power to stop it. Brian dared them to do it.

It was no contest. Even after eight years, nothing trumped a grieving dad.

———

The Columbine memorial was dedicated on a sunny afternoon in September 2007. A few thousand visitors filed quietly past the inner wall. There was no ruckus over the angry inscription. It did not draw more onlookers than the other twelve, even out of curiosity. There was no discernible reaction. No one seemed to care.

Patrick Ireland spoke on behalf of the injured. "The shootings were an event that occurred," he said. "But it did not define me as a person. It did not set the tone for the rest of my life."

Thirteen doves were released. Seconds later, two hundred more fluttered free—an arbitrary number, to signify everyone else. They scattered up in all directions. For a moment, they seemed to fill the entire sky. Then they found one another and coalesced into a single flock, a massive white cloud weaving from left to right and back again, against the clear blue sky.

Timeline: Before

SOPHOMORE YEAR

January 1997	The missions begin.
February 28, 1997	Wayne Harris starts his journal.
March 31, 1997	Dylan starts his journal.
Summer 1997	Eric and Dylan start at Blackjack; build first pipe bomb.
July 23, 1997	Dylan first mentions killing in his journal—possibly figuratively.
August 7, 1997	Eric's Web site is reported to the police. It lists his "I HATE" rants.

JUNIOR YEAR

October 2, 1997	Eric, Dylan, and Zack are suspended for breaking into lockers.
November 3, 1997	Dylan first mentions a killing spree in his journal.
Unknown	Eric and Dylan steal from the school computer room.
January 30, 1998	Eric and Dylan are arrested for breaking into a van.
February 15, 1998	Deputies find a pipe bomb near Eric's house.
February 16, 1998	Eric begins seeing a psychiatrist and soon starts taking Zoloft.
Spring 1998*	Eric's dad catches him with a pipe bomb.

* Unknown date, approximately this period.

March 18, 1998	Dylan warns Brooks Brown about Eric's death threats.
March 19, 1998	Eric and Dylan conduct their intake interview for the Diversion program.
March 25, 1998	Eric and Dylan are formally sentenced in court.
April 1998	Investigator Guerra drafts an affidavit for a warrant to search Eric's house.
April 8, 1998	Eric receives his Diversion program contract.
April 10, 1998	Eric begins his journal.
by May 9, 1998	Eric and Dylan outline the attack, write about it in each other's yearbook.
May 14, 1998	Eric has switched from Zoloft to Luvox.

SENIOR YEAR

October 22, 1998	Eric begins pipe bomb arsenal production; resumes journal writing the next day.
November 13, 1998	Eric turns in his paper on Nazis.
November 17, 1998	Eric describes his sadistic rape fantasies in his journal.
November 22, 1998	Eric and Dylan buy two shotguns and a rifle at the Tanner Gun Show.
December 2, 1998	Eric fires his weapon for the first time.
January 23, 1999	Eric and Dylan buy the TEC-9 from Mark Manes.
January 20, 1999	Eric and Dylan complete the Diversion program, and Dylan resumes his journal.
February 7, 1999	Dylan submits his prescient story about killing "preps."
March 6, 1999	Eric and Dylan practice shooting at Rampart Range.
March 15, 1999	Eric and Dylan begin filming the Basement Tapes.
March 20, 1999	Eric attempts to recruit Chris Morris.
April 5, 8, 15, 1999	Eric talks to a Marine recruiter.
April 17, 1999	The prom.
April 20, 1999	The massacre.

Acknowledgments

This book is possible because of the survivors who graciously shared their stories. Thank you all. John, Kathy and Patrick Ireland, Brian Rohrbough, Linda Sanders, Frank DeAngelis, Dwayne Fuselier, Dr. Frank Ochberg, Dr. Robert Hare, and Kate Battan were especially generous. Reverend Don Marxhausen and Lucille Zimmerman were particularly kind.

Joan Walsh initiated this project by publishing my early stories at *Salon*. She gave me confidence and helped me find my voice. No writer could ask for more. David Plotz, David Talbot, Dan Brogan, Mim Udovich, and Toby Harshaw helped me continue reporting at other publications.

Early on, when I needed it, three veterans surprised me with e-mails of encouragement: Richard Goldstein, Frank Rich, and Jonathan Karp. You'll never know what that meant.

Jonathan first suggested the book. Mitch Hoffman later championed the project, guided early efforts, and helped me establish the tone. Jonathan returned for the crucial edit. I was struck by the clarity he brought. Jonathan gathered a wonderful team at Twelve and Hachette: his assistant, Colin Shepherd, added insightful notes on the manuscript; Karen Andrews did a thorough legal review; Bonnie Thompson redefined the term *copyedit;* managing editor Harvey-Jane Kowal was patient with my changes; Henry Sene Yee, Anne Twomey, and Flag Tonuz provided a great design. Cary Goldstein and Laura Lee Timko publicized the book well enough to get it into your hands.

This book went through several incarnations. From first reporting to publication, it took ten years. The one person who never lost faith in it or me was my agent Betsy Lerner. She earned my deepest gratitude. She's also a great editor, advisor, shrink, and rock.

I built on the work of other great journalists, especially Dan Luzadder, Alan Prendergast, and Lynn Bartels. I owe them a great debt. Michael Paterniti reinspired me with his brilliant *GQ* story on the tragedy. Wendy Murray generously shared her field notes. Mark Juergensmeyer's book gave me a deeper understanding of terrorists. Michelle Lopez and Mike Ditto were relentless researchers and fact-checkers. Dr. Frank Ochberg, Bruce Shapiro, Barb Monseu, and everyone at the Dart Center helped teach me about compassion for victims and for myself.

I was stunned by the number of friends willing to volunteer their time and contribute so greatly to this book. David Yoo, Ira Gilbert, Joe Blitman, David Boxwell, Jeff Barnes, and Alan Becker provided great feedback as early readers. Alan stepped in countless times, like lending me his PC and babysitting my hard drive at Best Buy for hours on a Sunday night when it crashed just before a deadline. My mom typed and formatted the bibliography, and cheered every development. Thanks to the folks at Alexian and Health Futures for keeping me solvent with an intermittent day job and the flexibility to put the book first. Lydia Wells Sledge stands alone. She devoted a year of her life to serve as full-time unpaid reader, proofer, fact-checker, researcher, organizer, assistant, and tackler of every conceivable odd task. She claims to have enjoyed it.

Jeff Moores, Marilyn Saltzman, Rick Kaufman, Keith Abbot, and Bobbie Louise Hawkins helped in many ways. So many volunteers pitched in at my Web sites, especially Melisande, Greg Smith, and the moderators, tech staff, artists, and editors. Thanks to the writers and bloggers who featured my work, especially David Brooks, Hanna Rosin, Jeralyn Merritt, Duncan Black, Stephen Green, Scott Rosenberg, Will Leitch, Rolf Potts, Michelangelo Signorile, Cyn Shepard, and all the members of the Brokeback forum and Open Salon.

Ten years on a massacre can be tough on the soul. Great friends got me through. Extra thanks to Tito Negron, Gregg Trostel, Elizabeth Geoghegan, Staci Amend, Tom Kotsines, Jonathan Oldham, Patrick Brown, Jessica Yoo, Miles Harvey, Kevin Davis, Bill Kelly, Maureen Harrington, Andy Marusak, Tim Vigil, Karen Auvinen, Tom Willison, Pat Patton, Scott Kunce, Greg Dobbin, Ira Kleinberg, Justin Griffin, Chuck Roesel, Bill Lychack, Alex Morelos, the cabin group, Natalie and the Muckrakers in New Orleans, my eight siblings, seven nieces and nephews, and my parents, Matt and Joan Cullen. All the early readers deserve a repeat here, but especially David Yoo, for keeping me amused.

I've had thirty years of great teachers, ending with a string of insightful editors. I got there because of Reg Saner, Peter Michelson, Lucia Berlin, and my other profs at CU; Linda Tufano way back at *The Daily Illini;* and my high school journalism advisor, Mrs. Barrows. Mrs. Thacker, thanks for what you told me graduation day in 1979. I didn't forget.

Those people helped me. I'm grateful to them and to everyone who helped the kids. Thanks to every paramedic, firefighter, cop, victim's advocate, teacher, custodian, shrink, Red Cross volunteer, detective, doctor, nurse, parent, sibling, friend, and anonymous stranger who came to the aid of the kids, the widow, and their families April 20 and afterward.

Notes

This book relies heavily on the evidence compiled by investigators, including videos, photographs, and more than 25,000 pages of documents. Where the notes say a piece of evidence was released, it was my primary source, except as noted. Jeffco stamped most pages with a unique number in this format, JC-001-000009, where the 9 indicates it was the ninth page compiled. (The prefix "JC-001" is constant.) I provide the JC numbers and online links to most documents in the expanded Web version of these notes, at www.davecullen.com/columbine. Links to many other sources are also maintained there.

I also drew on my own reporting, and the work of other journalists. Three were exceptional: Dan Luzadder led a crack investigative team at the *Rocky Mountain News* to reconstruct the events of April 20; Alan Prendergast of *Westword* tirelessly and brilliantly pursued the questions of what police knew before the murders and the cover-up afterward; and Lynn Bartels of the *Rocky Mountain News* covered nearly every aspect of the story with an unrivaled thoroughness, thoughtfulness, and empathy. I built on their work and am profoundly grateful. Tom Kenworthy's flawless reporting for the *Washington Post* was also an early inspiration.

Quotes from witnesses and survivors come from my reporting and reliable published accounts. All are attributed in the expanded online notes section. Significant outside sources are identified here.

Through their attorney, Sue and Tom Klebold verified much of the biographical information about their family and their activity after the attacks, adding small bits of information.

CHAPTER I. MR. D

He told them that he loved them: Most scenes involving Mr. D's speeches relied heavily on my interviews with him and were generally corroborated by others present. In many cases after the murders, I was present. I was the first journalist granted an in-depth interview with DeAngelis, which took place on July 4, 1999, in his office, for approximately two hours. I interviewed him more than twenty times over the next nine years.

twenty-four of Mr. D's kids: Twenty-four differs slightly from the figure in the introduction to the *Sheriff's Office Final Report,* and from those in some other accounts. The number varies depending on whether those with relatively minor injuries are counted. Twenty-four students were listed, with the names of the hospitals providing treatment, on JC-001-011869 and JC-001-011870. The governor's commission also settled on twenty-four. Twenty-one were shot, and three injured trying to escape.

CHAPTER 2. "REBELS"

pectus excavatum: Eric's medical records were released by Jeffco. He also discussed his reactions to the condition in several of his own writings.

Dylan went by VoDKa: Capitalization varied. Eric posted it that way on his Web site. Sometimes Dylan wrote VoDkA, or just Vodka or V.

Cold didn't deter the smokers: I made numerous trips to the smokers' pit over a nine-year period and found the students' behavior remarkably similar, with one exception: for several years after the shootings, students were suspicious of strangers and extremely hostile to the press. In time, that would change.

~~a friend videotaped him:~~ This scene came from video footage shot by a friend of the killers and released by police. They taped quite a bit of routine behavior.

CHAPTER 3. SPRINGTIME

argued in the *Washington Post:* Schiraldi, "Hyping School Violence."

A *New York Times* editorial: Egan, "Where Rampages Begin."

CDC data: The 2008 CDC study "School-Associated Student Homicides: United States, 1992–2006" added the most recent data and corroborated the research Schiraldi cited.

CHAPTER 4. ROCK 'N' BOWL

Both boys asked for cash advances: The new owner, Chris Lau, described the advances the boys requested and received and Eric's promotion in his police interview.

Eric had a phone engagement: Susan gave a detailed account of her interaction with Eric in her police interview.

CHAPTER 5. TWO COLUMBINES

in the Columbine Lounge: Most descriptions of the Lounge and its clientele were my observations from several Friday and Saturday night trips, all after the murders. The anecdotes and individuals were all real, down to the song titles, and were representative. Additional details were filled in by Linda Sanders and by friends of Dave's who hung out there with him. These interviews were the primary basis for my accounts of Dave and Linda, before and after the tragedy.

Dave Sanders taught typing: I am indebted to Marilyn Saltzman and Linda Lou Sanders for their book *Dave Sanders: Columbine Teacher, Coach, Hero,* which I drew on heavily. I corroborated and/or fleshed out the elements I used with Linda and friends of Dave's.

"He was never home": This quote was based on Linda Sanders's recollection of the response by Dave's ex-wife.

Cassie Bernall was not asked: Misty Bernall's memoir was extremely helpful in providing details about Cassie's life and about Brad and Misty's reactions to the tragedy. Additional information came from my interviews with Cassie's classmates, pastors, and church members, as well as TV interviews of the Bernalls. Journalist Wendy Murray also generously provided her field notes, including interviews with the Bernalls.

CHAPTER 6. HIS FUTURE

Dylan was giddy: Descriptions of Dylan at home that afternoon came from people who watched the video Tom Klebold shot. Thanks to Wendy Murray for sharing her interview notes for some of them.

CHAPTER 7. CHURCH ON FIRE

This is a church on fire: The descriptions of all churches and services were from my observations. I attended worship services at nearly a dozen local churches but focused primarily on three: Trinity Christian Center, West Bowles Community Church, and the Foothills Bible Church. I attended services at each of those three more than a dozen times, all after the murders.

CHAPTER 8. MAXIMUM HUMAN DENSITY

seven big bombs: It's possible there was an eighth. To avoid assisting copycats, Jeffco authorities will not specify certain details about the bombs. We know Eric produced two for the cafeteria, two for each car, and at least one decoy, using two tanks. The reports do not state whether that was a single device or two separate ones, and Kate Battan refused to say.

The main event was scripted: The killers' attack plan was reconstructed from a combination of their written and verbal descriptions, diagrams they made, and physical evidence, such as the placement of their cars (which they said would be used for initial firing positions). All those elements corroborated well.

he had nearly seven hundred rounds: Eric's journal chart for bomb production also included a section on ammo. He made a column for each gun, showing each acquisition and deducting for rounds spent in training. He did not label them, except for R (for Reb) beside one column and V (Vodka) next to another. Statements on the Basement Tapes a week and a half before the attack corroborate several entries and help identify what each column signifies. The chart tallies

143 rounds for Dylan's TEC-9, 129 for Eric's rifle, 295 for Dylan's shotgun, and 122 for Eric's (272 initially, less 150 fired off), for a total of 687. This was before Manes purchased the final hundred 9mm rounds, which could be split between the first two guns.

CHAPTER 9. DADS

It came up unexpectedly: Dave's conversation with Mr. D in the bleachers was re-created based on my interviews with DeAngelis.

team captain, Liz Carlston: The scene with Liz Carlston was based on her memoir.

Linda Lou was asleep: The Monday and Tuesday scenes with Linda vary slightly from the depictions in the book she wrote with Saltzman. In my interview, Linda recalled a few things differently, and added more details.

CHAPTER 10. JUDGMENT

the boys rose early: The killers' activities on Tuesday morning were compiled from several sources: 1) eyewitness testimony of parents and neighbors who saw them coming or going, 2) time-stamped receipts, 3) video surveillance cameras at two stores where Eric bought gas and in the Columbine cafeteria, and 4) the killers' handwritten schedules for the morning and taped descriptions of their plans. Several schedules appeared in their notebooks and on assorted scraps of paper, with minor variations. The external evidence indicated that they stuck close to plan.

They got something to eat: Dylan's autopsy report indicted 160 cc of gastric contents, including "fragments of what appears to be potato skins." Given Dylan's love for fast food, that could have meant French fries. Eric's showed 250 cc, no specific contents.

CHAPTER 11. FEMALE DOWN

At 11:19 they opened: For depictions of the shootings, I relied mostly on police interviews with witnesses, the Jeffco *Sheriff's Office Final Report,* the governor's report, and the El Paso County sheriff's report. Discrepancies were sorted out through interviews with investigators, particularly lead investigator Kate Battan. I treated all Jeffco statements related to its own culpability and police response skeptically. However, the team's documentation of the killers' activities on April 20 was generally thorough and meticulous. Notable exceptions, such as information about Danny Rohrbough's killer, have been corrected. The El Paso County sheriff's department thoroughly reinvestigated Danny's shooting, reinterviewing about 130 witnesses and approaching 65 others who refused. Its 450-page report supersedes the Jeffco report on most of the outside gunfire.

Times came from the *Sheriff's Office Final Report,* and were arrived at through a variety of means, including: witness testimony and time stamps on 911 calls, dispatch calls, and the surveillance video in the cafeteria. Patti Nielson's 911 call was particularly useful. She dropped the phone but left it off the hook, and 10 minutes, 48 seconds were recorded. The audio was then enhanced by the FBI crime lab. Every shot, crash, scream, and loud verbal exchange described by witnesses could be sequenced against a solid physical record.

Sean burst out laughing: Sean's perceptions of what was happening came from his police reports, conducted by both Jeffco and El Paso counties.

CHAPTER 12. THE PERIMETER

The story took twenty-eight minutes: I relied on transcripts from ABC, CBS, NBC, CNN, and NPR for all descriptions and analysis of real-time TV and radio reporting. CNN stayed live for at least four hours. It had access to feeds from four local stations—affiliates of the three networks and one other station—and cut between them, providing a good cross section of local coverage as well.

CHAPTER 13. "1 BLEEDING TO DEATH"

Always the same question: Most of the descriptions and quotes from the Columbine library were based on my observations. I spent about an hour there, in the early afternoon. Misty Bernall's thoughts and statements at the library are an exception; they were drawn from her book.

The Leawood scenes came from my later interviews with kids and parents there and from live TV reports I watched later on video.

The grousing increased when: Assessments of police reaction that afternoon came from several sources who were present and in a position to hear.

a SWAT team made its first approach: Actions of the SWAT team came from the *Sheriff's Office Final Report* and from numerous other documents released by Jeffco. The movements outside were corroborated by news chopper footage. Sources for Dave Sanders's nonrescue are described in the notes for Chapter 26.

Rachel Scott: Some witnesses reported that Rachel cried for several minutes, and the story gained great currency. However, Investigator Kate Battan makes a convincing case that Rachel's gunshot to the temple killed her immediately.

Robyn Anderson watched it all: Most depictions of the killers' friends' reactions came from their police interviews. Additional details came from TV interviews some of them gave.

Nate dialed his house: All the action involving the Klebolds here comes from a combination of their police report, TV interview transcripts from Nate, and news stories documenting Byron's interaction with coworkers. The calls between Nate and Tom were described by each of them, with only minor discrepancies.

kicked Byron out: Dylan's Diversion file contains several references to

Byron's eviction. The "Drug/Alcohol History" section of the summary states Byron "was kicked out of the house for continued drug use."

CHAPTER 14. HOSTAGE STANDOFF

Two to three hundred: This is Kate Battan's estimate.

The cops were livid: Police reactions to news coverage were based on my interviews with senior officers and school officials among them that day. Their statements in news reports served as a secondary source.

CHAPTER 15. FIRST ASSUMPTION

Detectives arrived at the Harris place: Several officers filed detailed reports about their encounters at the Harris and Klebold homes.

Fuselier got the call: Most scenes involving Agent Fuselier were drawn from interviews with him; his wife, Mimi; and their two sons. Much of it was corroborated by police reports, his published work, and research by other journalists. I questioned Agent Fuselier more than fifty times between 2000 and 2008.

CHAPTER 16. THE BOY IN THE WINDOW

Mr. D arrived in the hallway: The account of Mr. D's rescue of the girls' gym class was based on interviews with him and some of the girls in the class.

John and Kathy Ireland knew: Most scenes involving the Ireland family and their earlier life were drawn from my interviews with them. Additional sources are noted in later chapters.

CHAPTER 17. THE SHERIFF

The SWAT teams: I am indebted to the *Rocky Mountain News,* whose wonderful piece "Help Is on the Way" provided the basis for much of my description here. Kate Battan added and corrected details.

Lead investigator Kate Battan: Accounts of Kate Battan's involvement were drawn from my interviews with her, police reports, and the excellent "Inside the Columbine Investigation" series, led by investigative reporter Dan Luzadder and published in the *Rocky Mountain News* in December 1999. I also discussed Luzadder's findings with him, and I am grateful for his generous support.

At 4:00 P.M., Jeffco went public: Quotes and descriptions from this fateful press conference were based on my observations and the audiotape I recorded. I spent most of the late afternoon near the command post in Clement Park. Stone and Davis spoke regularly. Students kept wandering through to provide their evolving perspectives.

"We ran for our lives": Several quotes from Tom and Sue Klebold—including this one and the ensuing statement by their lawyers—were made to David Brooks in 2004. He reported them in his *New York Times* column.

CHAPTER 18. LAST BUS

Brian Rohrbough gave up: Most of my accounts of Brian Rohrbough and Sue Petrone were based on numerous interviews with them. I also used their TV interviews and countless news reports quoting them. My accounts of John and Doreen Tomlin came from Wendy Zoba's book *Day of Reckoning,* which was based on her interviews. The descriptions of the Red Cross volunteer Lynn Duff came from my interview with her. Details involving DA Dave Thomas and the coroner came from police reports and news accounts, particularly Luzadder's "Inside the Columbine Investigation" series.

CHAPTER 19. VACUUMING

Marjorie Lindholm had spent: Marjorie Lindholm's reflections came from her memoir.

CHAPTER 20. VACANT

There is a photograph: The *Rocky Mountain News* did an outstanding job in capturing the pain of this tragedy visually, and won the Pulitzer for those photos. Fourteen of the most iconic can be viewed at the Pulitzer Web site.

the survivors had changed: Virtually all accounts of students' reactions that week came from my observations and conversations with survivors. I spent most of that week in Clement Park, area churches, and student hangouts. I interviewed perhaps two hundred students during that time, and observed hundreds more. The depiction was also informed by media accounts I absorbed at the time and revisited later.

Light of the World seats eight hundred and fifty: This scene was drawn from my observations and audiotape. The event was not announced to press, and the major news outlets were asked not to go inside. I was told about it by students in Clement Park. As a freelancer, I got no notice not to avoid it, and no signs were posted. I saw TV crews outside and assumed that cameras were forbidden but reporters were allowed. Consequently, to my knowledge, this scene has not been depicted in print, except in my profile of Frank DeAngelis a few months later in *5280,* Denver's city magazine.

It's shocking: Quotes from the *Rocky Mountain News.*

the crime of the century in Colorado: For depictions of the police investigation I relied heavily on thousands of pages of police files and my interviews with Agent Fuselier and senior Jeffco officials, including Kate Battan and John Kiekbusch. Luzadder's "Inside the Columbine Investigation" series was extremely helpful for corroboration. Dan spent months working on the series and was generous and candid in discussing his observations and perceptions with me.

30,000 pages of evidence: This figure includes approximately 4,000 redacted pages.

CHAPTER 21. FIRST MEMORIES

It didn't start: Information on Eric and Dylan's childhoods and activities during their final years came from a wealth of sources, including hundreds of pages of their writings, appointments in their day planners, their videos, extensive police interviews with their friends, television interviews with those friends, my interviews with investigators who examined all the evidence, news accounts by trusted journalists (particularly Lynn Bartels), and my interviews with some of their friends, including Joe Stair, Brooks Brown, and several kids who had known them earlier. Some of their closest friends chose not to cooperate with me but gave detailed statements to police detectives. Tom and Sue Klebold provided a wealth of details about Dylan's childhood in their police interview. Bartels and Crowder's *Rocky Mountain News* profile "Fatal Friendship" was particularly helpful; I relied heavily on it. Other key profiles were Simpson, Callahan, and Lowe's "Life and Death of a Follower," Briggs and Blevin's "A Boy with Many Sides," and Johnson and Wilgoren's "The Gunman: A Portrait of Two Killers at War with Themselves."

"I just remember": The quotes from childhood friends and neighbors of Eric's in Plattsburgh and Oscoda were drawn from the Jeffco *Sheriff's Office Final Report* and the profiles cited above. The accounts were remarkably similar and fairly unrevealing: Eric seemed like an average kid prior to high school. This corresponded to both Eric's depictions of his younger self and friends' accounts to police.

Major Harris did not tolerate: My characterizations of Wayne Harris's parenting style came from several sources: his own twenty-five pages of notes in a steno pad he labeled "Eric"; Eric's frequent complaints about his dad's punishment in his writings; eight- and ten-page questionnaires about the family filled out by Eric and his parents for entrance to Diversion; Eric's statements to his Diversion counselor, which were recorded in his file; and statements by Eric's friends, primarily in their police reports but also in interviews with me and in some TV interviews.

"Fire!" Eric screamed: Most of the scenes in this chapter came from Eric's school assignments, recalling his youth. I chose material he returned to repeatedly.

CHAPTER 22. RUSH TO CLOSURE

Ministers, psychiatrists, and grief counselors cringed: The *Denver Post* headline was merely the most appalling example of early proclamations of healing. They were everywhere. I interviewed a great number of ministers, psychiatrists, and grief counselors during those first weeks, as well as over the following nine years. From the beginning, virtually all thought the premature assessments were a terrible mistake.

a throbbing teen prayer mosh: I was present for the mosh, which went on for several minutes. The *Rocky Mountain News* featured a giant photograph of the incident. Whenever possible in this book, I checked my observations against photographs, television footage, and news accounts by other journalists.

"I smell the presence of Satan": I attended the worship services where Reverends Oudemolen and Kirsten are quoted. I obtained additional information by interviewing them, attending services periodically for months, listening to cassettes of other sermons by Reverend Oudemolen, and enrolling in Bible study at West Bowles Community Church, with the consent of Reverend Kirsten, who led the class.

Most of the mainliners: I interviewed a few dozen local ministers, as well as countless attendees of local Sunday services during the first few weeks of the aftermath. A powerful consensus developed against active recruitment in most congregations and among most ministers. The scene described by Barb Lotze came from my interview with her and was confirmed by many students attending.

The kids kept pouring into the churches: Huge numbers of students described meeting up at the churches that week.

They turned the corner: DeAngelis and Fuselier independently described this scene in separate interviews with me.

They traced Dylan's TEC-9: Information on the TEC-9 ownership came from the search warrant for Manes's bank records. The relevant descriptions are on JC-001-025739.

Detectives interviewed Robyn: Robyn's interrogation was documented in great detail in her police report. It devoted twenty single-spaced pages to the back-and-forth of the questioning. The passages in italics are paraphrases of her statements. This same report laid out her activities the previous day and her admissions about what she knew and when she suspected Eric and Dylan's involvement. Eventually, she confessed to strong suspicions early in the shooting, so there was little reason to doubt her.

CHAPTER 23. GIFTED BOY

By third grade: Many sources cite Dylan as starting in second grade, but he did not transfer to Governor's Ranch Elementary School until third. Tom and Sue Klebold provided many of the details of Dylan's early life in their report.

Judy first saw him: The creek bed scene was described by Judy Brown during my interview with her and her husband. Dylan's quote was from her recollection. The incident matched many relayed by reliable people who knew Dylan as a boy and through high school. I chose this one because it encapsulated much of Dylan's early experience and fragile psyche.

They celebrated Easter and Passover: Tom and Sue described their religious and family background in their police report. Reverend Marxhausen filled in details during interviews with me. Dylan's writings and videos provided more.

Tom described Dylan: Tom's quote came from his police report. He also described Dylan as being sheltered in the CHIPS program.

CHAPTER 24. HOUR OF NEED

He organized a vigil: Depictions of the vigil and the funeral came from my interviews with Reverend Marxhausen. Additional information came from his statements in news reports.

CHAPTER 26. HELP IS ON THE WAY

when the first shot hit him: Dave Sanders's four-hour ordeal was painstakingly documented before I covered that aspect of the story, so I corroborated existing accounts with sources from both sides of the eventual lawsuit, as well as the 911 tapes released by Jeffco. On most points, they concurred. The police issued voluminous reports documenting the department's take, and for the Sanderses' side I relied most heavily on Angela Sanders's legal team, which researched the case for months and eventually prevailed. This included interviews with lead attorney Peter Grenier, his excellent thirteen-page summary of the case after it was over, and the forty-two-page complaint filed in April 2000. The report by the governor's review commission and the accounts in the *Rocky* and the *Denver Post* were extremely helpful in providing additional details, especially the *Rocky*'s "Help is on the way: mundane gave way to madness..." In interviews, Linda Sanders and several friends of Dave's provided their perspective on what happened.

hurl a chair: This incident comes from the Sanderses' lawsuit and the case summary by their attorney Peter Grenier. It is consistent with other accounts.

CHAPTER 27. BLACK

He started shopping: The killers' friends gave fairly consistent accounts of their style of dress, in police interviews and media interviews. These are corroborated by videos the killers shot of themselves and by details scattered throughout their writings—for example, Eric mentioned that he had taken to shopping at Hot Topic and the surplus store.

For Halloween: Police believe Dutro got the first duster, but reports conflict, because no one was really tracking it at the time. Other accounts have Thaddeus Boles kicking off the trend. Boles was an acquaintance of the killers.

CHAPTER 28. MEDIA CRIME

We remember Columbine: To gauge national print coverage, I analyzed every news story published in the first two weeks, as well as hundreds of later stories from the following papers: the *Denver Post, Rocky Mountain News, New York Times, Washington Post,* and *USA Today.* I also studied a large number from AP,

Reuters, and other sources. The two local papers each created a special Columbine archive online, recording all their stories, which allowed me to gauge the frequency of their coverage for the next several years and ensure that I did not miss anything.

The killers were quickly cast: The scenes in Clement Park in this chapter and all related quotes came from my observations and audiotapes. Much of it was published in my stories that week for *Salon*. The stories concerning "the rumor that won't go away" were by me.

***Salon* published:** "Misfits Who Don't Kill" was produced by *YO! (Youth Outlook)*.

There's no evidence: Mr. D's quotes are from my interview with him July 4, 1999, and were published in the August/September issue of *5280*, Denver's city magazine. The pierced-out girl was Jo-Lee Gallegos, a senior I interviewed in June and quoted at greater length in the same story. I talked to hundreds of students in the months after the tragedy, and Gallegos was one of the few I could find with a negative impression of Mr. D, though the killers' friends were lying low. Gallegos joined the majority in praising DeAngelis's behavior after April 20. "He really made it a point to reach out to everyone after that," she said.

CHAPTER 29. THE MISSIONS

The mischief started as a threesome: Most of the details and the quotes about the missions came from Eric's postings on his Web sites. They were corroborated by a large number of people who got involved at the time, including Randy, Judy, and Brooks Brown, who called the police several times, after which officers filed reports; a Columbine dean who got involved and talked to parents, including Wayne Harris; and Wayne Harris, who documented conversations with the dean, the Browns, and another family in his journal.

Eric got mad at Brooks Brown: For the showdowns between Eric and the Browns, I relied on several sources: Wayne's journal; Brooks's memoir; my interviews over a period of years with Randy, Judy, and Brooks; Eric's numerous statements about it; and Agent Fuselier's assessment of what took place, based on all the evidence presented to him by the detective team. The Browns and Harrises saw the underlying conflict very differently, but they were pretty consistent on the details of the incidents relayed here.

Wayne came home: Wayne documented his responses and many of his opinions about the feud in his steno notebook, which was seized by Jeffco and released years later. Eric's version of Wayne's behavior also provided a fairly close corroboration.

Dylan was miserable: Dylan didn't even mention the missions until much later, in passing—as an adventure he shared with Zack, rather than Eric.

CHAPTER 30. TELLING US WHY

Guerra would finally confess: Guerra made that statement to the attorney general's investigators.

Chris agreed to a wiretap: The FBI transcribed the full conversation. It ran twenty-two pages.

On Sunday an ATF agent: Details of the ATF interviews with both Duran and Manes, and the full history of purchases, came from the warrant to search Manes's bank records.

CHAPTER 31. THE SEEKER

Dylan's mind raced: Virtually everything from this chapter comes from Dylan's journal, where he expressed his thoughts vividly. He repeated a handful of ideas relentlessly, and I focused primarily on those. I wove much of Dylan's vocabulary and expressions into the paraphrased sections—for example, "that asshole in gym class," and "eternal suffering in infinite directions through infinite realities" are his words, woven into my sentences.

CHAPTER 32. JESUS JESUS JESUS

Afterward, the crowds trekked: The account of the memorial service was based on my observations there, as well as on my review of live television coverage I recorded.

Pastor Kirsten proclaimed: Quotes and descriptions from Kirsten came from my observations of his sermons, his recounting of passages at Bible study, and his interviews with me. Quotes from Oudemolen came from services I attended and audiotapes of his sermons.

Much of the Denver clergy was appalled: I interviewed a large number of local clergy about the dispute that week. Reverend Marxhausen's remarks were made to the *Denver Post*. I discussed them with him later.

One thoughtful Evangelical pastor: He was Reverend Deral Schrom of South Suburban Christian Church. He spoke with refreshing candor, and shared his wisdom about this tough dilemma for his peers. I thank him on both accounts.

Craig Scott was: The preponderance of evidence pointed heavily to the martyr story having originated with Scott.

He had hidden: All depictions of shooting inside the library were based on an examination of all witnesses' accounts, consultation with investigators who had access to the enhanced 911 tape, and a wealth of physical evidence. Kate Battan was especially helpful. There was pervasive agreement on most significant details, aside from the ones discussed in the narrative.

her mother was unsure: Brad and Misty discussed the evolution of their responses in various TV interviews, as well as in Misty's memoir. Journalist Wendy Murray also graciously gave me access to her interview notes with the family.

CHAPTER 33. GOOD-BYE

He got excited: He noted his license day in his day planner. That and his other writings provided additional insights into his mental state.

CHAPTER 34. PICTURE-PERFECT MARSUPIALS

Patrick Ireland was trying: Patrick's story is based primarily on my numerous interviews with him and his parents. It was supplemented and corroborated by video footage, televised interviews, news accounts and photographs, my observation of him giving speeches and attending events, and photo albums of his youth, graciously provided by his mother.

Something was missing: The account of the crosses came from my observations in Clement Park, interviews with most of the principals, live news coverage, news photographs, print news accounts of these events and the carpenter's earlier work, and a few hours of video provided by the carpenter to journalist Wendy Murray, who generously loaned it to me. The latter included video a friend shot of him returning with the new crosses, ongoing commentary from him, shots of his home life, and numerous TV appearances. His name was intentionally omitted.

DAD DESTROYS CROSSES: The *Rocky* uses a tabloid format, and ran just headlines and the photo on page 1 that day. It printed the story on page 5, under a different headline: DAD CUTS DOWN KILLERS' CROSSES. It can be found online under the longer title.

CHAPTER 35. ARREST

The Harris and Klebold parents responded: Information on the locker break-in came primarily from police files, which included interviews with the dean, and Wayne Harris's journal notes. Further reflections came in the Diversion program questionnaires filled out by the killers and parents.

Sometimes she would laugh: The depictions come from Dylan's journal.

Brenda was almost twenty-three: Brenda Parker's account and quotes came from her police interview and her interviews with Denver papers.

a crime of opportunity: My account of the break-in and its aftermath relied heavily on the forty pages of police reports, which included written confessions from each boy, and accounts from several officers, one of whom quoted exchanges with the boys. Other sources include the boys' writings; their statements in court; Wayne Harris's journal; the Diversion program questionnaires; and session notes by their Diversion counselors. I discussed the events at length with investigators.

CHAPTER 36. CONSPIRACY

Detectives returned to question her: Detectives filed a detailed description of the interrogation, including much more information from the notes passed in

German class. Agent Fuselier provided additional insights on the full text of the German-class notes.

Eric had never known: Staff Sergeant Mark Gonzales called investigators at ten the morning after the murders to apprise them of his contact with Eric, citing all the dates when they'd met. On April 28, police interviewed him and documented his statements in a police report one day before the news story broke. A full account appears in Chapter 50, based on this testimony and on my discussions with investigators. Gonzales was firm about his contention that Eric never learned of his rejection.

officials met with the Klebolds: Virtually all of this scene comes from Investigator Kate Battan's nine-page police report.

National Rifle Association convened: The scene is based primarily on news reports, as well as my later reporting on the gun control debate. I'm especially grateful to Jake Tapper of *Salon,* and his excellent piece, "Coming Out Shooting."

"We deal with facts": Kiekbusch's quotes came from a 1999 phone interview with me, which appeared in *Salon*. He made similar statements to other media.

What Kiekbusch meant: I discussed the team's approach with several investigators, including Kiekbusch, and with officers and experts outside the case.

He was driving his team nuts: I spoke to many investigators and officials in close contact with them.

Columbine coverage ended abruptly: Sixty-six tornadoes struck between May 3 and 6, including a Category 5 twister that killed thirty-six people, damaged more than 10,000 buildings, and wreaked $1.1 billion in damage. I was at an event with many of the national reporters when they got the word and quickly fled. Several of the largest papers maintain a Denver bureau, consisting of one or two national reporters. These individuals returned to Denver after the storms, while many others did not. Regardless, the lull in coverage abruptly ended Columbine as a daily national story.

CHAPTER 37. BETRAYED

Their rates varied: Wayne took detailed notes on possible lawyers and shrinks.

Eric told Dr. Albert: Dr. Albert refused to talk to any other journalist about Eric. He told me that too many people could be hurt. However, Eric had discussed the sessions with his parents and his Diversion counselors, who recorded Eric's thoughts at the time (i.e., long before the murders). Their notes provided the basis for all of my information about Dr. Albert's sessions.

Dylan leaked the URL: Brooks described Dylan's leak to reporters soon after the murders. Police records confirmed that the Browns called Jeffco detectives the night of the leak and produced several pages from Eric's Web site. I drew on interviews with Brooks and his parents, his memoir, the police report, the Web pages, and discussions with investigators.

Only one parent: The meetings with the boys and their parents were well documented by Andrea Sanchez in their Diversion files. The full questionnaires were released.

Sanchez worried: She documented her concerns in their files at the time.

But he was impressed: DeVita recalled their appearances and expressed his thoughts a year later, in media interviews following the murders. The court released documents related to the case.

The affidavit was convincing: It was released April 10, 2001. I discussed its merits with officials and experts both inside and outside the case.

A plausible explanation: The official was Undersheriff John Dunaway, who told the *Denver Post* in 2004: "After several weeks that he [Guerra] was called away, he had nothing that he could credibly argue to the courts that was timely. Part of securing a search warrant is that your information is timely and accurate." Dunaway was not in office when the affidavit was written.

CHAPTER 38. MARTYR

"She's in the martyrs' hall of fame": I did not attend Cassie's funeral. Later, I interviewed Reverend Kirsten, who provided the passages. I also discussed it with many congregants who were present.

It had been possession: My accounts of Cassie's possession and "rebirth" came primarily from a series of interviews I did with her youth pastor, Dave McPherson, who closely advised her parents and worked with her the following years, and from Misty's memoir. Additional sources included Reverend Kirsten, television interviews of Brad and Misty, and my contact with the Bernalls at a handful of functions at their church following the murders. Direct quotes from Cassie and the letters her friend wrote came from Misty's memoir.

Val dropped to her knees: Val's account came from her police report and my interviews with her and her mother, Shari, in September 1999.

Emily Wyant watched: Emily's account of April 20 came primarily from her police interview on April 29. My description of her struggles in the ensuing months were based on my two interviews with her mother in September 1999 and my conversations with Dan Luzadder, the *Rocky*'s lead investigator. I respected her mother's request that I not contact Emily directly.

Bree Pasquale was sitting there: Bree exhibited a stunning recall of events in the library, conveying the tiniest details of Eric's movements in her police interview. Her testimony was corroborated by nearly all witnesses, the physical evidence, and the 911 tape. Because her exchange with Eric was so memorable, it was reported in similar form by a great number of witnesses. Therefore, I have used quotations, relying on Bree's version of the precise wording.

something unexpected happened: Craig's experience in the library was recorded in detail in his police report, beginning on JC-001-000587. I abbreviated his exchange with detectives.

CHAPTER 39. THE BOOK OF GOD

Fuselier found answers: Fuselier's deductions came from my numerous interviews with him.

CHAPTER 40. PSYCHOPATH

the Psychopathy Checklist: All characterizations of psychopathy in this book were based on the latest research, founded primarily on the work of Dr. Hervey Cleckley and systematically refined by Dr. Robert Hare. Hare's revised Psychopathy Checklist (PCL-R) is used to assess the subject on twenty characteristics, organized into two categories: emotional drivers and antisocial behavior. The twenty are: 1) glib and superficial charm, 2) grandiose estimation of self, 3) need for stimulation, 4) pathological lying, 5) cunning and manipulativeness, 6) lack of remorse or guilt, 7) shallow affect (superficial emotional responsiveness), 8) callousness and lack of empathy, 9) parasitic lifestyle, 10) poor behavioral controls, 11) sexual promiscuity, 12) early behavior problems, 13) lack of realistic long-term goals, 14) impulsivity, 15) irresponsibility, 16) failure to accept responsibility for own actions, 17) many short-term marital relationships, 18) juvenile delinquency, 19) revocation of conditional release, 20) criminal versatility.

The item titles cannot be scored without reference to the formal criteria contained in the PCL-R Manual. It is issued only to qualified practitioners, who are instructed to combine interviews with case histories and archival data. But in many cases, such as Columbine, the subject is not available for an interview. Studies by outside researchers have concluded that the tool is reliable without the interview in situations where extensive, reliable data is available. Eric left a massive trove, which experts considered far more than enough data to assess him.

Evaluators rate the subject on each trait, assigning a score from 0 to 2: 2 if it clearly applies, 1 if it applies partially or sometimes, 0 if never. The maximum score is 40, and a 30 is required for the designation of "psychopath." There are degrees of psychopathy, but most subjects turn out to be either highly psychopathic or not at all. Average criminals score about 20; they share some behavior with psychopaths but few of the underlying drives.

In 1885: *The Oxford English Dictionary* (1989 edition) cites 1885 as the first time the term *psychopathy* was used in its present meaning. German researchers used it earlier in the century, with a somewhat different purpose.

Varying definitions: Nothing comparable to the PCL-R exists for *sociopath*, though some therapists use the checklist and then assign the subject the designation of "sociopath."

psychopaths and unstable homes: "We do not know why people become psychopaths, but current evidence leads us away from the commonly held idea that the behavior of parents bears sole or even primary responsibility," Hare wrote. But if a child is born with dangerous traits, bad parenting can make him or her infinitely worse.

The family backgrounds of psychopaths turn out to be surprisingly consistent with those of the overall prison population. In both cases, the incidence of significant family problems is high. With nonpsychopathic criminals, a troubled youth correlates closely with the age and seriousness of the first offense. Those with family trouble appear in court by age fifteen, on average. Those without show up nearly a decade later, at twenty-four. Psychopaths arrive earliest of all—at fourteen, on average—and their family background shows no effect on that number whatsoever. But the home life has a huge impact on the type of crime committed by psychopaths. Those from unstable upbringings are far more likely to be violent. In the rest of the prison population, a troubled home seems to drive criminals toward earlier and more serious offenses, but not violence.

screening device for juveniles: It is called the PCL:YV, for "Youth Version."

stated desire for a career in the Marines: In March 1998, Eric answered the "Career Goals" question on his Diversion questionnaire with "Marine or computer science."

Dr. Kiehl repeated: Summaries of Dr. Kiehl's work were based on his published work, as well as phone and e-mail correspondence with me and my researcher.

therapy often makes it worse: This is a widely recognized conclusion. Many studies have confirmed it. One found that convicted psychopaths who took part in therapeutic programs were four times more likely to commit violent crimes than those who did not.

CHAPTER 41. THE PARENTS GROUP

the FBI organized a major summit: Scenes from the Leesburg summit were described to me by several participants. Quotes were based on their recollections.

Several of the experts continued: Several continued studying Columbine. Drs. Fuselier, Ochberg, and Hare agreed to several interviews for this book and were of great assistance. Others requested anonymity but continued conferring behind the scenes and provided valuable insights not attributed to any individual.

The Bureau firmly prohibited: All agents were forbidden from speaking about the case, including those at headquarters, such as Mary Ellen O'Toole, who organized the Leesburg summit. All journalists, including me, were rebuffed repeatedly; *60 Minutes* sued for information and lost. An exception was made for Agent Fuselier to participate with Jeffco officers in the *Rocky*'s "Inside the

Columbine Investigation" series—discussing his role in the investigation, but not his conclusions.

Jeffco commanders were lying: After several years of withholding, Jeffco released documents that proved commanders had been lying on several counts—including repeated denials about possessing the documents.

Investigator Mike Guerra noticed: The actions of Guerra, Kiekbusch, and Searle came from the grand jury report. Guerra described his actions. Searle described actions by her and by Kiekbusch.

Anne Marie Hochhalter: Her progress was drawn from news accounts, particularly Bartels' "A Story of Healing and Hope."

Students reached the opposite consensus: The depiction of diverging attitudes among students and parents that spring and summer were based primarily on my numerous interviews and trips to the area at the time and interviews I conducted years later. I also pored over news coverage from the period.

Brian Fuselier was heading: The description of Brian's reactions that summer initially came from my interviews with both his parents; I confirmed them with him several years later.

It was an emotional day: I spent much of the day outside the school, interviewing students coming and going, and observing.

"This is not about money!": The description of the Shoelses' press conference was based on my observations.

CHAPTER 42. DIVERSION

their junior yearbooks: Scans of the yearbook pages were released by Jeffco.

Eric launched a new charm offensive: Diversion counselors documented each meeting—roughly two a month—which provided a more detailed record of the boys' activity for the last year. Both boys had also acquired day planners by this time, though Dylan used his more.

His grades dropped briefly: The school released grade reports indicating progress within each semester. For Diversion, the boys were also required to have teachers fill out monthly progress reports, with grade projections and comments.

write apology letters: Jeffco released Eric's letter.

Then he quit: Months later, Eric would resume using the planner, documenting much of his daily existence. Dylan filled in his planner as well. Jeffco released scans of the full contents of both.

Dr. Albert switched him: Eric's medications and his responses to them were recorded in his Diversion file. He had completed the switch from Zoloft to Luvox by May 14, 1998.

They got to make movies: Jeffco released many of their videos other than the Basement Tapes. The depictions here were based on my viewing.

Eric was gobbling up literature: Eric kept many of his school assignments, including papers on all the items cited in this chapter. I reviewed them all.

CHAPTER 43. WHO OWNS THE TRAGEDY

There is a house, outside of Laramie: Linda described their retirement plans, including the house, in an interview with me.

Columbine was set to reopen: I attended the Media Summit and the Take Back the School rally. Only pool reporters were permitted inside the human shield at the rally, so I relied on their briefings for that passage, as well as my later interviews with numerous people inside. I discussed objectives for the rally and the ideas behind it with several administrators responsible for designing it.

For one morning: I spent the morning in the Columbine commons, chatting with the kids as they painted their tiles.

CHAPTER 44. BOMBS ARE HARD

just before Halloween: From this point, Eric recorded the dates for all major milestones, as well as a slew of trivial ones. He also kept dated receipts for many of his purchases.

began assembling his arsenal. Eric let Nate watch him produce part of one batch. Nate described the process to police; their records served as the basis for my visual depiction.

CHAPTER 45. AFTERSHOCKS

Milestones were hard: I covered most of the events in this chapter for *Salon* and the bulk of the material was based on that reporting. (An exception was the football championship—I followed the team's progress but did not attend the games.) Years later, I gathered hundreds of pages of news stories on the events and mined them for additional quotes, including those from the Graves and Hochhalter families. All news quotes are cited in the expanded Web version of this Notes section.

another publication broke the news: It was my story in *Salon*.

The magazine ran an exposé: *Time* sent a team back to reinvestigate the tragedy and reexamined the entire case for that cover story. It did a great job, effectively correcting the major myths. But it did not cop to the correction. This was a grievous example of "rowback"—the term was resurrected in 2004 by *New York Times* public editor Daniel Okrent to critique Iraq War coverage; it's rarely heard even within the industry, because it denotes such an ugly sin. Okrent cites journalism educator Melvin Mencher describing it as "a story that attempts to correct a previous story without indicating that the prior story had been in error or without taking responsibility for the error." Okrent wrote that a more candid definition might be "a way that a newspaper can cover its butt without admitting it was ever exposed."

CHAPTER 46. GUNS

Eric named his shotgun: Arlene was the heroine from the *Doom* books Eric enjoyed. He scratched the word into her barrel and referred to her by name in writings and on video.

Eric fit both categories: Millon, Simonsen, Davis, and Birket-Smith created the ten subcategories to sort out very different types of psychopaths, but they are not designed to be mutually exclusive; nor are they necessarily the drivers of behavior. Eric exhibited symptoms consistent with malevolent and tyrannical personalities, and Dr. Fuselier concurred that Eric appeared to be a cross between those two.

"I want to tear a throat out": I edited this passage down. It went on much longer, and more viciously.

On January 20: The Diversion program files cite February 3 as the termination date, but that's not an accurate reflection, particularly from the boys' perspective. In both files, Kriegshauser documented meeting with them on January 20 to close their cases.

Eric was also working hard: Eric wrote about his efforts to "get laid" frequently during the final months.

CHAPTER 47. LAWSUITS

Mr. D told a magazine: He said it to me. I covered the events of this chapter extensively for *Salon,* and most of it was based on that reporting.

the Rohrboughs: For simplicity, I used "the Rohrboughs" periodically to denote both sides of Danny's family, the Rohrboughs and Petrones.

gun-control legislation: In April 2000, a few bills were pending to allow concealed weapons in Colorado. Those were quickly defeated in the wake of the tragedy.

CHAPTER 48. AN EMOTION OF GOD

a big problem: Eric cited getting the bombs in as a major issue.

If only he had a little more cash: Eric expressed frustration about his limited funds and drew up budgets for his arsenal.

Dylan wrote a short story: Jeffco released the story, with Judy Kelly's notes.

Three friends went with them: The boys videotaped quite a bit of the target practice, and Jeffco released the tape.

They made three target-practice trips: Manes told lead investigator Kate Battan they made three trips, but she could not determine whether they were before or after the videotaped trip.

Dylan leaked again: Zack told police his conversation with Dylan occurred in February. His memory might have been off slightly, or Dylan might have begun training earlier—with or without Manes.

Desperado: Robert Rodriguez directed the film. Tarantino appeared as an actor and is closely associated with Rodriguez.

CHAPTER 49. READY TO BE DONE

Most of the Parents Group attended: The scenes at the opening of the atrium came from my observations.

Jeffco was forced to cough up: I followed the slow release of the information over several years and examined most items as they came out, but I did not write about these events at the time. *Westword* and the *Rocky* did an excellent job covering the slow trickle, and I relied on their work. I considered the reports from the Colorado attorney general and the grand jury definitive.

the affidavit to search Eric's house: After months of silence, the DA responded to a written request from the Browns. His response letter alluded to Guerra's affidavit, which for two years his agency had insisted did not exist. Randy and Judy couldn't believe it. They took it to CBS, and *60 Minutes* cornered Thomas. Judge Jackson demanded to see it—it had been withheld from him as well.

The affidavit was more damning: Guerra was exceptionally convincing. He demonstrated motive, means, and opportunity. From a threat-assessment perspective, the specificity of Eric's attack raised it to high risk. The details regarding the weaponry increased it further. The capstone, though, came in connecting Eric's plans to physical evidence. The affidavit described the pipe bomb found near Eric's home and stated twice that it matched his descriptions of "Atlanta" and "Pholus."

"Based on the aforementioned information your affiant respectfully requests the court issue a search warrant for the residence," Guerra's affidavit concluded. The police would have found a great deal. Eric had made quite a few bombs by that time. The former chief justice of the Colorado Supreme Court, who had chaired a commission set up by the governor to investigate Columbine, eventually weighed in. He chided Jeffco for missing a "massive" number of clues. The massacre could have been prevented, he concluded. He lamented the perimeter response; if the SWAT team had stormed the building, he said, several lives could have been saved.

The affidavit also revealed that Division Chief Kiekbusch had told at least three whopping lies at the press conference ten days after Columbine: that the Browns had not met with Investigator Hicks, that the department couldn't find bombs like those in Eric's Web descriptions, and that it had been unable to locate his Web postings. The affidavit contradicted all three, and Kiekbusch had to have been familiar with it, since he had just attended the Open Space meeting with one topic: how to suppress it.

Jeffco responded with new lies. It issued a press release claiming it had disclosed the affidavit's existence a few days after Columbine—at the very time commanders were meeting to plot how to hide it. All the local media called Jeffco on the lie.

"It's amazing how long": Sue Klebold recalled this exchange to David Brooks in 2004. He reported it in his *New York Times* column.

The FBI and Secret Service: The FBI released its report, *The School Shooter: A Threat Assessment Perspective,* in 2000. Two years later, the Secret Service and the Department of Education teamed up for a broader analysis: *The Final Report and Findings of the Safe School Initiative.* Both reports were excellent, and I relied on them extensively. I also used news accounts to document foiled copycats in other cities. I interviewed school administrators, students, and mental health experts about zero tolerance policies.

two biggest myths: The Secret Service studied every targeted attack at schools from December 1974 to May 2000. There had been forty-one attackers in thirty-seven incidents. Disciplinary history and academic performance also varied widely. The loner myth was perhaps the single biggest misconception. Some of the attackers were loners; two-thirds were not.

they "snapped": "Nonviolent people do not 'snap' or decide on the spur of the moment to meet a problem by using violence," the FBI report said. Planning ranged from a day or two in advance to over a year.

in video games: Only an eighth were fond of violent video games. A larger group—about a third—exhibited violence in their own written assignments or journals.

Most perps shared: In many cases, bullying may have played a role: 71 percent of attackers had experienced persecution, bullying, threats, or injury. Initially that sounds dramatic, but the study did not address how many nonattackers suffer that sort of experience; it's pretty commonplace for a high school kid. Several of the shooters experienced severe or long-term bullying, though, and in some cases, it seemed to be a factor in the decision to attack.

suffered a loss or failure: Loss came in different forms: 66 percent had suffered a drop in status; 51 percent had experienced an external loss, which included the death of a loved one but was more commonly being dumped by a girlfriend. The key was that the attacker perceived it as significant and felt his status drop.

More than half told: There were at least two outsiders in the know 59 percent of the time. Someone had suspected the attack 93 percent of the time.

The danger skyrockets: The FBI offered this example of a high-risk threat: "At eight o'clock tomorrow morning, I intend to shoot the principal. That's when he is in the office by himself. I have a 9mm. Believe me, I know what I am doing. I am sick and tired of the way he runs this school."

Melodramatic outbursts: Melodrama and wild flourishes of punctuation are common—for example: "I hate you!!!!…You have ruined my life!!!!" Most lay-men assume that such drama signals greater danger. That's a common fallacy, the report said. Perpetrators are just as likely to remain calm. No correlation has been established between emotional intensity and the actual danger it foretells.

A subtler form of leakage: The FBI said a kid had reached the point of leakage when the same ugly ideas grabbed hold of him "no matter what the subject matter, the conversation, the assignment, or the joke."

list of warning signs: The FBI listed criteria in four different areas: behavior, family situation, school dynamics, and social pressures. The behavioral list alone included twenty-eight characteristics. It cautioned that lots of innocent kids exhibited one or two or even several of its warning signs; the key was evidence of a majority of the items from all four areas. The risk factors were also highly correlated with substance abuse.

A national task force: It included officers involved in Columbine, and leaders in the field, from the Los Angeles Police Department's SWAT team to the National Tactical Officers Association.

CHAPTER 50. THE BASEMENT TAPES

The first installment: Jeffco showed the Basement Tapes to *Time,* then the *Rocky,* and then to a small group of reporters at a single screening. I was not included and have not seen them. My depictions came from three sources: a detailed account in the police files, news stories from the reporters who viewed them, and descriptions by Agent Fuselier and Kate Battan, who each studied them for six months. The police report ran ten pages and documented each scene in detail, with extensive quotations.

After the initial press showing, Jeffco promised more but never held another. The Klebolds then filed a motion asserting that the tapes belonged to the killers' estates. Other suits followed. Most victims' families eventually fought for release of the tapes. Jeffco worked with the killers' families to suppress them, a legal alliance that infuriated the victims. In December 2002, U.S. District Judge Richard Matsch threw out the copyright claim with an angry rebuke. He called it "a transparent attempt to hide something of public interest." But Stone's department insisted that the killers' words were too dangerous to expose to the public.

A *Denver Post* motion worked its way up to the Colorado Supreme Court. The court ruled against Jeffco. It unanimously declared the material to be public records. Colorado law includes a loophole, though, stating that records may be withheld in cases of "public interest." It was then up to the new sheriff to rule whether the tapes and writings were a risk to the community. He decided that the killers' journals were safe but the Basement Tapes were not. The *Post* chose not to appeal. Any future sheriff has the power to release the tapes at any time.

The Colorado attorney general's Web site states the following: "The 'public interest' exception is a specific exception in the Open Records Act. According to this law, an agency may hold public records confidential if the records custodian decides that making them available to the public would cause substantial injury to the public interest. This is the case even if the record is something that would otherwise be available to the public under the Open Records Act. The reason this law exists is that the Legislature realizes that there will be situations in which information should be kept private, even though no law specifically states that it is private."

Eric made at least three attempts: Chris later reported the three attempts to police detectives.

Zack told the story: But both versions of Zack's account, as recorded in his FBI file, are confusing, so I presented the gist of what he conveyed.

Staff Sergeant Gonzales cold-called: Gonzales had gotten a list of seniors from the high school.

Eric hounded Mark Manes: Manes testified about the ammunition at his sentencing hearing.

Eric spent the night at Dylan's: Dylan's parents described the sleepover in their police interview.

Eric left his microcassette: In its response to the Supreme Court decision, Jeffco ignored the existence of the "Nixon" microcassette. Aside from Eric's odd label and the two sentences recorded in an obscure evidence log, nothing is known about the tape. Even Dr. Fuselier has never heard it. It remains in limbo. The Jeffco sheriff has the power to release it at any time.

CHAPTER 51. TWO HURDLES

to share his analysis: I interviewed Dr. Ochberg several times and eventually gained FBI approval to speak to Agent Fuselier. We began a series of interviews, and he directed me to the classic books on psychopathy and to other experts brought in by the FBI. After several years of research—while also working on other projects—I published the results in the piece cited in the text. It was called "The Depressive and the Psychopath," and ran in *Slate*.

the first and only media interview: David Brooks wrote an insightful and empathetic summary of his interviews with Tom and Sue Klebold. He was generous enough to share additional thoughts with me by phone.

Kiekbusch filed a formal objection: The *Rocky* also phoned former sheriff John Stone for a comment. He called the investigation a "bunch of bullshit." He told the reporter he was a "horse's ass" and hung up. The paper printed all that.

Undersheriff Dunaway told the *Denver Post* he had done nothing wrong and again pointed the finger at Brooks Brown. He repeated, on the record, the old accusation that Brooks had known about the murders in advance. No scrap of evidence has ever come to light supporting that charge.

Mr. D strode out dressed as Barry Manilow: I attended the assembly. I watched from the bleachers and took photos.

He lost big: Thomas lost to incumbent Representative Bob Beauprez (R) 55–42 percent, with all precincts reporting.

the Platte Canyon shooting: My depictions of this event came primarily from live television coverage, which I watched and recorded on two stations as it happened, as well as follow-up reports from authorities.

CHAPTER 52. QUIET

any crap this might instigate: Dylan's quote was slightly longer, with an inaudible word.

that fly CD: It's unclear whether he was using "fly" as an adjective (slang for "cool") or a title. In 2008, iTunes listed eighty-eight songs with fly in the title.

The boys wandered: They were observed by numerous witnesses, and surveillance cameras in the commons recorded their activity there, with time stamps. Jeffco released highlight footage, and Agent Fuselier described his impressions of the full tape to me.

Fuselier and a colleague: I was the colleague.

found the room quite different: Depictions of the library scene when the killers returned to commit suicide were based on several sources, including: autopsy reports; my interviews with investigators who observed the scene; police video of the room after the bodies were removed; and standard medical information on the decomposition of bodies in the first thirty minutes; and checked with investigators for applicability to the actual conditions in this case. The killers' suicides were reconstructed from testimony, autopsy reports, police diagrams, police reports, and police photos of the killers' bodies.

Patrick Ireland, gently breathing: Patrick went in and out of consciousness. It's possible, though unlikely, that he might have already begun to crawl away from his initial position. There's a remote possibility that he could have been conscious during the suicides. He has no memory of them.

CHAPTER 53. AT THE BROKEN PLACES

Two thousand mourners turned out: I attended both events for the memorial, in 2006 and 2007.

They married: Depictions of the wedding came from attendees.

Local churches felt a surge: I interviewed a large number of local pastors about activity in their congregations over the intervening years. The pattern was remarkably similar, and followed historical trends. The Barna Group did a major study on the religious impact of 9/11. It found a similar surge on a national level: half of Americans said their faith helped them cope; church attendance spiked—doubling in some churches the first Sunday; and a sizable minority of people actually altered their core beliefs. The latter change flouted conventional wisdom, though—turning *away* from fundamentalist beliefs: slightly fewer people believed in an all-powerful God, or in Satan as an actual entity. All the changes disappeared within four months. And five years later, rates on every measure were still indistinguishable from pre-9/11.

When a journalist stopped by: I was the journalist.

Bibliography

In addition to these sources, this book relies on my reporting for several periodicals, published in somewhat different form. The articles appeared in 1999 through 2007 in *Salon, Slate, 5280,* and the *New York Times.* Links to those and online versions of many works below are available on my Web site at davecullen. com/columbine. Instructions for obtaining evidence released by Jefferson County and other agencies are also available there.

GOVERNMENT REPORTS ON COLUMBINE AND SCHOOL SHOOTERS

Centers for Disease Control and Prevention. *"School-Associated Student Homicide: United States, 1992–2006." Morbidity and Mortality Weekly Report* 57, no. 2 (January 18, 2008): 33–36.

EI Paso County Sheriff's Office. *Reinvestigation into the Death of Daniel Rohrbough at Columbine High School on April 20, 1990.* April 10, 2002.

Federal Bureau of Investigation. U.S. Department of Justice. Critical Incidence Response Group. National Center for the Analysis of Violent Crime. *The School Shooter: A Threat Assessment Perspective,* by Mary Ellen O'Toole. 2000.

Jefferson County Sheriff's Office. *Sheriff's Office Final Report on the Columbine High School Shootings.* CD. May 15, 2000.

Lindsey, Daryl. "A Reader's Guide to the Columbine Report." *Salon,* May 17, 2000. http://archive.salon.com/news/feature/2000/05/17/guide/index.html.

The Report of Governor Bill Owens' Columbine Review Commission. Hon. William H. Erickson, chairman. May 2001.

U.S. Secret Service and U.S. Department of Education. *The Final Report and Findings of the Safe School Initiative: Implications for the Prevention of School Attacks in the United States.* May 2002.

THE KILLERS: EVIDENCE RELEASED

Colorado Bureau of Investigation. *Laboratory Report.* Released by Jefferson County on May 31, 2000.

Colorado Bureau of Investigation. *Laboratory Report.* CD. Released by Jefferson County on February 6, 2002.

Colorado Department of Law, Office of the Attorney General. *Columbine-Related Grand Jury Report: Supplemental Attorney General Investigative Report.* Released on September 16, 2004.

Colorado Department of Law, Office of the Attorney General. *Grand Jury Report: Investigation of Missing Guerra Files.* September 16, 2004.

Colorado Department of Law, Office of the Attorney General. *Report of the Investigation into Missing Daily Field Activity and Daily Supervisor Reports Related to Columbine High School Shootings.* September 16, 2004.

Columbine High School. *Cafeteria Surveillance Tapes.* DVD. Released by Jefferson County on June 7, 2000.

Denver Police Dispatch. *Denver Dispatch Cassette Tapes.* CD containing seven and a half hours of communication. Released by Jefferson County on March 6, 2003.

Federal Bureau of Investigation. Denver Division. *FBI Crime Scene Processing Team Reports and Sketches.* CD. Released by Jefferson County on September 5, 2001.

Federal Bureau of Investigation. Denver Division. *FBI Report of Interview with Randy, Judy and Brooks Brown.* CD. Released by Jefferson County on May 22, 2001.

Harris, Eric. *Harris Web Site: 1997 Police Report and Web Pages.* CD. Released by Jefferson County on October 30, 2003.

Harris, Eric. Journal, school essays, yearbook inscription, IMs, schedules, and hundreds of other pages of accumulated writing. Included in *936 Pages of Documents Seized from Harris and Klebold Residences/Vehicles.* CD. Released by Jefferson County on July 6, 2006.

Harris, Eric, and Dylan Klebold. *Klebold/Harris Footage.* Contains miscellaneous footage retrieved from Columbine High School or provided by citizens. VHS tape. Released by Jefferson County on February 26, 2004.

———. *"Rampart Range" Video.* VHS tape. Released by Jefferson County on October 21, 2003.

Harris, Wayne. Journal. Included in *936 Pages of Documents Seized from Harris and Klebold Residences/Vehicles.* CD. Released by Jefferson County on July 6, 2006.

Jefferson County Coroner's Office. Autopsy Summaries. Released on February 6, 2001.

Jefferson County Coroner's Office, Klebold Autopsy Reports. Released on February 23, 2001.

Jefferson County District Attorney's Office. Juvenile Diversion Program Documents (Harris). Released on November 4, 2002.

Jefferson County District Attorney's Office. Juvenile Diversion Program Documents (Klebold). Released on November 22, 2002.

Jefferson County Juvenile Court. Magistrate John A. DeVita. Hearing Resulting in Assignment to a Diversion Program for Eric Harris and Dylan Klebold. March 25, 1998.

Jefferson County Sheriff's Department, Case No. 98-2218, February 24, 1998. Westover Mechanical Services by Ricky Lynn Becker v. Eric Harris and Dylan Klebold. Arrest report, case synopsis, and supplemental reports about the January 30, 1998, van break-in.

Jefferson County Sheriff's Office. *11,000 Pages of Investigative Files.* DVD. November 21, 2000. (The largest single release of police reports.)

———. *Additional Investigative Files.* Contains CD of additional ancillary reports (tips, Internet pages, threats, and related reports, plus audiocassette of Jefferson County 911 dispatch tape and missed side of tape from previous release) and two large crime scene diagrams. August 8, 2001.

———. *Crime Scene Processing Team Reports and Sketches.* CD. Released on June 19, 2001.

———. *"Crowd" Video.* VHS tape. Approximately 38 minutes of crowd footage filmed by the Jefferson County Sheriff's Office Crime Lab outside Columbine High School after 1.00 P.M. on the day of the shooting. Released on February 26, 2004.

———. *Evidence Books.* CD. Released on May 11, 2001.

———. *Jefferson County 911 and Dispatch Audio.* Two CDs. Released on August 7, 2000.

———. *Miscellaneous Items.* CD. Contains the draft search affidavit, audio of the shoot team interviews, written transcript of an interview with Columbine High School community resource officer Neil Gardner, and the executive summary of the library investigative team. Released on April 10, 2001.

———. *Miscellaneous Missing Documents.* CD. Released in 2003.

———. *Tracking Sheets, Investigative Index and Other Columbine Documents.* CD. Released on January 8, 2003.

———. *Warrants Book.* CD. Released on June 9, 2003.

Klebold, Dylan. Journal, school essays, yearbook inscription, schedules, and other pages of accumulated writing. Included in *936 Pages of Documents Seized from Harris and Klebold Residences/Vehicles.* CD. Released by Jefferson County on July 6, 2006.

Littleton Fire Department and KCNC-TV. *Littleton Fire Department "Training" Video and Raw Helicopter Footage.* VHS tape. Released by Jefferson County on April 26, 2000.

THE KILLERS: PROFILES AND CHILDHOOD HISTORY

Achenbach, Joel, and Dale Russakoff. "Teen Shooter's Life Paints Antisocial Portrait." *Washington Post,* April 29, 1999.

Anton, Mike, and Lisa Ryckman. "In Hindsight, Signs to Killings Obvious." *Rocky Mountain News,* May 2, 1999.

Bartels, Lynn, and Carla Crowder. "Fatal Friendship: How Two Suburban Boys Traded Baseball and Bowling for Murder and Madness." *Rocky Mountain News,* August 22, 1999.

Briggs, Bill, and Jason Blevins. "A Boy with Many Sides." *Denver Post,* May 2, 1999.

Brooks, David. "Columbine: Parents of a Killer." *New York Times,* May 15, 2004.

Dykeman, Nate. "More Insight on Dylan Klebold." Interview of Nate Dykeman by Charles Gibson. *Good Morning America,* ABC, April 30, 1999.

Emery, Erin, Steve Lipsher, and Ricky Young. "Video, Poems Foreshadowed Day of Disaster." *Denver Post,* April 22, 1999.

Gibbs, Nancy, and Timothy Roche. "The Columbine Tapes." *Time,* December 12, 1999.

Johnson, Dirk, and Jodi Wilgoren. "The Gunman: A Portrait of Two Killers at War with Themselves." *New York Times,* April 26, 1999.

Johnson, Kevin, and Larry Copeland. "Long-Simmering Feud May Have Triggered Massacre." *USA Today,* April 22, 1999.

Kurtz, Holly. "Klebold Paper Foretold Deadly Rampage." *Rocky Mountain News,* November 22, 2000.

Lowe, Peggy. "Facts Clarify but Can't Justify Killers' Acts." *Denver Post,* March 12, 2000.

Prendergast, Alan. "Doom Rules: Much of What We Know About Columbine Is Wrong." *Westword,* August 5, 1999.

———. "I'm Full of Hate and I Love It." *Westword,* December 6, 2001.

Russakoff, Dale, Amy Goldstein, and Joel Achenbach. "Shooters' Neighbors Had Little Hint." *Washington Post,* May 2, 1999.

Simpson, Kevin, and Jason Blevins. "Mystery How Team Players Became Loners." *Denver Post,* April 23, 1999.

Simpson, Kevin, Patricia Callahan, and Peggy Lowe. "Life and Death of a Follower." *Denver Post,* May 2, 1999.

Wilgoren, Jodi, and Dirk Johnson. "The Suspects: Sketch of Killers; Contradictions and Confusion." *New York Times,* Friday April 23, 1999.

PSYCHOPATHY

Babiak, Paul, and Robert D. Hare. *Snakes in Suits: When Psychopaths Go to Work.* New York: HarperCollins, 2006.

Barry, Tammy D., Christopher T. Barry, Annie M. Deming, and John E. Lochman. "Stability of Psychopathic Characteristics in Childhood: The Influence of Social Relationships." SAGE Publications, Thousand Oaks, CA. *Criminal Justice and Behavior* 35, no. 2 (February 2008): 244–62.

Cleckley, Hervey. *The Mask of Sanity.* 1st ed. St. Louis: C. V. Mosby Co., 1941.

———. *The Mask of Sanity: An Attempt to Clarify Some Issues About the So-Called Psychopathic Personality.* 5th ed. 1988.

D'Haenen, Hugo, Johan A. Den Boer, and Paul Willner, eds. *Biological Psychiatry.* 2 vols. New York: Wiley, 2002.

Greely, Henry T. "The Social Effects of Advances in Neuroscience: Legal Problems, Legal Perspectives." In *Neuroethics: Defining the Issues in Theory, Practice and Policy,* edited by Judy Illes, 245–63. New York: Oxford University Press, 2005.

Hare, Robert D. *Hare Psychopathy Checklist—Revised (PCL-R).* 2nd ed. Toronto: Multi-Health Systems, 2003.

———. *Psychopathy (Theory and Research).* New York: Wiley, 1970.

———. *Without Conscience: The Disturbing World of the Psychopaths Among Us.* New York: Guilford Press, 1999.

———. "Without Conscience." Robert Hare's Web page devoted to the study of psychopathy. http://www.hare.org/.

Hart, Stephen, David N. Cox, and Robert D. Hare. *Psychopathy Checklist: Screening Version (PCL:SV).* Toronto: Multi-Health Systems, 2003.

Kiehl, K. "Limbic Abnormalities in Affective Processing by Criminal Psychopaths as Revealed by Functional Magnetic Resonance Imaging." *Biological Psychiatry* 50, no. 9 (November 2001): 677–84.

Kiehl, Kent A., Alan T. Bates, Kristin R. Laurens, Robert D. Hare, and Peter F. Liddle. "Brain Potentials Implicate Temporal Lobe Abnormalities in Criminal Psychopaths." *Journal of Abnormal Psychology* 115, no. 3 (2006): 443–53.

Kiehl, Kent A., Andra M. Smith, Adrianna Mendrek, Bruce B. Forster, Robert D. Hare, and Peter F. Liddle. "Temporal Lobe Abnormalities in Semantic Processing by Criminal Psychopaths as Revealed by Functional Magnetic Resonance Imaging." *Psychiatry Research: Neuroimaging* 130 (2004): 297–312.

Kosson, David S. "Psychopathy Is Related to Negative Affectivity but Not to Anxiety Sensitivity." *Behaviour Research and Therapy* 42, no. 6 (June 2004) 697–710.

Larsson, Henrik, Essi Viding, and Robert Plomin. "Callous-Unemotional Traits and Antisocial Behavior: Genetic, Environmental, and Early Parenting Characteristics." *Criminal Justice and Behavior* 35, no. 2 (February 2008): 197–211.

Millon, Theodore, and Roger D. Davis. *Psychopathy: Antisocial, Criminal, and Violent Behavior.* New York: Guilford Press, 1998.

Millon, Theodore, Erik Simonsen, Roger D. Davis, and Morten Birket-Smith. "Ten Subtypes of Psychopathy." In Millon and Davis, *Psychopathy: Antisocial, Criminal, and Violent Behavior,* pp. 161–70.

Moran, Marianne J., Michael G. Sweda, M. Richard Fragala, and Julie Sasscer-Burgos. "The Clinical Application of Risk Assessment in the Treatment-Planning Process." *International Journal of Offender Therapy and Comparative Criminology* 45, no. 4 (2001): 421–35.

Newman, Joseph P. "The Reliability and Validity of the Psychopathy Checklist—Revised in a Sample of Female Offenders." *Criminal Justice and Behavior* 29, no. 2 (2002): 202–31.

Oxford English Dictionary, s.v. "psychopath." 1989. (Indication of first use.)

Patrick, Christopher J., ed. *Handbook of Psychopathy*. New York: Guilford Press, 2007.

Ramsland, Katherine. "Dr. Robert Hare: Expert on the Psychopath." Crime Library. http://www.trutv.com/library/crime/criminal_mind/psychology/robert_hare/index.html.

Stone, Michael H. "Sadistic Personality in Murderers." In Millon and Davis, *Psychopathy: Antisocial, Criminal, and Violent Behavior*, pp. 346–55.

JUVENILE PSYCHOPATHY

Forth, Adelle, David Kosson, and Robert D. Hare. *Psychopathy Checklist: Youth Version (PCL:YV)*. Toronto: Multi-Health Systems, 2003.

Glenn, Andrea L., Adrian Raine, Peter H. Venables, and Sarnoff A. Mednick. "Early Temperamental and Psychophysiological Precursors of Adult Psychopathic Personality." *Journal of Abnormal Psychology* 116, no. 3 (2007): 508–18.

Loeber, Rolf, David P. Farrington, Magda Stouthamer-Loeber, Terrie E. Moffitt, Avshalom Caspi, and Don Lynam. "Male Mental Health Problems, Psychopathy, and Personality Traits: Key Findings from the First 14 Years of the Pittsburgh Youth Study." *Clinical Child and Family Psychology Review* 4, no. 4 (December 2001): 273–97.

Lynam, Donald R., Rolf Loeber, and Magda Stouthamer-Loeber. "The Stability of Psychopathy from Adolescence into Adulthood: The Search for Moderators." *Criminal Justice and Behavior* 35, no. 2 (February 2008): 228–43.

Munoz, Luna C., Margaret Kerr, and Nejra Besic. "The Peer Relationships of Youths with Psychopathic Personality Traits: A Matter of Perspective." *Criminal Justice and Behavior* 35, no. 2 (February 2008): 212–27.

Murrie, D., D. Cornell, S. Kaplan, S. McConville, and A. Levy Elkon. "Psychopathy Scores and Violence Among Juvenile Offenders: A Multi-measure Study." *Behavioral Sciences and the Law* 22 (2004): 49–67.

Pardini, Dustin A., and Rolf Loeber. "Interpersonal Callousness Theories Across Adolescence Early Social Influences and Adult Outcomes." *Criminal Justice and Behavior* 35, no. 2 (February 2008): 173–96.

Salekin, Randall T., and John E. Lochman. "Child and Adolescent Psychopathy: The Search for Protective Factors." *Criminal Justice and Behavior* 35, no. 2 (February 2008): 159–72.

Vitacco, Michael J., Craig S. Neumann, Michael F. Caldwell, Anne-Marie Leistico, and Gregory J. Van Rybroek. "Testing Factor Models of the Psychopathy

Checklist: Youth Version and Their Association with Instrumental Aggression." *Journal of Personality Assessment* 87, no. 1 (2006): 74–83.

Vitacco, Michael J., and Gina M. Vincent. "Understanding the Downward Extension of Psychopathy to Youth: Implications for Risk Assessment and Juvenile Justice." *International Journal of Forensic Mental Health* 5, no. 1 (2006): 29–38.

PSYCHOPATHY TREATMENT

Caldwell, Michael F., David J. McCormick, Deborah Umstead, and Gregory J. Van Rybroek. "Evidence of Treatment Progress and Therapeutic Outcomes Among Adolescents with Psychopathic Features." *Criminal Justice and Behavior* 34, no. 5 (2007): 573–87.

Caldwell, Michael, Jennifer Skeem, Randy Salekin, and Gregory Van Rybroek. "Treatment Response of Adolescent Offenders with Psychopathy Features: A 2-Year Follow-Up." *Criminal Justice and Behavior* 33, no. 5 (October 2006): 573–87.

Caldwell, Michael F., and Gregory J. Van Rybroek. "Efficacy of a Decompression Treatment Model in the Clinical Management of Violent Juvenile Offenders." *International Journal of Offender Therapy and Comparative Criminology* 45, no. 4 (2001): 469–77.

Caldwell, Michael F., Michael Vitacco, and Gregory J. Van Rybroek. "Are Violent Delinquents Worth Treating? A Cost-Benefit Analysis." *Journal of Research in Crime and Delinquency* 43, no. 2 (May 2006): 148–68.

Cohen, Mark A., Roland T. Rust, and Sara Steen. "Prevention, Crime Control or Cash? Public Preferences Towards Criminal Justice Spending Priorities." *Justice Quarterly* 23, no. 3 (September 2006): 317–35.

Skeem, Jennifer L., John Monahan, and Edward P. Mulvey. "Psychopathy, Treatment Involvement, and Subsequent Violence Among Civil Psychiatric Patients." *Law and Behavior* 26, no. 6 (December 2002): 577–603.

Wong, Stephen C. P., and Robert D. Hare. *Guidelines for a Psychopathy Treatment Program.* Toronto: Multi-Health Systems, 2006.

OTHER MENTAL HEALTH

American Psychiatric Association. *Desk Reference to the Diagnostic Criteria from DSM-IV-TR.* Arlington, VA: American Psychiatric Publishing, 2000.

Anderson, Scott. "The Urge to End It." *New York Times Magazine,* July 6, 2008.

Ekman, Paul. *Telling Lies: Clues to Deceit in the Marketplace, Politics, and Marriage.* 2nd rev. ed. New York: Norton, 2001.

Millon, Theodore, and Roger D. Davis. *Disorders of Personality: DSM-IV and Beyond.* New York: Wiley, 1996.

Ochberg, Frank. "PTSD 101." DART Center for Journalism and Trauma. http://www.dartcenter.org/articles/special_features/ptsd101/00.php.

SURVIVORS: MEMOIRS AND INTERVIEW TRANSCRIPTS

Bernall, Brad, and Misty Bernall. "Columbine Victim Cassie Bernall's Story." Interview by Peter Jennings. *World News Tonight,* ABC, April 26, 1999.

Bernall, Misty. *She Said Yes: The Unlikely Martyrdom of Cassie Bernall.* Farmington, PA: Plough Publishing, 1999.

Brown, Brooks, and Rob Merritt. *No Easy Answers: The Truth Behind Death at Columbine.* Herndon, VA: Lantern Books, 2002.

Carlston, Liz. *Surviving Columbine: How Faith Helps Us Find Peace When Tragedy Strikes.* Salt Lake City: Shadow Mountain, 2004.

Ireland, Patrick. "The Boy in the Window." Interview by Diane Sawyer. *20/20,* ABC, September 29, 1999.

———. "Headline Follow-ups: What's Happened in the Aftermath of Explosive News Stories." *Oprah Winfrey Show,* May 22, 2002.

Kirklin, Lance, and Sean Graves. Interview by Barbara Walters. *20/20,* ABC, October 1, 1999.

Lindholm, Marjorie. *A Columbine Survivor's Story.* Littleton, CO: Regenold Publishing, 2005.

Nimmo, Beth. *The Journals of Rachel Scott: A Journey of Faith at Columbine High.* Adapted by Debra K. Klingsporn. Nashville: Thomas Nelson, 2001.

Saltzman, Marilyn, and Linda Lou Sanders. *Dave Sanders: Columbine Teacher, Coach, Hero.* Philadelphia: Xlibris Corporation, 2004.

Sanders, Angela. "Angie Sanders Talks About Her Father, Only Teacher to Die in Colorado School Shooting, Who Is Now Being Remembered for His Bravery." *Today Show,* NBC News, April 22, 1999.

Scott, Darrell, Beth Nimmo, with Steve Rabey. *Rachel's Tears: The Spiritual Journey of Columbine Martyr Rachel Scott.* Nashville: Thomas Nelson, 2000.

Taylor, Mark. *I Asked, God Answered: A Columbine Miracle.* Mustang, OK: Tate Publishing, 2006.

SURVIVORS: NEWS ACCOUNTS

Bartels, Lynn. "Mom Had Been Hospitalized for Depression: Carol [sic] Hochhalter Had Struggled with Depression for Three Years." *Rocky Mountain News,* October 26, 1999.

———. "Some Families Arguing over Money: Accountability, Means of Distribution Lead List." *Rocky Mountain News,* May 26, 1999.

———. "A Story of Healing and Hope: Faith and Friends Helped Paralyzed Student Overcome a 'Very Dark Place.'" *Rocky Mountain News,* April 20, 2004.

Callahan, Patricia. "Dream Turns to Nightmare." *Denver Post,* April 22, 1999.

Michalik, Connie, and Jo Anne Doherty. "Connie Michalik and Jo Anne Doherty Discuss Death of Carla Hochhalter, Mother of Paralyzed Columbine Shooting Victim." Interview by Charles Gibson. *Good Morning America,* ABC News, October 25, 1999.

Curtin, Dave. "Suicide, Arrest Spur Columbine Calls." *Denver Post,* October 24, 1999.

"Distribution Plan." *Rocky Mountain News,* July 3, 1999.

Edwards, Bob, anchor, and Andrea Dukakis, reporter. "Controversy over How to Spend the Millions of Dollars Donated Since the Columbine High School Shooting." *Morning Edition,* NPR, June 22, 1999.

Fox, Ben. "School Shooting Suspects Appear in Court." Associated Press, March 26, 2001.

"Grace Under Fire: Columbine High School Teacher Dave Sanders Dies a Hero, Saving the Lives of Others." *48 Hours,* CBS News, April 22, 1999.

Green, Chuck. "Columbine Receives, Asks More." *Denver Post,* March 31, 2000.

———. "Enough Milking of Tragedy." *Denver Post,* April 3, 2000.

Johnson, Dirk. "The Teacher: As They Mourn, They Are Left to Wonder." *New York Times,* April 28, 1999.

Kurtz, Holly. "Columbine-Area Groups Reap Funds: Nine Agencies, Charities to Use Money for Victim Counseling, Anti-violence Teen Programs." *Rocky Mountain News,* August 14, 1999.

———. "Healing Fund Gives to Families: Columbine Victims Satisfied with Plan; Half of Distribution Goes to Students, Staff." *Rocky Mountain News,* July 3, 1999.

Lowe, Peggy. "Aired Video Irks Sheriff." *Denver Post,* October 14, 1999.

———. "Columbine: They Are 5A Champions; Team Triumphs After Tragedy." *Denver Post,* December 5, 1999.

Lowe, Peggy, and Kieran Nicholson. "CBS Airs Cafeteria Tape." *Denver Post,* October 13, 1999.

Obmascik, Mark. "Healing Begins: Colorado, World Mourn Deaths at Columbine High." *Denver Post,* April 22, 1999.

Olinger, David, Marilyn Robinson, and Kevin Simpson. "Columbine Victim's Mom Kills Herself: Community Grief Continues with Pawnshop Suicide." *Denver Post,* October 23, 1999.

Paterniti, Michael. "Columbine Never Sleeps." *GQ,* April 2004, pp. 206–20.

Paulson, Steven K. "Aftershocks Assail Columbine Community: Will It Ever End?" Associated Press, October 23, 1999.

"Phenomenon of the Goth Movement." Interview by Brian Ross. *20/20,* ABC, April 21, 1999.

Prendergast, Alan. "Deeper into Columbine." *Westword,* October 31, 2002.

Scanlon, Bill. "'Nothing but Cheers, Yells and Tears': First Day Back Starts with Music, Parents Forming Human Chain." *Rocky Mountain News,* August 17, 1999.

Slevin, Colleen. "Mother of Columbine Victim Kills Self in Pawn Shop." Associated Press, October 22, 1999.

Sullivan, Bartholomew. "In Memory of Daniel Rohrbough." *Rocky Mountain News,* April 27, 1999.

"Video from Inside Columbine: Students, Teachers Seen Fleeing Cafeteria." CBS News, October 12, 1999.

LAWSUITS: COURT FILINGS AND CASE SUMMARIES

Grenier, Peter C. "Civil Litigation Arising Out of the Columbine High School Massacre." National Crime Victim Bar Association. Continuing Legal Education. http://www.ncvc.org/vb/main.aspx?dbID=DB_Biography170.

Rohrbough, Brian E., and Susan A. Petrone, individually and as personal representatives of the estate of Daniel Rohrbough, deceased, et al. v. John P. Stone, the Sheriff of Jefferson County, Colorado, et al. Civil Action No. 00-B-808, April 19, 2000.

Ruegsegger, Gregory A., and Darcey L. Ruegsegger, et al. v. The Jefferson County Board of County Commissioners, et al. Civil Action No. 00-B-806, April 19, 2000.

Sanders, Angela, personal representative of William David Sanders, deceased v. The Board of County Commissioners of the County of Jefferson, Colorado, et al. U.S. District Court for the District of Colorado. Civil Action No. 00-791, April 19, 2000.

Schnurr, Mark A., and Sharilyn K. Schnurr, et al. v. The Board of County Commissioners of Jefferson County, et al. Civil Action No. 00-790, April 19, 2000.

CHRISTIANS

For Christian-oriented books, see also the section "Survivors: Memoirs and Interview Transcripts."

The Barna Group. "Five Years Later: 9/11 Attacks Show No Lasting Influence on Americans' Faith." *The Barna Update,* August 28, 2006. http://www.barna.org/FlexPage.aspx?Page=BarnaUpdateNarrowPreview&BarnaUpdateID=244.

Bartels, Lynn, and Dina Bunn. "Dad Cuts Down Killers' Crosses." *Rocky Mountain News,* May 1, 1999.

Bottum, J. "Awakening at Littleton." *First Things,* August–September 1999, pp. 28–32.

———. "A Martyr Is Born." *Weekly Standard,* May 10, 1999.

"Burying a Killer: Dylan Klebold's Funeral Service." *Christian Century,* May 12, 1999.

Crowder, Carla. "Martyr for Her Faith." *Rocky Mountain News,* April 23, 1999.

"Dad's Inscription Ties Columbine Deaths to Abortion, Immorality." Associated Press, September 22, 2007.

Dejevsky, Mary. "Saint Cassie of Columbine High: The Making of a Modern Martyr." *Independent* (London, U.K.), August 21, 1999.

Fong, Tillie. "Crosses for Harris, Klebold Join 13 Others: Killers Remembered in Memorials on Hillside Near Columbine High School." *Rocky Mountain News,* April 28, 1999.

———. "Fifteen Crosses Traced to Mystery Builder." *Rocky Mountain News,* April 30, 1999.

Go, Kristen. "Pastor Criticizes Security." *Denver Post,* May 6, 1999.

Haley, Dan. "Protesters Fell Church's Trees." *Denver Post,* September 27, 1999.

Kass, Jeff. "Angry Parents Cut Down 2 Trees: Church Planted 15 for Those Who Died at School, Including Harris and Klebold." *Rocky Mountain News,* September 27, 1999.

Kirsten, Reverend George. "When God Speaks." Sermon. West Bowles Community Church, Littleton, CO, May 9, 1999.

Littwin, Mike. "Hill of Crosses a Proper Place to Confront Ourselves." *Rocky Mountain News,* April 30, 1999.

Luzadder, Dan, and Katie Kerwin McCrimmon. "Accounts Differ on Question to Bernall: Columbine Shooting Victim May Not Have Been Asked Whether She Believed in God." *Rocky Mountain News,* September 24, 1999.

Miller, Lisa. "Marketing a Columbine Martyr: Tragedy Leads Victim's Mother to Media Stage." *Wall Street Journal,* eastern ed., July 16, 1999.

Oudemolen, Reverend Bill. "Responding to 'Every Parent's Worst Nightmare.'" Sermon. Foothills Bible Church, Littleton, CO, May 9, 1999.

Richardson, Valerie. "Columbine Trees Splinter Church, Victims' Parents: Killers' Inclusion Sparks Protests." *Washington Times,* September 28, 1999.

Rosin, Hanna. "Columbine Miracle: A Matter of Belief; The Last Words of Littleton Victim Cassie Bernall Test a Survivor's Faith—and Charity." *Washington Post,* October 14, 1999.

Scanlon, Bill. "*She Said Yes* to Tell Cassie Bernall's Story." *Rocky Mountain News,* June 4, 1999.

Sullivan, Bartholomew. "Hallowed Hill." *Rocky Mountain News,* April 29, 1999.

Vaughan, Kevin. "Divided by the Crosses." *Rocky Mountain News,* May 2, 1999.

Zoba, Wendy Murray. *Day of Reckoning: Columbine and the Search for America's Soul.* Grand Rapids, MI: Brazos Press, 2001.

MEDIA COVERAGE OF THE ATTACK

Bai, Matt. "Anatomy of a Massacre." *Newsweek,* May 3, 1999.

Brokaw, Tom. "Shooting at Colorado High School Leaves at Least 14 Persons Shot, Gunmen Still Not Apprehended." NBC, 3:48 P.M. ET, April 20, 1999.

Crowder, Carla. "For Friends, Long Wait Is Painfully Tense." *Rocky Mountain News,* April 22, 1999.

Crowder, Carla, and Scott Stocker. "Teen-agers Battle to Help Wounded Science Teacher; Students Try to Stem Blood from Gravely Injured Man." *Rocky Mountain News,* April 21, 1999.

Eddy, Mark. "Shooter Told Friend: 'Get Out of Here.'" *Denver Post,* April 21, 1999.

Johnson, Kevin. "Teacher with Critical Wound Saved Teens." *USA Today,* April 22, 1999.

LeDuc, Daniel, and David Von Drehle. "Heroism Amid the Terror: Many Rushed to the Aid of Others During School Siege." *Washington Post,* April 22, 1999.

Roberts, John. "Shooting at High School in Littleton, Colorado." CBS News, 2:07 P.M. ET, April 20, 1999.

Ryckman, Lisa Levitt, and Mike Anton. "'Help Is on the Way': Mundane Gave Way to Madness with Reports of Gunfire at Columbine." *Rocky Mountain News,* April 25, 1999.

Savidge, Martin, et al. "Gunmen Rampage Through Colorado High School." CNN, 1:54 P.M. ET, April 20, 1999.

HOSTAGES AND TERRORISTS

Fuselier, G. Dwayne. "A Practical Overview of Hostage Negotiations (Part 1)." *FBI Law Enforcement Bulletin* 50, no. 6 (June 1981): 2–6.

———. "A Practical Overview of Hostage Negotiations (Part 2)." *FBI Law Enforcement Bulletin* 50, no 7 (July 1981): 10–15.

Fuselier, G. Dwayne, and John T. Dolan. "A Guide for First Responders to Hostage Situations." *FBI Law Enforcement Bulletin* 58, no. 4 (April 1989): 9–13.

Fuselier, G. Dwayne, and Gary W. Noesner. "Confronting the Terrorist Hostage Taker." *FBI Law Enforcement Bulletin* 59, no. 7 (July 1990).

Gilmartin, Kevin M. "The Lethal Triad: Understanding the Nature of Isolated Extremist Groups." *FBI Law Enforcement Bulletin* 65, no. 9 (September 1996): 1–5.

Juergensmeyer, Mark. *Terror in the Mind of God: The Global Rise of Religious Violence.* Comparative Studies in Religion and Society, vol. 13. University of California Press, 2001.

Noesner, Gary W. "Negotiation Concepts for Commanders." *FBI Law Enforcement Bulletin* 68, no 1 (January 1999): 6–14.

Reich, Walter, and Walter Laqueur. *Origins of Terrorism; Psychologies, Ideologies, Theologies, States of Mind.* Washington, D.C.: Woodrow Wilson Center Press, 1998.

POLICE ETHICS AND RESPONSE PROTOCOLS

Brown, Jennifer, and Kevin Simpson. "Momentum for School Safety at Standstill." *Denver Post,* September 28, 2006.

Delattre, Edwin J. *Character and Cops: Ethics in Policing.* 5th ed. Washington, D.C.: AEI Press, 2006.

Fuselier, G. Dwayne, Clinton R. Van Zandt, and Frederick J. Lanceley. "Hostage/Barricade Incidents: High-Risk Factors and the Action Criteria." *FBI Law Enforcement Bulletin* 60, no. 1 (January 1991): 7–12.

Garrett, Ronnie. "Marching to the Sound of Gunshots." *Law Enforcement Technology,* June 2007.

Khadaroo, Stacy Teicher. "A Year After Virginia Tech, Sharper Focus on Troubled Students: Many Campuses Have New Practices." *Christian Science Monitor,* April 16, 2008.

Lloyd, Jillian. "Change in Tactics: Police Trade Talk for Rapid Response." *Christian Science Monitor,* May 31, 2000.

COLUMBINE POLICE RESPONSE, INVESTIGATION, AND COVER-UP

Able, Charley. "Police Want Columbine Video Copier Found and Prosecuted." *Rocky Mountain News,* October 14, 1999.

"America's Police Suppress Columbine Killers' Videos." *Special Report: Denver School Killings.* BBC, November 12, 1999.

"Cop Cleared in Columbine Death." CBS News, April 19, 2002.

Kenworthy, Tom, and Roberto Suro. "Nine Days After Rampage, Police Still Under Fire." *Washington Post,* April 30, 1999.

Lusetich, Robert. "Anger Grows at Two-Hour Police Delay." *Weekend Australian,* April 24, 1999.

Luzadder, Dan, and Kevin Vaughan. "Inside the Columbine Investigation Series, Part 1." *Rocky Mountain News,* December 12, 1999.

———. "Inside the Columbine Investigation Series, Part 2: Amassing the Facts." *Rocky Mountain News,* December 13, 1999.

———. "Inside the Columbine Investigation Series, Part 3: Biggest Question of All." *Rocky Mountain News,* December 14, 1999.

McPhee, Mike. "Sheriff's Former No. 2 Man Denies Coverup." *Denver Post,* September 17, 2004.

McPhee, Mike, and Kieran Nicholson. "Deputy in Columbine Case Fired Sheriff: Taylor Admits Lying to Families; Rohrbough Kin Calls Confession a Ruse." *Denver Post,* January 10, 2002.

Prendergast, Alan. "Chronology of a Big Fat Lie." *Westword,* April 19, 2001.

———. "In Search of Lost Time." *Westword,* May 2, 2002.

———. "The Plot Sickens." *Westword,* November 6, 2003.

———. "Stonewalled: The Story They Don't Want to Tell." *Westword,* April 13, 2000.

———. "There Ought to Be a Law." *Westword,* March 7, 2002.

Vaughan, Kevin. "Police Dispute Charges They Were Too Slow." *Rocky Mountain News,* April 22, 1999.

OTHER SCHOOL SHOOTINGS

The Brady Campaign. "Major U.S. School Shootings." http://www.bradycampaign .org/xshare/pdf/school-shootings.pdf.

Egan, Timothy. "Where Rampages Begin: A Special Report; From Adolescent Angst to Shooting Up Schools." *New York Times,* June 14, 1998.

Glaberson, William. "Word for Word: A Killer's Schoolmates; Guns, Mayhem and Grief Can Flourish When Good Friends Do Nothing." *New York Times,* August 6, 2000.

"Gunman Kills 2, Wounds at Least 13 at School near San Diego." Associated Press, March 5, 2001.

"Mass Shootings at Virginia Tech, April 16, 2007: Report of the Review Panel." Presented to Governor Tim Kaine, Commonwealth of Virginia, August 2007.

Morse, Russell, Charles Jones, and Hazel Tesoro. "Misfits Who Don't Kill: Outcasts Who Grew Up Without Resorting to Violence Talk about What Kept Them from a Littleton-style Massacre." *Salon,* April 22, 1999. http://www .salon.com/news/feature/1999/04/22/misfits/.

Paulson, Amanda, and Ron Scherer. "How Safe Are College Campuses?" *Christian Science Monitor,* April 18, 2007.

Schiraldi, Vincent. "Hyping School Violence." *Washington Post,* August 25, 1998.

GUN CONTROL

Abrams, Jim. "House Tempers Background Checks for Guns." Associated Press, Washington, June 14, 2007.

Bortnick, Barry. "Passed/Amendment 22: Background Checks—Gun Shows." (Colorado Springs) *Gazette,* November 8, 2000.

"Colorado Kills Gun Laws." Report by Vince Gonzales. CBS News, February 17, 2000.

Ferullo, Michael. "Clinton Implores Colorado Voters to Take Action on Gun Show Loophole." CNN.com, April 12, 2000.

Hahn, Robert A., Oleg O. Bilukha, Alex Crosby, Mindy Thompson Fullilove, Akiva Liberman, Eve K. Moscicki, Susan Snyder, Farris Tuma, and Peter Briss. "First Reports Evaluating the Effectiveness of Strategies for Preventing Violence: Firearms Laws: Findings from the Task Force on Community Preventive Services." Centers for Disease Control and Prevention. http://www .cdc.gov/mmwr/preview/mmwrhtml/rr5214a2.htm, October 3, 2003.

Havemann, Joel. "Gun Bill Passes with Aid of NRA." *Los Angeles Times,* June 14, 2007.

Holman, Kwame. "A Quick Draw." Report by Kwame Holman. *NewsHour with Jim Lehrer,* May 14, 1999.

———. "Gun Control." Report by Kwame Holman. *NewsHour with Jim Lehrer,* June 18, 1999.

O'Driscoll, Patrick, and Tom Kenworthy. "Grieving Father Turns Gun-control Activist." *USA Today,* April 19, 2000.

Paulson, Steven K. "Governor Signs Four Gun Bills, Says Compromises Necessary." Associated Press, Denver, CO, May 19, 2000.

Schwartz, Emma. "Gun Control Laws." *U.S. News & World Report,* March 6, 2008.

Soraghan, Mike. "Colorado After Columbine: The Gun Debate." *State Legislatures Magazine,* June 2000.

Tapper, Jake, "Coming Out Shooting: In the Wake of the Littleton Massacre, the NRA Holds Its Convention in Denver, Less than 20 Miles Away from Columbine High School." *Salon,* May 2, 1999. http://www.salon.com/news/feature/1999/05/02/nra/index.html.

Weller, Robert. "Colorado Supreme Court Clears Way for Vote on Closing Gun Show Loophole." Associated Press, Denver, CO, July 3, 2000.

MISCELLANEOUS

Fragar, Russell. "Church on Fire." Hillsong Publishing, 1997.

Garbarino, James, and Claire Bedard. *Parents Under Siege: Why You Are the Solution, Not the Problem in Your Child's Life.* New York: Free Press, 2002.

Hemingway, Ernest. *A Farewell to Arms.* New York: Scribner's, 1929.

Jefferson County School District Profile of Columbine High School. http://www.jeffcopublicschools.org/schools/profiles/high/columbine.html.

Okrent, Daniel. The Public Editor. "Setting the Record Straight (but Who Can Find the Record?)" *New York Times,* March 14, 2004.

Shepard, Cyn. A Columbine Site. http://www.acolumbinesite.com.

Staff and News Services. "Inevitably, School Shootings Cause Ratings Spike." *Atlanta Constitution,* April 23, 1999.

Steinbeck, John. *Pastures of Heaven.* New York: Braver, Warren & Putnam, 1932.

Index

ABC, 118–19, 156

Absalom, 132

Active Shooter Protocol, 324

Adams, Devon, 185–86

alarm, at Columbine High School, 61, 140, 142–43, 145, 227, 353

alarm clocks, for detonating bombs, 32, 33, 45, 124

Albert, Kevin, 214–15, 218, 245, 261

alienation, 157–58, 323

Alpha Pawn Shop, 282–83

altar calls, 120

Anarchist Cookbook, The, 32, 68, 204

Anderson, Robyn, 210, 293
  as Dylan's prom date, 8, 26–27, 28, 109
  gun purchases by, 88–89, 90, 122–24
  the massacre (Tuesday, April 20, 1999), 40, 44, 62–63
  police interrogation of, 122–24

anger, 10, 187–88, 197, 217–18, 243, 307

antidepressants, 208–9, 214, 218, 261, 319, 334

anti-Semitism, 128, 131–32, 258

antisocial personality disorder (APD), 241

Arlene (shotgun), 293, 326, 327

arsenal. *See* bombs; crickets; guns; Molotov cocktails; pipe bombs

attire. *See also* trench coats
  of Eric and Dylan on Judgment Day, 34, 42, 53–54, 55, 335–36

Babcock, Lewis, 318–20

Bartels, Lynn, 363*n*

baseball, 8, 112–13, 126

Basement Tapes, 35, 41, 169, 288, 326–36, 385–86*n*

Battan, Kate, 109, 169, 213, 242, 248
  Cassie Bernall's martyrdom and, 232, 287
  conspiracy theories, 167
  first assumptions about case, 68–69
  juvenile records of Eric and Dylan, 84–85
  Klebolds' interview with, 209–10
  search warrants, 85, 315

battle positions, 33, 34, 45–46

Beauprez, Bob, 387*n*

Bella Ristorante, 26–27

Belleview Lanes, 27–28, 296, 309

bell schedule, at Columbine High School, 43

Bernall, Brad
  current update on, 346, 356
  day after massacre, 103–4
  martyrdom of Cassie and, 180–81, 222–26, 229–33
  the massacre (Tuesday, April 20, 1999), 58–59, 93, 97–98
  Sue Klebold's letter of apology to, 254–55

Bernall, Cassie
  day after massacre, 103–4
  library massacre (Tuesday, April 20, 1999), 43, 58–60, 92–93, 98, 180, 226–30
    Bree Pasquale's account, 226–29

Bernall, Cassie (*cont.*)
Emily Wyant's account, 226–30, 232–33, 287
Valeen Schnur's account, 224–25, 232–33
martyrdom of, 177–81, 222–33, 287
prom night and, 25
religious conversion of, 222–24
transfer to Columbine, 30–31, 224
Bernall, Chris, 13, 58, 93
Bernall, Misty
current update on, 346, 356
day after massacre, 103–4
martyrdom of Cassie and, 180–81, 222–26, 229–33, 287
the massacre (Tuesday, April 20, 1999), 58–59, 92–93, 94, 97–98
She Said Yes: The Unlikely Martyrdom of Cassie Bernall, 230–32, 287, 356
Sue Klebold's letter of apology to, 254–55
Bethel Regional High School, 14
bibliography, 389–403
bin Laden, Osama, 316
Blackjack Pizza, 6, 9, 16–17, 89, 185
black trench coats. *See* trench coats
Boles, Thaddeus, 372n
bombs. *See also* pipe bombs
friends knowledge of, 71, 88–89, 122–25, 330–31
the massacre (Tuesday, April 20, 1999), 41–44, 125, 349–51
the missions and testing of, 183, 184–85
planning for the massacre, 32–35, 275–76, 329–31, 332
bomb scares, 284, 347–48
bomb squads, 124–25, 215
Boston Red Sox, 8, 41
Bottum, J., 180, 222
Bowles Crossing Shopping Center, 177
Bowling for Columbine (documentary), 317
Brady Bill, 211, 280
brain and psychopaths, 242, 244–46
Branch Davidians, 31, 95, 108
Breckenridge, Colorado, 13
Brokaw, Tom, 301

Brooks, David, 339–40
Brown, Aaron, 127, 162, 220
Brown, Brooks
friendship with Eric and Dylan, 126–27, 134, 161–66, 217, 263
the massacre (Tuesday, April 20, 1999), 41, 42
No Easy Answers (memoir), 342
threats from Eric toward, 85, 161–64, 165–66
warnings from Eric and Dylan to, 42, 217
Brown, Judy, 126–28, 210
first recognition of threat posed by Eric, 161–63
warnings about Eric from, 85, 165–66, 217, 220–21, 248, 263
Brown, Randy, 85, 165–66, 185, 217, 220–21, 248, 263–64
bullying, 157–59, 258, 339–41, 384n
Burgess, Mark, 185
Butts, Brad, 308

cafeteria, at Columbine High School, 13–14
crime-scene investigation, 124–25
the massacre in the (Tuesday, April 20, 1999), 46–50, 61–62, 81–82, 350–51
preplanning attack, 305–6, 333
Carlston, Liz, 38–39
Castaldo, Richard, 46, 62, 282, 283
CBS, 281, 287
cell phones, 65–66, 67
Challenging High Intellectual Potential Students (CHIPS), 126, 129
Chatfield High School, 37, 118
Chatfield Reservoir, 114
Cherry Creek High School, 289–90
Cho, Seung-Hui, 348
choir room, at Columbine High School, 48, 51, 65, 81, 86–87
Christian Fellowship School, 30–31
Christian reawakening, 29–31
Cleckley, Hervey, 240–41, 243–44, 328
Cleland, Max, 354–55

Clement Park, 59, 86, 152, 155, 159, 339
  wooden crosses, 192–95
Clinton, Bill, 80, 93, 339, 354–55
Clinton, Hillary, 354
clothing. *See also* trench coats
  of Eric and Dylan on Judgment Day, 34,
    42, 53–54, 55, 335–36
CNN, 53, 65–66, 72, 76, 80, 150–51, 178
Cohn, Aaron, 283
Cohn, Steve, 283
Colorado Community College System,
    128, 317
Colorado Right to Life, 345
Colorado Rockies, 8, 112–13, 210
Colorado Springs, Colorado, 29
Colorado State University, 291, 320–21
Columbine Bible Study, 30
Columbine Curse, 289
Columbine Evangelicals, 29–31, 116–20,
    178–81
Columbine High School
  bell schedule at, 43
  bullying at, 157–59, 339–40
  cafeteria. *See* cafeteria, at Columbine
    High School
  football team, 289–90
  founding and construction of, 20–21
  girls' basketball team, 21–22, 37–39
  library. *See* library, at Columbine High
    School
  massacre. *See* Columbine High School
    massacre
  prom, 23–28, 336
  renovation of, 250–51, 312
  reopening of, 270–74
  second school year, 312–14
  Take Back the School rally, 271–74
Columbine High School massacre
    (Tuesday, April 20, 1999), 40–67,
    349–53
  aborted attempt on Monday, 35–36
  arrival at school of Eric and Dylan,
    41–42
  assembling arsenal for, 275–76, 280,
    293–95, 305–6, 309–11, 335
  battle positions, 33, 34, 45–46

bomb failures, 45, 125, 351
bomb placement, 42–43
cafeteria scene, 46–50, 61–62, 81–82,
    281, 350–51
choir room scene, 48, 51, 65, 81,
    86–87
crime-scene confusion, 53–54, 55–56
Dave Sanders and, 87–88, 96–97, 121,
    138–44
decoy plans, 32–33, 41, 44
eyewitness testimony, 53–56, 59–60, 84,
    86–87, 121, 151–52, 204–6
"female down," 49–50, 54–55
fifth anniversary, 338–39
final death toll, 85–86
finalizing details for, 35, 332–33
firing of first shots, 46–47
first anniversary, 297–301
first assumptions about, 68–72
gym scene, 73–74
hostage potential, 65–67
injury count, 76
library scene, 50–51, 61–62, 76–79,
    83–84, 151, 205, 226–32, 351–53
myths about. *See* Columbine myths
parking lots, 33–34, 41–42
Science Room 3, 48, 64, 76, 82, 87–88,
    93, 96–97, 139–44, 350
setting up the perimeter, 56–57, 58–59,
    64
six-month anniversary, 281–85
suicide of Eric and Dylan, 83–84,
    351–53
SWAT team, 61–63, 76–79, 142–45,
    352–53
timeline of events, 358–60
West Staircase, 45–46, 50, 55
Columbine Lounge, 19–22
Columbine Memorial, 339, 354–55,
    357–58
Columbine myths, 149–52, 155–59
  bullying, 157–59
  gay rumors, 155–56
  Goths, 72, 107, 149, 155, 156–57
  jocks, 125, 151, 208–9, 330
  outcasts, 72, 147, 149, 155, 157–59

Columbine myths (*cont.*)
    targeting jocks, 125, 151–52, 208–9, 330
    third shooter, 86, 150, 203–5
    Trench Coat Mafia, 72, 150–51, 156
Columbine Task Force, 122–25, 212–13
conspiracy theories, 71–72, 107–10,
        203–13
Couric, Katie, 157
Craig Hospital, 154–55, 191–92, 248–50,
        269–70
crickets, 33–34, 184–85, 332
crime-scene confusion, 53–54, 55–56
crosses, atop Rebel Hill, 192–95
Curnow, Bob, 104

Dairy Queen, 62
David, King, 132
Davis, Steve, 85–86, 144
DeAngelis, Brian, 38
DeAngelis, Frank ("Mr. D"), 297, 312–14
    bullying at Columbine and, 158–59
    current update on, 356–57
    Dave Sanders and, 37–38, 94–95, 121
    lunch duty of, 14, 16
    the massacre (Tuesday, April 20, 1999),
        43, 73–74, 94–95
    at Patrick Ireland's wedding, 355
    prom night and, 28
    PTSD symptoms of, 74, 313–14
    recollections of attack by, 121, 205–6
    renovation of Columbine, 251, 312
    reopening of Columbine, 272–74
    school shooters and, 348
    six-month anniversary, 346–47
    speech at Light of the World Catholic
        Church, 104–6
    speech at West Bowles Community
        Church, 117–18
    student assembly (April 16, 1999), 3–4,
        11, 335
death toll, 85–86
Deer Creek Canyon Park, 201
Deer Creek Mesa, 129
dental records, 93–94, 95
Denver Broncos, 200
Denver Design Center, 24–25, 27, 28

Denver Health Medical Center, 83–84
Denver Post, 88, 116, 144, 152, 178, 180, 271,
        300
DePooter, Corey, 77, 191
depressives, 187–88, 197, 198
Desperado (movie), 311, 383*n*
DeVita, John, 219–20, 282
DeWitt, Susan, 17, 18, 27, 340, 349
*Diagnostic and Statistical Manual of Mental
        Disorders* (DSM-IV), 241
Dobson, James, 345
Doom, 114, 137
Downward Spiral, The (album), 197, 353
Drudge Report, 156
Duff, Lynn, 94
Dunaway, John, 61–63, 288, 343, 377*n*
Duran, Phil, 89, 122, 167–68, 285–86,
        309–11
dusters, 34, 42, 147–48. *See also* trench
    coats
Dutro, Eric, 147–48
dyad phenomenon, 244
Dykeman, Nate
    friendship with Dylan and Eric,
        26–27, 136, 198, 200, 206–7, 215,
        259, 330
    knowledge of bombs by, 198, 200
    Kristi Epling and, 206–7, 296
    the massacre (Tuesday, April 20, 1999),
        42, 54, 63–64

early warning signs, 323–24, 385*n*
egocentrism, 239, 240
Ekman, Paul, 241
Epling, Kristi, 206–8, 296
Eubanks, Austin, 77
Euripides, 276, 351
Evangelicals, 29–31, 116–20, 178–81
Event Horizon (movie), 27
eyewitness testimony, 53–56, 59–60, 84,
        86–87, 121, 151–52, 204–6

Falwell, Jerry, 156
FBI (Federal Bureau of Investigation),
        31, 69–71, 85–86, 108–10, 124–25,
        247–48, 316, 322–24, 384*n*

"female down," 49–50, 54–55
Fieger, Geoffrey, 252
final report, 297–301, 343–45
Finegan, Robin, 252–53, 271–72
fire alarm, at Columbine High School, 61, 140, 142–43, 145, 227, 353
firearms, 33–36, 71, 86, 121–24, 280, 293–95. *See also* shotguns; TEC-9 gun
  purchase at Tanner Gun Show, 90, 122, 167–68, 293–94
first assumptions, 68–72
flamethrowers, 137, 305
Focus on the Family, 345
Foothills Bible Church, 30, 118, 178
Foothills Day Care, 327
forgiveness, 193–94, 268–70
Fort Benning, Georgia, 34
Fountain Real Estate Management, 128
Fox News, 178
Friesen, Kent, 140
frustration, 127, 243
Fuselier, Brian, 71, 75–76, 85, 95, 108–9, 251, 273, 316–17
Fuselier, Dwayne
  assessment of Eric and Dylan by, 168–70, 175–76, 187–88, 196–97, 235, 236, 239, 244, 247–48, 256–57, 258, 260, 265, 267, 277, 279, 311, 320, 339
  Basement Tapes and, 169, 328, 329, 330, 334
  charges against Mark Manes and Phil Duran, 285–86
  conspiracy theories and, 107–10, 203, 204–5, 208, 212
  crime-scene investigation, 108–10, 121
  current update on, 355
  FBI background of, 31, 95, 108
  the massacre (Tuesday, April 20, 1999), 69–71, 72, 75–76, 85–86, 108–9
  retirement of, 315–17
  Waco standoff, 31, 95, 108
Fuselier, Mimi, 71, 75–76, 95, 273, 317

Gallegos, Jo-Lee, 373*n*
Gardner, Neil, 43–44, 49–50, 51, 54–55, 57, 73
gay rumors, 155–56
Goethe, Johann Wolfgang von, 265
Gonzales, Mark, 332, 334–35
Gore, Al, 177, 178
Goths (goth culture), 72, 107, 149, 155, 156–57
Graham, Franklin, 177
Grant, Amy, 177
Graves, Sean, 46–47, 61, 250, 281, 282
Great Clips, 17, 27
Green, Chuck, 300
Green Mountain Guns, 295
Grenier, Peter, 298, 372*n*
Grove, Glenn, 220
Guerra, Mike, 124, 166, 220, 248, 315, 343–44, 383*n*
gun control legislation, 300–301, 382*n*
Gun Digest, 199
guns, 33–36, 71, 86, 121–24, 280, 293–95. *See also* shotguns; TEC-9 gun
  purchase at Tanner Gun Show, 90, 122, 167–68, 293–94

Hall, Makai, 77, 154
Hancey, Aaron, 140–43
Hare, Robert, 239–42, 244–47
Harold and Maude (movie), 134
"Harriet," 186–87, 197, 199, 215, 262–63
Harris, Eric, 6–10
  antidepressants and, 208–9, 214, 218, 261, 319, 334
  appearance of, 6–7, 41, 146
  assembling arsenal, 275–76, 280, 293–95, 305–6, 309–11, 335
  Basement Tapes, 35, 326–36
  birth of, 112
  Blackjack job, 6, 9, 16–17, 89, 185
  as Colorado Rockies fan, 8, 112–13, 210
  credit card scam, 200
  in Diversion program, 84–85, 215–20, 234, 245, 256–67, 279–80, 306
  dreams and fantasies of, 134–36, 137, 160

Harris, Eric (*cont.*)

drinking by, 114, 183, 218, 278–79

false apologies of, 162, 218–19, 259–60, 328–29

family life of, 111–15, 126–27, 262, 293

farewell video by, 349

first meeting with Dylan, 134

freshman year, 134–37

friends of, 88–90, 122–24, 155, 203–4, 278, 330–31

attempts at recruitment, 330–31

Brooks Brown, 42, 109, 134, 161–66, 217, 263

Chris Morris, 71–72, 89–90, 109, 136, 146, 330

Kristi Epling, 206–8, 296

Nate Dykeman, 42, 54, 63–64, 136, 198, 200, 215, 259, 296, 330

Zack Heckler, 88–89, 123–24, 136–37, 185–86, 196, 198, 331

future plans of, 16–17

German fascination of, 18, 89, 128, 208, 258, 265–66

girls and dating, 17, 18, 134, 199, 294, 295–96

guns and, 33–34, 35–36, 90, 113, 121–23, 167–68, 199, 280, 293–95, 309–11, 335

hate lists, 18, 183–84, 256–57, 326–27, 343

"I Am" (poem), 134–35

investigative file on, 84–85, 165–66, 185, 220–21, 248, 285, 315, 343–44

journal of, 35, 169–70, 175, 221, 234–36, 243, 260, 264, 266, 267, 276–77, 280, 287–88, 293, 332

junior year, 256–64

"Just a Day" (essay), 114

loss of computer privileges, 112, 196, 214, 262

Marine Corps and, 113, 208–9, 244, 332, 334–35

the massacre (Judgment Day, Tuesday, April 20, 1999), 40–67, 349–53

aborted attempt on Monday, 35–36

arrival at school, 41–42

attire, 34, 42, 53–54, 55

battle positions, 33, 34, 45–46

cafeteria scene, 46–50, 61–62, 281, 305–6, 350–51

Dave Sanders and, 138–40

decoy plans, 32–33, 41, 44

eyewitness testimony, 53–54, 55–56

firing of first shots, 46–47

first assumptions about, 72

library scene, 50–51, 61–62, 83–84, 227–29, 350, 351–53

police engagement with, 51, 54–55, 57, 61–62, 73

as primary suspect, 68, 84–85

suicide of, 83–84, 351–53

timing of, 332–33

the missions, 32–36, 40–41, 160–64, 173, 183, 196, 200–202

nickname of Reb, 6, 9

personality of, 9–10, 18, 113, 146

prom and, 6–7, 18, 27–28, 336

psychological motives explored, 168–70, 183–85, 187–88, 196–97, 216, 234–36, 239–40, 242–43, 244, 247–48, 256–58, 276–78

as a psychopath, 187, 239–48, 294

punishments of, 112, 196, 198, 214–15, 219

senior year, 264–67, 275–80

sophomore year, 146–48, 160–64, 173

target practice at Rampart Range, 167, 309–11

timeline of events, 358–60

Timothy McVeigh and, 32, 35

turning point for, 256–64, 307

van break-in and arrest, 200–202, 214, 219, 220, 256–57

Web site, 35, 163, 165–66, 170, 183–85, 197, 216–17, 217, 219, 220–21, 257, 343

yearbook exchange with Dylan, 256–58

Harris, Kathy, 112–15, 262

apology and condolence letters from, 254, 298

attorney hiring by, 107

current update on, 356
Diversion program and, 214, 215–16, 218–19
interview with investigators, 285
Judy Brown and, 161, 162–63
lawsuits against, 319–20
the massacre (Tuesday, April 20, 1999), 68
public blaming of, 107
vandalism missions and, 196, 202
Harris, Kevin, 112, 113, 114
Harris, Wayne, 112–15
  attorney hiring by, 107
  current update on, 356
  disciplining of Eric by, 112, 162–64, 196, 214, 262
  discovery of pipe bombs by, 197–98
  Diversion program and, 214, 215–16, 218–19, 261–62, 279
  guns and, 293, 295
  interview with investigators, 285
  journal of, 162, 214, 261–62
  lawsuits against, 319–20
  the massacre (Tuesday, April 20, 1999), 68
  parenting style of, 112, 162–64, 196, 214, 262
  prom night and, 27
  public blaming of, 107
  vandalism missions and, 183, 196, 202
Harris house, 68, 110, 220, 315
Healing Fund, 252–53
Heath High School, 14, 118–19
Heckler, Zack
  friendship with Eric and Dylan, 136–37, 185–86, 196, 263, 311
  knowledge of bombs by, 88–89, 123–24, 183, 198, 204, 331
Hemingway, Ernest, 354–55
Heston, Charlton, 211–12
Hicks, John, 166, 185, 220
Himmler, Heinrich, 266
Hobbes, Thomas, 264–65
Hochhalter, Anne Marie, 49, 61, 249–50, 281–84, 338–39

Hochhalter, Carla June, 282–84, 339
Hochhalter, Ted, 281, 283, 284
Horvath, Peter, 9–10
hostages, 65–67, 70–71, 83, 316
Hot Topic, 146
Huron National Forest, 113

Infantry School (Fort Benning), 34
injury count, 76
interlocking fire lanes, 34
Ireland, John, 75, 80–81, 153–54, 191, 270, 321
Ireland, Kathy, 75, 80–81, 153–55, 189–91, 268–70, 291
Ireland, Maggie, 80
Ireland, Patrick, 290–92
  at Colorado State University, 291, 320–21
  current update on, 341, 355
  forgiveness of killers by, 268–70
  graduation of, 301–2
  Laura and, 23–25, 43, 291–92, 355
  love of waterskiing, 24, 270, 321
  the massacre in the library (Tuesday, April 20, 1999), 43, 75, 76–80, 142, 352
    boy in the window, 78–80, 142, 190
    SWAT rescue, 76–77, 78–80, 142
  prom and, 23–25, 28
  recovery of, 153–55, 189–92, 248–49, 268–70
  reopening of Columbine and, 274
  school trip to England, 290–91
  six-month anniversary and, 282

Jackson, Brooke, 298, 299, 314–15
Jeffco cover-up, 84–85, 165–67, 185, 220–21, 247–48, 285, 315, 343–44, 383–84n
Jeffco Sheriff's Office Final Report, 297–301, 343–45
jocks, 125, 151–52, 208–9, 330
Johnson, Doug, 141
Judgment Day (Tuesday, April 20, 1999), 40–67, 349–53
  aborted attempt on Monday, 35–36

Judgment Day (*cont.*)
  arrival at school of Eric and Dylan,
    41–42
  assembling arsenal for, 275–76, 280,
    293–95, 305–6, 309–11, 335
  battle positions, 33, 34, 45–46
  bomb failures, 45, 125, 351
  bomb placement, 42–43
  cafeteria scene, 46–50, 61–62, 81–82,
    281, 350–51
  choir room scene, 48, 51, 65, 81, 86–87
  crime-scene confusion, 53–54, 55–56
  Dave Sanders and, 87–88, 96–97, 121,
    138–44
  decoy plans, 32–33, 41, 44
  eyewitness testimony, 53–56, 59–60, 84,
    86–87, 121, 151–52, 204–6
  "female down," 49–50, 54–55
  final death toll, 85–86
  finalizing details for, 35, 332–33
  firing of first shots, 46–47
  first assumptions about, 68–72
  gym scene, 73–74
  hostage potential, 65–67
  injury count, 76
  library scene, 50–51, 61–62, 76–79,
    83–84, 151, 205, 226–32, 351–53
  myths about. *See* myths
  parking lots, 33–34, 41–42
  Science Room 3, 48, 64, 76, 82, 87–88,
    93, 96–97, 139–44, 350
  setting up the perimeter, 56–57, 58–59,
    64
  suicide of Eric and Dylan, 83–84,
    351–53
  SWAT team, 61–63, 76–79, 142–45,
    352–53
  timeline of events, 358–60
  West Staircase, 45–46, 50, 55
Juergensmeyer, Mark, 277–78
"Just a Day" (essay), 114
Justice Policy Institute, 15

Kamin, Sam, 298
Kaufman, Rick, 272
Kechter, Matthew, 179, 180, 289–90

Kelly, Judy, 307–9
Ken Caryl Middle School, 129, 134
Kiehl, Kent, 245–46
Kiekbusch, John, 109, 212–13, 248, 344,
    383*n*
Kirgis, Robert, 9, 17
Kirklin, Lance, 46–47, 61, 250, 253
Kirsten, George, 30, 119, 224, 225–26
Klebold, Byron, 63–64, 107, 132, 198, 327,
    356
Klebold, Dylan, 7–11
  appearance of, 7, 41
  assembling arsenal, 293–94, 305–6,
    309–11
  Basement Tapes, 35, 326–36
  birth of, 126
  Blackjack job, 9, 16–17, 89, 185
  college plans of, 16–17, 27
  in Diversion program, 84–85, 215–20,
    256–67, 279–80, 295, 306
  drinking by, 9, 183, 187, 217, 278
  family life of, 126–29, 209–10, 262,
    327–28
  farewell video by, 349
  first meeting with Eric, 134
  first mention of killing, 185–86
  freshman year, 134–37
  friends of, 88–90, 122–24, 155, 203–4,
    210, 278, 330–31
    Brooks Brown, 109, 126–28, 134, 217
    Chris Morris, 71–72, 89–90, 109, 136,
      210
    Nate Dykeman, 26–27, 54, 63–64,
      136, 200, 215
    Zack Heckler, 88–89, 136–37, 185–86,
      196, 198, 263, 311
  funeral of, 131–33
  guns and, 33–34, 35–36, 90, 121–23,
    167–68, 186–87, 309–11
  "Harriet" and, 186–87, 197, 199, 215,
    262–63
  homicidal thoughts of, 187, 215, 340
  journal of, 173–76, 182–83, 185–87, 197,
    198–99, 215, 216, 296, 306, 309, 334,
    336–37
  junior year, 256–64

loneliness of, 174, 186
the massacre (Judgment Day, Tuesday,
     April 20, 1999), 40–67, 349–53
  aborted attempt on Monday, 35–36
  arrival at school, 41–42
  attire, 34, 42, 53–54, 55, 335–36
  battle positions, 33, 34, 45–46
  cafeteria scene, 46–50, 61–62, 281,
     305–6, 350–51
  Dave Sanders and, 138–40
  decoy plans, 32–33, 41, 44
  eyewitness testimony, 53–54, 55–56
  firing of first shots, 46–47
  first assumptions about, 72
  library scene, 50–51, 83–84, 227–29,
     350, 351–53
  as primary suspect, 68, 84–85
  suicide of, 83–84, 351–53
the missions, 32–36, 40–41, 160, 164,
     173, 183, 196, 200–202
nickname of VoDKa, 9
outbursts by, 10, 127–28, 146–47,
     187–88
prom and, 7–8, 26–27, 28, 336
psychological motives explored, 175–76,
     187–88, 196–99, 235, 244
punishments of, 196, 198–99, 214–15,
     219
school suspension, 196, 198–99, 200
senior year, 264–67, 278–80
short story about killing "preps," 307–9
sophomore year, 160, 164, 173–76
spiritual quest of, 173–76, 182–83,
     186–87
suicidal thoughts of, 173, 174–75, 186,
     188, 198, 263
target practice at Rampart Range, 167,
     309–11
timeline of events, 358–60
turning point for, 307–9
van break-in and arrest, 200–202, 219,
     256–57
yearbook exchange with Eric, 256–58
Klebold, Eric, 126
Klebold, Sue, 126–29, 339–41
  apology letters from, 254–55, 298

attorney hiring by, 107
current update on, 356
Diversion program and, 217–18
family counseling, 198
lawsuits and, 285, 319–20
the massacre (Tuesday, April 20, 1999),
     68–69, 90–91, 335
  Nate Dykeman's call to, 63–64
police interview with, 209–10
public blaming of, 107
Reverend Marxhausen and, 128, 130–33,
     253, 317–18
vandalism missions and, 196, 202
Klebold, Tom, 126–29, 339–40
attorney hiring by, 107
current update on, 356
Diversion program and, 217–18, 219
family counseling, 198
lawsuits and, 285, 319–20
the massacre (Tuesday, April 20, 1999),
     68–69, 90–91, 335
  Nate Dykeman's call to, 63–64
police interview with, 209–10
prom night and, 26
public blaming of, 107
Reverend Marxhausen and, 128, 130–33,
     253, 317–18
vandalism missions and, 196, 200, 202
Klebold house, 68–69, 90–91, 110, 126–27
Kmart, 317
KMFDM, 18, 258, 317
knives, 33–34, 335
Koresh, David, 31, 108
Kosovo, 15, 52
Kreutz, Lisa, 83–84, 352
Kriegshauser, Bob, 245, 264, 265, 279–80,
     295, 306

Laman, Troy, 83–84, 143–44
Lancaster, Kacie, 321, 355
lawsuits, 297–300, 314–15, 318–20
Leawood Elementary School, 59, 65, 74,
     86, 92
Leo Yassenoff Jewish Community Center,
     128
Lewinsky, Monica, 233

library, at Columbine High School
  crime-scene investigation, 108
  the massacre in the (Tuesday, April 20,
      1999), 50–51, 61–62, 76–79, 83–84,
      151, 205, 226–32, 351–53
  rebuilding of, 250–51, 312
Light of the World Catholic Church,
      105–6, 119–20
Lindholm, Marjorie, 97, 139, 140, 141, 143
Littleton, Colorado, 21
Littleton Fire Department, 299
Littwin, Mike, 193
Lockheed Martin, 231
Long, Rich, 51, 94–95, 138–40
Lost Highway (movie), 197
Lotze, Barb, 120
Lumberman's Monument, 113
Luvox, 208–9, 261, 319, 334
Luzadder, Dan, 230, 363*n*
lying, and psychopaths, 240–41, 260
Lynch, David, 197

Macbeth (Shakespeare), 43, 226
McPherson, Dave, 223–24, 230, 287
McVeigh, Timothy, 31, 32, 35, 278
Manes, Mark, 36, 167–68, 285–86,
      309–11, 335, 337
Manwaring, Terry, 61–63
Marilyn Manson, 149, 155, 211, 317
Marine Corps, U.S., 17, 113, 208–9, 244,
      332, 334–35
Marxhausen, Don, 119–20, 128, 130–33,
      178, 253, 317–18
Mask of Sanity (Cleckley), 240–41, 243–44
massacre. *See* Columbine High School
      massacre
Matsch, Richard, 385*n*
Mauser, Daniel, 211, 301
Mauser, Tom, 211, 286, 300–301
maximum human density, 35
Medea (Euripides), 276, 351
media coverage, 101–2, 106, 159, 178–79,
      271–72. *See also* television coverage
  myths and, 149–52, 155–59
Media Guidelines Summit, 271
medications, 208–9, 214, 218, 261, 319, 334

melodrama, 323, 384–85*n*
Mencher, Melvin, 381*n*
Meyer, Diane, 314, 356
Michalik, Connie, 283–84
Millon, Theodore, 294
Mink, Ted, 343
Mitchell, Andrew, 157
Molotov cocktails, 33–34, 351, 353
Montana Freeman, 108
Moore, Ivory, 4
Moore, Michael, 317
Morris, Chris, 109
  friendship with Eric and Dylan, 136,
      146, 210, 266, 330
  police interview with, 71–72, 89–90,
      122, 167
Murrah Federal Building, 31, 32
myths about Columbine, 149–52, 155–59
  bullying, 157–59
  gay rumors, 155–56
  Goths, 72, 107, 149, 155, 156–57
  jocks, 125, 151, 208–9, 330
  outcasts, 72, 147, 149, 155, 157–59
  targeting jocks, 125, 151–52, 208–9, 330
  third shooter, 86, 150, 203–5
  Trench Coat Mafia, 72, 150–51, 156

napalm, 16, 203, 305, 331
National Rifle Association (NRA),
      210–12, 300–301
National Right to Life, 345
NATO, 15, 52
Natural Born Killers (movie), 197
Nazism, 89, 128, 258, 265–66
NBC, 286, 301
Nelson, Jerry, 177
New Columbine, 19–21
New York Times, 15, 132, 145, 165, 178, 208,
      287, 290, 339–40
Nielson, Patti, 50–51, 84, 226
Nieto, Henry, 286
Nietzsche, Friedrich, 9, 264–65
9/11 terrorist attacks (2001), 278, 316,
      387–88*n*
911 calls, 49, 51, 52–53
Nine Inch Nails, 197

"Nixon" microcassette, 337, 386n
Northwestern Mutual Financial Network, 321
NRA (National Rifle Association), 210–12, 300–301

Ochberg, Frank, 153, 247, 289, 339
Ohio State University, 126
Oklahoma City bombing, 31, 32, 35, 252–53
Okrent, Daniel, 381–82n
Old Columbine, 19–21
open records request, 297–300, 314–15, 319–20
Open Space meeting, 166, 343, 344, 345
Oprah Winfrey (TV show), 181, 341
O'Toole, Mary Ellen, 379n
Oudemolen, Bill, 30, 118–19, 178
Outback Steakhouse, 336–37
outcasts, 72, 147, 149, 155, 157–59
Owens, Bill, 177, 301

Parents Group, 252–53, 300, 312
Parker, Brenda, 199, 257, 294, 295–96
Pasquale, Bree, 151, 181, 227–29
Pastures of Heaven, The (Steinbeck), 160–61
Pearl High School, 14
performance violence, 277–78
perimeter, 56–57, 58–59, 64
Perry, Robert, 203–4
Petrone, Nicole, 73–74
Petrone, Rich, 194
Petrone, Sue, 102, 194, 312, 324, 357
photographs, 101–2
pipe bombs
    Browns's knowledge of, 166
    friends knowledge of, 71, 88–89, 123–24, 330–31
    the massacre (Tuesday, April 20, 1999), 41–44, 349–51
    the missions and testing of, 183, 184–85, 200, 214–15, 216
    planning for the massacre, 33–34, 275–76, 280, 329–31, 332
    Wayne Harris's knowledge of, 197–98

Place, Dean, 164
Platte Canyon High School, 347
Plough Publishing, 230–32, 233
post-traumatic stress disorder (PTSD), 74, 152–53, 289, 313–14
prayer in schools, 177
Prendergast, Alan, 363n
prom, at Columbine, 23–28, 336
propane bombs, 32, 33, 34, 40, 44, 124–25
psychopaths, 187, 239–48, 257, 294, 378–79n
Psychopathy Checklist, 241, 378n
psychosis, 187, 240
PTSD (post-traumatic stress disorder), 74, 152–53, 289, 313–14
public donations, 252–53
public interest considerations, 299, 320, 385–86n

rage, 243, 327
Rammstein, 18
Rampart Range, 167, 309–11
Random House, 233
Rebel Hill, 10–12, 346–47
    wooden crosses, 192–95
Rebel News Network, 8
Red Cross, 94
Reno, Janet, 31
Revelation, 119
Revival Generation, 225–26
Rivera Live (TV show), 156
Rock 'n' Bowl, 17–18
Rocky Mountain News, 97, 107, 116, 118, 144, 149, 152, 180, 193, 230–31, 253, 271, 287, 308, 347
Rocky Mountains, 10–11, 13
Rogers Federal Building, 69
Rohrbough, Brian, 102–3, 345
    Columbine Memorial and, 357
    financial compensation and, 253
    lawsuits and, 285, 297–300, 312, 314–15, 345
    the massacre (Tuesday, April 20, 1999), 92, 94
    memorial garden incident and, 288

Rohrbough, Brian (*cont.*)
  mythologizing of Danny's death and, 116
  Rebel Hill crosses and, 193–95
Rohrbough, Danny, 102–3, 108, 116
  the massacre (Tuesday, April 20, 1999), 44, 46–47, 61–62, 73–74, 75–76, 92
Ross, Brian, 156
rowback, 381–82*n*
Ruegsegger, Kacey, 179, 180

SAFE Colorado (Sane Alternatives to the Firearms Epidemic), 301
St. Anthony Central Hospital, 79, 153–54
St. Philip Lutheran Church, 128, 130–31
Salazar, Ken, 343–44
Salon, 157
Sanchez, Andrea, 215–16, 217–19, 234, 258–59, 260–61
Sanders, Angela, 21–22, 23, 96–97, 138, 298, 319
Sanders, Coni, 22, 286
Sanders, Kathy, 22
Sanders, Linda Lou, 22–23, 39, 324–25, 341–42
  current update on, 357
  the massacre (Tuesday, April 20, 1999), 87–88, 96–97, 138, 142
  police notification of death of Dave, 104
  retirement plans with Dave, 268
Sanders, William "Dave," 21–23, 324–25
  appearance of, 22–23
  coaching of, 19, 21–22, 37–39
  at Columbine Lounge, 19–20, 21
  Frank DeAngelis and, 37–38, 94–95, 121
  lawsuits and, 298, 318–19
  the massacre (Tuesday, April 20, 1999), 138–45
    saving students, 47–48, 50, 51
    in Science Room 3, 87–88, 96–97, 121, 139–44, 350
  retirement plans, 268
Satan, 29–30, 107, 117–20, 180
Sawyer, Diane, 156

Schiraldi, Vincent, 15
Schnurr, Mark, 225, 233
Schnurr, Shari, 225, 233
Schnurr, Valeen, 224–25, 231, 232–33
school prayer, 177
school shooters (school shootings), 14–15, 66–67, 199, 247–48, 322–24, 347–48
Schrom, Deral, 374*n*
Science Room 3, at Columbine High School, 48, 64, 76, 82, 87–88, 93, 96–97, 139–44, 350
Scott, Craig, 179–80, 231, 232–33
Scott, Rachel, 8, 46, 62, 75–76, 106, 108, 179, 180
Searle, Judy, 344
Second Great Awakening, 29
Secret Service, 322–23, 384*n*
Serbia, 15, 52
Shakespeare, William, 9, 43, 226, 308, 333–34
Sheriff's Office Final Report, 297–301, 343–45
She Said Yes: The Unlikely Martyrdom of Cassie Bernall (Misty Bernall), 230–32, 287, 356
Shoels, Isaiah, 94, 179, 180, 252
shotguns, 33–34, 36, 90, 122–23, 293–94, 309–11
Smoker, Paul, 55, 56
social cliques, 125, 151, 208–9, 330
sociopaths, 241, 378*n*
South Platte River, 21
Special Operations and Research Unit (SOARU), 108
Stair, Joe, 203–4
Starkey, Kevin, 141–43
Steepleton, Daniel, 77
Steinbeck, John, 160–61
Stone, John, 60–63, 85–86, 93–94, 165, 204, 213, 248, 285, 288, 343, 345
Subway, 44
suicide, of Eric and Dylan, 83–84, 351–53
"suicide by cop," 351, 352
survivor's guilt, 153

SWAT teams
  in the cafeteria, 81–82
  in the choir room, 81
  Dave Sanders and, 96–97, 142–45
  first approach to school, 61–63, 352–53
  in the library, 83–84, 98
  Patrick Ireland rescue, 76–79, 142
Swedish Medical Center, 96

Take Back the School rally, 271–74
Tanner Gun Show, 90, 122, 167–68, 293–94
targeting theory, 125, 151–52
Taylor, Mark, 253
TCM (Trench Coat Mafia), 72, 147–51, 156
TEC-9 gun, 33–34, 36, 48, 122, 167–68, 285–86, 322, 335
television coverage, 52–53, 56–57, 64, 65–67, 140–42, 159. *See also specific television stations*
  myths and, 72, 149–52, 150–51, 155–59
Texas Seven, 316
third shooter myth, 86, 150, 203–5
Thomas, Dave, 93, 104, 110, 166, 315, 345
Time (magazine), 288
timeline of events, 358–60
Today Show (TV show), 165, 195, 233
Tomlin, Doreen, 92, 93–94
Tomlin, John, 93, 118
Tortilla Wraps, 259
Townsend, Dawn Anna, 250, 319, 354
Townsend, Lauren, 118, 224, 250
Trench Coat Mafia (TCM), 72, 147–51, 156
trench coats, 34, 53–54, 55, 63, 71–72, 147–48, 335–36
Trinity Christian Center, 29–30
TV coverage. *See* television coverage
20/20 (TV show), 156, 181, 233
2001: A Space Odyssey (movie), 242–43

United Way, 252–53
universal-witness concept, 152
University of Arizona, 17
University of Wyoming, 21, 268
USA Today, 151, 152, 157, 158, 178

video games, 10, 107, 134, 137, 197, 323, 384n
violent media, 107, 197, 222, 323, 384n
Virginia Tech, 348

Waco, Texas, 31, 32, 95, 108
Walcher, David, 61
Wall Street Journal, 233
Walsh, Timothy, 201–2, 307
warning signs, 323–24, 385n
Warren, Diane, 355
Washington Post, 15, 208
Webb, Wellington, 210–11
Weekly Standard, 180, 222
Weintraub, Alan, 154–55
West, Randy, 254
West Bowles Community Church, 30, 117–18, 119, 223–24
West Paducah, Kentucky, school shooting, 14, 118–19
William Morris Agency, 233
Without Conscience (Hare), 241
witnesses. *See* eyewitness testimony
wooden crosses, atop Rebel Hill, 192–95
Woods, Tiger, 256
World Trade Center terrorist attacks (2001), 278, 316, 387–88n
wrongful death suit, 252, 298, 318–19
WWJD (What Would Jesus Do), 30, 224
Wyant, Cindie, 229–30, 232
Wyant, Emily, 226–30, 232–33, 287

Yassenoff, Leo, 128
Yugoslavia, 15, 52

Zanis, Greg, 192–95
zero-tolerance policies, 322
Zeus, 137
Zimmerman, Chris, 232, 233
Zoloft, 214, 218, 261
zombies, 182, 215, 235

ABOUT THE AUTHOR

DAVE CULLEN is a journalist and author. He has contributed to the *New York Times,* Slate.com and Salon.com, and is considered the foremost authority on the Columbine killers. He has also written extensively on Evangelical Christians, politics, and pop culture.